THE GREATEST GAME
EVER PLAYED

THE
GREATEST GAME
EVER PLAYED

HARRY VARDON, FRANCIS OUIMET,

AND THE BIRTH OF MODERN GOLF

M A R K   F R O S T

 KINGSWELL

LOS ANGELES • NEW YORK

For information address Kingswell, 1101 Flower Street,
Glendale, California 91201

Editorial Director: Wendy Lefkon
Editor: Laura Hopper

   Library of Congress Cataloging-in-Publication Data
Frost, Mark
   The greatest game ever played : Harry Vardon,
Francis Ouimet, and the birth of modern golf.—1st ed.
      p. cm.
   ISBN 0-7868-6920-8
      1. Golf—History.   2. Vardon, Harry, 1870-
3. Ouimet, Francis.   I. Title.

GV963 .F76 2002
796.352'09—dc21

                                    2002068930

       Original book design by Richard Oriolo

            FIRST PAPERBACK EDITION

       Paperback ISBN: 978-0-7868-8800-9
            FAC-020093-18018

                    10

THE PLAYERS

AMERICAN HOMEBRED PROFESSIONALS

TOM MCNAMARA, Boston, Massachusetts, 1885–1957

MICHAEL "KING" BRADY, Brighton, Massachusetts, 1887–1972

JOHN J. MCDERMOTT, Philadelphia, Pennsylvania, 1891–1971

WALTER HAGEN, Rochester, New York, 1892–1969

AMERICAN AMATEURS

WALTER J. TRAVIS, Maldon, Australia, 1862–1927

JEROME TRAVERS, New York, New York, 1887–1951

JOHN G. ANDERSON, Boston, Massachusetts, 1884-1933

HEINRICH SCHMIDT, Boston, Massachusetts, 1878–1951

CHARLES "CHICK" EVANS, Indianapolis, Indiana, 1890–1979

FRANCIS OUIMET, Brookline, Massachusetts, 1893–1967

EDDIE LOWERY, Newton, Massachusetts, 1903–1984

THE GREATEST GAME
EVER PLAYED

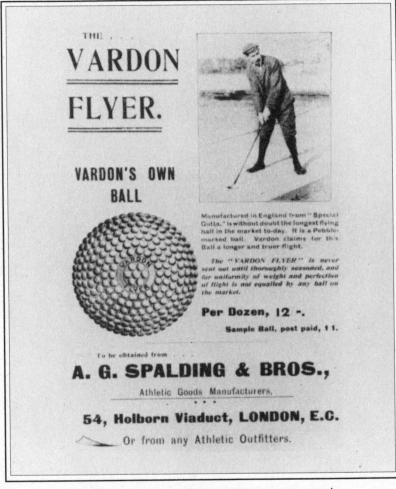

THE . . . .
VARDON
FLYER.

VARDON'S OWN BALL

Manufactured in England from "Special Gutta," is without doubt the longest flying ball in the market to-day. It is a Pebble-marked ball. Vardon claims for this Ball a longer and truer flight.

The "*VARDON FLYER*" is never sent out until thoroughly seasoned, and for uniformity of weight and perfection of flight is not equalled by any ball on the market.

Per Dozen, 12/-.

Sample Ball, post paid, 1 1.

To be obtained from . . .

A. G. SPALDING & BROS.,

Athletic Goods Manufacturers,

. . .

54, Holborn Viaduct, LONDON, E.C.

Or from any Athletic Outfitters.

PART ONE

FRANCIS AND HARRY

Golf develops the good qualities of a man's nature and softens the poor ones. It is a developer and builder of character without a peer. It is a leveler of rank and class, where rich and poor meet on common ground. It cultivates patience and endurance under adversity and yet keeps alive the fires of hope.
—WALTER J. TRAVIS

Keep your head down, and keep your eye on the ball.
—EDDIE LOWERY

FRANCIS, AGE 7, WITH HIS PARENTS IN
FRONT OF 246 CLYDE STREET.
(COURTESY OF THE COUNTRY CLUB)

FRANCIS

IT BEGINS WITH the simplicity of a fairy tale.

A small boy, combing through fields of grass for buried treasure, uncovers a magical talisman: a gleaming white ball, pristine, perfectly round, untouched by wear. Two words emblazoned on its cover: VARDON FLYER. That name, so suggestive of powerful, confident, dreamlike flight, burns itself into the boy's impressionable psyche. After seven-year-old Francis Ouimet races home to place the ball in the dented tin box that guards his growing cache of riches, the VARDON FLYER immediately becomes his most prized possession. A gift from an unknown god named Vardon.

GEOGRAPHY MAY BE destiny, but in the case of Francis Ouimet, destiny may have been more a result of real estate. The day before Harry Vardon's twenty-third birthday in 1893—the year he entered his first British Open Championship—Francis DeSales Ouimet was born in Brookline, Massachusetts, a sleepy Boston suburb. Four years later, his family purchased a modest little two-story clapboard house directly across from The Country Club, on a dusty dirt road called Clyde Street.

Francis's father, Arthur Ouimet, a French-Canadian Catholic immigrant, depended on odd jobs to make ends meet; occasionally he'd find them as a coachman or gardener for The Country Club's affluent members. After six generations in Quebec, Arthur was the first of his family to leave Montreal, fleeing the oppressive thumb of the English-Protestant majority to seek his fortune in America; what he found instead was heartbreak. Uneducated, his English clotted with a thick Quebecois accent, the best Arthur could manage in Massachusetts was a life of menial labor governed by the subtle but still profound prejudices of the nineteenth-century Boston gentry. Bostonians called this wave of immigrants "Frenchies," consigning them to servile positions that the city's second-generation Irish no longer considered suitable to their rising station.

After establishing himself on Brookline's lower margins, at the age of twenty-eight Arthur Ouimet fell in love and married a beautiful Irish girl named Mary Mahoney. Three years later Mary died in childbirth and their sickly child, named Joseph after Arthur's father, followed her in death only ten weeks later. The disaster scarred Arthur for life; from that point forward he was described only as a cold, hardworking man with a hot and ready temper. He married again in 1888, to another Irish lass, twenty-seven-year-old Brookline native Mary Ellen Burke. Although she was a warm, loving, and infinitely patient woman, for Arthur this second marriage exuded less romance than an air of nineteenth-century practicality, creating a family in order to solidify his economic standing. Within eight years Mary gave him four children: Wilfred, the oldest by three years, then Francis, a daughter, Louise, and finally Raymond, the youngest, born in the house on Clyde Street that Arthur had bought that year. Haunted by nightmarish visions of sliding back down into abject poverty, Arthur had nevertheless put enough aside to buy some of the vacant land behind the house as well. They raised chickens, grew vegetables, sank their own well. Arthur drummed into his children the hard necessity of contributing to the family's welfare; his oldest son, Wilfred, began to caddy at The Country Club not long after the Ouimets moved into their new home.

The house on Clyde Street sat directly across from The Country

Club's seventeenth fairway and green, the sight Francis woke to every morning outside his second-floor bedroom window. Soon after they moved in, his mother used to routinely find Francis, at the age of four, standing across the street, staring at players on the fairway through a stand of beech trees. He didn't know how, he could never later even adequately explain why, but from his first glance, Francis found the forms and rituals of the game mesmerizing. Golf seeped into his young mind; it may be no exaggeration to say Francis was America's first golf addict who grew up with the game. His family's earliest recollection of the boy would be right at home in a nineteenth-century tall tale, befitting the kind of legends told about Mike Fink or Paul Bunyan; he walked around the house crying for his brother Wilfred's first golf club. When he finally got his hands on it—a cut-down driver, nearly as tall as he was—Francis spent countless hours swinging that club in their backyard. He began attending the one-room Putterham Schoolhouse the following year, and discovered a trespassing shortcut that traversed The Country Club's fairways. Francis soon developed an uncanny eye for locating lost golf balls on his daily commute and by the age of seven had amassed that precious trove he kept in the old gingersnap tin under his bed.

Francis and Wilfred began their playing careers on the seldom traveled dirt surface of Clyde Street in front of the Ouimet home, digging out holes with the heels of their boots at the base of two streetlamps a hundred yards apart, knocking balls endlessly back and forth. Before they made much headway as players, they turned themselves into golf course architects. When their father brought home a new lawn mower to use on his gardening jobs, the boys waited until Arthur was away at work, then appropriated the mower to hack a primitive three-hole course out of the overgrown cow pasture behind their house.

The first hole required a hundred-yard carry off the tee over a creek to a small oval green. The second provided a breather, a fifty-yard par three. The third returned back across the creek to a circular green they stamped into their own backyard. Before long that home green required no mowing at all; they trampled it so often, they wore out the grass. Tin cans from the family kitchen served as cups. Their equipment consisted of Wilfred's one club and Francis's hoard of lost balls. He was fortunate

The Country Club continually replenished his supply because their training ground demanded unerring accuracy; it consisted more of hazard than fairway—marsh, gravel pit, swamp, high weeds. Hitting any ball more than a few yards off line into the unmown wilderness meant kissing it good-bye. Francis said later that as a result of learning the game on this primitive layout, every real course he subsequently played, no matter how ragged the fairways or threadbare the putting surfaces, felt as luxurious to him as White House lawns and green felt billiard tables.

Francis found little companionship at first for his mysterious attraction to the game; American golf was only five years older than he was, making him both prodigy and pioneer. The same could be said for the club across the street that sparked and nurtured his obsession; only a handful of courses in the United States predate The Country Club and few that came into existence afterward ever took to the game with equal alacrity. Because they opened their doors in 1882, The Country Club at Brookline makes an airtight argument for itself as sui generis; they were a club and it was in the country, hence its members became the first American organization to use the now generically applied name for private sporting establishments. But they didn't start out playing golf. Although The Country Club immediately attracted a solid, prosperous membership of Boston Brahmins, the Scottish game was still six years away from setting down roots in New England soil; horse racing and riding at hounds were The Country Club's original organizing interests. The hundred acres they acquired for that purpose centered around a half-mile racetrack called Clyde Park that had been in continuous operation since the 1860s. The legal structure of The Country Club allowed its members to assume financial responsibility for an annual racing season that filled the track's grandstand with spectators from miles around at fifty cents a head; with that income underwriting their ambitions, facilities for target shooting, archery, tennis, polo, ice-skating, and curling soon followed. A simple two-story roadhouse and former hotel on a bluff overlooking the heart of the property became their clubhouse, and over the years expanded in all directions into the genteel, rambling, pale yellow mansion that still plays host to its members today.

In March of 1893, two months before the birth of that boy who'd soon be scavenging her fairways, in response to increasing member curiosity

The Country Club added a rudimentary six-hole golf course that leapfrogged back and forth around the racetrack. Built in its entirety for the modest sum of fifty dollars spent on a few bags of grass seed, sand for primitive bunkers, and nine tin cans for holes. When early enthusiasts conducted their first exhibition of the game that spring, golf at The Country Club made an astonishing debut, hinting at the magic to come. The first shot struck off the first tee by a Mr. Arthur Hunnewell ran like a scared rabbit ninety yards to the green and dove neatly into the cup for a hole in one. Since no one knew any better, the small crowd who had turned out to watch the proceedings didn't even react; since they'd been given to understand that putting the ball in the hole was the whole point of the exercise, they just assumed this was business as usual. Arthur Hunnewell played golf passionately for another thirty years. He never scored another ace in his life.

Golf attracted so much interest so quickly that within months The Country Club expanded its course to nine holes. Twenty sheep were soon imported from Devonshire, England, to keep the fairways clipped. Soon afterward the club's first professional, Willie Campbell, arrived from Scotland and was paid the princely sum of $300 a year. Demand for golf lockers soon became so great, they had to be assigned by lottery. Friction resulted; on two holes where the course intersected their bridle paths, the club's equestrians complained they were frequently attacked by flying balls. Players hooked on golf openly defied their state's ancient blue laws forbidding the playing of games on the Sabbath. After complaints that golf was corrupting morals by emptying local churches, over thirty members were arrested and hauled off the course one Sunday after a busybody neighbor called the cops. When the neighbor died before the case ever went to court, the charges were dismissed. Not long afterward, with a push from Brookline's influential membership, the Massachusetts legislature quietly removed the Sunday ban. By mid-decade, The Country Club needed more golf course to accommodate its burgeoning roster of players; they purchased some adjacent properties and built eighteen new holes that threaded their way through verdant countryside adorned by granite outcroppings and stands of mature hardwoods. Only one of the original nine holes survived; the par three seventh. No architect was hired—a few already existed—but members didn't feel that expense was justified. The club already possessed the most important prerequisite for a great golf course; varied and interesting ground. Although they did bring in drivers and mule teams to move a little dirt around and make these new holes more challenging than their predecessors, for the most part the course laid out exactly as the land presented itself. At a cost this time of $5,000, the new course was completed and ready for play by October of 1899.

Brookline's golfers stood at the forefront of the game's vanguard. The Country Club participated in the first American interclub matches held in 1894, in the process joining Shinnecock Hills, the Chicago Golf Club, St. Andrews in Yonkers, New York, and the Newport Country Club, Rhode Island, to form the Amateur Golf Association of America. The group soon changed its name to the United States Golf Association, the birth of the game's governing body. The following year, in 1895, the USGA conducted the first United States Open Championship in Newport. The game caught on with the East Coast's upper crust like birthday cake; it was fun, it was outdoorsy, it could be, if socially required, coeducational, and it nearly qualified as exercise. Businessmen quickly found it an ideal recreational vehicle for the social lubrication so vital to the flow of commerce.

Before long the country's most successful sporting goods manufacturer, A. G. Spalding & Brothers, examined the new game's potential and smelled money. After pitching the Boston Red Stockings to five pennants, Albert Spalding in 1876 had opened a Chicago emporium to sell bats, baseballs, and gloves to America's first generation of baseball fanatics, and soon turned this single outlet into the first nationwide sporting goods chain. Eager for new worlds to conquer, in 1894 Spalding introduced a line of golf clubs and before long bought a foundry to handle the upsurge in orders. Four years later he plunged into the golf ball business, buying the rubbery raw material gutta-percha in bulk and molding a ball he marketed as the Spalding Wizard at his own factory in Chicopee, Massachusetts.

With a company that early on and ever since has understood the importance of marrying a sports product with a glamorous name, Albert Spalding in the spring of 1900 identified the one man in the ascendant game to whom he was willing to tie his company's fortunes. Spalding wasted no time making his move. He cabled the golf club at Ganton, Yorkshire, England, to extend to their resident professional, 1899's reigning British Open champion, Harry Vardon, an invitation to make a barnstorming, all expenses paid exhibition tour of America, in support of a new, state-of-the-art golf ball.

He planned to call it the "Vardon Flyer."

VARDON, 25, ON THE EVE OF HIS FIRST OPEN VICTORY.

(HULTON ARCHIVE/GETTY IMAGES)

HARRY

WHY DO SPORTS fans, or even people with faint interest in the game itself, get so worked up about professional golfers? The adoration of athletes in every other sport is a cinch to decipher; their physical gifts astonish us, our jaws drop at their defiance of earthbound limits; their triumphs over obvious adversities—pain, injury, the clock, Father Time, enraged behemoths trying to remove their heads—hardly require explanation to a child of five.

But golfers? They arouse passionate feelings while engaged in what appears to be nothing more than a meandering stroll, interrupted by minor, repetitive exertion. Most modern professionals exhibit on the course all the hot-blooded zeal of an accountant double-checking his books over a cup of chamomile tea. But the ones who come along once in a generation, immortals who transcend the game's pedestrian boundaries, hook us by the soul and inflame our imaginations like a holy figure. Unlike the stars of other sports, golf's great ones inhabit a world we readily recognize. With no stadium walls to separate us, we share their stage with them; they go about their work while walking among us, dressed in casual Friday clothes. Physically they conform almost exactly to our idea of average while at the same time embodying an irresistible human ideal—the unyielding pursuit of perfection, and its occasional attainment, under pressure that could crush a nuclear sub.

Although golf's first four centuries offer a parade of legendary figures, they pass before your eyes like shadows, remote and insubstantial as seaside mist. The first individuals remembered for the quality of their golf aren't the refined gentlemen amateurs of Stuart Scotland who invented the game on the seaside links for their own amusement, but the first generation of pioneering professionals eking out a living from the back of a toolshed. Not unlike boxers, the first wave of golf pros used the sport to elevate themselves from lives of gnawing poverty. The earliest nineteenth-century photos from the Scottish links show us groups of men dressed like itinerant hobos, armed with primitive tools bearing enigmatic names like cleek or baffie, traversing ragged landscapes that resemble nothing the modern eye associates with golf. They don't invite examination; grim, closed faces, fringed with shaggy Amish whiskers and a shiver of Old Testament fortitude, Ahabs in pursuit of some landlocked whale. Stoic, proud, self-reliant, long-suffering; now that, my friends, is a golfer.

A handful of them advanced their games far enough to still be remembered today. Three men from St. Andrews, Scotland, dominated the era: Alan Robertson, Old Tom Morris, and his tragic son, Young Tom, who dropped dead from grief at the age of twenty-four after losing his wife during childbirth. Between 1830 and 1870 this pioneering trio virtually invented the role of the modern golf professional, and along the way gave rise to the sport's most enduring tradition, the British Open Championship, contested for the first time in 1860. Hundreds of others followed their trailblazing footsteps into the profession, many of them brilliant players. Most entered life at a staggering deficit, proving the axiom that as often as necessity is the mother of invention, hunger is the father of immortality. One name towers above the rest. Little argument comes from any quarter to dispute the fact that Harry Vardon was the greatest of them all. Exactly what forces drove the man to such unprecedented levels of perfection are not hard to discern; as far as overcoming misery and suffering was concerned, no one had farther to travel than Harry Vardon.

When Harry was seven years old, the same age as Francis when he found his Vardon Flyer, he awoke one morning to an incomprehensible vision outside his bedroom window: six English gentlemen in frock coats and stovepipe hats measuring the sandy seafront waste behind his house with surveyor's tools. Curious, a bit fearful, Harry's mother ordered him to run outside and ask these strangers what they were up to. "There's a golf links going in here, laddy," he was told. Reluctant to question the man further, Harry had no idea what "golf links" meant—he'd never heard the words before. Six months later, three weeks before they broke ground, developers evicted the Vardons from their shack on the southern coast of the Isle of Jersey, to make way for the construction of the Royal Jersey Golf Club, a playground for the British leisure class to ply their exotic new pastime. Harry and his brothers were forced to carry their few possessions away from the only home they'd ever known, into the shanties that crowded the streets on the wrong side of the town. The year was 1877.

The tired truism that France has never produced a great golf champion is only a half-truth; Harry Vardon's mother, Eliza, was French. Although the Isle of Jersey lies just fifteen miles west off the coast of France and eighty-four miles south of the nearest English soil, it has existed under English authority since William the Conqueror crossed the Channel in 1066. The Romans called the island Caesaria and built forts and harbors there as they made their way to Britain; Napoleon constructed fortifications against English invasion during his time on Europe's throne; the Nazis invaded and occupied it during World War II. Geographically grouped with the smaller islands of Guernsey, Alderney, and Sark as the Channel Islands, Jersey's land mass adds up to less than forty-eight square miles. The islands are governed by England's Hampshire County, under the religious auspices of the Episcopalian diocese of Winchester, and most of its citizens speak both English and French. Shipbuilding, potato fields, and dairy farms were its leading nineteenth-century industries. During the next century Jersey became better known for a more exotic and completely unanticipated export: championship professional golfers.

In 1865, Harry's father, Phillip, had migrated down from London to work as a carpenter in the thriving Jersey shipyards; flush for a time, he married Eliza, a local Catholic girl. Their first child, Harry, was born within a year; seven more children followed him in annual succession. Halfway through this impressive run of the Vardon production line, the volcanic rise of the steamship sent England's wooden shipbuilding industry into precipitous decline; the Jersey yards, and the local economy that depended on them, collapsed almost overnight. After being laid off, Harry's father struggled to make ends meet as a local handyman, angry and resentful at the raw deal the world had handed him. The family's fortunes plummeted, culminating in their humiliating descent to the Grouville slums. Staring young Harry in the face was a negligible life as a manual laborer that would never take him off the rock, until the same cloud that had dimmed his horizons let through a pale ray of light: When the Royal Jersey Golf Club opened in 1878, Harry's father ordered him to seek employment there as a caddie. The boy's only other option was to continue spending his free hours gathering seaweed from the beach to sell as fertilizer, twelve pounds to the penny. Harry decided he'd rather carry gentlemen's golf clubs, whatever that meant.

Slowly the game captivated him. He watched the better players closely and mimicked their moves on the sly, building a swing of his own that incorporated the best of what he'd taken in. Inspired to experiment, Harry carved a primitive club from the branch of a hawthorn tree, hammered a square of tin onto its face to create a uniform striking surface, and practiced at night with an oversized marble as his ball. Harry's younger brother Tom, now a fellow caddie, took to the game with equal enthusiasm, and together they contested imaginary championships played in some distant, impossible future. The game became the repository of their dreams, and the only tangible form for their visions of escape.

At the age of twelve, his father now drifting toward despair as the family spiraled deeper into poverty, Harry was forced to forgo what little formal education he'd been allowed to work on a nearby dairy farm; his two shillings a week for sixty hours of cold, menial labor went directly to his mother's pocket before his father could pour it down his throat. Caddie work was now confined to weekends; he looked forward to the fresh sea air and the warmth of the sun on his face, but Harry was often so exhausted by Sunday, he fell asleep standing up, leaning on the clubs, while his gentlemen golfers putted on the greens.

Two years later the Vardons' financial straits caught another down-draft, and now Harry's farmwork wages fell short of the family's dire needs. Creditors hounding their door, drunken rages, whispered nighttime conversations; some primitive survival instinct told Harry his precarious status was about to plunge down a rabbit hole of its own. A week later Harry came home to find his mother packing his clothes into a bundle. When he asked her what was going on, she tried to put on a bright face as she held up a freshly washed servant's uniform and broke the news: His parents had bound Harry over into domestic service as a wealthy doctor's houseboy.

"How long?" he asked.

She couldn't look him in the eye. "Three years," she said.

His bundle draped over his shoulder, the next day Harry walked across town alone to the doctor's front door. A butler directed him to the servants' entrance, where he was shown to his room, a windowless closet below the stairs. The doctor, a friendly but remote man, treated Harry decently enough; the violence he suffered at the hands of the house's senior staff was routine and severe. In his short, unhappy life, Harry had discovered only one source of joy, but now even that was denied him; the only rounds of golf he played for the next three years took place on moonlit summer nights after his fourteen-hour workday had ended and he and his brother Tom would sneak out onto the Royal Jersey links while the rest of the island was fast asleep.

When he reached seventeen and the end of the obligation his parents had arranged, despairing for a better life, in fear he'd never escape a brutish backstairs existence, Harry refused to continue in the doctor's house. Cutting himself off from his family's plans for him, Harry struck out on his own, applying for and receiving a position as an apprentice gardener. His new employer, Major Spofforth, a retired military man, happened to be the presiding Captain of the Golf at Royal Jersey; his house and gardens adjoined the links. One day the major returned home unexpectedly and found Harry in the backyard swinging one of his handsome, handcrafted clubs. The major immediately ushered him out onto a nearby Royal Jersey fairway and ordered him to repeat that swing, this time with a ball in front of him. Afraid for his job and unsure of the major's intentions, Harry obeyed. The ball flew straight and far.

"Again," said the major, dropping another ball. Again. A dozen shots later the major broke into a smile.

"Present yourself at the first tee tomorrow morning, Harry," he said, walking away. "Nine o'clock."

"Why, sir?"

"Why? We'll be playing together. A swing like that. Good heavens."

The man's simple kindness pierced Harry to his core; he turned and walked away before the major could see all the pent-up suffering and sadness of his last four years flow out of him.

When he arrived at Royal Jersey the next morning, Major Spofforth presented Harry with a full set of hand-me-down clubs. "Follow me," he said. Harry walked out onto the links to play the first complete round of his life; a best-ball match, with the major as his partner, against two of the club's better players. Tested under competitive pressure from his first tee shot, Harry played as if his life depended on it. By the time they reached the twelfth green, within sight of where Harry's old house had stood, the match was over; Harry and the major had won going away. Determined to repay the major's faith in him, for the first time Harry undertook a systematic study of the game. More competitive matches followed, and within months the major and his protégé were beating every twosome the club could throw at them. The major began to cut Harry in on a small percentage of their winnings from the lucrative side bets he wagered and cut back on his gardening chores, with the proviso that Harry use the extra hours to work harder on his golf. He didn't have to be told twice. The course whose creation had forced the Vardons from their home soon welcomed their oldest son as a rising star. Within two years Harry had worked his way down to a single-digit handicap and conquered every player on the island, including Major Spofforth and the club's resident professional. He could beat most of the members at Royal Jersey while playing left-handed.

That spring Harry received a letter from his brother Tom; sharing Harry's passion for the game, younger by two years, Tom had set off for England nine months earlier to see if he could earn a living as a club maker. He had settled for a menial position as an assistant greenkeeper, but now his news was sensational: Tom had won second prize at a tournament in Musselburgh, Scotland. Twelve pounds! Harry had never taken home more than sixteen quid in an entire year.

Within a week, at the age of twenty, Harry stepped off the Isle of Jersey for the first time in his life; he bought a second-class ticket on the ferry to Portsmouth, then rode the train to join Tom in the north of England. He carried with him all he owned in the world—one tattered valise, one set of golf clubs. He accepted the first job that was offered him, greenkeeper at a nine-hole course on a private estate in Yorkshire, owned by Lord Ripon, an older member of the House of Lords. Harry's new employer didn't play the newfangled game himself; he put the course in strictly for the amusement of weekend guests, for whom Ripon insisted the largely vacant links be kept in immaculate condition. During the long hours of Harry's six-day workweek he was a gardener again. The little time he had to himself in the late afternoons Harry devoted to practice, working his way methodically around the course, fine-tuning his swing. Six months later, on the advice of one of Ripon's weekend golfers who knew enough about the game to admire his skills, Harry secured a position as resident professional at a legitimate nine-hole club in Bury, Lancashire. His salary was one pound a week; ninety dollars in today's money.

Between these two jobs, Harry had returned to Jersey and married his hometown sweetheart, Jessie, a move born out of Catholic necessity, not choice; Jessie was seven months pregnant. A shy, retiring girl Harry had known for years, unsure of herself socially, entirely unschooled, intellectually unsophisticated. Sports in general and golf in particular held no interest for Jessie whatsoever; she found the game impenetrable and pointless. Given the heights to which Harry's career was about to take him, a more unsuitable life partner would have been hard to construct from scratch.

When the young couple's first child was born soon afterward, the marriage climbed onto more solid ground, but the health of the infant boy who carried their shared dreams failed shockingly; after a cruelly slow and painful decline, he died at the age of six weeks. Heartbroken, Jessie could not attend the funeral, retreating into inconsolable isolation. Bereft and grieving himself, Harry's hard-won instincts for survival told him life nevertheless must go on, but even after a month nothing Harry said or did could persuade his wife to leave the island with him and return to his new job in England. This mournful parting defined the pattern their entire married life would follow: Jessie stayed at home, while Harry, denied as a man the comforts of a supportive family life he'd never known as a child, set off like a bachelor to pursue his solitary dreams. Not so many years later, after he had become the world's most celebrated golfer, Harry wrote down the two words that had sustained him throughout those calamitous twenty-one years, delivering him from a life of servitude to his place in the sun: Never despair.

Harry found lodgings in the spare room of a kindly, childless couple who lived near his new club in Lancashire. He worked long hours ingratiating himself with the members, but his desolate private life now allowed him to develop the most rigorous practice regimen any golfer in the game's history had ever followed and no one until Ben Hogan would duplicate. Harry had learned the hard way that the only difference between realizing a dream and losing oneself in fantasy was backbreaking work. He spent weeks learning the secrets of every stick in his bag, mentally rehearsing every on-course scenario, and assembling an armory of shots. Once he felt he'd mastered a club, he moved on to one that gave him trouble, always striving to improve any weaknesses, trusting his strengths like money in the bank.

A few months later Harry's brother Tom accepted a club-making job nearby and again became his only companion. A buoyant, lighthearted optimist, Tom had dodged many of the hardships that fell on his older brother's shoulders; he lacked Harry's brooding intensity and prodigious powers of concentration, which made him a perfect foil. Tom's presence rounded the hard edges of his brother's obsessive drive, balancing his single-minded ambition with the gentler virtues of simple human friendship.

Together Harry and Tom began to venture out and compete in small-stakes tournaments around the north of England, playing for pocket money but with one clear goal in mind: to one day compete on the game's highest stage, Britain's national championship, the Open. Their dream sent the Vardons down a hard, bleak road; professional golfers were considered common laborers in Britain, sons of the working class, admired for their playing or teaching skills but in the narrowed eyes of the gentry predisposed to drinking binges and petty larceny. Professionals who harbored any hope of advancement in the game all lived an itinerant existence, traveling by third-class rail and hitching rides on farm wagons to remote tournament sites, bunking in cheap rooming houses, eating common meals, and closing the local pubs. They occupied a lowly rung on the social ladder shared by nomadic music-hall performers, a station somewhere between traveling salesman and migrant farmworker. Most were rough characters, poorly educated if at all, with thick regional accents that grated on a gentleman's ear. Their legendary weakness for the demon rum appears to have been more than rumor, and they weren't sipping single malt scotch; many of them brewed their own backwoods moonshine, bottles of snake venom with a razor-blade chaser.

Gentlemen amateurs received warm welcomes as honorary members whenever they traveled to competitions at Britain's private clubs. Visiting pros were looked down on as the hired help, there to amuse the members on the course and remain out of their sight off it. It would take another thirty years before this class stigma faded from the sport and professional golfers were allowed to eat lunch or even change their shoes in a private course clubhouse in England or America; almost impossible to imagine now in an era of superstar athletes jetting around the globe to multimillion-dollar tournaments in their customized Gulfstream V's.

After his hardscrabble life on Jersey, these new privations only served to harden Harry's already formidable hide. Separating himself from his fellow wanderers, who were content to live a marginalized existence as long as it supported their golf habit, twenty-three-year-old Harry Vardon kept his eye on the sport's biggest prize. He had converted all those lean, hungry years into fuel for the engine of his dreams. Harry had no other marketable skills and almost no education; his future would ride on one roll of the dice.

After deciding their years of knocking around the game's lesser precincts had properly seasoned them for the sport's ultimate test, Harry and Tom Vardon entered their first Open Championship at Prestwick in 1893. When he arrived at the first tee, Harry found himself assigned to a twelve-year-old hunchback caddie who fed him a steady stream of bad advice about the difficult course, then abused him verbally whenever

Harry failed to execute the little tyrant's commands to the letter. Harry's inexperience in championship competition made him reluctant to go against his caddie's counsel, until the twelfth hole when his gut instinct told him the boy was dead wrong about the club he'd told him to use. Harry refused to accept the offered club, hit his own selection to within six feet of the pin, and drained the putt for birdie. His peculiar little caddie fell into a permanent sulk and refused to speak to him again. Whenever they reached Harry's ball, the boy held out the golf bag, let Harry pull out his own weapon of choice, then turned his back as if he couldn't bear the sight of him. Perhaps jinxed by this little Rumpelstiltskin, Harry dropped out of contention during the third round, but the pure quality of his shot-making turned the head of everyone who saw him play. When he completed play, no less august a presence than Old Tom Morris, the acknowledged godfather of all professional golfers, quietly took Harry aside to commend him on his swing and his level of play. For a novice competing in his first Open, this simple kindness meant more to him than all the trophies in the world, but as far as Old Tom Morris was concerned, his gesture was far from a casual act. With a master's eye Old Tom had recognized in young Harry the first worthy successor to the legacy handed down to him through Alan Robertson, the royal lineage of the game's immortals that had come to a halt with the tragic death of Tom's own son. Twenty years on, with Old Tom nearing his twilight, another heir apparent to the throne had appeared. It remained to be seen if Harry would live up to their great legacy.

Learning the sport of golf outside the homogeneous Scottish instructional system, Harry attacked the game in a way no one in England had ever seen before. Throughout the history of the sport, golfers had been holding the shaft of the club in the palms of both hands like a baseball bat. On his own, Harry had come up with an innovative overlapping grip that locked his huge, powerful hands into a single unit, delivering a harder, surer strike at the bottom of the swing. His hand-eye coordination was so precise, he clipped the ball off the turf without taking a divot. The ball obeyed him like a circus animal; fades and draws appeared on command, and his standard shots flew straighter than bullets. He had developed mastery of what he called a push shot; launching a low ball through any kind of wind until it stuck on the green like a surefooted bird. He managed all this with just eight clubs in his bag, well below the unlimited number many players used and the rules then allowed. By the time he entered his first Open, Harry was already the most accurate striker of the golf ball who ever lived.

Harry's demeanor and methods on the course appeared so deceptively effortless, fellow pros began to call him "The Stylist." He was the sport's first dedicated athlete and kept himself in superb physical condition, following a program of exercises he determined were specifically beneficial to golf. Although it had been forty years since the introduction of the gutta-percha ball, many pros still affected "the St. Andrews swing," a closed choppy hack at the ball designed to draw and run the old featherie ball below the stiff Scottish winds. Harry learned the game with the solid gutta-percha, moved the ball forward in his stance, squared his feet to it, stood upright, and made a powerful, efficient athletic swing that wouldn't look out of place on today's professional tour. His tempo flowed as rhythmically as a Strauss waltz. His was the first modern golf swing, and before long, dozens of pros tried to emulate his elegant, musical move at the ball. So many others soon began mirroring his innovative way of holding the club that they soon began calling it the "Vardon grip."

In addition to "The Stylist," Harry earned another nickname on the course: "The Greyhound," a reference to the relentless way he gained ground when coming from behind in a match. No one who held a lead in front of Harry ever felt secure, and this can be attributed to the one quality none of his admirers ever duplicated, hidden so thoroughly as it was behind his gentleman's manner: Harry Vardon's mental toughness. After the childhood he endured, any misfortune that befell him on a golf course was literally a walk in the park.

Another precocious English talent named John Henry Taylor made his Open debut in 1893. Known to his friends as J.H., a year younger than Harry, and like him the son of a manual laborer, Taylor grew up caddying and playing at Royal North Devon, also known as Westward Ho!; designed by Old Tom Morris, the course was England's first true seaside links. Taylor had developed an idiosyncratic flat-footed swing and derived considerable power from his heavily muscled legs; his thighs were so thick, he couldn't cross one over the other, and finding trousers to fit them presented a constant challenge. By 1893 Taylor had already risen to a job as a professional at Winchester, one of the finest English clubs. Like Harry, as a teenaged boy he had also endured a stint of Dickensian domestic service, but his nerves had suffered from the experience more than the sturdy Vardon's; although a ferocious competitor who asked or gave no quarter, Taylor was subject to black periods of self-doubt and plagued by chronic digestive disorders. A taut, high-strung terrier to Harry's sleek coursing hound, he and Harry realized the two ex-caddies had a lot to talk about and struck up an immediate friendship.

The following year, in 1894, the presiding figures of the Royal & Ancient Golfing Society expanded the rota for the British Open. They announced that for the first time in its thirty-four-year history the tournament would take place outside of Scotland, at Sandwich, Kent, on the links of St. George's. One of the first seaside courses in the south of England, St. George's was a worthy addition; the lush texture of its velvety turf resulted in the perfect lies players dream about. Harry improved to a fifth-place finish in his second Open Championship, but he watched fellow Young Turk J. H. Taylor dominate the field, win the tournament going away, and become the first Englishman to ever break the Scottish stranglehold on the Claret Jug. Harry paid close attention to how the victory transformed his friend's life; Taylor's home club immediately doubled his salary, and increased demand for private lessons tripled it. Appearances in exhibitions all over Britain came his way along with regular invitations to participate in high-stakes challenge matches. He was even asked to lend his endorsement to products in advertising from golf balls to beer, a new phenomenon in sports, one that cash-poor professionals were only too happy to embrace.

In 1895 J. H. Taylor proved his first Open victory was no fluke by successfully defending his title, this time on Scottish ground, mastering the sterner test of St. Andrews; Harry took a step forward as well, leading the tournament after the first round. The Scottish press fell into despondency; it was one thing for an Englishman to capture the Open while playing in England, but at St. Andrews, their sport's holiest shrine? The infidels had sacked Jerusalem. To these journalists' minds, Taylor's second win foretold evil portents for golf's future north of the Tweed; the man who would soon embody their worst fears was already in plain sight. Harry ended up finishing ninth in the Open that year, tied with his brother Tom, and it's a curious note in Vardon's career—of all the immortals, he's the only one who never developed a feeling of religious awe for the old course. For some reason Harry was unable to articulate, he never won on the Royal & Ancient's home turf; St. Andrews just didn't suit his game.

In early 1896 Harry climbed another step up the professional ladder and accepted a job at a club in Ganton, Yorkshire. Ganton's five-year-old course, a future Ryder Cup site, was later redesigned by Dr. Alister MacKenzie, a surgeon in the British army during the Boer War who would go on to create American masterpieces at Cypress Point and Augusta National. Ganton was one of England's first heathland clubs, built a few miles inland from the sea, a departure from the traditional links that pointed toward a more diverse future for the game's architecture.

Although Harry hadn't yet won the British Open, he had tested himself in the game's crucible, enabling him to assess the quality of his competition with a cool, dispassionate eye. He was privately convinced now that the only man standing between him and the championship was his good friend J. H. Taylor. He'd also spotted a flaw in Taylor's psyche he believed he could exploit; J.H. was a self-assured front-runner who played best when he ran out in front of the pack. Get him into a street fight and Harry suspected the tightly wrapped Taylor's abrupt, angular swing might fall off its hinges. He asked the members of his new club at Ganton to offer Taylor a challenge match to be played on Harry's home course three weeks before the 1896 Open. Eager to draw attention to both the course and their promising young pro, the members at Ganton agreed, and Harry's friend Taylor accepted. Newspaper coverage of the defending Open champion going against one of the game's rising young players turned the match into a major event.

A confident J. H. Taylor arrived at Ganton only the day before their match. Certain he had Harry's number, Taylor decided against playing a practice round on the unfamiliar course. On May 14, 1896, Harry and Taylor teed off in front of a sizeable partisan crowd; Harry shook Taylor's hand on the first tee. He didn't say another word to him until they walked toward each other on the eleventh green, when Taylor shook Harry's hand to congratulate him. The match was over and Harry had won 8 and 7, leading by eight holes with seven left to play. Harry Vardon had just wiped the floor with the defending two-time Open champion.

J. H. Taylor was no slouch; he won five British Opens before he was through, a French and German Open as well, became one of the founding fathers of the Professional Golfer's Association, and captained the second British Ryder Cup team. After caddying at Royal North Devon as a boy, Taylor was elected the club's president in 1937, thus becoming the first man to complete the arc of the professional's social ascendance. A prodigious talent by any era's standards, he was about to be surpassed by an even stronger player while still in his early prime, a turn-of-the-century Palmer to Vardon's Nicklaus. Taylor lived until 1963. Having personally watched and evaluated every major player to come on the scene for over seven decades, including Hogan and Nicklaus, he never wavered in his admiration for Harry Vardon.

"Little did I guess when playing him at Ganton," Taylor later wrote in his excellent autobiography, "that I was playing a man who would develop into—in my solemn and considered judgement—the finest and most finished golfer the game has ever produced."

Three weeks later the Honourable Company of Edinburgh Golfers— the game's oldest organization, predating the Royal & Ancient Golfing Society of St. Andrews by a decade—hosted the 1896 Open Championship at their new digs in Muirfield, east of Edinburgh. After fleeing an overcrowded course at nearby Musselburgh, the Honourable Company bought a sodden pasture that housed a primitive eighteenth-century links and almost overnight transformed it into one of the world's classic tests.

As all major tournaments were for decades to come, the British Open was still being played over just two days, with two rounds on each day. Harry finished the first day at Muirfield six strokes in back of defending champ Taylor, who sprinted out to his signature early lead. Denied the use of the members' clubhouse, the sixty-four competing pros were ordered to change their shoes and clothes in a rough wooden shed on low ground near a swampy cow pond. Unwilling to risk leaving their clubs in the shack unattended overnight, both Vardon and Taylor carried their bags back to a nearby boardinghouse. Following his formula for success at Ganton, Harry kept his own counsel and didn't speak to Taylor all night, who in the morning admitted to a sleepless night.

On the Open's second day Harry shot 78 in the morning round to Taylor's 81, erasing half his lead. In the afternoon the wind kicked up and the increasingly nervous Taylor posted another 81, but the wind was affecting everyone's game and Taylor walked into the—well, not the clubhouse, but the shack, still holding a slim lead. When Taylor heard that Vardon was mounting a charge, he made his way to the back of the eighteenth green to watch him finish. Harry stepped to the difficult 447-yard home hole needing a birdie three for an outright win; a par would secure a tie with Taylor. Harry's perfect tee shot took a cruel bounce off the fairway into light rough on the right. To reach the green in two and gamble for the win now he'd have to carry a treacherous bunker that stretched fifty yards in front of the green, a dangerous reef on which more than one championship hope had foundered. Bearing no resemblance to the groomed, beachy sandboxes found on courses today, bunkers then were rough, untended waste pits cluttered with rocks and loose debris. As he stood over his second shot, Harry's victory in his challenge match with Taylor determined his strategy. Confident he could handle his friend in a two-man play-off, Harry laid up short of that bunker, chipped onto the green, and coolly sank a ten-footer for the tie.

Their thirty-six-hole play-off for the Open Championship would have to wait a day; another tournament had long been scheduled at nearby North Berwick on the following morning, and both Taylor and Vardon had committed to appear. One of Scotland's oldest courses, hugging a rugged stretch of eastern coastline, the North Berwick links had played a central role in the game's development, without ever inspiring the emotional veneration of St. Andrews or Prestwick. North Berwick was and forever had been a lunch bucket, workaday layout; tough, honest, and plain.

Reserving himself for the next day's play-off, a relaxed Harry finished ninth at North Berwick, and came in delighted to see Taylor still grinding out on the course. Unable to curb his fierce competitive instinct, Taylor had pushed into a tie for first place and a nine-hole play-off. He eventually prevailed and won eight pounds, but at a spendthrift cost of nervous energy he could scarcely afford to waste. Another promising omen for Harry; before his morning round he happened across a derelict putter in the North Berwick pro's shop and liked the way it felt in his hands so much, he asked the man to reshaft it for him while he played. The only part of Harry's game that ever came in for criticism was his putting, and then only in comparison to the rest of his golf. When he came off the links late in the day, Harry stuck the newly shafted stick in his bag, traveled back to Muirfield that night, and slept the sleep of the just.

The 1896 Open Championship play-off at Muirfield began at nine the following morning. Tom Vardon caddied for Harry and his presence on the bag meant a lot to his brother's confidence; as a first-rate player himself who knew Harry's game backward and forward, no one had a better ability to offer perfect advice at precisely the right moment. Tom was also the only human being the passionately self-reliant Harry ever listened to or confided in, about golf, marriage, and whatever fell between. Their relationship transcended sibling differences; they were a team, Jerseymen against the world, and this was the most important day of their lives.

Harry showed up ready; he quickly ran out to a six-stroke lead on the front nine, but Taylor cut it back to two as they finished their first eighteen. According to the opinion of at least one reporter, the outcome of the championship was settled during lunch. In front of a crowd of five thousand people, laughing and chatting with anyone who happened by, a preternaturally serene Harry sat down to a hearty steak and a beer. Watching him from a distance, his stomach in knots, the fretful Taylor could barely wash down a digestive biscuit with a cup of weak tea.

On the first hole of the afternoon round, Harry knocked his tee shot over Muirfield's encircling wall, out of bounds. Taylor birdied. All square. Instantly putting the setback behind him, Harry never lost his faint little smile—"It's gone, no use worrying," he said quietly to Tom, as they moved to the second tee—while the gasping Taylor looked like he was about to blow a gasket. Three holes later Harry had his two-shot lead back and he held on to it tenaciously until the seventeenth. Both men reached the par five's green in three, thirty-five feet above the hole, Vardon's ball lying just inside Taylor's. Taylor's putt ran straight for home but skidded to a stop an inch shy of the lip. Having seen the line, Harry stroked his castaway putter and rammed his ball past Taylor's into the back of the cup. Birdie four. Three-stroke lead, one hole to play. Filled by a calm he later described as eerie, Harry stepped to the eighteenth tee and nailed his drive down the middle of the fairway. Forced to go for broke, Taylor went for the green on his long second shot, bunkered himself, and ended up taking six. Harry played smart, laid up short of the bunker, chipped on, and two-putted for a five. The crowd erupted. Harry Vardon had won the Open Championship.

His brother Tom ran over and embraced him, tears in both their eyes. They clung to each other, neither able to speak; the prayer Harry had offered years before for escape from obscurity on Jersey had been answered. Harry had written down some words he planned to speak at the presentation ceremony, but when they handed him the Claret Jug, and he held his sport's highest trophy in his hands for the first time, all the feelings he never gave expression to on the course or elsewhere in his life so overwhelmed him, Harry could only whisper a hoarse, simple "Thank you."

Harry's name joined the list of greats on the Claret Jug and he took home thirty pounds in prize money, the largest single sum he'd ever received. He hung that vagrant putter he'd rescued from North Berwick over his mantel at home, the first exhibit in what would become a crowded trophy room, but he never played with it again. The privileges of championship followed in short order; he was besieged for lessons on his course at home, invitations for lucrative challenge matches poured in from around the country, and within months he quadrupled his base salary.

Success became Harry; he dominated nearly every event he entered during the ensuing year, and as word spread about his achievements, as would happen later with Arnie or Tiger, larger crowds than golf had ever seen before began showing up just to watch Harry Vardon play. Instead of dingy rooming houses, he could now afford to spend all those lonely nights on the road in first-class hotels. His dark good looks and athletic form began gracing a variety of advertisements, none of which hurt his standing with a growing legion of female fans. Perhaps sensing a threat in the wind, five years after he'd left her on Jersey, his wife, Jessie, finally agreed to join him in England; they bought their first house a short walk from his club in Ganton. Harry's moment had arrived and he put an iron grip on it; driven by the specters of poverty he'd struggled so fiercely to escape, he was on his way to becoming the wealthiest professional golfer his sport had ever known.

"The Stylist" exhibited a sense of fashion that extended beyond his golf game. Annoyed at the way his pants legs bunched and muddied during a round and feeling pinched by golf's traditional tweed jacket, Harry assembled an outfit better suited to facilitate his fluid swing. In early 1897, on the first day of a tournament in Northern Ireland, he walked out to the first tee and unveiled his creation: a natty Norfolk jacket with a red rose in his lapel, suspenders, white shirt and tie, and a pair of knickerbocker trousers buttoned over knee-high woolen socks. He patiently explained to non-plussed reporters that the suspenders reminded him to keep his shoulders square and upright, while the knickers, long considered suitable apparel only for preteen boys, kept his cuffs from dragging through the dirt. (Also known as "plus fours" because they reach the knee, plus four inches.) The rumpled Scottish professionals grumbled that the dapper Vardon was putting on airs, trying to show them up; local Irish papers wondered if he'd lost his mind. Harry smiled through it all and suggested that the Scots might find a similar level of comfort if they wore kilts, then went out and lapped the field, winning the tournament by eleven strokes. Harry wore an identical outfit onto the links for the rest of his career. Within a year, knickers lined the shelves of nearly every British golfer's wardrobe.

Unlike many of the game's modern stars, Harry enjoyed the camaraderie of the locker room and became unfailingly popular with his fellow pros; they considered him the very model of a man's man. Every one of those competitors also knew that out on the course Harry's only purpose was to crush them into a fine dust; when pressure mounted in a match Harry could reach down and engage a gear no one else seemed to possess. His concentration was so complete, he seldom spoke during a round and played with an enigmatic, perpetual half-smile on his face so central to his on-course behavior that one writer labeled it "vardonic." Harry often lit up a pipe when he played, which further enhanced his image as a man supremely at ease with himself, regardless of what was going on in his game. He appeared never to notice a single shot his opponents made, good or bad, which affected their state of mind a lot more than it did his. Remember Jack Nicklaus during his prime on the back nine of Sunday in any major and you'll catch a glimpse of the blue carbon steel in Harry's spine. Whether by chance or by choice, Harry came into his own equipped with the ideal emotional thermostat for this complex and maddening game; always engaged but never upset. That ability to compartmentalize, separate emotion from outcome, is part of what separates every champion from the pack. He later claimed, without bragging, that his nerves never bothered him during a match, although it's easier to verify that if they did no one else ever knew it by looking at him.

A horse cost Harry the 1897 Open; the event was played at Hoylake, England, near Liverpool, which shared its course with a racetrack, a not uncommon mix of sporting pastimes in those early days. On the crucial hole of the final round, his drive went flying onto the track and landed in a deep, unnegotiable hoofprint. Knowing the breaks of the game required every man to take the bad luck with the good, Harry offered no complaint, and suffered a double bogey, which knocked him from the race. He finished a quiet sixth.

The following year in 1898's Open at Prestwick, Harry battled Scotsman Willie Park Jr. down to the wire. A successful golf course architect and relentless self-promoter, Park was a former two-time Open champion (1887, 1889) and author of the first best-selling golf instruction book. Only a touch past his prime, he was also a bit of a crackpot with the braggadocio of a professional wrestler.

The British Open's original home, Prestwick remains to this day a monument to the game's quirky origins: blind shots, fast and bumpy fairways, harrowing pot bunkers and fierce swirling winds. Adapting to the Scottish style on his second try at the old links, Harry played smart, conservative golf and trailed Willie Park by two going into the final round. Playing a few holes ahead of him, Harry caught Park with a birdie at the tenth. Long before the introduction of scoreboards, young caddies ran back and forth across the course keeping players apprised of each other's score. Quickly made aware that Vardon had matched him, Park knuckled down and their tie stood until the eighteenth, a rare par three finishing hole. Harry missed the green off the tee, chipped up, and drained a testing ten-footer for a final round 76 to preserve the tie. Twenty minutes later the tournament's entire crowd mobbed the eighteenth green to watch Park come in. Jockeying for sight lines grew so intense that as Harry walked back toward the green to have a look, he found himself elbowed to the back of the pack; they didn't even realize he was there.

Park hit his tee shot to the front fringe of the eighteenth green. As he walked up to his ball, all Harry could see was the top of Park's head. He faced a makeable twenty-foot putt, straight uphill, no break; if he sank it, Willie Park Jr. would win the 1898 Open. Park called his faithful putter "Old Pawky" and his inspired work with it on Britain's greens had always been one of his notable strengths. A hush. Harry turned away and listened. Moments later, an animated buzz began but no cheers; Park had left his approach three feet short. As he stepped up to hole the routine tap-in and secure the tie, Harry walked away, mentally preparing himself for the next day's play-off. He stopped cold when he heard that distinctive moan so peculiar to a golf crowd, eight thousand voices breaking absolute silence like a single enormous creature that had just lost a bet: "Oooohhh!" Park choked. As if woken from a dream the crowd around Vardon realized he was standing there among them and a cheer went up. Harry had won his second British Open.

His loss seemed to unhinge Willie Park Jr. He declared, insupportably, that the Claret Jug had been stolen from him. Ugly rumors circulated that Park missed that last putt on purpose because he had wanted to take on Vardon in the play-off, only to then learn that Harry's supporters in the gallery had lied to him about Harry's score as Park approached the green, thereby cheating him out of the win. After learning that Willie Park himself had generated these damnable lies, Harry didn't dignify them with a response. That only made matters worse.

Now proclaiming himself the defender of Scotland's honor as the birthplace of golf against the upstart Englishman, Willie Park began issuing outrageous monthly challenges in *Golf Magazine*, calling Harry out to face him again in a one-on-one match to settle the imaginary offense. He proposed unheard-of stakes: one hundred pounds, winner take all. Early negotiations to arrange the contest broke down; Park blamed Vardon, Vardon blamed Park. When they ran into each other at tournaments later in the season, the Scotsman taunted Harry publicly. Harry somehow restrained himself from busting Park in the chops. He had constructed a persona of impeccable civility in response to his harsh upbringing, but Harry could not abide boorish disrespect; he answered the insult in print in the pages of *Golf Magazine*, casually dismissing Park in an interview as "not much of a golfer." Inflated by the press, their dispute escalated beyond the personal to one of national pride, with newspapers in Scotland and England each lining up behind their respective champion.

It's more than possible Willie Park started all this breast-beating to boost his off-the-course career; he was the first pro golfer to market a personally endorsed line of clubs and balls for department stores, and sales of his weird fifty-six-sided golf ball—the modestly titled "Park Royal"—had gone begging after his loss in the Open. (On hot days Park stored his "Royals" in a bucket of ice to keep them hard and round.) In fairness, Park's enmity may have been merely a showman's attempt to drum up brand-name recognition for his struggling product line. If that was his reason, Willie Park never let Harry in on the plan; by creating an international incident out of his defeat at the Open, all he succeeded in doing was turning Harry's anger to a cold, white flame. Letting Park cool his heels, Harry refused to commit to a rematch until after the Open Championship was held at Royal St. George's the following year in 1899.

By that time, the Greyhound had reached cruising speed. Amidst the hottest streak of his entire career Harry jumped out to a first-round 76 at St. George's, led wire-to-wire, and breezed to the finish line five strokes ahead without a backward glance for his third Open Championship in four years. With the press now dubbing him "The Napoleon of Golf," Harry appeared poised to lead his sport to a popularity undreamed of, but first there was the small matter of Willie Park Jr. to dispense with. To remove the jabbering magpie from his back, Harry finally agreed to a seventy-two-hole challenge match; two rounds at North Berwick—Park's home course in Scotland—with the finale to follow at Harry's home turf at Ganton. Each man deposited a hundred pounds of his own money—a sizeable chunk of Harry's net worth—in escrow with the editor of *Golf Magazine*. The press treated the event like a modern heavyweight title fight, and the showdown captured the imagination of both men's nations. Special trains had to be added on the English rail schedule to handle crowds traveling north for the first round. Aggressive Scottish partisan fans at blue-collar North Berwick had badly abused English golfers in cross-border matches for years, and friends privately urged Harry not to set foot in front of them without an armed escort. Unwilling to back down from anyone, let alone a lying braggart who'd slapped the gauntlet in his face, Harry traveled to North Berwick with only his brother Tom, who appointed himself to serve as both caddie and bodyguard.

Harry walked the links and discussed strategy with Tom the evening before the match; as they rounded a tall dune, a figure appeared directly in front of the two brothers and hurled a huge horseshoe at Harry's head. Only his lightning reflexes prevented the iron from braining him. His assailant turned out to be a well-known local caddie, a demented eccentric named "Big" Crawford who ran the ginger beer concession on the North Berwick back nine. Far from trying to injure him, Crawford claimed he'd wagered every penny he had on Harry and was only tossing the shoe over his head to bring him luck. Harry walked back to his rooming house with the odd feeling that their bizarre encounter with Crawford might do exactly that, but only after restraining Tom from returning Crawford's horseshoe at a significantly lower altitude.

The next morning over eight thousand people flooded North Berwick's links to watch their opening round. Lined up ten deep along the path from the pro shop to the first tee, the hometown crowd cheered wildly when Willie Park appeared. When Harry stepped out to follow, a nasty chorus of boos and catcalls greeted him. Harry stopped and stared down the hostile section of the crowd. For Scottish golf fans steeped in the game's tradition, even an Open champion who had the misfortune to be born English possessed an aura of majesty; they quieted. Harry smiled, and continued to the tee. For the rest of the day, at least whenever he held a club in his hand at address, Harry's dignity, composure, and manifest skill silenced the rowdy Scottish partisans.

Tom carried Harry's clubs in one of the new canvas bags that had recently hit the market, but Park's regular sherpa, a red-faced old-schooler nicknamed "Fiery," disdained the contraption, bunching the clubs under his arm, whipping the appropriate stick out in time-honored fashion before his man requested it. Inspired by the crowd's fervent support, Willie Park played out of his head, driving the ball solidly, dropping putts from all over the greens. Instead of folding, Harry displayed his unflappable command of every aspect of the game and stood up to Park's assault. Expecting a donnybrook, the crowd was treated to one of the finest exhibitions of golf Scotland had seen since the days of Alan Robertson and Old Tom Morris. The two men halved every one of the first ten holes; both were two under par.

On the eleventh, after Park split the fairway with a perfect tee shot, Harry stepped up and drilled an equally impressive drive. As the astonished gallery looked on, Harry's ball landed directly on top of Park's ball, knocking it forward another fifteen yards while sending Harry's sideways into a scraggly, unplayable lie. Cashing in this uncanny piece of luck, Park won the hole and he hung on to finish the morning round by that same margin, one up. In the afternoon, Harry evened the match on the first hole and they again halved the next eight holes in a row. After canning a birdie putt at fifteen and a misplayed iron by Park on the next, Harry finished their initial thirty-six leading Park by two holes. Judging by Park's strutting banty rooster reaction on the eighteenth green, the Scotsman apparently believed that any outcome short of a fatal thrashing by the great Vardon represented high moral victory. After watching Park cavort around among his adoring fans, Harry first calmed Tom, livid at Park's unsportsmanlike display, then walked off the course with that same thin enigmatic smile on his lips. His eyes told a different story.

When a few days later Park and his twenty-man entourage traveled down to Ganton for the return match, Harry made sure that the Scotsmen were treated to every courtesy. He arranged first-class lodging and meals and saw to it a fawning line of English journalists paid homage to Park throughout his two-day visit, inflating the self-absorbed Willie until his seams stretched. The next day when the action moved onto the course, the star treatment ended abruptly. Playing at a level even he only rarely achieved, from the opening tee to his final putt, Harry demolished Willie Park; he won the match 11 and 10, bringing the afternoon round to an unceremonious end after only eight holes. When they shook hands at the close, Park couldn't even look Harry in the eye. His shocked legion of

Scots supporters drifted off the course in anesthetized silence. The editor of *Golf Magazine* turned over the prize of two hundred pounds to Harry; Willie Park Jr. slipped onto the train back to Scotland that night a broken man. Although his success as a golf merchandiser and course architect continued for many years—at one point he traveled to America for six months to serve as John Jacob Astor's personal instructor on his private course—Park never issued a challenge match to another golfer in his lifetime. Because of what it meant for both him and England, Harry later called his match with Willie Park Jr. the most important event of his professional career.

Having beaten their champion, Harry followed up his victory over Park with a triumphal tour of Scotland, thumping every provincial pro he faced on their own home course. During one thirty-six-hole match he holed out from over a hundred yards in both the morning and afternoon round, on the same hole. After bearing the brunt of one of these routine steamrollings, a proud former Scottish champion told the press afterward that going up against Harry would break the heart of an iron ox. As his tour continued and their hopefuls fell to Vardon one after another, the Scottish press drifted into progressively deeper anguish; for good reason, as it turned out. Although from time to time Scotland would send forth dozens of first-rank players into championship competition, their domination of the game they gave the world was officially at an end.

Harry Vardon was twenty-nine years old and stood alone at the top of Britain's sporting culture. He'd finished the century with a performance of sustained excellence the game had never before seen and few champions would subsequently match. One writer who covered him throughout this period claimed Harry hadn't missed a fairway off the tee for two years. During the heart of his hot streak Harry reeled off fourteen straight tournament victories, a mark that never has and never will be broken. He won more British Opens in the 1890s single-handedly than all of Scotland's finest combined, and in doing so concentrated the interest of the English public on the sport of golf like no one man had ever done before.

As the turn of the new year ushered in the birth of the twentieth century, Harry's gaze turned to the west. Out of the blue, in the spring of 1900, he received an irresistible offer to make another exhibition tour, designed to promote a new golf ball bearing his name, in an even bigger country waiting to be conquered. He took them up on it.

Harry was going to America.

THE COUNTRY CLUB, 1900.

(COURTESY OF THE COUNTRY CLUB)

1900

ALTHOUGH HE ACCEPTED Spalding's offer, and agreed to play with and promote his namesake ball during the tour, Harry declined a contractual percentage of sales and instead settled for a flat fee: two thousand pounds for ten months of work. Since he would also be allowed to pocket any purses he won in exhibition matches throughout his travels, this turned out to be a farsighted decision; by the time it was over, he would net a small fortune, more than $20,000. Delighted to further Harry's career, Ganton agreed to let its resident pro out of his contract for the tour's duration. When Jessie predictably refused to accompany him on the voyage, Harry arranged for her sister Annie to sail over from Jersey and stay with her in his absence.

Amid great public fanfare, and no little grousing in the British press about a mercenary champion selling out to an American seductress tossing buckets of money at him, Harry sailed for America on January 27, 1900. Six days later a mob of American press assaulted him as he stepped off the gangway in New York. The hyperbolic headlines they cooked up seemed to suggest a head of state had arrived for a presidential summit. Harry quickly learned to keep his answers to these ravenous pack animals short and to the point; brazenly ignorant about his sport, they wrote whatever flights of fancy they wanted to concoct about Harry no matter what he told them. He didn't need to worry since every word they printed, fictional or otherwise, turned out to be slavishly favorable. As true then as it is now, New York loves a winner, and the public backed up the news hawks' intuition that this Brit golfer could be a big-ticket item: Harry Vardon sold a ton of newspapers. When he played his first exhibition a few days later in New Jersey, during a swirling snowstorm, a crowd of over two thousand showed up and followed him every step of the round.

HARRY'S TOUR OF America plays like one of those feverish headline montages from an old Hollywood biopic. The moment he set foot in America, he became the best player the country had ever known. By his own estimate he covered over one hundred thousand miles by boat, train, horse-drawn wagon, and, for one memorable day in Colorado, mule. Public curiosity about the handsome, dynamic champ never waned; eager crowds and hordes of press dogged his every step. When he played an exhibition at Van Cortlandt Park in New York, the country's first public golf course, the Stock Exchange shut down for the day so Wall Street's hotshots could ride to the Bronx and watch him tee it up. Moguls with a golfing addiction on the order of Andrew Carnegie went one better; they took Harry out to lavish dinners and picked his brain like scientists searching for the fountain of youth. Local grandees threw glittering parties for Harry whenever he rolled into their town; his Spalding tour manager nearly suffered a breakdown trying to sort out a social calendar that changed more often than a four-year-old's mind. Harry never complained. Feeling these public obligations were as important a part of his job as the golf, he soldiered on, honoring a remarkable number of mind-numbing engagements. As he usually appeared at these affairs with a succession of good-looking babes on his arm, it seemed fame in America had begun to offer Harry some of the comforts he was apparently no longer finding at home.

But golf came first, and here's how good he was: With the exception of some high-profile singles matches against established pros like current U.S. Open champion Willie Smith or future U.S. and British Amateur champ Walter J. Travis, every other exhibition he took part in pitted Harry against a city's top two golfers, pro or amateur, playing the better of their two balls, as a team; sometimes three golfers ganged up against him. Most of these pros were journeyman Scots, skilled players who'd recently sailed across the pond to accept positions at the mushrooming number of American clubs; their keen awareness of Vardon's reputation back home helped fan the flames of public interest wherever he turned up to play. Some of them regarded Harry with such wonder, they could barely swing a club in his presence; just as many others went out and played the round of their lives against him. Not that it made much difference.

On over half of the courses he visited, having never set foot on them before and without time for a practice round, Harry Vardon shattered the club scoring record. He took part in eighty-eight matches during his American tour and he lost exactly once, 2 and 1, to a pro in Miami named Alex Findlay. Harry can be forgiven this blemish; agronomists hadn't gotten the hang of growing grass in southern Florida yet. This course's fairways were fashioned out of compressed dirt, with greens made of oiled and rolled sand, a semitropical mutation the Englishman had never imagined before.

Harry himself said that for some reason even he didn't understand, during this season of his life the world's hardest game became easy for him. He found America's milder climate delightful; the dry spring heat loosened up his muscles in a way he'd never felt before and it seemed to liberate his swing. Shedding his customary Norfolk jacket, he played in shirtsleeves, relaxed by America's relative informality. As the trip gathered steam, he began to entertain escapist fantasies about shedding the baggage of his past and becoming an American himself. He found the country's brassy big cities dazzling, the variety and scale of the American landscape captivated him, and the less class-conscious social atmosphere charmed his working-class disposition. For the first time in his life, Harry wasn't just allowed into private clubhouses, their members threw an arm around his shoulder and welcomed him in as an honored guest. His new fans were fascinated by the mechanics of Harry's golf swing; a nation of go-getter engineers, breaking down a foreign technology to mine its secrets. Far from being annoyed by their insatiable curiosity, Harry realized America perceived him as the sport's ambassador, and he was only too happy to hold question-and-answer sessions after his work on the course was finished.

The only complaint Harry ever voiced had to do with American caddies; he never found one who could begin to measure up to the high British standard. During a round in Florida the only spark of interest his diffident club bearer showed all day came when he asked if he could borrow Harry's niblick to go kill a snake. Another flatly refused to clean Harry's ball after a muddy landing, telling him in no uncertain terms that such menial work was beneath his dignity. Difficult as the absence of a useful caddie made his competitive rounds, he reminded himself the game in America was only twelve years old; the former caddie in Harry realized that respect for the game's traditions had not had time to develop in its humblest foot soldiers.

During his journey Harry entertained a boatload of lucrative side deals that thickened the engorged lining of his pockets. One offer he couldn't turn down brought him to the sporting goods department of Jordan, Marsh & Co., a bellwether Boston department store. For a fee so generous he was too embarrassed to ever mention the amount, Harry agreed to hit balls into a net inside the store—half an hour hitting balls, half an hour off—from nine-thirty in the morning until five in the afternoon.

When Harry stepped out onto the showroom floor of Jordan Marsh on the appointed day, he was stunned to discover an eager crowd of over a hundred people waiting for him. He greeted them with a shy tip of his cap. A young volunteer teed up his balls from a wire bucket and the crowd watched him perform in hushed silence as he drove one perfect shot into the net after another. When the first half hour was over, they burst into thunderous applause, and when he exited to take his scheduled break, the ovation didn't stop; he felt compelled to come back out for an encore. By that time new faces had refreshed the crowd and when he finished his second session, the applause lasted even longer. Harry couldn't for the life of him imagine why anyone wanted to watch this monotonous routine that was no more interesting to him than hammering a long row of nails, but these folks were so mysteriously aroused by his exotic skill, they wouldn't let him stop.

At this point, bored with hitting the driver, Harry took out his niblick, picked out a target, and began skying balls toward a metal tap in the room's cavernous ceiling. As each successive shot came closer to hitting its mark, the store's panicked manager ran out to stop him; the ceiling tap connected to the store's sprinkler system and if he hit it solidly, the taps would open and flood the entire ground floor. Harry went back to the driver. Before long, spectators jammed every inch of the store that offered a glimpse of him; Harry saw kids hanging off the lampposts outside staring through the windows. A man who believed in living up to his agreements, Harry ended up hitting balls for eight straight hours, then fled the store as fast as his feet could carry him. (Department store exhibitions eventually became such a common promotional device, and one professionals found so demeaning, that in 1928 the PGA issued a ruling saying its members would no longer participate in them.) Tumultuous applause and cheering followed him for a block. He later found out that within two hours after his appearance, Jordan, Marsh & Co. had sold out every golf club and ball they had in the store.

Somewhere in the crowd that afternoon, with his mother, Mary, stood seven-year-old Francis Ouimet. Francis had spied an advertisement for Vardon's appearance in a Boston newspaper and begged his father, Arthur, for a chance to see the man behind his beloved Vardon Flyer. For the first time in his life, Francis's runaway love for golf smacked into a wall. Embittered by his inability to break through Boston's hard-drawn class lines, Arthur's resentments about his stalled station in life dominated his thoughts and he tended them in brooding silence. Although Francis's older brother, Wilfred, always adapted himself to their father's will, and would pay for it dearly in later life, Francis possessed an innate cheerfulness and optimism that Arthur found maddening and inexplicable. Francis was the model of an obedient son, but he had come into the world with an irrepressibly sunny spirit that deflected Arthur's every attempt to grind into him his own tragic view of life. Nothing he could do or say to the boy got across his baseline belief, that all that awaited an open-hearted unsuspecting soul was cold, hard disenchantment. Arthur flatly refused Francis's request to see Harry Vardon perform at Jordan Marsh.

Mary had seen early on the quality of the dreamer in Francis; she knew this drew breath from something she'd always admired on her side of the family, the Irish romancer, a poetic softness, and she did what she could to nurture and protect it in her son. Wilfred suffered under his father's harsh discipline, problems with the bottle lay in his future, and Mary already sensed that some part of his spirit had been broken. Not so yet with Francis; she knew he'd learn the harsh lessons of the world soon enough, but in the meantime the dreamer in him needed looking after. After hearing Arthur turn Francis down, and seeing the young boy's disappointment, later that night Mary quietly went up to his bedroom. She told Francis she happened to be planning a shopping trip to Boston on the day Harry Vardon was making his appearance. If they chanced to pass by Jordan, Marsh & Co., Mary was certain she could find something the family needed on sale in the housewares section. Francis nearly hit the ceiling; she hushed him. It would have to remain their little secret.

When they entered the doors of Jordan, Marsh & Co. that morning, the sight across the room of Harry Vardon—that name emblazoned on his treasure, standing before him in the flesh—created in young Francis a state of spiritual transcendence. Harry's elegant attire, his self-contained manner, the sleek blade in his enormous hands repeating a precise, metronomic swing with no visible physical effort; he indeed appeared to be some sort of deity, descended from a plane of physical perfection. As Francis watched Vardon's club carve the same flawless arc through the air, ball after ball zooming up into the overhanging net, he made up his mind in that moment he wanted nothing more from his life than to be just like this avatar in front of him. Staring long and hard at Harry Vardon focused Francis's childish, unstructured fantasies like sunlight through a magnifying glass.

Harry interrupted his tour in May at the three-month mark, just long enough to return to Scotland and defend his British Open crown at St. Andrews. After enjoying a balmy American spring, the cold blustery winds blowing off the North Sea put an unexpected chill in his bones.

Even chillier after the lengthy absence was his reception at home; although he brought back a trunk full of thoughtful gifts and made all the proper gestures of the loving husband, Jessie showed scant interest in his scrapbook of American headlines or the colorful stories of this strange new land. A miscarriage earlier in the year had further undermined her brittle sense of self; the scope of Jessie's universe barely reached the front gate outside their door, let alone across the Atlantic. She was willing to enjoy all the fruits of her husband's achievements without showing the slightest interest in the excitement they generated in the rest of the world. Although Harry no longer practiced the faith in which he'd been raised, Catholic stoicism had equipped him with the capacity to suffer in silence, which went hand in hand with the overwhelming lesson of his wretched early life. He expected to suffer, period.

It was a critical turning point for Harry: Standing unhappily in his own living room, his wife again turning coldly away from him, the freedom and happiness he'd experienced in America suddenly presented a clearcut avenue of escape. A new life free of this domestic mousetrap and England's straitjacket caste restraints. The idea hit him hard enough to discuss with his brother Tom; Harry seriously considered sailing across the water again and never coming back. Tom was supportive. Harry wavered. His growing success and stature in Britain, his deeper need to live within the borders of a life he'd worked so long and hard to build carried tremendous weight. Harry was a breaker of sporting records, not social conventions. The moment passed. Instead of pulling up stakes for a new life, Harry packed for St. Andrews and prepared to defend his title. Jessie hardly noticed. Their deepening estrangement was made even more evident by her refusal to accompany him for the third straight Open Championship he'd returned to pursue. Harry left home and took the short train trip to Scotland with only his faithful brother Tom.

A number of his colleagues remarked on how tired Harry looked during the Open that year; whether it was the ongoing strain of a failing marriage or the rigorous demands of his foreign tour, something had chiseled away at the once indefatigable Vardon's reserves. When he arrived at St. Andrews, Harry found his old rival J. H. Taylor lying in wait for him, on the same course where J.H. had won his second Open five years before. After the firing of a cannon near the clubhouse, in a tradition that gave birth to the one now observed every year at the Masters, eighty-year-old Old Tom Morris hit a ceremonial first drive to open the championship, the last Open the father of the game would preside over on his home ground. Retired from tournament play now, Old Tom watched and walked along in Harry's gallery as the two-time defending champion followed him off the tee.

Tom and Harry played early in the day and set the pace, but by the end of the first round the determined Taylor had worked himself into a tie with both Vardon brothers, and built a two-stroke lead by the conclusion of the second. Without a strong answer from Harry, Taylor found his favorite front-running stride; during the third round the next morning, he increased his lead to six, then flat-out won the 1900 Open with a remarkable 75 at the last, played in a howling wind. Early on in the final eighteen Harry whittled Taylor's lead down to three, but he once again faded during the stretch at St. Andrews and had to settle for second place, eight strokes back. J. H. Taylor had now caught his friend and rival Harry Vardon on the larger career scoreboard, three Open Championships apiece.

After another brief stay with Jessie and her sister Annie, who had now taken up permanent residence in the prosperous Vardon household, Harry boarded the ocean liner *St. Paul* to head back to America on June 20. As summer warmed the northern half of the country, the pace during the second half of Harry's tour increased; New England, New York, New Jersey, Michigan, Colorado, Montreal, Toronto. He played an exhibition every other day, followed by a day of travel. The entire country followed his progress now; headlines of his exploits regularly appeared in cities Harry never came close to visiting. But now Harry Vardon wasn't the only British champion touring the United States.

In August, his win in the 1900 British Open still fresh in the public's mind, J. H. Taylor decided to follow Harry back to America. Taylor had recently purchased an interest in a Pittsburgh factory that manufactured and sold clubs in the States, and a visit on the heels of his latest victory made sound business sense. He announced a two-month exhibition tour scheduled to climax at the U.S. Open in October.

On the heels of Harry's return, newspapers reacted to Taylor's arrival like the Second Coming. When a babbling cyclone of reporters enveloped him as he stepped off the ship in New York, the uneasy Taylor blurted a curt "Don't know" to every question they peppered at him. A man more comfortable in the company of friends and familiar surroundings, J.H. found less to admire in America than Harry did. Constant travel aggravated his delicate stomach, and the presence of so many strangers increased his anxiety. Among Taylor's stops, an exhibition at The Country Club in Brookline; thirty-six holes of better ball against the two best players in Boston. Francis Ouimet spent the entire day across the street watching every shot he attempted, adding J. H. Taylor's to the bank of golf swings he was assembling in his memory.

Eager to create a newsworthy controversy, the American yellow press went to work drumming up a feud between the English champions. Although they remained spirited rivals throughout their careers, Harry and Taylor were solid friends off the course and never spoke a word in anger to each other. To read contemporary American accounts of their time in the States together, you'd think they'd threatened to eat each other's children. Some accused Taylor of trying to steal the thunder from Harry's tour. One reporter claimed he spotted J.H. spying on Harry from the crowd during an exhibition, disguised in a phony beard and glasses. Harry was reported to have offered an insane challenge, à la Willie Park Jr., to play Taylor *mano a mano* for the total salary of both men's entire tour, winner take all. Patent nonsense, willfully designed to draw the two men into a challenge match prior to the U.S. Open. For reasons not hard to discern—neither man had much to gain and everything to lose by competing against each other before the championship—both refused to take the bait. As the tall tales about their "blood feud" grew continually more outrageous, Taylor considered pursuing a libel suit until the two friends finally met in Chicago and Harry reassured J.H. this was just the way the press went about their business on this side of the briny.

Even in 1900 there was no such thing as bad publicity. When J. H.

Taylor opened his locker at the Chicago Golf Club the day before the first round of the U.S. Open, he found inside a courteous note and a tin box of a dozen balls from Mr. Coburn Haskell, a bicycle manufacturer from Akron, Ohio. The ball was of Mr. Haskell's own design; a small, solid rubber core surrounded by tightly wound rubber threads enclosed by a thin gutta-percha, and later balata cover. The ball's inspiration had occurred to Haskell while visiting a friend at the Goodrich Tire factory. Waiting in his friend's office, Haskell idly gathered up some loose rubber threads from the wastebasket, winding them into a tight ball. When the strands accidentally slipped from his hands, the wad of rubber shot across the room like a bottle rocket; its violent trajectory caused some synapse in Haskell's mind to fire up the words "golf ball." Two years of persistent experimentation later, Haskell and his partners received a U.S. patent for their "golf ball winding machine." Haskell began shipping unsolicited boxed samples to as many top professionals as he could find, hence this delivery to visiting British Open champion J. H. Taylor. His curiosity piqued, Taylor hit a few shots at the practice ground with Haskell's creation before the next day's competition. Because his game depended on bull's-eye accuracy, the way this new ball jumped off the club face and its soaring flight, at least thirty yards longer than the gutty, so alarmed J.H., he put the rest of the Haskells, as they were soon to be called, back in their box and left them in his locker for the duration of the tournament. Harry, on tour promoting his own well-publicized gutty ball, did not receive a box from Mr. Haskell.

The 1900 U.S. Open took place on October 4 and 5 under perfect skies before the largest crowd to ever witness a game of golf in America. None of the USGA's five previous professional championships had captured even a fraction of the public's interest; only scantily reported and barely attended, they had taken place largely in a void. Stoked by the grudge match angle whipped up by the press, thousands showed up at the Chicago Golf Club in Wheaton, Illinois, expecting to witness a bitter, two-man fight to the finish between the invading Brits. When Harry and J.H. finally got around to teeing it up, their performances exceeded every expectation. Both men coveted this championship; Harry in order to supply the ideal exclamation point to his American sojourn, Taylor because he wanted to be the first man in history to complete the double slam, hold both the British and American titles simultaneously.

The first five U.S. Opens had all been won by transplanted Scotsmen working as American club professionals; all five were in the field at Wheaton, led by defending champ Willie Smith, who'd taken the tournament in 1899 by a record eleven strokes. Along with Willie came his older brother Alex, a future two-time Open winner; the brothers had immigrated together from Carnoustie in 1898. (Their youngest brother, Macdonald, the best player in the family and a future member of the PGA Hall of Fame, wouldn't make the trip over for another five years.) Also contending at Wheaton was Willie Dunn Jr. of Musselburgh, son of another of Old Tom's ancient rivals and recent designer of the great American course at Shinnecock Hills. The best and brightest of America's "Willies" turned out to be Willie Anderson, a recent arrival from North Berwick who would win the U.S. Open the following year and two years later run off a record streak of three consecutive Open victories that has never been equaled.

After his win streak, Willie Anderson became the first American golfer, albeit an adopted one, to draw comparisons with Young Tom Morris. The comparison proved apt in more ways than one; he was the son of a renowned greenkeeper, he won four Opens in six years, and at the age of thirty, still poised at the top of his game and in apparent good health, he carried those comparisons with Young Tom to their ultimate sorry conclusion by suddenly dropping dead. An autopsy revealed advanced arteriosclerosis; as with Young Tom, alcohol abuse played a considerable part in Willie Anderson's shocking death.

All players of considerable talent, these expatriate challengers represented the best competition America had to offer. Harry had already beaten all five of them during the course of his tour, in two cases by staggering margins. None of them ever came close to being a factor in this tournament.

Harry teed off during the first round just after Taylor, paired in the last twosome with 1899's defending champion Willie Smith. The Chicago

Golf Club course set up better for Harry's lofted straight game than Taylor's low-running links shots, but a strong wind blowing off Lake Michigan in the morning rewarded Taylor's control and he carded a 76, leading Harry by three strokes. That afternoon Harry adjusted his game for the wind and came in at 78, while Taylor fell back to 82. At the halfway mark the nearest American stood five shots behind them and never came closer; the two-man race everyone had hoped for was at hand. Harry led Taylor by one stroke at the halfway point, but it should have been two; attempting to tap in a two-inch gimme for par at eighteen, Harry stubbed his putter into the ground and whiffed. It happened so quickly that not another soul saw him do it. True to the spirit of the game, Harry called the extra stroke on himself.

The next morning the Greyhound broke fast right out of the gate and extended his lead over Taylor to four strokes. Six holes into the afternoon's final round, Harry's lead had grown to five. At the long par four seventh, with the wind behind him, Harry nailed his Vardon Flyer over 270 yards, driving it through the fairway and into a bunker that for the first three rounds had been out of reach. Taylor pressed to take advantage of this slip but could only manage par. Harry nipped his ball neatly out of the bunker from 150 yards out to within three feet of the hole, and then sank the putt for birdie and a six-stroke lead. Taylor fought back; by the time the two men came to the final hole, he had narrowed Harry's lead to two. Taylor outdrove Harry off the tee at eighteen, but then the Stylist reached into his bag of tricks and slaughtered a two-wood over 225 yards, where it fluttered down onto the back of the green, in the immortal words of Sam Snead, like a butterfly with sore feet. Both men made par, but Harry Vardon had prevailed in their memorable duel and added *1900 U.S. Open Champion* to his list of titles. A striking photograph, taken just after his win, shows a spent and satisfied Harry seated outside the clubhouse in shirtsleeves, an open collar, and a bandana looped around his neck, looking considerably happier and more satisfied than he ever appeared after any victory in England.

J. H. Taylor later bitterly regretted leaving that gift box of Haskells in his locker on the tournament's first day, certain in retrospect that the rubber ball's additional length could have meant the difference for him. Fretting over such choices years afterward was vintage J. H. Taylor; Harry never gave a missed shot or a lost tournament a second thought for more than a couple of minutes. After he played a full practice round with his Haskells a week later in New York, Taylor became a permanent convert; J.H. never teed up a gutty again. Within three years every other golfer of note, on both sides of the Atlantic, would follow his lead.

Harry set sail back to England in early December on a ship appropriately christened *The Majestic*. His visit could only be viewed as a personal and professional triumph, and its importance to the development of the game cannot be underestimated. Harry's barnstorming tour did more to publicize and popularize golf in the United States than any single event in its history. His private search for perfection had resulted in a display of athletic excellence young America had never seen before. Wherever he played, he left in his wake a planted seed of interest that sprouted overnight; at private clubs and public courses, thousands of men, boys, and women who'd never even considered golf before all took up the game. After a century of exploring and taming the frontier that comprised most of their continent, Americans ready to settle down found in golf the perfect ritual to reenact their primal struggles. A player walked out into a manufactured "wilderness" armed only with primitive weapons, conquered the challenges and hazards of the landscape, and returned home to tell about his trials safe and sound. The metaphor embedded in the game proved irresistible to the psyche of the American male. By the end of Harry's ten months in the United States, over two hundred new golf clubs had announced plans to break ground.

Harry accomplished all of this alone. No caddie, no agent, no traveling swing coach or sports psychologist, no physical therapist, conditioning guru, nutritionist, or chiropractor. He played the game without a formfitting Cabretta leather glove, custom designer spikes, moisture-wicking shirts, titanium metal woods fitted with tempered shock-absorbing steel shafts, or balls with the latent explosive potential of nitroglycerin. His irons weren't part of some tungsten-injected, frequency-matched progressive set featuring a muscle-backed sweet spot; each one was as quirky and idiosyncratic as its owner. Harry conquered America with ten hickory shafted homemade clubs in a canvas bag and an ungainly aerodynamically challenged ball handcrafted from the hardened sap of an Indonesian palanquin tree.

It's impossible to find a modern equivalent in any sport for the impact of Harry's 1900 American tour; Babe Ruth, Wayne Gretzky, Michael Jordan, Arnold Palmer, and Tiger Woods come to mind, but each entered an established, widely popular game and raised it to a higher level of public interest. Harry encountered an entire country with little or no awareness of an obscure British pastime and so inspired the people who witnessed his exploits that within twenty-five years the country's players achieved a world dominance in the game they have never relinquished. These forthright Americans, strangers unfamiliar with his sport, had embraced him with a universal warmth and affection he would never experience in his own country until very near the end. Two subsequent tours would increase that high regard to an even deeper affection; the acknowledged godfather of American golf, Harry was accorded the love of an adopted son, and he considered his days in the United States among the happiest of his life. Although they always professed to admire his achievements in Britain, the clubby aristocracy that dominated the game's social side still looked down on a man even as supremely gifted as Harry Vardon as the issue of an inferior class. Adding a U.S. Open victory to his other championships also guaranteed Harry Vardon's immortality within the sport itself; in the intervening century only three other British golfers have engraved their names on the American national trophy.

Curiously, the only failure of Harry's tour turned out to be the Vardon Flyer. Thanks to Harry's tireless campaign, American golfers took up golf by the tens of thousands, but not with the product he'd come over to sell them on; for beginners, the new wound rubber ball made the perplexing game much easier to handle than Harry's redoubtable gutta-percha. A topped gutty went nowhere; mis-hit a Haskell and it still ran a hundred yards. As a novice hacker, which ball would you rather play? This exquisite piece of bad timing doomed the excellent Vardon Flyer to commercial failure, soon to be savored only as a collector's item by the young Ouimets of the world.

Harry Vardon single-handedly generated the first great wave of American interest in golf, and when he unknowingly awakened the ambitions of seven-year-old Francis Ouimet in Brookline, he set in motion events that would produce its second, even more explosive expansion. Although living in worlds that couldn't have been farther apart, their paths were now locked onto a course that would bring them together in an epic showdown thirteen years later on the serene lawns of The Country Club, only a few steps across from Francis's own front door.

CADDIES AT THE COUNTRY CLUB, 1904.
(COURTESY OF THE COUNTRY CLUB)

THE CADDIE

THE GAME IS deceptively simple—put the ball in the hole. But it reveals itself at a stately pace, one secret at a time, to even the most ardent practitioner. Francis endured a full year of frustration trying to clear that creek on his backyard course's opening hole. Refusing all his brother Wilfred's offers to move the tee box closer, Francis insisted on beating the course on its own terms or not at all. The day he first landed a ball on the far side of that brook was the proudest of his eight years on earth, even if he couldn't quite duplicate it for Wilfred when he returned home from the club; Francis plunked three straight balls into the water. Within days he managed to reproduce the tee shot on a regular basis, which created something more useful to him in the long run than satisfaction: ambition.

During the season, Francis spent his free days watching from the wrong side of Clyde Street as The Country Club regulars made their appointed rounds. When better players showed up, he'd pay even closer attention, often tagging along after them at a respectful distance. Francis had clipped stories from the Boston newspapers about Harry Vardon's tour and his stirring win in the 1900 U.S. Open at Chicago, pasting them into a scrapbook. Because Brookline's august heritage earned it a regular stop on the sport's premier circuit, The Country Club frequently hosted tournaments or exhibition matches that attracted the country's top players. This gave Francis the opportunity to scrutinize all the greats of his age, most of whom he would eventually compete against; U.S. and British Amateur champion Walter Travis; U.S. Amateur champ Jerry Travers; two-time U.S. Open champ Alex Smith; immortal Willie Anderson. Whenever some quality in a swing worth emulating caught his eye, a change in stance, hand action, or tempo, he'd pick up his brother Wilfred's only club and practice the move obsessively, weaving it into muscle memory. Anything that made the grade into Francis's own evolving swing had to live up to that template of Harry Vardon's smooth perfection he always carried with him.

On summer afternoons Francis stood outside the professionals' workshop at The Country Club and watched through the window as resident Scottish pro Willie Campbell and his two brothers practiced their craftsmen's alchemy: transforming raw blocks of ash or persimmon into sleek, varnished club heads. Campbell's charge of seventy-five cents for an hour golf lesson lay outside the reach of the Ouimet pocketbook, but Francis read every book or magazine he could get his hands on about the game. Getting fully outfitted for the game in the first years of the twentieth century set you back $25.00; clubs ran about $2.50 apiece, a golf bag $4.00. Rubber tees sold for twenty-five cents each and Haskell balls cost three for a dollar. All of which put first-rate equipment well beyond the young Ouimet brothers' budget, until Wilfred discovered on a day trip to Boston that the man in charge of sales at Wright & Ditson's Sporting Goods was willing to take used golf balls—ever since Vardon's visit, local stores couldn't keep enough in stock—in trade for brand-new clubs. Francis was horrified to open his tin can one day and discover his precious reserves had been diminished by three dozen balls. He calmed down as soon as Wilfred returned from Boston and presented Francis with his first real golf club: a cut-down brassie, a fairway two-wood that derived its name from a brass sole plate that protected it from wear.

With that brassie in hand, Francis first honed his full swing off the tee, and then learned to clip the ball from the turf without one, a shot that would become the most reliable in Francis's repertoire. A few months later, after replenishing his surplus, Francis sacrificed a second batch of balls for a used mashie, equivalent to the modern five-iron, and learned the mid-iron game. A weathered niblick, today's wedge, followed soon after. Full swing, then irons, then the pitching and chipping game; quite by accident, Francis learned how to play golf in exactly the right sequence, tee to green. Whenever he was awake from that moment forward, one or another of those precious clubs rarely left his hand.

Around this time Francis found his first Haskell in The Country Club's weeds; instead of enshrining the ball beside his aging Vardon Flyer, he teed it up and put it to work. The innovative Haskell's added distance and control only increased his anxiety about losing it in the weeds; as a result Francis came to value accuracy as the game's cardinal virtue. He played with that ball for so many consecutive rounds, the paint wore off. After repainting it in his father's workshop, Francis set it on a cookie sheet in his mother's oven to bake it dry. An hour later he returned to find a stinking puddle of stringy rubber; his Haskell had met an untimely end. When Mary returned home, she at first thought her house was on fire. The kitchen filled with acrid smoke and her oven disabled, Mary's tolerance for her son's controlling passion took a downward turn. The family ate cold chicken that night, but Mary conspired with Francis to keep the reason for the oven's demise from his father.

During his ninth summer, as soon as he was old enough to carry a bag, Arthur ordered Francis to join Wilfred at The Country Club as a caddie. He agreed, almost too readily for Arthur's peace of mind; then later that week his career began by accident before Francis could even apply for the job. He was making one of his periodic sweeps for golf balls through the rough by the fifteenth fairway with his mashie in hand when an arriving member, assuming he was a caddie, asked if Francis wanted to carry for him. Francis leaped at the chance and from that day forward the club's caddie master couldn't keep him away. You don't cure an alcoholic by asking him to tend bar; Arthur didn't realize what he'd bargained for.

Francis already knew which of the members could really play and made a point of hurrying out to present his services to the best of them whenever he saw one arrive; now he studied these golfers up close and personal. For four hours of muling their clubs around he earned twenty-eight cents a round, usually squeezing in two loops a day. A bright, well-behaved, eager-to-please boy, he found his services were soon welcomed by discriminating members. One of those veteran players—some accounts say it was the club's grizzled Scottish pro Willie Campbell—recognizing a kindred spirit helpless in the grasp of the game, presented his young caddie with four used clubs: a driver, a mid-iron (today's three-iron), a mashie niblick (today's five-iron), and a putter. With these additions to his original three sticks, Francis now sported a complete set of tools in his bag, and he applied himself to the study of their use with the devotion of a temple acolyte. During his caddying rounds, he studied The Country Club's course like a book of holy writ, breaking down the strategic secrets of every hole, learning angles of attack and approach, committing the contours of every inch of green, every blade of grass to memory. He soaked up whatever insider's knowledge of the game the members would share with him, taking home new ideas for experimentation on his primitive workshop in the pasture behind their house.

At the age of ten Francis finally bested his brother in a nine-hole match. Victory at last. The game's grasp on him tightened another notch. Wilfred's interests had begun to drift toward baseball but Francis's dedication never wavered. Contemporaries from school and the neighborhood gradually assumed Wilfred's place in the Ouimets' home course matches. Francis began making small wagers with his new competitors; golf balls were the customary stakes. Francis never had to comb The Country Club's fairways to replenish his stash again.

Arthur treated his son's passion for the rich man's game with habitually growing scorn, browbeating him frequently about it in front of the rest of the family. He could find no patience or sympathy for such a self-centered indulgence; his objection to the sport became ideological, making golf a convenient target for all of Arthur's social and economic bitterness. Francis's love for the game left him standing right in front of the bull's-eye. Arthur hectored him about his passion so relentlessly that Francis learned never to speak about it in front of him. Arthur never expressed any of the same scorn for caddying—it was work, it brought in money—but playing this game for pleasure as far as he was concerned amounted to nothing less than a venal sin.

Not even his father's contempt could deter Francis. Although his mother, Mary, tried to shield Francis from Arthur's temper, she watched her son's obsession with growing alarm of her own; one night, hearing strange sounds from overhead well after midnight, she crept upstairs and peered through the partially open door. Francis stood bent over, staring anxiously down at something on his hardwood bedroom floor by candlelight. He tapped whatever it was, then watched it slowly roll across the floor. Mary pushed the door open and entered; the object was a golf ball. He held a cut-down putter in his hand. So engrossed that he didn't even notice her come in, Francis crossed over to the ball and tapped it back the other way.

"Francis?"

Finally he looked up. "Oh. Hello, Mother."

"What in the world are you doing?" asked Mary.

"I was just lying there and I figured out how to improve my stroke," he said. "I've been gripping the putter all wrong."

"You couldn't wait until morning?"

He looked at her incredulously. "Well, no."

He began rising an hour before dawn to sneak over onto The Country Club course and get a few holes in before school, playing in his bare feet so he wouldn't mark up the greens. More than once he was forced to flee when a greenkeeper chased him away. On cold, stormy afternoons that kept the club's members indoors, Francis would put on his boots and slicker and play the empty course through fog, drizzle, driving rain. This extensive foul-weather experience would years later come in particularly handy. When complaints from The Country Club about his surreptitious forays followed him home across the street, Mary sat Francis down before Arthur heard word of it and gave him an urgent talking-to.

"No good will come from this, Francis," she told him. "Golf can never offer you any kind of life or living. It's time you concentrate on your education; that's what matters."

"Do we have to tell Father about this?" Francis asked.

Mary hesitated. Any grievance from the outside world that reflected badly on his son would bring a fearsome reply from Arthur.

"We'll keep this between us, Francis," said Mary. "For now."

By the time he was thirteen, on the few days he didn't caddie, Francis's typical summer day went like this: Rise at dawn, begin a two-hour trek on three connecting streetcars into town, carry his clubs another mile to Franklin Park, the only public course in Boston, play five or six rounds until sunset, then catch the last streetcars back to Brookline, reaching home an hour after dark. Convinced her son was headed for juvenile delinquency—or worse, professional golf—Mary tried to steer Francis away, encouraging his brother Wilfred, who had by now abandoned golf entirely for baseball, to take him along to ball games. Francis played some sandlot ball, like every kid his age, but it never threatened to supplant his first love. When his father told him to look for a second job and bring in more money that summer, Francis even applied for a position as batboy with the Red Sox; so did every other teenaged kid in Boston. The Red Sox turned him down.

One day at work late that summer of 1906 the caddie master assigned Francis to carry for Theodore Hastings, one of The Country Club's more eccentric members who always insisted on playing alone. As they walked to the first tee, Hastings asked his young caddie if he played the game. After a sudden summer growth spurt, Francis stood nearly six feet tall now and weighed a spindly 110 pounds; not the most obviously promising build for a golfer. Instead of a simple "Yes, sir," Francis poured out his heart to Hastings, expressing his enthusiasm in great gulping bursts.

"Where do you live, Francis?" Hastings asked, amused but respectful.

"Over there, sir." Francis pointed across the street to 246 Clyde Street.

"Well, you'd better go get your clubs then, hadn't you?"

Francis ran like his hair was on fire. When he returned, Hastings handed him a ball on the first tee and told him to tee it up. Facing his first test of nerves on a real golf course, Francis launched a solid drive straight down the middle. Nodding sagely, Hastings watched the ball settle, then turned back to Francis and smiled.

"Let's play," he said.

Carrying both their bags, Francis finished his first complete nine holes at The Country Club in only three over par, besting Mr. Hastings by five strokes. Concerned he might be showing his client up, Francis considered going in the tank for a few holes to even things up, but Hastings remained focused on his own game and didn't seem to mind. Francis's outstanding play continued after they made the turn, right up until they approached the fifteenth hole, when he simultaneously remembered three things: After a blind tee shot over and down a hill, the caddie shack held a commanding view of the fifteenth fairway. At this time of day the caddie master always sat outside the caddie shack smoking his pipe. Caddies were not allowed to play at The Country Club.

Ever.

Francis laced his tee shot, climbed the hill, and spotted his ball lying dead center in the fairway. He also saw Dan McNamara, the club's stern caddie master, pipe in hand, seated at his post outside the shack. And he saw that Dan saw him. Francis took his stance, topped his second shot, whiffed his third, dropped his fourth into a greenside bunker, took three to get out, and then three-putted. For a ten.

McNamara watched closely but didn't say a word. As they moved to the next tee, out of Dan's sight, Francis's rattled nerves settled down and he finished out his round with an 84; if it hadn't been for his meltdown by the caddie shack, thirteen-year-old Francis Ouimet would have broken 80 his first time around The Country Club's championship-caliber course. Every bit as pleased as Francis was by the final result, Mr. Hastings shook his hand and as they stood near the clubhouse reliving the highlights of their round, Dan McNamara wandered up. Certain the axe was about to fall, Francis stepped back and kept his mouth shut. Hastings greeted Dan and told him, with protective emphasis, what a wonderful afternoon he and Francis had just enjoyed. Dan nodded with seeming interest, and turned to the boy.

"What'd you shoot, Francis?" he asked.

"Eighty-four, sir," said Francis.

"Really? That's an outstanding score," he said with a straight face. "But now tell me; what in the world happened to you on fifteen?"

After letting Francis squirm for a moment, Dan laughed and let him off the hook; he'd actually followed them the rest of the way in without Francis noticing. A strong player himself, with a younger brother, Tom, who was on the verge of becoming one of the country's finest, Dan had seen a lot to admire in Francis's performance. Suspecting they had a gamer on their hands, from that day forward whenever a member at Brookline asked to play a round with Francis, and they did in days to come with increasing regularity, the club's caddie master looked the other way.

With permission to play at The Country Club assured, under the watchful eyes of Dan McNamara the rest of Francis's apprenticeship fell neatly into line. He skated during the winters and walked or ran everywhere, developing strong, lean legs while the rest of him filled out. Combine Woodrow Wilson with Stan Laurel and the result is a reasonable image of the young Francis Ouimet: elongated face, prominent ears, bright eyes, broad, ready smile, with the habitual chin in the air, loose-limbed, up-on-his-toes stride of a congenital optimist. People remember best about the young man a clarity of spirit and his straightforward manner: happy, courteous, good-humored, well-adjusted, and uncomplicated. A remarkable personality, considering it developed in the deep shadow of his tyrannical father. In all the photographs of Francis on a golf course, even in competition when the pictures aren't posed—and this holds true from youth to old age—a striking detail emerges: He's smiling at the conclusion of nearly every swing. Playing this game gave him sweet and simple joy. At this age and throughout his life Francis projected a singular quality devalued and almost scorned in today's ironic mass media youth culture—plain, earnest goodness.

Francis also possessed a native ability from his mother's Irish side: the gift of gab. He visited Brookline High School the summer before his freshman year with the intention of talking himself onto the golf team; when he discovered the school didn't even have a golf team (still a relatively exotic sport), Francis promptly convinced the principal to organize one. (He emphasized the game's character-building qualities.) Not long afterward he was voted the team's first captain and then helped organize six other Boston schools, public and private, into an informal league with matches played twice weekly. The boys at Brookline caught more flak on game days for carrying their clubs to school than they would have for a violin, but Francis rose above it. Within a year, now sixteen, he became Brookline's number one player.

When the five-man Brookline High squad showed up one day that spring for a league match with the Fessenden School, Francis was shocked when an older man he instantly recognized introduced himself as his opponent. John G. Anderson was twenty-six, an English teacher and coach of Fessenden's golf team. John had inherited his love of the game from his Scottish immigrant parents and had won at least one tournament in every year of his life from the age of eleven onward. After graduating as a four-letter man from Amherst College, John began his teaching career at Fessenden, where at his suggestion they formed a golf team. The school had only five boys enrolled who even played the sport, and when one called in sick that morning, John had decided to play in his place. John Anderson was the two-time defending Massachusetts State Amateur champion; during last year's win he had scored the longest hole in one in the history of state competition, at the 328-yard par four tenth hole of Brae Burn Country Club. Anderson was head and shoulders the most accomplished golfer Francis had ever gone up against. He couldn't remember ever feeling more nervous as they stepped to the first tee and then . . . Francis nailed his drive down the middle of the fairway and John topped his twenty yards into the weeds. Francis went on to shoot the first 72 of his life, apologized every time he won a hole, and beat John Anderson 5 and 3. A generous soul, truly a teacher at heart, Anderson seemed to enjoy Francis's victory even more than he did.

When he turned sixteen, Francis reluctantly decided to give up caddying at The Country Club in order to retain his amateur status. In these early days the USGA's stringent partition of church and state forbade amateur players from receiving money for any job or service connected to the sport—including caddying—after reaching the age of sixteen. Still thinking of the game as a calling but not a potential profession, after seven years Francis reluctantly said good-bye to Dan McNamara and the boys at the

Brookline caddie shack. A deeper misunderstanding over the USGA's controversial position on what separated amateur from professional would only a few years later provoke the most unpleasant episode of Francis's life in the sport.

During his junior year Francis led Brookline to the Massachusetts State High School Championship. Individually he captured the Boston Interscholastic Championship by defeating John Sullivan of Voltman High School, 10 and 9. The two boys became so friendly during their final match that John invited Francis home for supper afterward and introduced him to his younger sister Stella. Six years later Francis married Stella Sullivan, and stayed married to her for nearly fifty years. With that clear-cut certainty of vision peculiar to sixteen-year-olds, Francis gazed back at his youthful career from this lofty summit as Massachusetts's schoolboy champion and decided he had no more worlds to conquer. Perhaps his father was right after all; it was time to get serious about a career in the real world. This burst of adolescent laurel-resting lasted exactly one week.

The Country Club's caddie master Dan McNamara had a younger brother named Tom, who, like Francis, had developed his game on local Boston courses. Now one of the country's first homegrown professionals, working at nearby Wollaston Golf Club, McNamara was beginning to grab headlines. At the 1909 U.S. Open in Englewood, New Jersey, Tom became the first man to ever break 70 in a competitive American tournament and came within four holes of becoming the first native-born American golfer to win his country's national championship. Played under crippling hot conditions, on the last day that coveted victory appeared to be in Tom McNamara's pocket; he held a three-stroke lead as he made the turn into the final back nine, when he staggered and collapsed with heatstroke on the fourteenth hole. Doctors managed to revive him and Tom insisted on finishing his round, but he faded down the stretch and finished second to an expatriate English pro who later worked at Chevy Chase Country Club outside Washington, D.C., a former assistant to Harry Vardon at Ganton by the name of George Sargent.

Despite his disappointing second-place finish, Tom McNamara returned home to Boston after the 1909 Open and received a hero's welcome. Local papers covered his exploits exhaustively, raising local interest in the game to an unprecedented level. When his brother visited The Country Club, Dan made a point of arranging a private round between Tom and Francis.

As they walked the course, Tom shared his war stories about the recent championship and grilled Francis about his ambitions to compete on the national level. Already committed to the idea of retaining his amateur status, Francis's innate modesty made it difficult for him to admit he aspired to such lofty goals. As Francis played him dead even on the front nine, Tom poured on the encouragement. Making the turn, Francis pulled even with him and began entertaining thoughts of winning the match, until McNamara thrashed him soundly on the last few holes. Holding his own against one of the country's top professionals, measuring himself against the older man shot for shot and then just coming up short, reignited Francis's competitive fire. After his round with Tom McNamara, Francis told Dan he had decided to dedicate the next year to getting his game ready for the National Amateur Championship.

Dan thanked his brother afterward; he'd had a private agenda for putting their match together. For the first time in its fifteen-year history, the 1910 National Amateur Championship would be played in Massachusetts, right there at The Country Club. Because he had such faith in the boy's potential, Dan desperately wanted Francis to compete in that tournament; he secretly believed Francis had the talent to win it. Francis's own incentive for winning the National Amateur soon took on unexpected urgency. Announcing he intended to play in next year's championship provoked another bitter scene between father and son. Francis was nearly seventeen, a grown man as far as his father was concerned, already two years older than Arthur had been when hardship kicked him out the door to make his own way in an unwelcoming world. The argument turned ugly, Arthur pursuing him out the door, into the yard, shouting in his face.

"No more! No more living off the sweat of my brow; this game makes a mockery of everything I work for! You know how I feel about it—why do you insult me like this? Why? Why?"

Francis stammered; he couldn't answer, stunned to silence. Mary tried to intervene; Arthur turned his anger on her.

"If he wants to keep living under my roof and waste his life, then he'll find a real job. You quit school—"

"But I have one more year—"

"No more! You find a job!"

"All right," said Francis. "All right then, I will."

Francis walked away, wiping his eyes, his father's taunts continuing, as Mary tried to restrain her husband from following Francis across the street. There was only one way to prove golf meant much more to him than just a game; that it encouraged physical and mental discipline, ethical rectitude, and, in order to excel, demanded skills, resolve, and courage that would serve a man superbly in any walk of life. But a line had been crossed; fighting about it with his father no longer served any purpose. That was a battle Francis couldn't win with words.

So . . . by an accident of birth, you grow up with a first-rate golf course on your doorstep. Your immigrant father finds only erratic work as a manual laborer; the family's precarious financial state requires you to enter the adult workplace before the age of ten. By virtue of this serendipitous proximity you take up caddying and discover a soulful affinity for the game. Your brother precedes you in the sport and provides constant competition, if not inspiration, helping you rapidly develop your skills until eventually you surpass him. An obsessive autodidact, you never take a lesson in your life, tackling the world's toughest sport on your own terms. At a crucial moment, the kind intervention of an older benefactor who takes an interest in you provides access to a top-flight golf course that allows those developing skills to flourish. You determine, against all odds or logic, that golf will be the center of your life, but regardless of your ambitions, your ability to rise above your humble circumstances is by no means assured. Without support at home for your interests, your education cut short by cruel necessity, you're forced to fend for yourself at an early age. Whatever success comes your way will be a direct consequence of your desire to better your lot in life through the gift this game has given you and your tenacious persistence to make the best of it, come hell or high water.

Although neither of them knew it yet, Francis Ouimet and Harry Vardon had a remarkable amount in common.

VARDON AND HIS GREATEST BRITISH RIVAL, J. H. TAYLOR.

THE KING OF CLUBS

WHEN THEIR CONQUERING hero returned from his American tour at the end of 1900, the British newspapers ran out of superlatives and rolled Alan Robertson's old title out of retirement to bestow upon Harry Vardon: The King of Clubs. The English press was so worried their champion might be enticed into emigrating by his American odyssey that Harry felt compelled to write an open letter to *Golf Illustrated* reassuring his public he had no intention of leaving Britain. Although he welcomed the attention and reaped the rewards of his growing celebrity, as so many winners before and after Harry have discovered, life at the top of any competitive profession leaves you with only one direction in which to travel. Just at the moment he'd consolidated his position as the game's premier player, the ground beneath his feet began to shift. When Queen Victoria died in 1901, punctuating the end of an astonishing century with the end of England's longest reign under one monarch, the King of Clubs saw threats to his own sovereignty converge on him from every direction.

The controversial new Haskell ball followed Harry back to England like an airborne virus. Harry himself began to sound like Alan Robertson preaching against the evils of the gutta-percha ball, the innovation that had threatened his livelihood as a manufacturer of featheries. In 1848 the great crisis of Alan's life, which subsequently ruptured his partnership with Old Tom Morris, arrived in the form of a new golf ball called the gutta-percha, or gutty for short. The origin of the game's greatest innovation in two hundred years is worth telling: The gutta-percha ball came to golf as a gift from a Hindu god.

When the English Empire spread into the Far East, the harvesting of tropical forests in Malaysia led to the discovery of the towering *Palaquium gutta* tree and the remarkable properties of its latex sap. Collected via tap as a milky liquid, the substance dried and hardened into leathery strips that were rolled into large bundles and shipped back to England. Early experimentation revealed that when this resinous bulk was boiled in water, it softened into a malleable putty that held whatever shape it was molded into when it cooled. Completely waterproof, gutta-percha soon found vital application as insulation for underwater cables, allowing the connection of telegraph lines between England and the Continent. Gutta-percha made possible the development of replaceable belting in machinery, a huge advance for commercial production lines. No one had foreseen it, but it was also about to revolutionize the ancient Scottish game.

Vishnu entered the story in 1843 when Dr. Robert Paterson, a professor of divinity at St. Andrews University, received a marble statue of the god sent by a colleague from the Orient. Vishnu functions as the protector of moral order and, curiously, is often depicted standing with a weapon, for example a club, in his hands. To protect Vishnu en route, the statue had been packed in a dense wad of rubbery black shavings. Recognizing the material as gutta-percha, the thrifty Dr. Paterson collected the shavings, boiled them down, and rolled them out into rubbery sheets he then used to resole his family's shoes. The professor's youngest son, Rob, a student at St. Andrews University, was a fanatic golfer whose ability to play had been restricted by the high cost of featheries. When after two years these new soles on his shoes betrayed no sign of wear and tear, in 1845 Rob experimentally heated a hunk of gutta-percha, rolled it by hand into a ball, painted it white, and snuck it out onto the St. Andrews links. Although it split into pieces after a few blows, he saw enough promise in its flight to carry on, and after three years of tinkering with his formula, the first batch of bona fide gutta-percha golf balls appeared on the Old Course in 1848. The heavier gutty's sharp, boring flight pattern and superior distance astonished the average player. Because it was the first truly round golf ball, its rolling consistency on the greens also won immediate converts. Even more telling, because of its nearly indestructible durability, mass quantities of the new ball could be produced at a fraction of the featherie's cost, all of which threw St. Andrews's ball-making establishment into a blind panic.

After coming of age as a devoted gutta-percha player, Harry Vardon claimed the Haskell ball, which he derisively called the "bounding billy," would ruin the sport and he refused to even consider putting it in play. Length at the expense of accuracy violated Harry's dearest held convictions about the game. The less powerful but more sensitive gutty required the touch and feel of a master, in Harry's hands turning the high achievements of a sport into an art. A ball like the Haskell devalued those hard-earned skills, bringing less talented players within reach of Harry through golf's coarsest unit of measurement—sheer brute distance. Even when Harry did finally submit, just as Robertson had before him with the gutty, he never felt as confident with the wound rubber ball, particularly with a putter in his hands. While his competitors soon embraced the new technology and their games took a corresponding leap forward, Harry hesitated. As a result his game was about to suffer the first decline he'd ever experienced. It would last, with one brief exception, for over ten years.

Although the golf boom Harry inspired was just taking off in the United States, Britain's own late-century explosion had by now brought over 150,000 players into the fold. Golf's headlong popularization had resulted in a Tower of Babel regarding local interpretations of the game's original thirteen rules. Responding to the need for centralized authority, in 1897 the Royal & Ancient Golfing Society of St. Andrews became by national consensus the game's official ruling body, codifying a standard set of rules and arbitrating future disputes. One of the most fateful rulings they were ever called upon to deliver involved making no decision at all.

Scarcity made the Haskell difficult to find at first, but the golf establishment and press reacted as if foot-and-mouth disease had arrived on their shores in spherical disguise. The fledgling British Professional

Golfers Association led the chorus of condemnation, representing top professional players who feared for their livelihood, foreseeing an apocalyptic future where the ball's ungodly length rendered every existing course obsolete. Club professionals were up in arms as well; they lacked the technology to manufacture the ball in their own shops, limiting their markups and taking cash from their pockets. The only people who didn't think the sky was falling by having the ball in their bag were the 150,000 recreational hackers who couldn't have been happier about it, and their argument was simplicity itself: When they hit it, the Haskell went farther.

No less an authority than England's prime minister, Arthur J. Balfour, an avid amateur golfer, tried to settle the raging dispute by suggesting that enforced standardization in any part of the game would stifle innovation and unfairly limit a player's freedom to choose their own equipment. Influenced by Balfour's plea for moderation, when the PGA demanded the rubber ball be banned from the British Open and Amateur Championships, in early 1903 the R&A voted to decline taking any action on the issue. The decision about which ball to play would be left up to every individual golfer. Their edict made an immediate impact at the game's loftiest level.

After his loss to J. H. Taylor in the 1900 British Open, Harry suffered two more second-place finishes—in 1901 to rising Scottish player James Braid at Muirfield, then in 1902 at Hoylake to another Scotsman, Alexander "Sandy" Herd. This third straight runner-up finish particularly galled Harry because Herd, who along with Vardon had been one of the Haskell's most vocal critics, was the first professional to break ranks and play an Open Championship with the pernicious pellet. A perennial contender for over a decade and four-time runner-up in the Open who had never broken the Vardon-Taylor lock on the country's major championship, Sandy Herd played a final practice round with a free Haskell that persuaded him it might provide the advantage he needed to get past his illustrious contemporaries. Haskells were so hard to come by in England at that time, Herd played the entire tournament with that same ball.

Sticking with his old reliable Vardon Flyer, Harry led at the halfway point by four strokes over Herd. On the second day of competition, Harry found himself paired with a lesser player who was also hitting a Haskell. Still outdriving the man, Harry found himself constantly misjudging distances on approach shots to the greens after watching his partner first hit his "bounding billy." Although unwilling later to lean on this as an excuse, Harry scrambled to get up and down from short of the green on almost every hole, missed two key putts, and lost his lead and the 1902 Open to Sandy Herd by a single stroke. Herd's win opened the floodgates for the Haskell invasion and just like that up went the white flag; no British professional ever won another Open with a gutta-percha ball. In 1903, one month after the R&A's non-ruling on banning the Haskell, just as Alan Robertson gave in to the gutty, Harry Vardon began playing with the heretical new ball himself. It was not the only shake-up in Harry's life that year.

Restless for a more exciting life after his international adventures, and feeling the need to be closer to London where his growing off-course business now revolved, Harry accepted an offer to become professional at the South Herts Golf Club in Totteridge, a north London suburb. The purchase of a new, brick four-bedroom house around the corner from the club, a mansion by the Vardons' unassuming standards, helped Harry convince his wife, Jessie, to uproot herself from her quiet life in Ganton and make the move south to the big city.

While his world travels and triumphs had built Harry's confidence to a level befitting a renowned national figure, Jessie had never grown out of her insecure small-town shell. Harry's fame now carried him into social circles in London unimaginable only a few short years before; captains of industry, lords, ladies, and politicians eagerly sought his company. Increasingly this public side of his life he lived alone. Jessie had her house and garden, Harry his admiring fans and thriving career. Nothing Harry ever said encouraged a soul to imagine his marriage satisfied his deepest needs, but if divorce was ever on the table, neither party mentioned that to anyone either. Socially conservative by nature and obedient to convention by choice, Harry still felt deeply tied to Jessie by their common past. His loyalty to her exacted a heavy, silent toll; their unfulfilling relationship compounded by the pressing demands of stardom he felt obliged to answer slowly undermined his physical well-being.

After complaining of sluggishness and declining energy throughout the spring of 1903, the thirty-three-year-old Vardon prepared for the Open Championship to be held that June at Prestwick on Scotland's Ayrshire coast. Compounded by the stress of establishing their household in London during a long, wet winter all the while trying to manage Jessie's precarious emotional stability, Harry's health had been troubling him for weeks. Weighing himself in the locker room at the club one morning, he was shocked to discover he'd lost over twenty pounds. Harry had also been experiencing periodic dizzy spells, and a persistent hacking cough that occasionally yielded flecks of blood in his handkerchief. His doctor strongly urged Harry not to make the trip to Scotland for the Open and instead use the time to rest. Used to bulling his way through physical ailments the way he attacked any impediment in his life, Harry didn't listen.

As he traveled north on the train with Tom, Harry didn't even confide in his closest friend about his weakened condition. He hardly needed to; Harry's labored breathing and sallow, gaunt appearance made it clear to Tom that something had gone seriously wrong, but when he brought it up, Harry would only admit to being drained by the trying move to London. His brother decided not to press him on it. As far back as Tom could remember, Harry had never missed a day of work in his life because of illness. A Jerseyman took pride in his endurance. Arrival at death's door was the only acceptable excuse for shirking one's professional obligations, and it was considered bad form to ask a Jerseyman about his health; he'd tell you all you needed to know about his troubles in his own good time. At which point it was usually time to measure the man for his casket.

Designed by Old Tom Morris, the links at Prestwick served as the Open's original home for its first nine years in the 1860s; both Old and Young Tom Morris won each of their four titles at Prestwick, engraving their names on the game's record book. In spite of his faltering health, Harry Vardon arrived with plans to join them. The appreciative crowds at Prestwick saw nothing in Harry's behavior that led them to believe he was ailing, and their rousing cheers wherever he showed his face revived his spirits.

Harry dropped a long putt for birdie on eighteen that gave him a first-round 73 and raised him into a tie with Sandy Herd for the lead. As soon as he walked away from the crowds and the course, Harry's gallant smile vanished. Instead of sharing lunch in the locker room with the other players, his long-established custom, he disappeared into the professional's shop and quietly asked for a place to lie down, the first and only time in his life he'd ever felt compelled to rest between two rounds of tournament golf. His caddie arranged some seat cushions on the floor, then fetched a light lunch and a cup of tea.

Harry couldn't catch his breath. His hands shook. His heart fluttered in his chest like a captive bird. He told no one. He closed his eyes, lay back, and tried to sleep; a deep, dangerous blackness reached out for him and he woke with a start. Brushed by the wings of something dark and final, the walls closed in. He struggled to breathe. Mortal terror had introduced itself to Harry Vardon.

When his caddie called him out to the first tee an hour later for the afternoon round, Harry dragged himself to his feet. On legs as wobbly as a foal's he walked out into the sunlight among the adoring crowd. Harry didn't even know they were there. From some precious buried reserve he reached down and borrowed the energy to go out and play his game; over time, the terms of the arrangement would cost him dearly—loan shark rates he could ill afford, but work came first. On a day when no one else mounted a charge, Harry labored his way around Prestwick through high winds to a workmanlike 77 and ended the first day's competition with a six-stroke lead over Sandy Herd and the rest of the field.

Tom Vardon ate a quiet dinner with his brother that night at their hotel, shocked at how pale and drained he appeared. Harry's hand shook as he lifted his fork. The Jerseyman code of self-reliance be damned, Tom felt compelled to speak.

"You're sick," said Tom. "Tell me what's wrong."

Harry denied it. Exhausted, not sick. The wrenching move, looking after Jessie, his professional obligations, the public's demands. All of it. Crashing down on him. He couldn't meet Tom's eye. Tom knew Harry wouldn't leave the field of any Open in which he held the lead unless they carried him off feet first, which on this night seemed an all too vivid possibility.

"If you feel as bad as you look," said Tom gently, "maybe you shouldn't play tomorrow."

Harry looked at him; a flash of anger. Not himself.

"Withdraw? Is that how it is?"

"I don't know what you mean—"

"That's one way to clear out a path to the title for yourself, isn't it?"

Tom was stunned. At the tournament's halfway point he remained in serious contention, three strokes behind Sandy Herd; victory in an Open had never been closer, an achievement that had until now eluded the younger Vardon. A good player for a long time, but never a great one, Tom had a cheerful, restless nature—he had never married and switched jobs frequently—that turned out to be ill-suited for the single-minded obsessiveness demanded by championship golf. One of those stainless steel temperaments per family appeared to be the limit. Maybe because he'd achieved less in life without expecting as much from himself, it didn't take as much to make Tom happy, but if living in Harry's shadow had ever troubled him, he never spoke a word to anyone about it.

Tom looked straight into Harry's eyes. Something foreign lodged there. A cornered animal. Tom chose his words carefully. Kept his tone as light as he could to hide the hurt he felt at Harry's unjust accusation.

"That's right, Harry, I'll take it any way I can get it," said Tom. "Have another pint or two. Go out for a walk in the rain. And while you're at it, make sure you don't sleep tonight. I'll thank you tomorrow."

Tom's characteristic good humor cut through and aroused his brother's better nature. The accusing glare in Harry's eye blurred, then receded. Turned inward. Searching.

"That's what they want," said Harry. "They want me to fail."

"Who? Who's that then?" asked Tom.

Harry's eyes turned bright and feverish again as he looked at his brother. "We're Jerseymen," he said in a fierce whisper. "Professionals. We're not good enough for them."

"I'd say people treat you more than well enough—"

"Like Thoroughbreds. Prize animals the lords and ladies have their picture snapped with after you've won a race."

"Even so, Harry. Better a champion than a draft horse pulling a Blackpool beer wagon—"

"They can take it all away, don't you see? Everything we've worked for. The moment you show weakness, if you break down, they'll take it all back."

Tom regarded his brother carefully before he spoke. Harry's fear and instability amplified his own deepest worries—Harry had always been his rock, even if one Tom occasionally wished he could climb over—but he somehow set them aside.

"Then what you'll do is this," said Tom calmly. "You'll see to it you go out there and play your best game. Don't you dare let up. If I beat you tomorrow, it'll be on even terms or not at all, Harry. I want you on the mark the day I win my Open."

The discussion stopped abruptly. A crossroads. The brothers said their good nights and retired to their rooms. Purged of his demons, Harry fell into a peaceful, dreamless sleep. As he was discovering with this unpredictable malady, when he woke the next morning, his strength had mysteriously returned. When he joined Tom for breakfast, not a word was spoken about last night's conversation. Back to business.

Whenever victory was in his sights no one in the history of the game ever played better golf than Harry Vardon; on that final morning at Prestwick he showed complete command of his game, shot a 72, and established a new Open record for the lowest total score through fifty-four holes. His lead increased to seven strokes. Tom Vardon, playing ahead of Harry in the pack, made a sustained charge of his own, separating himself from the pack into a third-place tie with Sandy Herd.

Then, after Harry's morning exertions, the loan shark came calling. Between rounds he once again sought shelter in the professional's shop. A coughing fit gripped him; alarming gouts of blood appeared on his handkerchief. He concealed it from his caddie, hiding the handkerchief in his pocket. Feeling too ill to eat, he sipped a pint of Guinness, lay down, and tried to focus on the last lap ahead of him. Even in his weakened state, Harry knew a seven-stroke lead should see him through the Open's final round, but J. H. Taylor was behind him in the field that day, Sandy Herd, his brother Tom, and the up-and-coming James Braid, all gunning for him. The championship crown hadn't been his for three years now and he had no intention of letting this chance slip away without a fight. Victory shimmered before him like a fever dream. Another win would keep him at the top of the game and who knew when, or if, he'd ever have another opportunity like this again?

His eyes closed. He mumbled incoherently. Alarmed, his caddie hurried out to fetch Tom. Disoriented, slightly manic, to keep himself from facing his deteriorating health Harry's mind fixed on becoming the first man to tie the record of Young and Old Tom's four Open wins; and he obsessed about breaking the tournament scoring record in the process. Both goals lay tantalizingly within his reach, but only if he could find a way to coax his failing body through the final eighteen holes.

Tom charged into the shop and saw his brother flat on his back, pale as parchment, drenched in sweat and shuddering with fever. He insisted Harry see a doctor. Harry refused, knowing full well any responsible physician would recommend to tournament officials that he not be allowed to continue.

"This was Old Tom's shop," said Harry, waving a hand at the spartan room. "It all started here; the work we do, the Open. If it hadn't been for him we'd still be clipping hedges back on Jersey—"

"Harry, it's just a tournament. There'll be others—"

"Old Tom never quit. He's playing still, bless him. Young Tom won his fourth here—"

"Young Tom didn't quit when he should have, and it killed him."

"Don't exaggerate. I'll be fine," said Harry. "A bad cold. Had worse. Many times."

Tom saw the determination in Harry's eyes, shining through the pain, fear, and frailty.

"I can do it, Tom. I can do this."

"I know, Harry," said Tom.

Harry's eyes filled with tears. "You've always stood by me. You're the only one, Tommy. You've never gotten your due. Not fair. Any of it. You should have your own wins by now. Never could have done it without you. Never thanked you properly—"

Tom took his hand. "No need, Harry. No need."

Silence seemed to return Harry to himself, although his eyes still burned with a frightening intensity that, for the moment, cut right down to his core. "I don't know what's wrong with me," he whispered.

"We'll know in good time, Harry. Don't think about that now. Since I can't stop you—look at me—since I can't stop you going out there . . . make it count today."

"I will. I can do this, Tommy."

"I know you can, Harry."

Tom looked to the caddie. He pointed to the clock outside; it was time. Harry gestured for help to rise; Tom and Harry's caddie had to lift him to his feet. Harry stopped and shook them off when they reached the door—he didn't want the crowd to see them assisting him—and walked out to play his final round.

He never spoke of it, so it's impossible to know what sustained Harry that afternoon. Courage? Sheer obstinacy? Foolishness or pride? We define and admire greatness not only by the magnitude of achievement but also for the degree of difficulty that person has to overcome. On this day, judged by that standard, Harry shattered every standing record in the book. Although so weak he nearly collapsed half a dozen times—once only his caddie's quick hands prevented him from toppling into a steep bunker—Harry plodded his way around the Prestwick links for a final round that afterward he could barely remember. Tunnel vision. Ball, lie, distance, and club. Swing. One foot in front of the other. The round became an exercise in brute, animal survival. His resolve to finish was so great, the massive crowds that swarmed around him never realized how dangerously fragile their favorite was that day.

Harry shot 78. Carding a total score for the tournament of 300, Harry won his fourth British Open Championship and, just as he'd set out to do, smashed the tournament scoring record by five shots. While Sandy Herd and the other contenders fell away, Tom Vardon shot a brilliant closing 74 that afternoon and stood alone in second place, six strokes behind his ailing brother. Tom had played in two groups ahead of Harry and waited for him as he finished his round. When he sank his final putt, the brothers embraced on the eighteenth green, Harry visibly sagged and nearly collapsed in Tom's arms; he had to brace himself to keep Harry from falling.

"Easy on," said Tom quietly. "Easy on now, Harry."

The tears in each brother's eyes this time held a far different meaning than they had at Harry's first Open win at Muirfield, only eight years earlier. Before they could say another word, the crowd mobbed around them, clapping Harry on the back as they walked off the green. Still blissfully unaware of his illness, they greeted Harry with such joy and enthusiasm that their energy was able to sustain him through the presentation ceremony. Years later, expressing no regrets about the terrible price the win extracted from him physically, Harry's only sorrow came in realizing what it had cost his dearest friend. Tom, to his undying credit, never begrudged Harry what history now considers to be his greatest professional victory, but it was the closest Tom would ever come to a major victory in over thirty years of trying. He took home fifteen pounds and a silver watch.

When Harry raised the Claret Jug to the sky, the crowd went wild; the British press concluded no Open had ever experienced a more popular victory. In the only interview he gave immediately afterward, Harry hinted at the physical toll his effort exacted: "I feel that this championship has aged me by at least ten years and I do not think I shall face such another four and a half hours."

Harry waited in the pro's shop—resting quietly as his fellow players stopped by to offer their congratulations, until the crowds dispersed, the excitement passed, and the sun reached down below the Irish Sea. When the last players had left, Harry looked now as if he'd aged forty years. Tom and his caddie had to nearly carry Harry back to their hotel. He rested overnight and then, over Tom's strong objections, Harry insisted on fulfilling a commitment to play in a one-day tournament at Western Gailes near Troon. Tom was beginning to understand; as long as Harry could play, he fended off the shadows gathering around him for another day.

The brothers boarded a train at dawn to reach the nearby course for their early tee time. Despite his advancing illness, in a field that once again included J. H. Taylor, Sandy Herd, and the scores of others who were chasing the King of Clubs, Harry walked out that morning and broke the course record. Straining again against the absolute limits of endurance, he went on to win the tournament that afternoon, with Taylor and Herd tying for second, two strokes back. His last obligation fulfilled, only now would Harry return to his new home near London. After a few restful weeks during which his health and emotional outlook improved, he pronounced himself fit and went out to play a casual round with some members at South Herts. At the twelfth hole, suddenly and alarmingly stricken, a coughing fit seized Harry and shook him like a rag. He staggered to his knees, expelled a torrent of blood, and collapsed under a tree. The members carried him back to his workshop, then summoned a cab and quickly drove him home.

This time his doctor did not hesitate to deal with his patient more sternly: Harry had suffered a severe lung hemorrhage and the man ordered him confined to bed until a more precise diagnosis could be determined. The next morning, over Jessie's pleas for him to rest, once again refusing to yield to his body's needs, Harry disobeyed his doctor's instructions, got out of bed, dressed, and prepared for his day's work at South Herts. As he bent over to tie his shoes, a second more devastating hemorrhage flattened him. He lost consciousness and nearly choked to death on the blood that filled his mouth; Jessie screamed for help, their cleaning woman helped drag Harry back onto the bed. His spiking fever hit 104 degrees. When the doctor returned later that day, he brought with him the word Harry had secretly been dreading he would hear for the last three months.

Tuberculosis.

FRANCIS, 16, IN FRONT OF 246 CLYDE STREET.

THE AMATEUR

IN ORDER TO compete in the 1910 National Amateur Championship, seventeen-year-old Francis Ouimet needed to produce proof of membership in a recognized USGA-affiliated golf club. Membership at The Country Club remained miles out of his economic reach, not that he would have dared ask Arthur for a nickel now. But with the Amateur fast approaching, Francis desperately needed a club to call home; he secretly applied for a junior membership at Woodland Golf Club, six miles farther to the west, where Francis had played many of his high school matches.

Francis learned he'd been accepted at Woodland when the club mailed him a bill for twenty-five dollars. His heart sank; although he had just begun work as a stockboy in a Boston dry goods store, he hadn't yet brought home a single paycheck. When Francis confided in his mother about his pending membership at Woodland, she was furious. After calming her down, Francis spun the greatest sales pitch of his life; convincing her that finding success in the Amateur tournament held the key to all his life's designs, he talked Mary into lending him the twenty-five dollars, swearing he would pay her back by the end of the summer out of his four-dollar weekly salary. She reluctantly agreed, and secretly altered the family account books to hide the loan from Arthur, but her deepest fears about the game's pernicious influence on her son darkened to a shade resembling his father's.

"Golf will ruin you," she warned him, not for the last time.

Francis worked six days a week that summer to make good his promise to Mary, and played less golf than at any other time in his life, once a week at best. By September his debt to Mary was repaid and he arranged for the club secretary at Woodland to submit his entry to the National Amateur; it arrived at the USGA offices in New York on the last day they accepted applications. Francis made the entry list, but due to the tremendous number of players applying nationwide, surpassing 300 for the first time in its history, to reach the match-play portion of the championship, he would have to pass through a thirty-six-hole medal qualifier that would advance only the top sixty-four finishers. Fulfilling his financial obligation to Woodland had deprived Francis of a full season's practice; going into the tournament for which he'd made so many sacrifices, he had never felt less confident about his game.

As the National Amateur neared, the upper-class dignitaries and mandarins of the amateur game from around the country descended on The Country Club. Francis watched the high social goings-on from his porch across the street: lines of gleaming jet black automobiles, bright-colored lights, Chinese lanterns, men in black ties, beautiful young girls in evening dresses, a live band spilling dance music into the warm summer evenings. They all seemed to inhabit a world as dreamy and unapproachable as the Arabian Nights. Yearning filled him like rain in a well. To make that hundred-yard walk, step through the looking glass out of his drab existence into their world and become a part of it, Francis faced a task as simple and daunting as one of the labors of Hercules; all he had to do was win.

With a Massachusetts country club hosting the National Amateur for the first time, pressure on the local entries to make a good showing was sky-high; that's what the Boston newspapers said, anyway. Francis

brought his own reasons. When he arrived on the morning of the qualifying round, Francis discovered his tee time had been switched at the
last minute, moved back without explanation to the late afternoon.
Fraught with nerves, he practiced and puttered around without focus,
killing time at the club all day. When his tee time finally came, at nearly
five o'clock, he played only fitfully well, then a thunderstorm and darkness prevented him from completing his first round. Francis spent a
sleepless night worrying about his 6:00 A.M. start the next day and when
he woke, he neglected to eat breakfast; his father wasn't about to tolerate Mary getting up that early to fix it for him. Forced to complete yesterday's round first and then begin his second without a break, weak from
hunger and emotional strain, his focus wavered and then faltered; he
dropped precious shots that removed any margin for error but still came to
the final hole needing only a bogey to qualify. His drive hooked left; a
low percentage recovery that fell short compounded the mistake; a
missed putt cinched the deal. Francis double-bogeyed the eighteenth
hole . . . and missed the cut line by a single stroke. Heartbroken, Francis
endured his father's taunts that night in silence. The next day Francis
went back to work at his dingy downtown stockroom for ten cents an
hour. He couldn't bring himself to watch another shot in the championship. Lying in his bedroom late that Saturday afternoon, as cheers for
the winner swelled and echoed from the course, that lyrical, elegant
world he'd glimpsed across the street remained as out of his reach as a
mirage.

This near miss established a bedeviling pattern for his next two
years; Francis excelled in local events, winning with increasing regularity against the toughest players New England had to offer, but every
time he reached the qualifying round for the National Amateur Championship, some bad bounce or evil piece of luck trumped his chances
and he fell one single, maddening stroke short of making the cut. Francis later called this period of his life "something of a disappointment."
Taking into account the modest understatement with which he habitually expressed himself, this amounts to a tortured cry of anguish. Not
long after his failure in the 1910 Amateur, while browsing through a

Cambridge bookstore, Francis came across a used copy of Harry Vardon's first book, *The Complete Golfer*. Over the next two years he committed it to memory; it became his bible, and he wholeheartedly adopted Harry's sound, sensible approach to the game in practice and in competition.

"Do not reflect upon the possibility of defeat; you become too anxious and lose your freedom of style."

"Remember that the player who first settles down to the serious business of a hard match has the advantage. Concentrated purpose is the secret of victory."

His swing, founded on the image of Harry's from the conception of his interest in the game, began to take on an eerie similarity to Vardon's—upright, flowing, and effortless. Efficient hand action and timing gradually increased his length off the tee, while his accuracy continued to sharpen. He was pleased to learn that Vardon's favorite club had long been his own mainstay as well, the brassie two-wood. Francis's proficiency with a newer version of the first club he'd ever owned soon meant that no matter where his tee shot ended up, no green was ever out of reach.

IN 1911, AFTER leaving his job in the dry goods store stockroom, his luck took a turn for the better; Francis found work as a salesclerk in the Boston sporting goods store Wright & Ditson, the same establishment where his brother had made the fateful trade for Francis's first golf club. George Wright, the company's founder, a brilliant ex-shortstop and executive for the Cincinnati Red Stockings and hometown Boston Red Stockings throughout the 1870s, was a future member of baseball's Hall of Fame. Wright had been an essential contributor to the development of golf in Boston; after buying some clubs from an English catalog, he became the first man in all of New England to take up the game. When they didn't arrive with a set of rules, not knowing what else to do with them, Wright stashed the clubs in his storefront window, until a visiting Scotsman spotted them, walked in, and explained the game to him. Now eager to give it a try, in 1889 Wright convinced the skeptical Boston Parks Commission to let him knock some gutta-percha balls around the lawns of Franklin Park.

Consulting a printed rules booklet the Scotsman had sent him and with one set of imported clubs among them, Wright and four friends buried nine tomato cans in strategic locations and introduced golf to Massachusetts. During their first go-around on the improvised course Wright shot a low score of 59 over nine holes, won the match, and was hooked on the game for life. At his urging the city eventually turned Wright's tomato can layout into the city's first eighteen-hole public course, where Francis would soon be taking three streetcars to play, still Boston's most trafficked public track today. George Wright soon afterward began manufacturing his own golf clubs for sale in his store; they were some of the finest sticks produced in the country. Within a few years his old baseball colleague Albert Spalding purchased a controlling interest in Wright & Ditson and eventually absorbed them, but Spalding continued to sell Wright & Ditson golf clubs under its own established label for another fifty years.

By the time Francis came to work for him, George Wright knew all about the young man's potential in the game and took a personal interest in the ex–Country Club caddie. As a former professional athlete, he understood only too well the pressures a gifted young player faced as he neared adulthood, searching for the limits of how far his talent could take him. Francis reached the second round of the Massachusetts Amateur in 1911, then made it to the finals and lost the following year. As the summer of 1913 approached, just after Francis had turned twenty, the peppery, sixty-six-year-old George Wright sat down with him and asked about his plans for the upcoming season.

"This is the year," said Francis. "I have to win the National Amateur. I have to do it this year or not at all."

"That's putting a lot of weight on your shoulders, Francis, don't you think?"

"I'm twenty, sir. It's becoming time, if you know what I mean, for me to get on with life."

Wright nodded patiently. "So how will you do it then? Win the Amateur."

"Well, sir," said Francis, unsure of exactly what he was asking. "I figure first I'd enter the tournament. And then I'd win it."

Wright lit his pipe, leaned back in his chair. "We were playing a game in Chicago once. Late in the season, thick of the pennant race. Fell behind eight to nothing in the first inning. Terrible fix. We came to bat in the bottom of the first, every one of our guys goes up to the plate trying to hit an eight-run home run. After two innings of this, I take some of the boys aside and tell 'em there's only one way we get back in this game, and that's one run at a time. One base at a time. One pitch at a time."

Francis leaned in intently. "Did you win?"

"We got slaughtered, fourteen to six. That's not the point. You're looking way up here at the National and it already seems out of reach. You got to get to first before you can touch second, and from there you can see home. Do you follow?"

"I think so, sir," said Francis.

"Win your home tournament at Woodland. Play in whatever they got going at Brae Burn. Then try your hand at the Massachusetts Amateur. You did pretty well in it last year as I recall?"

"I was runner-up."

"See, there you go. Where is it being held this year?"

"It's at Wollaston, sir. I've played there quite a lot."

"So that's first base," said Wright. "Are you with me?"

Francis formulated a tactical plan for his game that summer, but still felt he lacked a consistent source of inspiration to guide his mental and emotional approach. He found it, of all places, at an opera. Opera companies offered a far more populist form of entertainment in the early twentieth century than the high cultural temples they've become today, albeit one that his father still found easy to resist. Having grown up herself in a musical family, Mary determined to instill in her favorite son an appreciation of the arts—he had in fact inherited her musical talent; he played the piano well without instruction and possessed a pleasing tenor with perfect pitch—with to date only limited success. In April 1913, Mary dragged Francis along with her to see a local production of a Verdi melodrama downtown, from cheap seats in the balcony. He found the music engaging enough but the story didn't exactly grab him; how could it when he didn't understand the words? But then a young singer, a soprano, took the stage to perform a tragic aria.

Good Lord, thought Francis, *will you look at this woman?* She had committed herself to this song so completely, she appeared to be in a kind of trance. Then the source of it came clear to him; a clean, concentrated light in her eyes that Francis intuitively understood to mean she'd given up her very soul to let this music come through her, nothing stood in the way of it, he could see she wasn't even aware anyone else was watching her, and at that moment, the tumblers in the lock he'd been trying to open to reach the heart of his own talent all clicked into place.

"That is just what I want for golf," he said to himself.

Skill guided by belief. Practiced without fear and with absolute commitment. Believe shots could fly on line and they did. He slowly gave up his fear of being judged, his fear of failing. His distance increased dramatically. Putts dropped. With this new philosophy guiding him, Francis followed the practical plan he'd outlined for himself after his conversation with George Wright. He set every other earthly concern aside to concentrate on his game, and his years of dedication finally paid dividends. During an early summer run up to the 1913 Massachusetts state tournament, Francis began breaking amateur scoring records left and right around the Boston area. A second-place finish at Brae Burn, then a first at Woodland.

On June 19, 1913, the Massachusetts Amateur Championship began at Wollaston Golf Club, a links-style course on a bluff overlooking a tidal marsh and river, half an hour south of Boston. Match play. Francis's game appeared as sharp as the crease in a motorman's cap, the local papers considered him a bona fide contender, but there weren't any walkovers in this field; all the best players in the state showed up when the championship was at stake. Working through some first-day nerves, it took Francis nineteen holes to edge past his first-round opponent, but he got it going when it counted, down the stretch, ratcheting up his confidence another crucial notch. In the second round Francis drew an old adversary from the Boston high school league, Ray Gorton, ranked third in the state. Francis didn't feel like himself from the jump. Tempo was off, putts he rolled on line wouldn't drop. Never a fast starter, a couple of bad breaks early on put him off his game. He had to grind his way through the front nine on raw nerve just to stay even. Easily distracted. Thinking too much. Then his luck ran out and Ray got hot; Francis dropped the ninth, the eleventh, and the twelfth holes. Three down now with only five holes to play. Francis walked toward the fourteenth tee, his mind racing.

It's slipping away, everything you've hoped for, all your life, all the hard work that's brought you to this moment and you were ready, you were ready this time, you were sure of it, you felt it in every corner of your heart and soul. One more slip now and it's over. And when it's over, be honest with yourself; you can say good-bye to your dreams.

And do you think you'll ever get a better chance? Will you ever again be able to take the time to practice this hard, to play this often, to bring you back to this moment? The world's going to make that impossible. Making a living, raising a family, all the paths you're going to travel not so long from now will pull you away from what you believe you were put on earth to do; the only perfection you've ever experienced or hoped for in life, the kind you find right here, on the golf course. The feeling, if you can only sustain it, that will point your way through the world like a lighthouse.

If it was going to happen, just once in his lifetime, it had to start right now. But begin where?

Fundamentals. Back to basics: What are your strengths, what's brought you this far? Temperament; controlling your emotions under pressure. Temperament and concentration; seeing your path in spite of all distractions. Lose one and you lose the other; with both gone, you're stone dead. What the mind can conceive, the body can achieve. Believing you're capable of putting them together is what got you this far. Pulling it off on command, in a desperate moment of need, well, we'll see . . .

When you announced two years ago, in a burst of atypical audacity, that you one day planned to win the National Amateur Championship—the sport's most coveted American title—your friends at Woodland fell all over themselves laughing. What in the world got into you, Francis? they said. You might as well say you're going to win the U.S. Open.

And why not? Johnny McDermott's won it now two years running.

Yeah, and he's the only American to ever pull it off; plus he's a professional and a hard case, as hard as they come. No amateur's ever gotten close to winning the Open. Who the heck do you think you are?

Good question. One that Francis had come to Wollaston to answer, but the cold, hard truth had him three down with only five to play. What was he going to do about it, *right now?*

Temperament and concentration; these are your cornerstones. And you start by playing the way you know you can. One shot at a time.

Francis kicked up a tuft of turf and set his ball on the improvised tee.

Stare down at the ball, look at the target, feel the shot before you hit it. Look at the ball, hard. Since his revelation at the opera, he'd realized that when his game came together, it was triggered by an intensity of seeing, as if the will projected itself through his eyes. When he summoned up that look and the confidence that came with it, a one-piece connection between mind, hand, and club, everything else disappeared: the course, the score, the guy who was trying to beat his brains out. He made the shot with his mind first, and if the vision was strong and sure enough, the ball ended up exactly where he'd just seen it land.

Believe you can play this way and you will. Your opponent's going to make mistakes. Make fewer than he does and you'll win, it's that simple and it all starts with the simple act of seeing. This is how you've taught yourself to play the game.

Francis took a deep breath, looked around. That was odd; his opponent, Ray Gorton, what was that look? Isn't that interesting; he's up three with five to play, but standing on the fourteenth tee Francis only saw one thing on Ray's face.

Fear.

All you need to know. Not another glance at Ray. Francis stared at the ball, hard. Will it to the target. Now make the swing.

A bullet, straight down the fairway. And just like that, it all fell into place for the next four holes. Four straight pars. Francis played his game and waited for the other man to make a mistake . . . and he did, the fear got him; Gorton faltered twice down the stretch, two bogeys.

One down with one hole to play.

Now with the home hole in sight, somehow Ray Gorton got his hands back on the wheel. He'd beaten Francis before, in a pivotal match three years ago when they were both still in school—*yes, that memory's come back to him, you're sure of it, you can see it in his posture, there's a spring in his step again, he's back in the match—*

Hold on, enough of that: Ray Gorton is not your problem now.

At eighteen Francis hit another solid tee shot. Ray responded. Francis followed with a fine approach onto the green and again Ray matched him; both men lying two. Down to his last chance, Francis needed a birdie to keep the pressure on Gorton. He examined the line: twenty feet, slightly left to right, downhill; all about speed. He took his stance.

Steady. Make the stroke. Yes, it's on line, tracking straight toward the hole—

No. No go. The birdie putt that would have momentarily secured a tie hung on the lip. A good run, but he'd come up one inch short. Empty, hollowed out inside, Francis made the tap-in for his par. Ray Gorton surveyed his fifteen-footer from every angle; putting was the strongest part of his game. He'd get down in two from where he was. Ray would win, one up, and Francis would go home empty-handed. The match was over.

There's always next year. If Mr. Wright gives you a week off from work maybe you can still qualify for the National Amateur at Garden City next month—no, that's out of the question, you didn't even want to ask unless you won this state title first, that was your plan, but it didn't work out—

Gorton lined up his putt.

—of course this puts the U.S. Open completely out of reach; there's an even bigger disappointment, and it's at Brookline this year, right across the street. The chance to finally show your father, and everyone else who ever doubted you what you know you're capable of—

Francis cut off the thought. There would be no feeling sorry for himself; things happened for a reason. He had come up short. Today the better man won. That was the end of it.

Remember what Harry said: "Never despair."

Gorton stroked his putt smoothly, the ball lagged up and settled a foot and a half below the cup. Ray glanced at Francis, looking for a handshake and a concession. Everyone knew Francis was a great sportsman, in the amateur game it was the gentlemanly thing to do. Francis took a step toward Ray Gorton, involuntarily felt his hand start to rise . . .

Something stopped him. He rooted his feet to the ground, stuck that hand back into his pocket, and yanked the loser's smile off its tracks before it ever reached his face. Words from Vardon came immediately to mind, backing up his instinct:

Never concede the putt that beats you.

Francis stood ready to offer his congratulations and Ray Gorton's future success in the tournament. After he made this eighteen-inch putt.

Ray looked the slightest bit rattled. He stepped back up to his ball, taking less time than usual before he made a casual stroke—

—*holy mother of pearl, Gorton yanked it right.*

Ray stared at that ball still lying on the green. He couldn't believe his eyes. Then he tapped in. Bogey five.

You've caught him—no, frame that thought the way you've learned to see the game; you kept your temperament and he lost his. An hour ago you nearly gave yourself up for dead and now look where you are.

Francis knew beating Ray now was just a formality; a man can't swing a club with a millstone around his neck. On their first play-off hole, Gorton drove deep into the weeds; bogey all the way. Francis made a routine par and just like that the match was over. But Francis knew his victory hadn't happened at eighteen and had nothing to do with Ray Gorton missing that gimme putt; that was just Ray's half of the equation. Beating Gorton became possible at the fourteenth tee when Francis stared down hard at his ball and the rest of the world went away.

The following day, in the eighteen-hole semifinals, Francis went out to play John G. Anderson, the former two-time Massachusetts Amateur champ and coach of the Fessenden School's team whom Francis had beaten in their memorable high school match. John had recently moved on from teaching to try and become one of the country's first golf journalists, covering the sport for the *Boston Traveler,* and he was still one of the most dangerous players in the state. Anderson had remained friendly with Francis, always taking a keen interest in his progress. This time out, with the

1913 State Amateur Championship on the line, he seemed more interested in evening the score.

Francis played steadily, Anderson played better. Through twelve, Anderson had Francis down two, with six holes left to play. Finding himself in a similar hole to the day before, it was time to make a move or go home.

And then suddenly, as he walked to the thirteenth tee Francis felt that concentrated vision seize hold of his mind like it never had before. Every ray of light, every blade of grass tunneled down into a sharp, crystalline line of sight, his vision clear and single-minded, each shot he made following a pattern that already existed in some seamless future he could somehow suddenly see into, a feeling so overpowering he wouldn't even fully realize the degree to which it had him in its grip until . . .

One hour later, at the seventeenth hole, when Francis stuck a blind approach shot one foot from the cup, tapped in for birdie . . . and the match was over, 3 and 1. John Anderson was so amazed by what had just been done to him, he insisted that Francis finish out the round and walked in alongside him as he played the last hole alone.

Drive, approach short, putt. Birdie three at eighteen.

Francis played the back nine as follows: par, birdie, par . . . and then, from the thirteenth on, this was how he finished: 2-3-3-3-3-3. *Six birdies in a row*. He had just shot 28 on the back nine at Wollaston, shattering the club record.

Francis interrogated himself afterward, how had it happened? Without effort or strain, for the first time in his life he hadn't forced a single move, he'd just stepped into the feeling; aware of everything, distracted by nothing. Perfect clarity between intent and result; he'd only had to picture what he was about to do in his mind and then get out of the way. As Francis went to bed that night, prepared to play his first final in the state championship the next morning, a lingering doubt haunted him: Would he ever experience it again?

The next day during the thirty-six-hole final, Francis got his answer. His opponent this time, not that it mattered, was his good friend from Woodland Country Club, Frank Hoyt. There it was; the feeling was with him from the moment he walked onto the first tee. This time he never questioned the gift. Halfway through their afternoon round the match with

Frank was over, 10 and 9. When he played with this kind of connection and confidence, a strange, unutterable thought occurred to him: It was just possible that not another player in the world could beat him.

Who was he now?

He was Francis Ouimet, the 1913 Massachusetts State Amateur champion.

MUNDESLEY SANATORIUM.

ABYSS

IN THE YEARS between the discovery of its bacterial origins in 1882 and the development of antibiotics after World War II, tuberculosis became the leading cause of death in Western industrialized countries, striking down people from every walk of life. Although tuberculosis is currently mounting a comeback in Third World countries, it's hard to imagine today the terror the "white plague" conveyed in 1903. Theories for fighting the disease abounded, but the only effective treatment to this point involved a concentrated program of complete isolation, bed rest, restricted diet, and fresh air. For the fortunate few who were diagnosed and treated early, these methods proved effective; private sanatoriums in the countrysides of England and America sprang up to treat the afflicted. For hundreds and thousands of others, hearing that dreaded word whispered meant a death sentence.

Harry may have been exposed to the lethal bacteria during his year in America. The pathogen could have been in the unpasteurized milk he drank as a boy in Jersey, lying dormant all these years; the cumulative fatigue of his long tour might have suppressed his immune system, allowing it to flourish. More recent studies have suggested that individuals burdened by an overload of repressed emotional distress, particularly involving troubled intimate relationships, are especially vulnerable to the disease. Revealing, then, to note that Harry's paramount concern in the immediate aftermath of his diagnosis became trying to reassure Jessie about his prospects for recovery. His hands shook so violently when he told her the terrible news that he had to clamp them behind his back, but terror never cracked the confident half-smile on his face. Jessie predictably fell apart; despite their estrangement, her husband was still the foundation upon which she'd built her entire world. Harry continued to prop her up, assuring her his prognosis looked bright and positive. This may have been as much for his benefit as hers. Harry had been putting on a brave face against a hostile world since he was eight years old and it had taken him to the heights; now it would have to save his life.

His doctors made discreet and immediate inquiries for Harry to enter the sanatorium at Mundesley, in Norfolk, near the North Sea coast. Dispensing with their lengthy waiting list, Dr. Burton-Fanning, Mundesley's chief physician and founder, who just happened to be an avid golfer, admitted Harry at once. Celebrity affords many privileges, not all of them deserved. On this occasion the good will Harry's reputation gave him probably saved his life; Mundesley was England's foremost facility for treatment of the disease, and its most expensive. Days later Harry took a train north, accompanied only by a hired nurse. Too distraught to face their parting, Jessie didn't even make the trip to the London station. For the first time in his adult life, Harry left home without his golf clubs; Dr. Burton-Fanning had forbidden it. A carriage met Harry at the local depot and drove him to the Mundesley facility, a former private country estate converted to a convalescent hospital, nestled in a deep pine wood within sight of the sea. Harry's corner room featured a wall of southern-facing windows with a splendid view of one of the doctor's therapeutic innovations for his recovering patients, a nine-hole golf course.

Denied all visitors and a little light reading the only activity allowed him, Harry spent his first three weeks at Mundesley confined to his bed. A sound conceit lay behind this treatment; cessation of physical activity reduced oxygen consumption, enabling lung tissues damaged by the diseased bacteria to heal. For a man with the constitution of a Clydesdale who'd spent his entire life outdoors, striding over some of the great landscapes of the world, submitting to an invalid's life while staring at a lush green course just outside his windows felt like a fiendishly personalized torture. Would he ever play again, let alone compete at the world's highest levels? More to the point, would he even survive?

Once he'd admitted the presence of the disease and given up struggling against it, Harry collapsed physically; for the first time he allowed his body to dictate its needs ahead of his ambitions. He slept twelve hours a day. During waking hours he stared out at the meditative green lawns, closed his eyes, and replayed rounds from his past, not daring to visualize others yet to come. When clouds of depression closed in around him, the mental discipline and fortitude he'd developed as a champion formed his last inner line of defense. Never despair.

In the second month they let him out of bed for one hour a day. He shuffled to a terrace, out of breath after fifty paces, sat down wrapped in a blanket on a reclining chair, and gazed out toward the lush flower beds; the former gardener in him admired the roses. Occasionally his nurse wheeled him out to spend warmer afternoons on a daybed in a wooden cabana on the lawn, open on one end and equipped with gimbals to turn it away from the wind. When the wind came from the east, the smell of the salt sea air reminded him of Jersey. He drifted into a miasma of dreams, memories from childhood weaving in and out of his fractured reality.

As each week passed, the doctors allowed him another hour on his feet. Card games on the porch. Books in the library. Desultory turns at the billiard table. The days whispered by in hushed slow motion, patients drifting from room to room, purgatorial spirits waiting to learn if they'd be allowed to return to their former lives. In his third month he insisted on dressing every morning and began taking his meals in the dining room downstairs with the other patients. Fame meant nothing inside these walls; the disease leveled all those fine distinctions. Meeting people from every walk of life, Harry formed new friendships on the basis of what they all had in common—saving their lives. No one in the hospital better understood that belief one was going to heal made healing possible. Harry took the lead in encouraging his fellow inmates to keep faith with their treatment. Courage, he told them; we'll beat this thing yet.

In private moments, when Harry read newspaper and magazine accounts of his sport, his mood took a grimmer turn as he realized the world had gone on without him. Articles about Britain's greatest champion appeared less frequently as the months crept by. Now all he came across were progressively briefer updates of his status that never called the disease by its name; that perversely delicate Victorian sensibility forbade such an indiscretion: Harry had an "illness." Harry had "gone away." He didn't miss the implication: They didn't expect Harry to survive, let alone ever play again, but all best wishes for a speedy recovery nonetheless. Their mechanical, arm's-length cheerfulness chilled him to the core. Alone in his sterile room, Harry faced the ice-water reality that the outside world that used to revere him like a king had already turned its back on him. Thanks for the thrills, old boy, but sporting fans wanted no part of Harry Vardon's mortality; if the reaper could come without warning for a hero, its bony finger could at any moment tap their own shoulder.

An abyss. The end of everything he'd lived and worked for, stolen from him. A solid life built brick by brick demolished in a single phantom blow. A kind of blind hope had always sustained him, but for once the indomitable engine of his will alone wasn't up to the task. Harry had abandoned his native Catholic faith years before; now he confronted a godless universe that had without warning thrown him back into the squalid misery he thought he'd escaped for good.

Never despair. The words had never rung more falsely. He never needed them more. He narrowed his focus, surviving one hour, one minute at a time. You don't wrestle the devil to the ground with a single throw, he told himself; patience, persistence, a slow-rooted refusal to fall. Hang on. Endure. Maybe he'll lose interest. Maybe you can outlast him. Slowly his weight came back as his appetite and a small portion of his strength returned. At the end of his fourth month, they allowed Harry an afternoon walk out on the grounds. One day, wandering without direction, he found himself on the edge of the hospital golf course. Just setting foot on tended grass again lifted his spirits. The smell of cut grass, sea air, a green, a bunker, a fairway. The reassuring grammar of his professional life. Two recovered patients near the end of their treatment came by, playing a casual round, chipping and putting; Harry watched silently. As they passed, engrossed in their game, neither man noticed the other patient standing by the green. Harry hadn't set foot on a golf course without being recognized in ten years.

He looked down at his right hand; a steady tremor ran through it now that he couldn't control. He still had bad days, days he could barely climb out of bed, but on that day on the edge of the golf course, Harry felt some vital part of himself return; he was furious about his right hand. Damn this thing. Betrayed by his own flesh and bone. He balled it into a tight fist and struggled to still the shaking. In that moment, enraged at his own helplessness, he realized he had enough left in him to win this fight.

Walking back to the clinic Harry spotted a large wooden chalet hidden back in the woods and asked his nurse about it.

"That's where our most seriously ill patients are housed," she said.

"By that you mean they're not expected to recover."

"We never like to give up hope," she said.

"I'd like to visit them," said Harry.

"But that isn't done, Mr. Vardon."

"Why? Why so? It can't be fear of contagion. I've got it already, haven't I?"

Harry made his first visit to the critical ward the next day. Many of the victims were children in their teens, separated from their families for months. Wasting bodies, eyes bright with a fever using their flesh as kindling. Now Harry stared straight into the abyss. He went there as often as the hospital staff would allow. He sat by their bedsides, read to them, signed autographs and pictures, spoke quiet words of encouragement. Never despair, he told them. In this world or the next.

During his fifth month, Harry asked to borrow a club from Dr. Burton-Fanning. No full swings yet, he was told; too violent on the lungs. He negotiated a putter and ball, not surprised to learn that Burton-Fanning played with Haskells. Harry walked out to the course's first green on a late fall afternoon, low syrupy golden sun pouring through the pines. He dropped the ball and took his first stroke with a golf club in half a year. His right hand trembled uncontrollably, the putter jumped in his hand, and the ball sped eight feet past the hole. Again and again he tried in vain to steady his hand but got the same perplexing result.

When he told Burton-Fanning about his problem, the doctor asked if Harry had ever suffered an injury to his right hand; he had, a broken bone near the outside of the wrist, the result of an old football collision. Although Harry was slowly winning his overall fight with the disease, Burton-Fanning explained that once they breached the body's defenses the *tubercle bacilli* sought out and opportunistically attacked any vulnerable tissue they could find, in bones and joints as well as internal organs.

"That in all likelihood is what's happened to your hand, Harry."

"Irreversible nerve damage."

"Yes. I wish I could tell you we have a remedy, but . . ."

"So what you're saying is, this tremor is there to stay," said Harry.

"In all likelihood."

Harry walked to the putting green every afternoon. The tremor teased him, subsiding on occasion, only to leap like a running salmon in the middle of his transition from takeaway to downswing, sending the ball drastically, disastrously off line. He spent hours on the green, calling on his old practice disciplines, determined to find a way around this catastrophe. He varied his stance, his grip, his stroke. Nothing worked. Sometimes, at dusk, if he ignored the line to the hole and just stared at the ball, he could ease his hand through a full stroke smoothly. Once in ten tries. The results discouraged him, but the effort had a salutary effect; immersing himself in a golf problem, even one as potentially devastating as this, set him down the road toward recovering the rest of his health.

Christmas came and went. Harry ordered in cases of champagne for his new circle of friends and hosted an elaborate holiday dinner. For those depressed and missing their families, he organized a series of supervised outings to nearby towns and the seaside to bolster their spirits. On one of those outings Harry left the group to make a private, sentimental journey; the course that had first employed him when he came to England was near enough to visit. As he walked the grounds, he happened upon the simple cottage belonging to the couple that had let him his first lodgings. The same sweet-natured husband and wife lived there still, elderly and infirm now; the man almost blind, the woman deaf as a post. Neither recognized him. When he identified himself as Harry Vardon, their former tenant, they refused to believe him.

"Couldn't be," the old man said. "Harry Vardon's famous."

"That's what I'm trying to tell you; I'm Harry."

"No. Not possible. A man as great as Harry Vardon. He'd have nothing to do with the likes of us."

Nothing Harry could say or do would persuade them he was the same young man who had lived in their spare room.

In early February, Harry persuaded Dr. Burton-Fanning to accompany him on a round of the hospital's golf course. Harry hadn't made a full swing at a ball since his last round at South Herts eight months earlier, but he suspected neither the long layoff nor the persistent tremor in his hand would affect that part of his game. On the fourth hole that day, a short par three, Harry scored the only hole in one he made in his entire career. Since his intention had been to impress his doctor that he was fit enough to return home, he never struck a more important shot in his life; Burton-Fanning agreed to let Harry go back to London at the end of the month.

Harry didn't like everyone he met at Mundesley. A loutish, overbearing lawyer named Aubrey, nearing release himself, had for months been insisting he could beat Harry Vardon at golf straight up, raising the possibility he may have mistakenly been transferred from a mental institution. Tired of his arrogant posturing, and eager to teach this bore a lesson, Harry agreed to meet Aubrey for a nine-hole match on the local links. Harry intended to throw the match in order to set up the elaborate joke, but when they finally got on the course Aubrey turned out to be so horrifically inept Harry had to work harder to lose than he normally did in winning; if perfection is ingrained in your swing, shanking on purpose takes serious concentration. Being called on to back up his boasts, Aubrey was such a nervous wreck that even with Harry hitting tee shots out of bounds and flubbing every chip shot, losing to him was a close run thing. Pale and shaken by his unexpected "victory," Aubrey believed his impossible achievement was for real and to the co-conspirators' amusement, began regaling the other patients—who were already in on the joke—with a blow-by-blow account of his conquest of the great Vardon.

A few days later Aubrey received a letter from the editor of *Golf Illustrated*, Britain's leading golf magazine, expressing interest in running a story about his victory over Harry. Aubrey could hardly contain his excitement and showed the letter to everyone he knew. A few days later Harry arranged for two friends to arrive posing as a reporter and photographer from the magazine; Harry, of course, had sent the inciting letter. The two "reporters" sat with Aubrey, taking notes, nodding earnestly as he recounted his version of the match, embellished with more heroic details in every retelling until it reached mythic proportions. They snapped Aubrey's photograph out on the golf course, club in hand, bursting with pride, and assured him the story would be published in the magazine within days. Aubrey broadcast this glorious news to the hospital population, who by now could hardly keep from laughing whenever Aubrey appeared. The following week he marched down to the village and bought out every copy of the magazine he could find. After searching in vain for the account of his triumph, Aubrey dashed off an angry letter to the editor. Silence. Weeks later, he finally went to Harry wondering if he could offer any explanation as to why the story hadn't appeared as the magazine had promised. Harry comforted him.

"Never mind about them, old chap. We all know what you did," he said with a wink. "Your story's safe with us."

When he saw the twinkle in Harry's eye, it finally dawned on Aubrey he'd been had. Satisfied he had at last made his point, Harry stood up and walked away. His victim never admitted his humiliation to another soul.

His friends threw a surprise dinner for Harry on his last night. He paid a final visit to the chalet in the woods to say his good-byes. The next morning, the same silent driver and black carriage that had brought Harry to Mundesley eight months earlier drove him to the station. Harry felt as if he were being ferried back across the river Styx to the land of the living. His convalescence continued at home in Totteridge. For the first time in their lives together, circumstance reversed the Vardons' marital roles; Jessie became Harry's support now and to her credit she accepted the responsibility with energy and discipline. She followed his doctor's orders to the letter, changing linens, regimenting his diet, keeping Harry's room obsessively free of dust and filled with fresh air.

Restless for a project to fill his idle days, Harry began work on a book he would eventually publish as *The Complete Golfer*. For a boy who'd left school at ten, and regretted it as long as he lived, the four volumes Harry authored in his life—without benefit of ghostwriters—were among his proudest accomplishments. For the victims and survivors of tuberculosis, the disease still carried the distinctly Victorian stigma of shame associated with the body and its physical processes; although he described his illness in sketchy detail in all his later books, he never identified it by name. Neither did a single newspaper account ever mention it when he made his return to the game.

Away from the regulated order of the sanatorium, Harry's bullish nature compelled him to test his limits; within a month he suffered another hemorrhage, a serious setback, but he refused to return to Mundesley. His doctors suggested Harry consider moving to the drier climates of California or South Africa. He refused to even discuss it; to do so now would mean admitting his weakness had become a permanent condition. This illness was a passing thing, Harry insisted, and now that he was home, he'd be back to his old self before they knew it. The spring of 1904 passed with Harry living in this twilight state. When later that summer his doctor finally pronounced him fit enough to return to his daily chores at South Herts, Harry and Jessie remained in their now separate bedrooms. For the remainder of their lives together, this new arrangement never changed.

Harry received a warm welcome back at South Herts, but he was nowhere near ready to give up his pursuit of the sport's highest titles for the humdrum existence of a full-time club professional. He discovered that in his absence his health had become a national preoccupation, although not quite with the sympathy he expected. The question the press posed most frequently now was this: Now that Harry was no longer fit enough to compete and his playing career finished, who would take his place? Another columnist, mourning the disappearance of the gutty golf ball, concluded that the great Vardon had vanished along with it. The public wanted thrills from its sports heroes, not lessons in mortality. These coarse assumptions and coldhearted dismissals made his blood boil; that was all Harry needed to hear.

With the 1904 Open and Harry's defense of his title less than a month away, his brother Tom approached Harry with a plan. Tom had recently taken a job as professional at Royal St. George's in Kent, southeast of London, where the 1904 Open would be held. He asked for a two-week leave of absence and accompanied Harry to a spa and golf resort in France. Together they worked around the clock to get Harry's body and game back into form, then returned to St. George's for a week of practice before the tournament began.

One hundred and forty-four players entered the 1904 Open, another new record. When the first day of the tournament arrived, nerves holding steady, Harry marched out, shot 76–73, and beat every last one of them. Harry held the lead at the halfway point. The press rejoiced at his success; *he's back,* they cried, *it's as if he'd never left. God bless you Harry, we knew you had it in you, we've always kept the faith.* That night, hoping against hope, Harry dared to believe them.

The next day on the greens at St. George's, the tremor returned to haunt his right hand like a vengeful spirit. Nerves firing at random, muscles jumping, he butchered half a dozen putts inside four feet and shot 79.

Harry not only failed to defend his title, he fell out of contention before the final round in a way his followers had never seen before.

The whispers in the press began again in the aftermath of this disaster: Was Harry Vardon finished as a force in his sport?

Harry looked down at his trembling, alien hand. He didn't know the answer.

JOHN J. McDERMOTT, 1910, WITH THE U.S. OPEN TROPHY.

RISE OF THE HOMEBREDS

WHEN HE FINALLY pulled it all together at Wollaston Golf Club against John Anderson to win the Massachusetts Amateur Championship, Francis wasn't the only one who felt his game at last stood on legs sturdy enough to carry him to the next level. Francis was reluctant to ask Wright & Ditson for any unpaid time off, knowing news of it at home would bring down the wrath of his father. Then one day in late July George Wright called Francis into his office and insisted he take a week's paid vacation from the store for his fourth crack at the National Amateur title.

Predating its professional counterpart by a single year, the USGA's National Amateur Championship received the lion's share of attention America paid to the sport of golf during the first decade of the twentieth century. It was the main event played by the sport's founding fathers, upper-crust captains of industry. They and their social equals who could afford to play the time-consuming sport still looked slightly askance at the U.S. Open as a Masonic cloister of lower-class, foreign-born professionals, gathering like an annual tradesman's guild convention. The truth was neither the press nor the public could get that worked up about a bunch of hard-faced immigrant Scotsmen wrestling amongst themselves not simply for honor, but for a negligible pile of cash. From the beginning, only highborn American players contended for the United States Amateur Championship. These blue-blooded gentleman golfers, most of whom looked down their noses at the commingling of any sport and money as unseemly, wanted a champion from their own ranks and wouldn't have long to wait.

Jerome "Jerry" Travers, an attractive young New Yorker from a wealthy family, began competing in the National Amateur Championship at the age of fifteen, won back-to-back Amateur titles in 1907 and 1908, and became the country's first matinee idol golfer. Like Francis, Travers learned the game on a homemade three-hole course in his backyard—although in his family's case, it really was their backyard, amidst the Gatsby-like splendor of his father's estate in Oyster Bay, Long Island. Without having to worry about earning a buck, young Travers devoted himself full-time to developing his golf game; Jerry's father hired 1906 U.S. Open champion Alex Smith as his son's private teacher. When he won his back-to-back Amateur titles, Travers cashed in on his growing celebrity in time-honored fashion; he dropped out of competitive golf to pursue full-time work as a notorious Broadway playboy. After sowing enough wild oats to fatten a Thoroughbred, Travers pulled himself out of his recreational tailspin and returned to capture his third Amateur title in 1912. A cold, calculating, methodical craftsman on the course, who took few chances and exhibited zero personality in the heat of competition, Jerry Travers was easy to admire. For the casual fan of the game, he was fairly hard to get stirred up about.

By 1913, this much was clear: Before professional golf would ever be able to capture the imagination of the public at large and win mainstream acceptance as a frontline sport, American golf needed a standard-bearer. Boston's Tom McNamara mounted the first serious challenge in the 1909 U.S. Open at Englewood, but when the moment finally arrived, a nineteen-year-old pro named John J. McDermott from Philadelphia grabbed the brass ring.

The blue-collar son of a mailman and a former caddie, just like Old Tom, Johnny McDermott weighed 125 pounds soaking wet and attacked everything he tried in life like an overmatched, half-blind club fighter try-ing to slug out the last round of a title fight. Johnny never met a risky, low percentage shot he didn't immediately take a swing at; his game was a high-wire act relying on white-knuckle nerves, an approach not just to golf but to his life, one for which he would not so many years afterward pay a horrific price.

Young Johnny McDermott had never been considered anything more than a journeyman until the 1910 U.S. Open, when on the final day he battled his way into a three-way play-off with 1906's Open winner Alex Smith and his younger brother Macdonald, the transplanted pros from Carnoustie. Alex prevailed, collecting his second Open title, but McDer-mott had found something in himself to build on. The next year at 1911's Open, held at the Chicago Golf Club, McDermott mounted another last-round charge and forced a second consecutive three-way play-off. This time the pit bull McDermott wouldn't be denied; he grabbed the play-off by the throat and held on for a two-stroke victory over a top Massachusetts pro, Mike "King" Brady.

After returning home to Philadelphia with the U.S. Open trophy, cloaked in glory as the country's first American-born champion, Johnny McDermott issued a challenge to every other homebred professional on the eastern seaboard: a $1,000 standing bet against $100 from any and all comers. Johnny put his money where his mouth was, using his own bankroll as the stake. After he soundly thrashed the first three takers on his home course, no one else showed up to take him on. The following year, in the 1912 U.S. Open at the Country Club of Buffalo, Johnny outdueled his fellow Americans Tom McNamara and Mike Brady down the stretch to win his second straight Open title, both before the age of twenty-one. In the process he became the first player ever to break even par while win-ning the Open. To this day John McDermott remains the youngest man to ever win America's national championship.

On hand in the gallery at Buffalo in 1912 was a nineteen-year-old assistant golf professional from the nearby Rochester Country Club named Walter Hagen. A slick-fielding semipro shortstop with big-league aspirations, Hagen was another charter member of America's first golfing generation; he had been swinging a club since before he could walk and was quietly on the verge of becoming upstate New York's best player. In spite of which Walter had been unable to convince his boss at the club, Andrew Christy, that he was ready to compete with the top dogs in the Open, even though Hagen regularly hammered Christy, who was himself entered in the tournament. As a consolation Christy allowed Hagen two days off to travel over to Buffalo and watch the action. When they both returned to Rochester and his head pro, who had missed the cut at the Open by a country mile, asked Walter what he thought of the golf he'd seen, with typical matter-of-factness, Hagen replied: "Not much."

John McDermott's back-to-back Open victories accelerated America's interest in the sport from a trot to a gallop; for the first time major metropolitan newspapers hired beat writers whose sole responsibility was covering the game. The increased detail of their reportage fueled public awareness, more people came out to watch the big tournaments, more ink was spilled reporting the results; each advance in the cycle raked more players into the sport. For Johnny McDermott, the inevitable comparisons to the greats of golf past began and the postman's son from South Philly milked them for all they were worth. He quickly cleaned up on the business opportunities that came his way, lending his name to the manufacturing of clubs and balls, playing paid exhibitions around the country. Within the year he made two well-publicized trips to England, mixed with the high and mighty of both societies, and invested his newly gotten gains in the stock market. At last it appeared American golf had found the leader it needed.

Except for one small hiccup: Almost nobody could stand him. A bachelor who still lived at home with his parents, away from the course Johnny by all accounts conducted himself in a sober, gentlemanly manner; too bad they didn't play golf in a church. Never an accomplished technical player, too small to overpower courses, Johnny McDermott depended entirely on winding himself up into an irrational frenzy against everything around him and then venting his rage like a blast furnace—at the golf course, the officials, the USGA, and his opponent, most particularly if his opponent was foreign-born. When he lost that first Open play-off to Scotsman Alex Smith in 1910, McDermott tracked Smith down afterward in the middle of his locker-room celebration, jammed a finger in his face, and stunned everyone within earshot by warning the champ that he intended to beat him senseless next year. Readily dismissed as a wacko with a chip the size of an anvil on his shoulder, McDermott shocked Smith and the golfing world by backing up his threat the following year with a win. Given to straight-faced egotistical proclamations about his own greatness, he anticipated the in-your-face confrontational style of late-century athletes like Muhammad Ali, without the poetic charm. After landing in Britain as America's champ in 1911 and crowing to every reporter he spoke to that he'd arrived to win the British Open and show the people of the old country how golf was supposed to be played, Johnny shot a 96 and failed to qualify. He slipped out of town and back onto the boat under cover of night, an object of universal scorn throughout the United Kingdom. The London papers cut him to ribbons. Never one to forget a slight, from this point forward John wore his hatred of all things British like a tattoo.

In retrospect it appears McDermott required extreme psychological kick-starting just to drag a brittle psyche out of bed in the morning. His taut fury concealed a fragile, frightened soul who in the course of two days in 1911 had made the leap from utter obscurity to national prominence. Whatever the underlying pathology that fueled his anger against the world, his golf game benefited enormously, because when Johnny got on a roll during a tournament, he was almost impossible to beat. Despite his phenomenal success, which appeared to have no limits, the emerging, genteel American golf establishment found him impossible to embrace. Bravado was one thing, but Johnny McDermott ran around like a steroidal jockey with Tourette's syndrome and continually violated the one tenet the gatekeepers of the game simply wouldn't then and won't now tolerate: bad manners.

Golf in the United States had taken a quantum leap forward since Harry Vardon's 1900 tour. New courses nationwide numbered over a thousand, and the number of active players had grown from roughly 50,000 to nearly 350,000. For the first time, in 1912, America had produced native champions for both of the country's coveted titles: a silver-spoon amateur playboy the man in the street couldn't relate to, and a rough, half-crazed professional whom people crossed the street to avoid. As the climax of the 1913 season rolled around, with both major championships to be decided within two weeks of each other, the position of role model for the sport of American golf was still wide open.

Almost no one outside of Massachusetts had heard of the gardener's son from Clyde Street. Putting years of frustration behind him with a furious finishing kick, he saw his whole game come together in that 1913 season. After winning his state's amateur tournament in late June, then sustaining that high level of play throughout the summer, on the last day of August, Francis Ouimet, the reigning Massachusetts Amateur champion, took the train from Boston down to Garden City, Long Island, to compete in the 1913 National Amateur Championship.

VARDON, 1908, AT THE START OF THE COMEBACK.

RESURRECTION

HARRY PUSHED TOO hard. A relapse soon after the 1904 British Open landed him back in bed for weeks. The fact he'd taken up smoking again didn't help his fragile lungs, but out of economic necessity he'd recently signed an endorsement contract with Players Cut tobacco and felt obliged to be seen in public using his pipe. Again he returned too quickly, overworked himself, and suffered yet another setback; Harry had devoted eight months to his recovery at Mundesley and to his regimented mind, that should have been sufficient to conquer any disease. Surrender was simply not in his makeup, but for once life wouldn't yield; Harry missed almost all of 1905's competitive season. *The Complete Golfer* hit bookstores that fall and quickly became the best-selling golf book of the decade on both sides of the Atlantic. He found its success deeply gratifying but just keeping his name in the public eye wasn't enough; Harry had just turned thirty-five and understood the game better than any man alive. He believed his best years as a player rightfully belonged ahead of him.

After a third-place finish in the 1906 British Open, a special challenge match brought Harry back to center stage; a high-profile international four-ball tournament, England versus Scotland, for bragging rights and four hundred pounds. Harry and J. H. Taylor represented England against Scotland's Sandy Herd and James Braid, the tall, modest, former carpenter who had now won the last two Opens, reviving Scottish hopes for a return to glory. The match would be a marathon event over four courses, thirty-six holes played on one day each week for four weeks. Organizers marketed the match as Harry Vardon's return to golf, which brought crowds out by the thousands.

Even with Harry unable to sink short putts, by the end of their third round of competition the English duo had established a commanding seven-hole lead, with thirty-six to play. Exhausted by the effort, Harry returned home to rest before the final, and his doctor advised him to withdraw, but given the national interest surrounding the match, he refused to seek a postponement. On the night before their final round, Taylor found Harry collapsed in his hotel room after suffering another serious hemorrhage. Taylor attempted to summon a doctor but again Harry refused, all the hard lessons of Mundesley ignored, insisting all he needed was a good night's rest.

The next morning, Taylor rose early to check on his old friend and found Harry already downstairs and dressed, ready for action. They played the final match in high winds and a cold, driving rain. Harry never uttered a word of complaint, marched out and settled matters six holes into the second eighteen; they won the match for England 13 and 12. When he rushed home that same night, weak and feverish, Harry was forced to spend another month in bed. Harry had described in his book that the ideal temperament for golf was a man who kept quiet and never gave vent to his true feelings; Harry followed that advice to the top of his profession. It was also how he lived his life.

It took six full years for Harry's health to return. While his success on the course faded, Harry's reputation more than sustained him. Ventures on the business side of the game flourished as never before: lines of clubs, advertising, publishing, lucrative exhibition appearances. Chased by specters of poverty, Harry filled his calendar—and bank accounts—with as many lucrative sideshows as his stamina could accommodate. He played one bizarre match against a pair of javelin champions, spotting them a hundred yards a hole. Harry had to putt each hole out, the javelins only had to stick within three feet of the cup; Harry beat them 5 and 4. Financially he was nearly set for life, but it was a life with Jessie that had settled into a dull and distant routine. Theirs was a silent house; no children, no music, no laughter.

In early 1911, Harry invited his favorite seventeen-year-old niece, Marie, to sail over from Jersey to live with them and provide companionship for Jessie. A lively, vibrant girl who had always brightened Jessie's mood, she quickly became the perfect surrogate for the child Jessie never had. As Harry's health improved, Marie's presence allowed him to resume traveling again, back on the road living his old life. Tom Vardon frequently accompanied his brother to Paris, ostensibly to conduct various pieces of business and to play each year in the French Open. The city's notorious nightlife offered more alluring enticements; Harry's poor finishes in the French championship relate directly to the extracurricular distractions the brothers found off the course. The prototypical Victorian gentleman, always discreet in deference to his wife, Harry could not deny his own hungers forever. He was coming back to life.

Harry showed up for every major British tournament and top-ten finishes were almost automatic, but he never threatened to win; that phenomenal reserve he'd always drawn on when victory was at hand refused to deliver when he needed it. Harry felt the greater part of his ability remained as solid as ever, and mentally no one ever better grasped the underlying ebbs and flows of the game, but his damaged hand on that putter let him down time after time.

Putting has always been golf's most ephemeral component; players as supremely gifted as Ben Hogan felt it shouldn't even be considered part of the same sport. As a result, putters tend to be the one club about which players turn irrational and superstitious. In Harry's case, his well-publicized search for a club to help him overcome his terminal yips became a national preoccupation; cartoonists depicted Harry forging a crude homemade putter over an open fire, or carrying twenty-five different models in his bag like arrows in a quiver. Sympathetic fans, eager club makers, and fellow professionals alike shipped him oddball variations from every corner of the globe. He tried ones carved from exotic woods and forged from every kind of metal, one with a foot-long blade, others with heads as square as a block of cheese. Nothing did the trick.

In 1908 James Braid won his fourth Open Championship, matching Harry's record number, and the following year J. H. Taylor's fourth victory created a three-way tie at the top. The British press began referring to them as the Great Triumvirate, the Palmer, Nicklaus, and Player of their day. The title embarrassed all three men, who felt it slighted the many outstanding players with whom they played, but each recognized its value as a marketing tool to expand the game's audience.

Even though Harry's name still earned mention before the others, and both Taylor and Braid always acknowledged him as first among equals, Harry hadn't captured Britain's national championship now in six years. After Braid won his fifth Open title in 1910, surpassing Vardon, Harry felt the judgment of history was on the verge of consigning him to the dustbin. Other players still respected him, too much as an elder statesman for Harry's taste, because he sensed they no longer feared him. When Old Tom Morris lost his competitive edge after his touch on the greens deserted him, he made light of it in old age by introducing himself as "Tom Morris, misser of short putts." Harry viewed such bland acceptance of his sorry state with unrelieved horror. He refused to classify this as a psychological problem; it was physical, and for that there had to be an answer.

As the 1911 season approached, Harry confided in his brother that this would be the year he confronted the issue once and for all; had his skills irrevocably diminished, or could he reignite the competitive fires? Before calling it a day, Harry prepared to mount one last charge, and he took to the field with a secret weapon in hand.

A high roller friend of Harry's named Arthur Brown, a successful timber baron, designed a customized experimental putter for Harry and presented him with it in early 1911. This new, heavier, longer iron club altered Harry's stance; more upright now, both head and body still. Instead of popping the ball with a wristy slap controlled by his unreliable fingers, the palm of his right hand held the shaft for a more even, pendulum swing that involved gently rocking the shoulders; a modern putting stance to go with his modern swing. To Harry's enormous surprise, Arthur Brown's putter appeared to solve his problem, but he refused to say he'd put it behind him until testing the club in competition.

Germany conducted its first Open Championship early that summer, and the game's top pros traveled to the resort town of Baden-Baden for the inaugural event. Against an outstanding field, Harry shot 279 over four strong rounds—a scoring record that would stand until 1950—but the tournament came down to a four-foot putt Harry had to make on the final hole to maintain his one-stroke lead. Assuming his new stance, armed with Arthur's putter, he drained the ball without a hint of a twitch and captured his first title in eight years. (A mass-produced version of his new flat stick, marketed with Harry's stirring endorsement, went on sale a few weeks later.) Winning an inaugural event on the Continent pleased him enormously, but Harry knew his comeback wouldn't be considered complete until he recaptured the crown jewel of the game, the British Open. Public opinion be damned; he needed to prove his own worth to himself.

With the German win under his belt and the Open on the horizon, Harry traveled with his friend Arthur Brown to la Touquet, the same French spa he'd visited with Tom prior to the 1903 Open victory. Arthur Brown knew a little bit about physical conditioning; he had once held the world record time for a twenty-four-hour bicycle race. Following a fitness regimen designed by Brown, Harry played thirty-six holes a day, then stretched, lifted light weights, and ended the day with a brisk twelve-mile walk. No booze, no tobacco, no nightlife, strict diet. At the conclusion of this austere routine, feeling as fit and energized as he had in years, convinced his entire game had returned to form for the first time since falling ill, forty-one-year-old Harry traveled to Royal St. George's in Kent for the 1911 Open.

Tom Vardon, still working as Royal St. George's professional, greeted

Harry with disturbing news: He had recently received an unsolicited offer to become the resident pro at an established private club outside Chicago, in Lake Forest, Illinois. Tom had always found his brother's stories of the United States captivating and for years he had dreamed privately of finding there the rewards that had eluded him in England. Without an Open win to his credit and his skills on the decline, Tom had gone as far as his game could carry him in Britain. On the verge of turning forty and without a wife or family to support, he envisioned a fresh start and a brighter financial future for himself overseas. Implied, but not stated, was his urgency to cash in on the Vardon name before it lost its currency. Afraid of how Harry might advise him—and always reluctant to go against his advice—Tom had accepted the job without first consulting his brother. Inwardly devastated at the prospect of losing his lifelong companion and closest friend, when he heard the excitement in Tom's voice, Harry gave his approval with manufactured enthusiasm. Then, with his champion's mental discipline, he shut down his feelings about it and directed his thoughts to winning the Open.

Two hundred and twenty-six players competed in the 1911 British Open, another record number. For the first time in its history the size of the field required that the first two rounds of the tournament take place on separate days before the cut down. Harry played solidly and at the halfway mark found himself tied for second, two strokes behind George Duncan, a promising Scottish newcomer and future Open champion. His sole company in second place was a rising thirty-three-year-old golfer from Jersey named Ted Ray, who had not only idolized Harry growing up, he'd followed him off the island and replaced him as professional at Ganton when Harry moved to South Herts.

Ted Ray stood well over six feet tall, weighed in at a hulking 225 pounds, and whacked his tee shots thirty yards farther than any man in Britain. Ted had spent the last decade climbing the professional ladder amid mixed forecasts of success; to date a third-place finish in the 1908 Open had been his best championship showing. Sporting a lush walrus mustache and wearing a long, shapeless tweed jacket and slouchy bucket hat, as he lumbered his way around the course, Ted looked something like a bear in a human suit. He possessed a wry, needling wit, the constitution of a brick building, and a bulletproof disposition uncannily similar to Harry's. He also enjoyed a good pipe, although unlike Harry, Ted's never left his mouth, even while he played. When they'd first met twelve years before, the two Jerseymen had immediately hit it off, and over the intervening years a solid friendship had developed.

The 1911 Open's final two rounds were played according to tradition, on the morning and afternoon of the following day. Harry posted a 75 in the early session, good enough to vault him into first place, three strokes ahead of a cluster of challengers that included Duncan, Braid, Taylor, Ted Ray, and Sandy Herd. Also in the pack was a Frenchman named Arnaud Massy, winner of the 1907 Open, the sole Continental to ever win the title to that point in its history and the only man to crack the Great Triumvirate's twentieth-century stranglehold on the Claret Jug.

Wielding his full complement of shots with his old confident style, Harry sank a par putt at eighteen and came off the course to thunderous applause. He couldn't later explain why he now abandoned his disciplined regimen and, for unexplained reasons, Arthur Brown wasn't there to keep him on track. Instead of taking a light snack and a nap back in his hotel room, Harry sat down to a heavy midgame meal with his fellow golfers. Perhaps flush with the excitement of being back in the thick of an Open hunt again he simply forgot himself. Whatever the reason, Harry went out early that afternoon for his final round only to discover his swing had been left behind in the locker room.

Throughout his career Harry had been the straightest, most accurate driver off the tee the game had ever seen; on this afternoon he couldn't find a single fairway. Crowds swarmed around Harry and he struggled to fight his way through packs of excited fans to reach his errant shots. So eager were they to see good old Harry win another championship, they nearly trampled him on every fairway and between every tee and green. Not only was his long game missing in action, his recoveries were coming up short of the greens. Harry had to rely on getting up and down all afternoon and for the most part his putting stood up to the severest test he'd subjected it to since falling ill, but he still limped home with a deeply disappointing 80. The bad news rippled outward through the course; once again, Harry had faded down the stretch.

Holding a slender two-stroke lead he felt certain to lose, Harry positioned himself at the eighteenth green alongside Tom, lit his pipe, and grimly prepared himself to watch the men still out on the course surpass him. One by one his pursuers closed the gap and then inexplicably . . . one after another fell short. First J. H. Taylor collapsed, followed closely by young George Duncan; both out of the running. Then a close call: Harold Hilton, the reigning British Amateur champ, came to the eighteenth in a flat-footed tie with Harry, found a bunker off the tee, took bogey, and finished one stroke behind him. Ted Ray fell apart down the stretch and came home three shots back. Defending champion James Braid missed a ten-footer for par on eighteen, let loose a choice Anglo-Saxon expletive, and joined Hilton in second place by a stroke. The crowd stirred, warming to the idea that Harry's slender advantage might against all odds survive.

But not yet: Sandy Herd reached eighteen needing only a par four to win the 1911 Open outright. He drove into high rough, hacked out to the fairway, missed the green, chipped up, and two-putted for a six; dead and buried in second place with Hilton and Braid. The buzz in the crowd grew louder. Harry exchanged weighted looks with Tom as, trotting out more pratfalls than a music-hall comedy team, each man came up just short of his number. Harry filled and relit his pipe at least three times to keep his hands busy, but never changed expression.

Now only one man was left on the course with a chance to catch him; the diffident Frenchman Arnaud Massy. A stolid Basque from the Pyrenees who was often described as possessing the soul of a Scotsman, Massy faced this situation on the final tee; a par four at eighteen would gain him a tie and force a play-off with Harry, a birdie would win him his second British Open outright. Without a single soul within a hundred miles wishing him well, Massy split the fairway, airmailed a 200-yard brassie onto the green, and calmly two-putted for his par. Harry had left the door wide open but only Arnaud Massy followed him through it. Their play-off for the Claret Jug would take place the next day, no sudden death, a real test of golf: thirty-six holes.

Harry dined quietly at his hotel that night with Tom. How many times had they found themselves in this situation, facing a final championship round with a chance to grab the title? The first win at Muirfield, then at Prestwick, here at St. George's in 1899. Eight years ago, his second victory at Prestwick, with Harry languishing on his sickbed between rounds. Unable to ever find support or encouragement for his game at home with Jessie, Harry's only confidant and companion had forever been Tom, the most important person in his professional and personal life. Tonight would be their last such shared occasion, a bittersweet realization for them both.

On every other one of these evenings, even when Tom was still in the field, they talked only of strategy; how Harry could attack the course for maximum advantage, Tom offering his intimate knowledge of St. George's secrets. This time Harry asked for no advice. He turned their discussion to Tom's new life, Harry's memories of Chicago—where he'd won his U.S. Open—and the many influential people he'd met who might be of value to Tom once he made the move. Tom revealed then what he'd been reluctant to tell Harry earlier: His new employers, Onwentsia Country Club, had offered him the job made vacant by the death of the late, great Willie Anderson on the condition that he fill the position immediately. Tom had already booked passage for America within the month.

So the two brothers faced the fact that with few exceptions during whatever remained of their lives, this would be their good-bye. Harry realized the best way to help his brother now would be to send him off on the wings of a fifth Open victory that revitalized the Vardon legacy. Tomorrow's win would be for Tom. Refusing to give in to sentiment, or perhaps to hide it, Tom said his good nights and one last time turned cheerleader.

"Rest up, Harry. You've got an Open to win," he said. "And I'm going to carry for you."

The old Harry Vardon walked out to the tee at Royal St. George's the next morning. No unsteady nerves, no self-doubts, rested, physically sound, and calm as a quiet sea. He greeted Massy at the starter's hut with a handshake and a quick *"Bon chance."* No other words were spoken. With Tom beside him on the bag every step of the way, Harry wore that steely, confident smile again; more important, it showed in his game. With thou-

sands of British spectators cheering his opponent's every move, Massy
held up solidly under pressure and they went dead even through fourteen,
both men playing flawless golf. On the fifteenth, the first crack appeared;
Harry took par, Massy double bogeyed. Harry never even glanced at him.
Massy's confidence wilted. By the end of the first eighteen Harry had
amassed a five-stroke lead. Tom and Arthur Brown kept Harry away from
the common lunch table during the interval, sitting him down in the pro
shop, alone, allowing him only a cup of black tea and a single barbecued
chicken wing. Harry felt so damn good and alive, he called for a whiskey;
they refused to give it to him.

Harry turned back the clock that afternoon; his swing flowed like
music again. Every shot planned and carried out with precision, no jitters
on the green, putts dropped as gently as eggs in a basket, a perfect textbook round. As he advanced, the crowd felt swept up in the wave of an
inevitable outcome; the victory they'd been afraid to hope for appeared to
be at hand. Massy tried gamely to mount a rally, but Harry gave him nothing close to an opening. By the fifteenth hole, his lead had grown to
eleven strokes. On the seventeenth green, the Frenchman threw in the
towel—unheard of in stroke play, particularly in a championship. As
Harry prepared to putt, Massy walked over and offered his hand in surrender, then in a grand, Gallic gesture held Harry's hand aloft. The crowd
went mad.

"Long live the King," said Arnaud Massy. Only Harry heard him.

Harry's fifth Open victory landed him back in a tie with James Braid.
The leader of the Great Triumvirate had returned from the dead.

Tom pushed through the roaring mob around him to find Harry and
they embraced, holding on to each other until the crowd pulled them
apart, lifted Harry onto their shoulders, and carried him away.

THE AMATEURS AT GARDEN CITY. JOHN ANDERSON (SEATED, SECOND LEFT), WALTER TRAVIS (SEATED, THIRD FROM LEFT), FRANCIS (LOWER RIGHT).

GARDEN CITY

WITH THE EXCEPTION of 1965–1972, the United States National Amateur Championship has been since its inception in 1894 strictly a match play event. One hundred and forty-one players showed up for the Amateur in the first week of September 1913, nearly double the number from only the year before. Hosting the event was the Garden City Golf Club, in Garden City, New York, now the heart of suburbia but at that time still a remote Long Island outpost twenty-five miles east of Brooklyn. A qualifying stroke play round on the first day advanced the lowest sixty-four to the next round, when a second day of stroke play would further trim the field to thirty-two. Eighteen-hole match play contests between the survivors would commence on the second afternoon, narrowing the brackets to sixteen finalists, at which point thirty-six-hole matches would carry the tournament to its conclusion.

Francis arrived two days early with a contingent of fellow Massachusetts players, and spirits were running high; young men footloose and free on the road. A group of them paid a visit two days before the tournament to Coney Island, where Francis rode the roller coaster a dozen times and made the casual acquaintance of an English journalist by the name of Bernard Darwin. The forty-six-year-old grandson of famed evolutionist Charles Darwin, Darwin had for five years been the number one foreign golf correspondent for *Golf Magazine*, one of the leading American journals, and he was six years away from being named the first regular golf columnist for *The Times* of London. On this occasion he was also on the payroll of Lord Northcliffe, as were Harry and Ted Ray, and Darwin had arrived in America for the first time only the day before to cover the tail end of Vardon's 1913 tour for Northcliffe's newspapers, leading up to and including the U.S. Open.

An accomplished golfer himself who twice reached the semifinals of the British Amateur, Darwin was also an expert on the work of Charles Dickens and the very model of an English gentleman. A brilliant student so full of generalized promise after leaving Oxford, he became jack of all trades and master of none, and it took him a decade to stumble onto the appropriate outlet for his talent. Once he settled on writing about golf, Darwin single-handedly transformed what had never been more than perfunctory journalistic coverage of the sport into lasting literature. Less a sideline reporter covering shot-by-shot action than a gifted portraitist, Darwin always exhibited more interest in the players than the games they played. His innate sensitivity and understanding of the game resulted in empathetic, incisive studies of every major figure in the sport through the first half of the twentieth century.

On this night, however, Darwin was simply a homesick, disoriented tourist trying to make sense of a new country that seemed solely dedicated to inducing a state of sensory overload, and in his case, succeeding admirably. A tall, sturdy man of a warm, avuncular nature, Darwin was an inveterate homebody and his unhappiness at being so far from England found expression in an endearingly neurotic litany of small physical complaints: the violence of the roller coaster bruised his rear end, the rich ethnic food upset his digestion. Long Island's local mosquitoes found Darwin such a rare delicacy, his ankles were so swollen by their bites, he could hardly pull on his boots. Adding to his discomfort, a late-summer heat wave had arrived along with his ship and Darwin found his first exposure to tropical humidity unbearably oppressive.

When they were introduced, Francis was amazed to learn that the sweaty, suffering Darwin knew who he was, until he explained. Darwin had for the last few years been corresponding with an American colleague, John G. Anderson, to whom Francis had recently administered such a memorable thrashing in the Massachusetts Amateur. During the surge of interest generated by John McDermott's homebred U.S. Open Championships, Anderson had given up his teaching career to work as a part-time correspondent for *Golf Magazine*. He began comparing notes with the magazine's contributing English editor, Bernard Darwin, whose writing often graced its pages. After their match in the Massachusetts Amateur Championship Anderson had written Darwin a glowing report about Francis.

What a small world, they both agreed. When Darwin asked about his recent successes that summer, Francis modestly attributed much of it to luck.

"How do you feel about your prospects in the upcoming tournament?" Darwin asked him.

"I plan to try my best," said Francis, "but I'm really a lot better at stroke play than in matches."

"In that case," said Darwin, mopping the sweat from his brow, "maybe you'll do better in your Open at Brookline in a few weeks."

"I don't know about that, sir," Francis said with a self-effacing laugh. "I wasn't planning on playing. They've got some pretty good players in that tournament."

"Yes, you know Harry Vardon and Ted Ray are already here preparing for it. And I'm here to write about them."

"I don't think I'd stand much of a chance against Mr. Vardon," said Francis.

"Really? Are you familiar with his golf?"

"You could say so, yes, sir."

The roller coaster beckoned again. Francis jumped on board with unsophisticated glee, still just a twenty-year-old kid on a lark, insisting that the Englishman join him and his friends; Darwin rode the Dragon's Gorge with considerably more trepidation, and emerged with a bruised sacroiliac. Engaged by the young man's modesty and self-possession, Darwin filed their conversation away, wrote some notes about it that night, and made a point of watching Francis during his practice round at Garden City the next day. His poise on the course and solid arsenal of shots impressed the veteran correspondent further, and in his earliest dispatches to London, he expressed surprise at the American press's apparent lack of curiosity about Francis Ouimet. Most of their attention was quite rightly focused on defending Open champ John McDermott, but in their hunger to find a homebred who could beat Vardon and Ray, to Darwin's mind they were overlooking a golfer who clearly merited a closer look.

Built in 1898 and the site of the 1902 U.S. Open, Garden City Golf Club resembles an English links in more ways than one. At over 6,800 yards, immensely long for an American course at the time, it has punitive pot bunkers, small canted greens, and tight fairways that feature the hearty turf and spiky, fescue rough of a classic links. Walk out onto its narrow, unmarked, links-style fairways today, screened from the surrounding suburban sprawl by tall, encircling stands of trees, and you feel as if a 200-acre swath of Scotland heath has been magically airlifted to Long Island. Former U.S. Amateur champ Walter J. Travis—not to be, but nevertheless often, confused with much younger playboy amateur Jerry Travers—liked the course so much, he made it his second home and completed a redesign that stiffened the test and added distinctly Scottish-style bunkering. (When the membership objected to some of the severity of the bunkers, Travis replied: "Tough.") In preparation for hosting the Amateur Championship, the membership had authorized an additional expenditure of $30,000 to upgrade its locker room and baths.

Walter John Travis is one of the most important and neglected figures in American golf. Born in Australia in 1862, the fourth of eleven children born to British parents, he immigrated to the United States as a young man, began a successful career in a variety of businesses, and, famously, didn't take up golf until the age of thirty-five. When a casual round played without expectation of enjoyment ensnared Travis in the game's form and complexity. He became, at once, a hopeless addict. Using an eccentric, autodidactic, quasi-scientific method of instruction, only seven months later Travis pedaled up to a course near his home on a bicycle, unknown, unannounced, and won the first competitive golf tournament he ever laid eyes on. He took the next two he entered as well. Within two years Travis had transformed himself into one of the country's top competitive players and, almost unbelievably, won his first U.S. Amateur Championship on the links at Garden City at the age of thirty-eight.

An amiable, funny, and companionable man in private, Travis possessed one of the finest minds to ever analyze the game of golf through the medium of the written word. With the heart of an artist and the analytic precision of an engineer, he penetrated the soul of the game and broke it down to its bare essentials, without denying its mysteries, more eloquently than any writer who'd ever preceded him. His gruff, plain-speaking demeanor belied a deeply passionate disposition, revealed many years after his death by his lushly romantic correspondence with Anne Brent, the young woman he courted and married in 1890.

Although anything but antisocial, he was often accused of appearing misanthropic toward his fellow players because the moment Walter Travis set foot on a golf course, he was all business to friend or foe alike. Never seen without a long, well-chewed black cigar in his mouth, he not only didn't suffer fools, if they didn't shut up during a round of golf, he wouldn't tolerate geniuses. The real reason for his apparent discourtesy was much simpler: He believed the game demanded absolute concentration, and concentration demanded absolute silence. The results speak for themselves: Between 1900 and 1903, Travis won three U.S. Amateur titles and then shocked the world in 1904 by winning the British Amateur Championship, the first American golfer to fire a warning shot across the Atlantic.

Forty-two-year-old Walter Travis sailed to England a month before the tournament with a small circle of friends to prepare for the 1904 British Amateur. He spent two miserable weeks struggling to find his game on the unfamiliar Scottish links courses before traveling south to the tournament venue at Royal St. George's, Tom Vardon's home course, for a week of practice before the Open. A straight, short hitter off the tee, Travis relied heavily on his short game and was arguably the most gifted putter in the history of the sport—crouched low over the ball, gripping the putter far down the shaft, and sporting his long, ever present cigar, he looked a little like Groucho Marx—but when he crossed the ocean for the championship, even his flat stick had deserted him. This may have put him in a foul state of mind when he arrived, because Travis's no-nonsense, damn-the-torpedoes personality immediately set him at odds with his formal English hosts. By the end of his stay, it created an almost comically obvious antagonism.

From the moment he checked in at Royal St. George's, Travis felt convinced tournament officials were going out of their way to sabotage his chances. They vehemently denied his accusations and in turn accused him of Britain's ultimate capital offense, poor sportsmanship. His hosts claimed he skipped out on the tournament's social affairs; Travis claimed he hadn't been properly invited. They found him cold and unapproachable; he thought they were haughty and rude. And so on. Travis began to suspect a darker motive at work behind these perceived machinations. After all, as he explained to his traveling companions— quietly, when they were alone—it had been less than a hundred years since the British invaded America in 1812, trying to take back their former colonies, sacked Washington, D.C., and burned down the White House.

It's impossible to now identify who was more at fault, since whatever the first slight was, real or imagined, the misunderstandings quickly escalated to open warfare. There's no question that the English at Sandwich resented the presence of an American pretender to one of their sport's most revered titles, even though the Scottish game had only taken hold in England proper about ten years earlier than it had in the States. The problem may simply have been Walter Travis's taciturn personality on the course; with his slight, stooped frame, severe black beard, sunken bronzed cheeks, and glowering, inscrutable, dark-eyed stare leveling everyone who stood in his way—one writer described his aura as Satanic—he wasn't an easy man to warm up to under competitive conditions on even the sunniest occasion.

The night before the 1904 British Amateur began, after listening to

Travis bemoan his putting woes, one of the seconds in his group handed their champion a blunt, center-shafted putter of his own design; the man called it the "Schenectady putter," after his own hometown. It was about to become the most important and controversial putter in golf's history.

The War of 1904 began in earnest the next day, on the first tee of his first match, when Travis arrived to discover he'd been assigned a cross-eyed, idiot caddie. Officials denied all of Travis's requests to allow some-one else on his bag, insisting this knucklehead was one of their finest lads. After determining the little nitwit could barely count to four, knew nothing about the local rules, and was unable to follow the flight of the ball for more than six feet after it left the tee, let alone provide any useable advice about the difficult, unfamiliar course, Travis began referring to the poor soul as "the human abomination." Shortly after he completed his morning round in a sudden driving rainstorm, the same tournament officials would not provide the thoroughly sodden Travis access to the locker room to change his clothes—earlier, they had already denied him a locker—claim-ing he was due on the tee for his afternoon round in ten minutes and unless he wished to forfeit his match, he had best present himself there forthwith. Travis had to towel off in a hallway and soldier on, soaked to the skin, water sloshing in his boots.

If undermining his golf was these officials' intention, they picked the wrong man to mess with; pissing off Walter Travis only focused his rawhide will, and with the new Schenectady putter in his hand that day, the American shocked them speechless. Routinely draining putts from over forty feet all over the course, the stalwart Travis conducted the most astonishing clinic on St. George's greens the British had ever wit-nessed. With the same nincompoop carrying his bag—who by the end found gruff acceptance by his boss as something of a good luck charm— Travis slashed and hacked his way through six matches, mowing down one beloved British favorite after another until he reached the tourna-ment finals, during which he exchanged not a single word with his En-glish opponent, Edward Blackwell. The longest hitter off the tee in British Amateur ranks, Blackwell constantly outdrove him by fifty yards, then watched, mouth agape, as Travis chipped up and sank one long, demoralizing putt after another. Travis beat England's last hope soundly, 4 and 3. When his final putt dropped to win the match and the tournament, the crowd of 6,000 greeted Travis's victory with a deafening silence.

The unthinkable had happened: An American—even though Australian by birth, to English-born parents, a detail that somehow eluded the local press throughout the campaign—had captured the British Amateur Championship. Yorktown all over again. If you thought the conclusion of the bitter contest would put all things right and sportsmanship would prevail, guess again.

The captain of St. George's and presiding local aristocrat, ancient Lord Northbourne, reluctantly came down from his manse on the hill for the presentation of Travis's trophy. He began his speech to the crestfallen crowd with: "Not since the days of Caesar has the British nation been subjected to such a humiliation." After Northbourne droned on in this vein, lamenting the Empire's fading glory for over an hour, Travis wondered if he was going to have to jump up and wrestle the trophy out of the old geezer's hands. When Northbourne finally handed it over, with a dead-fish handshake and a "here's hoping such a disaster never happens again," Travis somehow bit his tongue long enough to offer a brief, polite acceptance speech. The next day he jumped on the first available ship back to the States; at that point he was so eager to leave England, he would have paddled home on a raft.

In the years to come Travis could never find it in his heart to forgive his English hosts for the treatment he'd received—most of whom questioned whether he had a heart to begin with—and he never set foot in Great Britain again. As their parting shot, less than a month after the tournament the R&A outlawed the diabolic Schenectady putter from all future British competitions. Many years later, this act of spite came back to bite another American. A top collegiate amateur, Sergeant Charles Rotar, on leave from his British post in the U.S. Army, qualified for the 1949 Open at Royal St. George's while playing with a Schenectady putter. Not a single English soul took note until the second round, when an old-timer among the marshals working in the gallery spotted the nefarious club in the sergeant's bag and blew the whistle; Rotar was immediately disqualified and had to walk off the course in disgrace.

If his fellow American competitors called Walter Travis "The Old Man" because he was, well, old, it was also a measure of their respect for his groundbreaking achievements. The country's up-and-coming players looked up to him as something of a national monument. During his run of three National Amateur Championships in four years, he also finished second in the 1902 U.S. Open at Garden City, the closest any amateur had ever come to claiming the country's other top prize. In 1908 Travis became founder and publishing editor of *American Golfer*, the self-proclaimed "authoritative organ of the Royal & Ancient game," one of two national monthly journals that began to chronicle the sport for domestic readers. In sharp, simple prose as spare and elegant as his golf game, Travis introduced an entire new generation of Americans to the merits of the venerated pastime. The debt owed Walter Travis by the sport of golf for his play on the course, and his influence in print on thousands entering the game, can hardly be calculated. Although by 1913, at forty-six, even Travis admitted his best golf was probably behind him, in match play he could still be as dangerous as a snake whenever that old Schenectady putter heated up.

Since he considered Garden City to be his home course, Walter Travis presided as unofficial host for the 1913 Amateur, where Jerry Travers, his frequent nemesis in the National for many years, would defend his title. When Jerry Travers and Walter J. Travis met each other in their first match play tournament final, late in 1904, seventeen-year-old Jerry shocked his older opponent by bringing out an identical Schenectady putter. After both men conducted a master's class on the greens and finished dead even after eighteen, young Travers won the match on the third playoff hole. The Old Man felt as though he'd encountered a ghost of his younger self; both were extraordinary putters, seldom spoke a word on the course, and played the game like grim death. Theirs was the greatest rivalry in the first thirty years of American golf and their matches became legendary within the sport. They inspired brilliance in each other, almost always battling down to shots played within sight of the final flagstick. For the first few years they locked horns, the two men traded victories, each giving as good as he got, but inevitably youth had the final word; Jerry personally eliminated The Old Man from five of the next seven match play National Amateur tournaments. During that time, Jerry climbed to the top of their sport; Walter Travis never won a fourth national championship.

SEPTEMBER 2, 1913 — THE GARDEN CITY GOLF CLUB

For the first time Francis walked into a locker room crowded with all the top players he'd been watching compete at Brookline since he was a boy, this time as a fellow competitor. The prospect didn't daunt him—he was so exhilarated, the idea of feeling frightened didn't even occur to him. He made his way around shyly introducing himself to all the golfers he'd so long admired from a distance, still a happy-go-lucky youngster delighted to be in their company. Francis later remarked he was shocked by the fierce intensity he felt simmering in the room, realizing afterward he didn't yet appreciate the seriousness of the competition. When Walter Travis shook his hand but didn't say a word, staring at him with those gimlet eyes through his Coke-bottle glasses, Francis began to grasp the idea he'd taken his first steps into a different world.

Francis returned the favor out on the course that day; he shot 75, one stroke ahead of The Old Man, close to the top of the pack and well inside the cut line; the first time he'd put together a complete round during an Amateur qualifying in his four years of trying. Walter Travis even stopped by his locker afterward to offer a grunt of congratulation. Carried on the wings of the confidence he'd been banking all summer, for the first time Francis advanced into the second round of the Amateur Championship. No cause for celebration yet; he still needed another solid performance on the second day of play to reach the match play portion of the event.

Typically self-effacing afterward, that night Francis explained his success to Bernard Darwin by saying, "I was lucky." Darwin, in his first dispatch to *The Times* on the Amateur Championship, was more flattering: "He has a fine build for a golfer; his style and execution are good, very good and his temperament is fine. With his wooden clubs he was long and straight; his short game was sound and also his putting. He should have a brilliant future ahead of him."

On the second day of qualifying, many of the men in the field struggled just to finish. Although Garden City's usually persistent winds never kicked up and skies remained clear, the blistering late-summer heat wave had parked over Long Island, turning the event into a test of endurance in addition to golf. Used to watching buttoned-up Englishmen in their Norfolk tweed jackets and waistcoats, Bernard Darwin marveled at the sight of fairways filled with players in shirtsleeves, neckerchiefs, and white flannel pants. After overindulging in concession stand refreshments to combat the heat, and unwilling to abandon his new favorite Francis in the middle of his round, the polite, tweedy Darwin spent an uncomfortable back nine trying to hold his lemonade. For his part, Francis backed up Darwin's glowing assessment of his game on the second day as well, carding a 76, and when he got back to the locker room after this round, the more experienced players began to welcome him like the new kid on the block.

As impervious to the steel factory heat as he was to nearly everything else, the Old Man Walter Travis shot a second consecutive 76, bringing him in one stroke behind Francis for the lead in the qualifying rounds, an honorific that on its own would earn the leader a coveted gold medal. When he came off the course, Francis insisted to anyone who'd listen he wasn't concerned about winning the medal, he was just so doggone happy to have qualified for match play, that was more than enough good news for him. The veteran players who'd finished their work before him, Travis and John G. Anderson among them, wouldn't listen to any of that piffle and insisted Francis walk out to the last hole with them to watch the rest of the field play in. The eighteenth green, a difficult and rare par three finisher over a small pond called Lake Cornelia, adjoins the back of Garden City's rustic clubhouse, offering a superb vantage point from which to survey the final drama. Francis took a seat on the edge of the green among a group of former and future champions, soaking up their salty observations, relishing every exchange, a boy among men in the middle of his initiation to the sport's highest fraternity.

No one else challenged Francis's outstanding effort until late morning, when news drifted back to the clubhouse that Charles "Chick" Evans had caught fire. A former caddie from Indiana, Chick was only three years older than Francis, but his game had matured a little faster; he won his first tournament at seventeen and after finishing second to Jerry Travers in the 1912 National Amateur, Chick was now widely recognized as the best player in the western half of the country. A lower-middle-class kid, always pressed for cash, who nevertheless maintained his amateur status throughout his life, Chick didn't make it out to Garden City until the night before qualifying began. Without ever laying eyes on the course he shot 77 on his first day, and on the second played the front nine with a fine 39, but as he made the turn, Evans still needed a flawless 34 to beat Francis for the gold medal. Not an easy number at Garden City today, let alone 1913.

His more experienced companions around the eighteenth hole assured Francis that gold medal was as good as in his pocket. Chick Evans was notoriously iffy on the greens, so uncertain of his stroke that he carried four putters in his bag, and if they all went south, he wasn't shy about falling back on his two-iron. Garden City's lightning-fast, multitiered green complexes were bound to do him in sooner or later; just that morning Evans had told a friend that some of the greens undulated so fiercely, "they made him sick to look at them." Not knowing any better, Francis allowed himself to buy into the older players' reassurances, floating off into a fantasy of glory.

His dream was short-lived. Chick Evans stayed red hot, played the back nine in a blistering 32, set a new course record of 71, and promptly captured the gold medal for top qualifier. The party around the eighteenth green ended abruptly, experienced hands scattering to prepare themselves for the match play half of the tournament. Francis felt like a flattened tire; not only had he lost the prize he'd begun to believe was already in his hands, the casual camaraderie he'd found so reassuring had vanished the moment Chick Evans sank his last putt at eighteen. Francis got up and made his way back to the practice ground; his first match would start in less than an hour.

But the qualifying ordeal wasn't over yet. Only the top thirty-two play-

ers would advance, and a tally of the morning's scores revealed an unprecedented logjam—a twelve-way tie for the last eleven slots; one more man
had to go. To the surprise of the field, after dropping two balls into the
pond and posting a disastrous seven on the eighteenth that he said "took
ten years off my young life," defending champion Jerry Travers was among
the twelve. The surviving qualifiers gathered with the crowd at the first tee
to watch the twelve men sort it out; Bernard Darwin found this exercise in
democracy fascinating, comparing it to a round of musical chairs. The
twelve teed off, one after another; golf balls littered the first fairway like
hailstones. Among the twelve golfers was a close friend of Francis's from
Massachusetts, an accomplished veteran named Heinrich Schmidt; he hit
the best drive of the bunch, caught a bunker on his approach, took three to
get out, made triple bogey, and drew the short straw. Schmidt had recently
returned overseas from an outstanding fifth-place finish in the British
Open and had brought back a stylish tweed suit of Vardon-esque jacket
and knickers, accessorized with red socks and matching bow tie. He was
so proud of the way he looked, Schmidt refused to take off his jacket in the
sweltering heat and afterward attributed his sudden-death collapse to a
loss of mental acuity due to overheating. The crowd heaved a collective
sigh of relief—three-time champ Jerry Travers had survived to defend his
title in the match play rounds.

In his first match that afternoon Francis drew an opponent named
C. B. Buxton from Huntingdon Valley, Pennsylvania—a moniker worthy of
W. C. Fields. As Francis shook the man's hand on the tee, Vardon's words
were the first that came into his head:

"Treat your adversary—with all due respect to him—as a non-entity.
Whatever brilliant achievements he may accomplish, go on quietly playing
your own game."

Francis followed Harry's instructions to the letter and dispatched Buxton easily, winning 4 and 3. He felt his confidence growing with every shot,
every putt, every step he took on the course, and after securing the win at
fifteen headed back toward the clubhouse walking on air. Journalists other
than Bernard Darwin, perpetually starved for a story, now began to measure him in ink. Much more important as far as he was concerned, Francis
had played his way into acceptance by his fellow amateurs. Their growing

respect began to make him feel he might have a chance to go deep into the tournament—until he stepped into the locker room, looked up at the brackets for the second round, and discovered that tomorrow's opponent in his first thirty-six-hole match in the Amateur would be defending champion Jerry Travers.

Francis spent a sleepless night across the street from the club at the Garden City Hotel, thumbing through his Book of Vardon, searching for guidance to see him through the coming ordeal:

"A nervous man who can control his nerves can beat anyone."

"When a man has thoroughly grasped the principles and practice of the game, there is nothing like match play for proving his quality."

Sound advice, but not much comfort. Fresh off his toast-of-the-town sabbatical, Jerry Travers was in the opinion of everyone who knew the game the greatest match play competitor the country had ever produced. Stroke play never focused and engaged his enormous talent to the same degree—witness his previous day's near-failure to advance past the qualifying rounds—but put him head to head with one other man and he almost always found a way to win, even when his game was hanging off its hinges. Jerry's driver often deserted him without warning, dispensing hooks that snapped at geometric angles; he could go entire rounds without hitting anything but a driving iron off the tee and still had trouble staying on the fairways. None of which mattered because Travers understood that match play is fundamentally a different game than stroke play, where consistency and low total scores aren't nearly as vital as the ability to nail the killing shot in the match's crucial moment and drive a stake through the heart of your adversary.

Walter J. Travis, Jerry's favorite victim, acutely described match play golf as "psychological warfare cloaked in the trappings of a gentleman's pastoral amusement." No one took that advice more to heart than Jerry Travers. Although he was the life of the party off the course, often to a fault, Jerry played competitive rounds in a diffident, self-absorbed bubble, never acknowledging his opponents, which contributed to keeping them off balance. Whenever he was given the slightest chance to close out a match, Travers brought the hammer down with pistonlike regularity. The great golf writer Herbert Warren Wind later pinpointed why Travers had mastered this lethal gift so early in his career: "Like most rich men's sons who have played a sport well, he could afford to play the game as if his next meal depended on winning."

Francis borrowed as much courage as he could from his Vardon book and still showed up on the first tee at Garden City the next morning scared out of his wits. This was the end of childhood's games. The largest crowd he'd ever played in front of had gathered to watch the match, and the responses to their introductions left Francis with little doubt these people not only expected Jerry Travers to bury him, they were rooting for it. Jerry had won his second Amateur Championship in 1908 at Garden City; he knew the course backward and forward, and as a New York native, locals were pulling for him anyway. More than in any other major sport, golf fans have always preferred their favorites at the expense of unknowns; that is, until the unknown pulls off something spectacular enough to turn into a favorite. Francis stepped up to the first tee, swallowed his fear, smiled—

Well, here we are, Francis; this is what you've been dreaming about all these years; better get on with it. Remember what Harry says: More matches are lost through carelessness at the beginning than through any other cause. Make a point of playing the first hole as well as you have ever played a hole in your life . . .

—and smacked his drive 240 yards down the middle of the fairway. After yesterday's near-disaster, Jerry Travers had worked for hours with the Garden City pro and identified his swing fault—he was breaking his left wrist in toward his body on the downswing, resulting in a quacking duck hook—but he still hadn't logged enough practice time to fully integrate the adjustment. He teed off with his black driving iron and trailed Francis in the fairway by twenty yards. Both men reached the green in two and made their pars. The game was on.

As his nerves settled down, for the first few holes Francis complimented Travers on his good shots, which Jerry treated with the same attitude as he did his poor ones; reptilian disinterest. When Francis realized his own best efforts received the same cold shoulder from his opponent, something clicked inside him: *So this is how the game is played.* Lighthearted by nature, Francis had always been temperamentally inclined to treat competitive golf as a sporting contest between friendly rivals, with nothing more at stake than a handshake and hearty congratulations for the winner at the finish. Against a master like Jerry Travers on a national stage like the Amateur Championship, the deadly serious nature of his current situation came home to him as a revelation. Instead of shrinking from the test, like a young racehorse who doesn't find his stride until he's first thrown in against a champion Thoroughbred, Francis welcomed the whip and the spur and on this day found out just exactly how fast he could run.

This is how he later remembered the realization: *This fellow is determined to do just one thing and that is to win the golf game. I made up my mind to do the same.*

Jerry Travers's troubles off the tee continued all morning; the only two times he took out his driver, he snap-hooked into the arms of disaster, then miraculously disengaged before it tightened its embrace. The man's uncanny ability to immediately forget a bad shot and focus on the next one amazed Francis, but he stood up to the challenge, played his own ball, and refused to let Travers's improbable recoveries throw him off his game. They came to the eighteenth hole of their morning round dead even, and although there were fifteen other matches going on simultaneously, as word of the unknown amateur holding his own against the defending champion spread around Garden City, their gallery continued to grow until it was the largest on the course.

Both men hit superb tee shots and reached the par three eighteenth green in one, Francis thirty feet from the cup, Travers ten feet inside him. Francis took his time, lined up the putt, and left it hanging on the lip of the cup. Now Jerry took a long look at Francis and for the first time all morning made significant eye contact; the slightest ghost of a smile appeared on his face. By this time Francis knew exactly what that look was about. Even more impressively, Travers added the exclamation point by sinking the putt for birdie. The morning round was over, both men carding 74, with Travers one up on the match.

After a quiet lunch, which Francis decided to spend alone with his thoughts, the two men met again for their afternoon round. The crowd now surrounded both sides of the tee box and fairway and would continue to swell throughout the rest of their match. No nerves for Francis this time out; to his amazement and delight, he felt completely relaxed. Jerry Travers picked up right where he left off and won the first hole. Francis calmly struck back by winning the second and third, to square the match. Now every time Travers made a challenging shot or putt, Francis answered right back. As they moved briskly along, their ever-growing gallery faded from view; Francis no longer even realized anyone was watching. The vision came on him, and under the circumstances, he discovered something even more extraordinary—he liked it here. The heat, the pressure, the milling crowd only increased his levels of concentration and enjoyment, all of which contributed to a confidence that continued to rise. At the par five seventh, Travers, who had now abandoned his driver altogether, got into a patch of high grass off the tee with his driving iron from which even he couldn't recover. Francis made a routine par and took a one-hole lead, his first of the entire day, as they moved to the 418-yard par four eighth.

Francis drilled a solid drive at the eighth straight down the middle. Using his driving iron, Travers followed with a low, running draw and passed him by a few yards. Francis faced a 180-yard second shot across a wide, bunkered ravine to a small, difficult uphill green, tilted severely front to back.

"It is a mistake to continually exercise extreme cautions. If you play a difficult shot successfully, the circumstances will have some effect on the other man."

Francis took his stance and stared at the ball, hard, reached down, and sent a high, beautifully arcing mid-iron toward the flag that landed softly and settled eight feet north of the cup. Now Francis turned to Travers and made eye contact for the first time since his last putt in the morning round, a look that said: "There, let's see you beat that one, mister."

Travers met his gaze and didn't look away; that spooky little self-possessed smile appeared on his face again. He turned to his ball, took his time, stared at the distant flag, took a gentle practice swing, waggled, settled into his stance, and made the stroke. From the moment Travers let it go, Francis knew it was trouble. The shot followed an almost identical arc to his, pitched onto the green on line to the hole, and looked for a moment as if it might roll all the way in. The ball stopped ten inches short of the cup, a kick-in birdie. Travers didn't look at Francis again—he didn't need to—he just started walking. As if someone had pulled a plug, Francis felt every last ounce of self-assurance he'd stockpiled throughout the previous three days drain out through the soles of his shoes. The vision left him; he couldn't find the line of his putt when he got to his ball and pulled his birdie attempt to the right. Jerry Travers, needless to say, made his. All square.

The two men played on but the decisive blow so crucial to victory in match play had been struck; the battle was already lost because Francis knew he was beaten. Francis's friend John Anderson, who had finished playing himself for the day, was watching their match and said to his friend: "That's going to win it for Travers." Bernard Darwin reported: "From that moment on, Mr. Ouimet faded away, not very obviously, not without fighting bravely, but still he faded." Smelling blood in the air, Travers pounced; he took the ninth, eleventh, and twelfth holes to go three up. Francis gamely won the thirteenth to trim the lead, but gave it right back on fourteen. They squared the next two holes and just like that after sixteen holes the match was over, 3 and 2. The crowd gave the brave young challenger a tremendous ovation. Travers immediately walked over, smiled broadly for the first time all day, shook Francis's hand, and clapped a friendly arm around his shoulders. Immensely relieved, only Jerry Travers realized just how close he'd come to losing to the unknown kid from Massachusetts. Francis smiled, acknowledging the gallery's applause, but inwardly, for the moment, his spirit lay in ruins.

After he saw the hurt and disappointment in Francis's eyes, Jerry Travers made a remarkable gesture. In the locker room shortly afterward, he sat down with Francis in front of his stall and went over their entire match, shot by shot, breaking down his performance and course management, quietly identifying his mistakes, teaching him more about the game and sportsmanship in one hour than most men learn in a lifetime. Welcome to the top flight of amateur golf, Francis, he seemed to be saying. Even more than his early success, or their thrilling duel on the course, this conversation with Travers made Francis believe he truly belonged. Now able to put the entire experience into perspective, the National Amateur tournament bolstered his sense of his own worth enormously; Francis had not only survived the qualifying rounds—the one and only goal he'd arrived with in mind—he'd nearly taken the qualifying medal and then advanced into the second round of match play only to lose to the defending and eventual champion.

Bernard Darwin sought Francis out later that afternoon and warmly congratulated him. He'd watched closely from their gallery all day, avoiding the lemonade stand despite the heat in order to see their match to its conclusion. As a seasoned match combatant himself, he knew better than most how close Francis had come to getting over on Travers. When he telegraphed his dispatch to London that evening he wrote, with typical Darwinian understatement: "Mr. Travers did not appreciate the capacity of his opponent as he should have. Mr. Ouimet was the find of the tournament." Although he remained convinced that Francis's game looked to be of great promise, he predicted that young Ouimet "wouldn't fully arrive for a year or two, but when he got older and stronger, he might do great things." In his own article summing up the tournament, John Anderson said: "I cannot say too much in praise of the play of Francis Ouimet."

Enjoying the many compliments now coming his way, Francis decided to linger in Garden City and watch the tournament to its conclusion. In the next day's third round, he saw Chick Evans, using every one of his four putters—sometimes more than one on the same green—play Walter Travis dead even through thirty-six, then beat him on their third play-off hole. Bowing once again to youth, the Old Man appeared to tire near the end in the suffocating heat. In an upset, Chick Evans lost the next day in the semifinals to Francis's old Massachusetts friend John G. Anderson, who the following day faced Jerry Travers in the final match. But after his wake-up call with Francis, Travers had grooved his swing and was never seriously challenged again, including the Championship's final, which he took handily from Anderson 5 and 4. Twenty-six-year-old playboy Jerry Travers had won his fourth, and last, U.S. Amateur title, a record that would stand until the ascendance of Bobby Jones. But in the larger scheme of things it may have been his wholehearted kindness to a novice competitor in the locker room after their second-round match that did more to alter the essential history of the game than the many great accomplishments Jerry Travers delivered on the course.

As president of the United States Golf Association in 1913, Robert Watson was a pretty fair golfer himself; he survived that twelve-man qualifying play-off ordeal at Garden City only to lose to Jerry Travers in the first round of match play. The next day Watson walked the course and followed their entire match from the gallery. When the crowds around Francis thinned out, Watson approached him that night in the clubhouse dining room, commiserated briefly on their mutual losses to Travers, then proffered an interesting invitation.

With 1913's U.S. Open at The Country Club only two weeks away, Watson and the USGA had for some time been eagerly looking, without success, to add just the right amateur entry to the field. On the basis of what he'd seen at Garden City, and given his hometown credentials in Brookline, Robert Watson felt convinced that in Francis Ouimet he'd found his man.

Francis hemmed and hawed. Although he'd often dreamed of playing in an Open, he suffered a momentary case of nerves. Holding his own against the field in the National Amateur was one thing; the Open would include not only the best amateur players but every top professional in the country, not to mention Harry Vardon and Ted Ray. After the strain of what he'd just been through, the prospect filled him with an unexpected dread. He had no ambition to turn professional, Francis was looking ahead to a career in business. He'd seen too many ex-caddies get hooked on the idea of turning pro, neglect their education in the blind belief the game might furnish them a living, and never get anywhere in life. Caddies were dreamers, boys with no prospects who all too quickly turned into young men with no hope. He was determined to somehow rise above that, and took his job in the outside world seriously. To that end, Francis had already been granted a week's vacation from Wright & Ditson to come to Garden City and he felt he'd be taking advantage of their generosity to ask so soon afterward for any additional time away from work.

"Why don't you let me worry about Wright & Ditson," said Watson with a chuckle.

After their conversation Francis left Garden City for home, with the clear impression he had politely, but firmly, turned Watson's invitation down.

Watson remembered it differently. He cabled his office at the USGA the next day and instructed them to start the paperwork. Francis Ouimet, amateur from Massachusetts, had agreed to enter the 1913 U.S. Open.

JERRY TRAVERS CONGRATULATES FRANCIS AT THE
END OF THEIR MATCH.

TED AND HARRY ARRIVE IN NEW YORK, 1913.

(HULTON ARCHIVE/GETTY IMAGES)

HARRY AND TED'S
EXCELLENT ADVENTURE

HARRY VARDON'S VICTORY at the 1911 British Open revived his celebrity in England to heights surpassing anything he'd previously achieved. You'd have to leap forward to Ben Hogan's comeback win at the 1950 U.S. Open after his devastating car wreck or Nicklaus's taking the 1986 Masters at age forty-six to find a comparably popular victory. Alfred Harmsworth, Lord Northcliffe, owner of the London *Times* and a founding member and friend of Harry's at South Herts, immediately proposed sponsoring another tour of America to capitalize on his latest accomplishment.

One of the original media barons, the brash forty-eight-year-old Northcliffe had a mogul's genius for putting his finger on the pulse of what his public wanted to read. He'd built his first fortune with the *Daily Mail,* a nationwide newspaper not unlike the modern *USA Today,* that called itself "The Busy Man's Daily." Northcliffe's eight-page *Daily Mail* was the first broadsheet to condense the whole of the day's news into small, easily digested chunks, and its enormous success revolutionized the British newspaper business. Northcliffe also had uncanny luck with promotions and special editions, buying exclusive interviews with controversial news-makers, offering a huge reward to the pilot of the first successful flight over the English Channel. Northcliffe's resulting fortune soon reached Citizen Kane–like proportions; the arrogant, imperious Alfred Harmsworth played at the big table, on a global scale.

An avid amateur golfer himself—at great expense he built a private eighteen-hole course on his countryside estate—and a fervent nationalist still smarting from Walter Travis's victory at the 1904 British Amateur, Northcliffe had for years secretly brooded about exacting a measure of revenge. In the intervening years England had forfeited most of its preem-inence in international sports, losing important titles to America in yacht-ing, tennis, polo, and track and field. Except for that aberrant blot of the 1904 Amateur, only golf remained the last undisputed bastion of British supremacy; by 1912 holding on to that edge had become for Lord North-cliffe a personal obsession. With the time and money to indulge his fixa-tion, he decided to bankroll an English invasion of America, neutralize the memory of Walter Travis's victory, and bring the U.S. Open trophy back to Britain. No one, in his seldom-humble opinion, had a better chance at doing it successfully than the only Englishman who'd ever managed it before, his good friend Harry Vardon. Northcliffe found the patriot in Harry more than receptive to the idea, and given the financial windfall he'd raked in from his last American tour, why wouldn't he be? Negotiations began in earnest and Northcliffe booked first-class passage for Harry on a grand ocean liner about to make its maiden voyage to New York. The impresario in Northcliffe knew this would add ink-worthy cachet to Harry's arrival. Two weeks before his departure, after two years of uninter-rupted good health, Harry suffered a slight physical setback related to his tuberculosis. Wary of the demands a whirlwind tour would make on him in his somewhat weakened condition, Harry advised Northcliffe he would reluctantly have to postpone his American trip until the following spring.

A fortnight later the ship on which Harry had been booked to travel left Portsmouth amid enormous fanfare. Two nights into its voyage the *Titanic* clipped an iceberg and presumably you know the rest of that story.

As Harry read the endless accounts of the tragedy in the days to come, he confessed to Lord Northcliffe that it was the first and only time he could say his illness had saved his life.

Tom Vardon's departure for his new job in America, on a ship that left six months before the *Titanic,* had created a void in Harry's life. In the felicitous way in which fate sometimes provides replacement after such a loss, a surrogate for Tom appeared and it turned out he'd been standing in plain sight for the last ten years—Ted Ray, the Vardons' fellow professional and Jerseyman.

The son of a man who mended fishing nets for a living, Ted Ray had grown up in the same small town of Grouville, where he had followed Harry's ten-league footsteps into the game. He caddied at Royal Jersey, carving the head of his first club from a wooden pin his father used to mend his nets. Using a red-hot poker to bore a hole into it, Ted attached a shaft he carved from a hickory branch. With this homemade beauty in hand, Ted looked down in scorn at the crude, carved hawthorn branches his mates were still using, until one of Jersey's gentleman golfers gave Ted his first real driver; he slept with it for months. Only seven years Vardon's junior, as a boy Ted had known and admired Harry from afar before he left to seek his fortune. By that time, Vardon's exploits were as well known to the proud residents of Jersey as the catechism to Catholics. When his handicap dropped to one, Ted felt sufficiently inspired to set out down the same path Harry had blazed and try his own hand at the game in England.

Ted Ray—huge, and hugely likable—and Harry had begun enjoying each other's company since the droll behemoth made his first appearance in the Open at St. George's in 1899. Paired together in the final round, after Ted watched Harry's godlike march to victory in that tournament he realized he needed a great deal more than raw skill to succeed at the championship level and redoubled his efforts on the practice ground. When Harry relocated to South Herts in 1903, his recommendation helped Ted secure Harry's old job as the pro at Ganton in Yorkshire. After Harry was released from Mundesley, Ted visited the Vardon home more frequently than anyone but brother Tom. Harry and Ted also shared a fondness, one might even say a weakness, for the fruits of the grain and the grape; bending elbows during many late nights on the road solidified their friendship. A classic late bloomer as a player—Tom Lehman comes to mind—by the end of the decade Ted's playing career was suddenly and sharply on the rise.

The News of the World, a leading English newspaper, sponsored the premier match play event for professionals in Britain during the century's first decade, the forerunner of what eventually would become the British PGA Championship. Since the event debuted in 1904, the year after the onset of Harry's illness, this new major title had always eluded him. He came closest when he reached the semifinals in 1911, where Ted Ray defeated him in a nail-biter and then went on to take the event for his first major championship. Hitting the peak of his career, Ted followed that win with a victory in the 1912 British Open at Muirfield—defending his fifth title, Harry finished second to him, four strokes back—making Ray only the second man in eight years to break through the impregnable line of the Great Triumvirate.

Although he wasn't in the Great Triumvirate's rank, Ted Ray had gained widespread fame as a sort of Edwardian John Daly, the longest driver of the ball in the history of the game. He began his swing by swaying away from the ball over the outside of his right foot, then hurled the whole of his ponderous weight back into the downswing, and when his timing was on, he simply massacred the ball. Never has an ungainlier process produced a more magnificent result, but when he was off the mark, even by a fraction, Ted visited regions of golf courses never seen by mortal man. Ted himself described his wild driving this way: "Many roads lead to Rome, but some take us there more quickly than others. I often complete the journey to that fair city in solitary company, my route untrodden by previous travelers." One journalist indelicately wrote that Ted's swing resembled the lurching charge of an enraged Cape buffalo. Try to give Ted Ray advice about his unconventional methods and you risked arousing his hair-trigger temper; he was a self-taught Jerseyman and proud of it. Not even Harry dared offer a suggestion, unless Ted asked, and Harry was the only man he respected enough to occasionally do so. For a big man, Ted also possessed a surpassingly delicate touch on the green, and his work with his wedges kept him close to the pin; much more than the long-ball trick-shot artist he was occasionally accused of being, Ted Ray possessed a complete game. And unlike Tom Vardon, who had the talent but not the determination to emerge from his brother's shadow, Ted never backed down from a fight, even with a friend like Harry.

Ted Ray was as plainspoken and uncomplicated as he appeared, but often displayed a baroquely colorful way of expressing himself. His ball wasn't stuck behind a tree, it was "stymied by a monarch of the forest." His simple philosophy about the game began and ended with his prodigious length off the tee; Willie Park Jr. had been famously quoted as saying, "The man who can putt is a match for anyone." Harry Vardon later added, out of sheer necessity, "The man who can hit an approach shot doesn't need to putt." Ted had the final word on the subject: "The man who can drive the ball like Zeus gets the chance to approach."

Ted Ray's game perfectly reflected his personality; know the rules, know the course, know your limits, and get on with it. Walk fast, swing faster. "To think when we ought to play," said Ted, "is madness." Slow golfers drove him out of his mind. He hated indecision about anything and would argue a point for hours, even if it didn't involve a firmly held conviction, because even more than indecision he hated giving in to anyone. Harry remembered one instance where Ted carried on a ferocious debate with a fellow pro over two days. When the other man finally conceded the point—the exact nature of which no one afterward could clearly recall— Ted quietly confessed to Harry he'd actually agreed with the fellow from the beginning, but disliked the idea of conceding so much he couldn't bring himself to admit it.

The News of the World Tournament in 1912 brought Harry and Ted together against each other again, this time in the championship; Bernard Darwin described it as the most exciting match in the competition's history. To see Harry Vardon and Ted Ray contend head-to-head was like watching a matador fight a bull, Harry administering one stylish slash after another, Ted roaring back with the snorting fury of a wounded beast. After a give-and-take morning round ended all square, Harry twice built a three-hole lead in the afternoon, only to see Ray claw his way back to all square. Harry seized the lead again at fourteen, then went up dormy two by winning the sixteenth; all he needed now was a tie, or half, on either of the last two holes to win the tournament. Facing a three-foot putt for par on seventeen that would have secured the victory, the fugitive nerve in Harry's hand jumped and he missed it left. Dormy one; the match came down to the final hole. Both men reached the green in two; Harry needed a ten-footer for par to halve the hole and take the trophy. Darwin later dubbed this the "sixty-pound putt," the margin in the size of the purse between first and second place. As Harry stood over the ball, he had the wherewithal to reflect on all the opportunities for victory he'd squandered in the years since illness crippled his putting. This time no thought of missing ever entered his mind; his right hand held steady, the putt was struck firmly and boldly, and, as he put it, "as it left the club, there was never any doubt as to its destination."

Their hard-fought encounter only increased the two men's high regard for each other. With Harry's postponed American tour coming up in the spring of 1913, Lord Northcliffe suggested an additional wrinkle; take along an accomplished playing partner, of Harry's own choosing, to heighten American interest and increase Britain's chances to win the Open. Harry didn't hesitate to name Ted Ray as his man. Having gone through his first visit alone, Harry knew Ted's rock-solid temperament made him the perfect companion for a long, grueling road trip. He also predicted Ray's Bunyanesque drives would captivate American audiences spellbound by any oversized human virtue. Although this time the tour would last less than three months, Harry was now forty-two, and well aware that the quality of American golf had taken a huge step forward since 1900. He suspected he no longer possessed the stamina to face all those best-ball challenge matches against pairs of the country's top players alone. Ted Ray had no quit in him, sharing the same dogged spirit that had propelled them both off the Isle of Jersey; Harry wanted that kind of man in his foxhole. Business was one thing—and this was first and foremost a business trip—but golf was still golf. Despite their camaraderie, when it came time to compete against each other in the U.S. Open at the conclusion of their tour, both men knew from the intensity of their previous tangles, it would be every man for himself, as long as an Englishman prevailed. When the offer was made to him, Ted didn't hesitate.

"Count me in, Harry," he said. Then he ordered another round of drinks.

The two Jerseymen made the crossing to America in early August on the luxury liner *Celtic*. This time Lord Northcliffe saw to it their departure prompted no complaints from the home press about greedy champions turning their backs on England in pursuit of the almighty buck. His London broadsheets positioned the duo as avenging knights errant, on a mission to bring back the thunder Walter Travis had stolen from their national pride when he won the 1904 British Amateur; the rest of the British press obligingly followed Northcliffe's lead. During the trip, Harry tried to prepare Ted for the overwhelming immersion in American culture he was about to experience; Ted didn't have any Yankee acquaintances and only knew what he'd read in the newspapers.

"They're . . . a bit . . . hasty," said Harry, searching for the right word, over a top-deck scotch.

"What do you mean, hasty?"

"They like to do things . . . quickly."

"Is that right?"

"Oh yes. Straight on. Never a moment's hesitation."

"Hmm," said Ted.

Both men refilled their pipes and took another sip.

"What about their golf?" asked Ted eventually.

"The same."

"Well," said Ted, relighting his pipe. "That's all right, then."

A shore-to-ship cable arrived on board that night from their tour manager in New York. Eagerly looking forward to their arrival, etc., etc., and by the way, he had arranged their first match for early Saturday morning in Philadelphia. The *Celtic* wasn't scheduled to dock in Manhattan until late Friday evening, which Ted found confusing.

"Where is this Philadelphia?" he asked.

"South. About a three-hour train ride," said Harry.

"How the deuce are we supposed to present ourselves to play a match first thing Saturday morning in Philadelphia if we arrive in New York Friday night?"

"I told you," said Harry. "They're hasty."

As they sailed into New York harbor on Friday evening, Ted found the sight of the city's downtown skyline startling, a fantasy world. Amazed by the sixty-story Woolworth Building, America's tallest skyscraper at the time, he remarked to Harry, "It'd be a long-iron from the top of that building to the ground."

The *Celtic* made landfall on the West Side docks at sunset. After escaping from a frothing crush of reporters, handlers hustled Harry and Ted through Customs—their clubs were excused from any duty as "tools of their trade"—and immediately onto a night train to Philadelphia that waited an extra half an hour at the station for them to board. As the train pulled out, still struggling to find his land legs after six days at sea, a dazed Ted felt as if he'd wandered into the path of a tornado. Harry concealed his amusement. He was less amused after a sleepless night that saw them reach their Philadelphia hotel at four in the morning, only to find more reporters lying in wait in the lobby.

Five hours later the two woozy Jerseymen presented themselves at the Whitemarsh Country Club outside Philadelphia for the start of their thirty-six-hole match. A pair of local pros they knew from England, expatriate Scottish brothers Gil and Bernie Nichols, and a crowd of nearly ten thousand people awaited them. They also stepped into the sauna-like, strength-sapping blast of a sulphurous heat wave. Harry had experienced peak summer weather like this during his last tour, but Ted had never felt anything close to it before. Sweat poured off the burly big man like rainwater. Stripping down to their shirtsleeves and rolling them up, they brushed off their disorientation and discomfort and went to work. Seven hours of grinding golf later they had eked out their first American victory, 3 and 2.

After only one match Harry knew both his predictions had come to pass; since his last visit, American professionals had exponentially raised the level of their game, and in Ted Ray he had brought along the perfect complement for his own style of play to fight them off. When an American reporter, admiring the prodigious power of Ted's drives, continued to pester him after the match about how he, the reporter, could lengthen his own paltry efforts, Ted finally replied briskly: "Hit it a bloody sight harder, man."

Their tour retraced the tracks of Harry's 1900 journey in condensed form; nearly the same number of locations, in less than half the time. Philadelphia, Cleveland, Detroit, then whistle-stopping their way across the country to the West Coast; San Francisco, Seattle, Vancouver, then back across Canada to Toronto. Throughout the trip the manifest improvement of North America's golf courses, many of which he'd visited years before, astonished Harry. The game itself had clearly grabbed hold of the American imagination; record crowds showed up to watch them play in even the smallest cities, in even the foulest weather. Back in 1900, the professionals Harry had faced in exhibitions complained to him about their difficulties in finding students at their home courses; now these same pros told him they were booked for lessons weeks in advance as thousands of newcomers took up the game. Enthusiasm for Harry's sport had not spread to every city they visited just yet; after winning their match in Victoria, British Columbia, the evening paper's headline read: "British Golfers Beat Local Players by 4 and 3—Whatever That Means."

Harry had returned just in time to catch the crest of the wave of interest he'd kicked off thirteen years earlier. Public curiosity about Harry and Ted resulted in blanket press coverage that far exceeded the headlines he had garnered alone in 1900. As the showman in Harry had anticipated, Ted's booming drives off the tee left American galleries gasping in disbelief. He routinely reached short par fours under 300 yards from the tee and only the longest par fives remained out of reach in two. One reporter who had covered Harry's first tour marveled at how well his own classic swing had held up, but didn't fail to notice that his putting, particularly from inside four feet, had suffered dreadfully. Despite Harry's decline on the greens and the heightened level of play by their American opponents, the results on the golf course for the Jerseymen were extraordinarily similar to his first trip: Forty matches in fifty days. Forty victories.

Leaving Canada as August rolled into September, the two men dropped south and worked their way back up the eastern seaboard, heading toward their date with the 1913 Open at Brookline. They stopped and stayed put for a few days to take part in a stroke play tournament at the Shawnee-on-Delaware, a new course built as part of a summer resort on the upper banks of the Delaware River in eastern Pennsylvania. The architect was a young Philadelphia resident by the name of A. W. Tillinghast, and Shawnee happened to be his first golf course project; before he was through Tillinghast counted Baltusrol and Winged Foot among his contributions to the game. Along with Donald Ross and Charles Blair Macdonald, Tillinghast is considered one of the three greatest designers in the first half of the twentieth century. His trying courses inspired such dread in touring pros, they began calling him "Terrible Tilly." The Shawnee Open had debuted in 1912 and this year would serve as the final tune-up before the professionals gathered for the country's national championship. Most of the top players they'd be facing in three weeks, many of whom they'd already defeated during their tour in best-ball matches, showed up to take one last measure of Vardon and Ray, this time in the same stroke play format they'd all be playing at the Open.

Harry and Ted didn't have to hoist the Union Jack at Shawnee alone; a short, slight, somewhat effete thirty-one-year-old named Wilfred Reid had just sailed over from England, where he had worked as the pro at Banstead Downs, a suburban club twenty miles outside London. A scratch golfer by the time he was fifteen, Reid had traveled north to Edinburgh as a young man to study club and ball making. After making the acquaintance of the great Vardon, Reid turned professional at seventeen, and with Harry's recommendation secured a job as club professional at La Boulie, the best private course in Paris, where Wilfred had spent the last five years. Something of a dandy and a confirmed political radical, Reid suffered a rude shock to his wallet when he returned to England in the last year; after living in laissez-faire France, he didn't mind telling anyone who'd listen that he considered the recent increases in the British tax rates criminally punitive.

Reid didn't mind saying so, but someone minded listening; after only one of these conversations, Ted Ray, a loyal Tory, bristled every time he laid eyes on the man. Although Harry was more tolerant of Reid's presence—the little man's Continental pretensions actually amused him—Ted viewed Wilfred Reid as an interloper, trying to ride the draft created by the hard work of their tour for his own benefit. Reid blithely admitted as much; he made no secret of the fact he had come across—at his own expense, he was quick to add—to take a shot at the U.S. Open title, with an eye toward making the States his permanent home if he found some success. For Wilfred Reid, "America the land of the free" translated to "America the tax haven."

The American contingent at Shawnee included former U.S. Open champs Fred McCloud, George Sargent, and Willie and Alex Smith—all expatriate Scotsmen. Willie and Alex's younger brother Macdonald—who would turn out to be the most talented player of the Smith clan—rounded out the group of top semi-American pros. Native-born American players featured Francis's two friends from Massachusetts Tom McNamara and Mike Brady.

Walter Hagen, that greenhorn assistant pro from upstate New York, had in the last year been promoted to head pro at the Rochester Country Club. After a twelfth-place finish in the Canadian Open, his first professional tournament, Hagen sweet-talked his members into another working leave of absence and caught a last-minute train down to Shawnee to compete. Sporting a beret and a natty red neckerchief, Hagen had begun to affect an early version of the sartorial splendor for which he later became famous, although on this occasion, for the last time in his life, almost nobody noticed him.

Leading the charge of the homebreds was defending two-time U.S. Open champion, twenty-one-year-old John J. McDermott, and he seized center stage from the moment he crossed the Delaware. The sight of Vardon and Ray treading on American soil caused the chesty little bantamweight to puff up like a blowfish. Painfully aware that the two Englishmen hadn't lost a match since their arrival—including one in which he had faced them, and lost badly—McDermott felt that the Shawnee Open was the right time and place to man the barricades and put a halt to their relentless march through America.

McDermott quite reasonably expected his country's press to position him as the man to beat. Not only was he the two-time defending Open champ, he was also coming off a recent, decisive victory in the 1913 Western Open, the tournament thought of as America's second major prior to the advent of the Masters or PGA Championship. Predictions of these foreign trespassers winning the upcoming U.S. Open without breaking a sweat practically caused smoke to pour out of Johnny's ears. McDermott had another axe to grind; while making a tour of England after his 1912 U.S. Open victory, the British press—still smoldering over Walter Travis's 1904 conquest—had blistered Johnny with what he felt to be excessive harshness, bordering on brutality, conveniently ignoring the fact that he'd foolishly guaranteed he would win the British Open in every newspaper in the land, and then finished eight strokes behind Ted Ray, in effect tacking the target to his own back. Although he saw an ill wind in every passing breeze, the unsophisticated McDermott was his own worst enemy. His two years in the winner's circle had done nothing to round off the ex-caddie's rough edges and he strutted around Shawnee like a prizefighter psyching himself up for a brawl, issuing one bold forecast of victory after another to any reporter who'd listen. Harry and Ted, weary from their travels and grateful for a few days of rest at the deluxe resort, watched the tiny McDermott's gyrations from the hotel porch, enjoying a scotch and a smoke.

"Queer little duck," said Ted.

"Mmm," said Harry. "Bit like Willie Park, isn't he?"

"Quite," said Ted. "Except he could fit in Willie's bag."

When it came time to play the Shawnee tournament, McDermott carried his furious dervish act out onto the course. Alex Smith led at the halfway mark, with two even-par rounds; McDermott trailed him by five, in second place. With nothing at stake, and neither rising to take McDermott's bait, Harry and Ted played desultory resort golf during the first day and stood eleven strokes behind, well back in the pack.

The next day Harry found himself paired with Johnny McDermott and, breaking with his usual practice of studied indifference, watched the twitchy little character on the course intently throughout the day. The English champion's proximity revved up Johnny's spiteful engines to a scorching heat and he played with verve and abandon; McDermott broke the Shawnee course record with a 70, then captured the tournament going away with an afternoon 74. Tactically playing possum in a tournament that meant nothing to him, Harry finished fifth, thirteen strokes down to McDermott; Ted Ray settled for a relaxed sixth-place tie, fifteen strokes behind.

The real fun started at the presentation ceremony. While they waited outside the clubhouse, Harry diplomatically told a reporter for *American*

Golfer that "McDermott is undoubtedly the most dangerous player in America and one of the best in the world." After dutifully receiving the Shawnee trophy and thanking the men of the hosting club for his prize, McDermott hauled out the U.S. Open trophy, which he'd been carting around with him all week, for everyone to see. (The Open winner was granted custody of the trophy for the year of his reign; still the custom today.) The crowd called, unwisely, for a speech. Hoisting the cup onto a table, Johnny jumped onto a chair beside it, turned to Vardon and Ray, standing politely in the crowd, and directed these comments at Harry and Ted.

"There's been a lot of loose talk about the 'great English champions' coming over here and competing in our Open. And I just want to say to you boys: Welcome, glad you could make it, we're happy to have you with us. We hope our foreign visitors had a good time here at Shawnee, but I don't think they did."

An ominous silence fell over the crowd.

"Mr. Vardon, I understand you won this baby once before," he said, looking directly at Harry and patting his Open trophy.

Then McDermott threw a fiercely possessive arm around the trophy, jabbed a finger at both Vardon and Ray, and added angrily: "But let me tell you this; you are not going to take our cup back!"

You could have heard grass growing. USGA president Robert Watson and his fellow officials turned to stone. Harry felt Ted tense beside him—he'd seen men bleed for lesser insults when Ted's anger was aroused—and laid a restraining hand on his arm before Ted could make a move; he could have killed the cocksure little man with a single blow. McDermott's fixed, toothy grin turned gruesome, as he realized his jaunty challenge had gone over like a skunk at a wedding. No one knew where to look; McDermott the loose cannon had fired off another jaw-dropper.

Within moments Johnny was surrounded by the USGA men who quietly but firmly moved him toward the clubhouse. Tom McNamara had the presence of mind to apologize to Harry and Ted for McDermott's outburst, and others followed suit; although they considered themselves American citizens now, many of the transplanted Scotsmen considered Johnny's disrespect for their distinguished visitors a shocking breach of honor. They were also eager to limit the damage with the English journalists on hand, knowing McDermott's inexcusable swipe guaranteed a cool reception for American golfers in Britain for years to come. Harry graciously accepted their regrets, all the while keeping a wary eye on Ted as he waited for the color to come back into the big man's face.

Minutes later, a chastened McDermott returned from the clubhouse, with USGA president Watson and others closely behind. Johnny approached Harry and Ted and offered the most sincere apology for his outburst, professing the utmost respect for the two men and their abilities. Harry and Ted had no sooner accepted and shaken McDermott's hand, prepared to write the whole thing off as an unfortunate burst of youthful exuberance, when like a drunk on a bender, unable to pass up that last bar on the corner, McDermott turned back to them and shouted: "But you are still not going to take our cup back!"

This time Harry had to practically tackle Ted to keep him off the kid. USGA officials hustled Johnny into the clubhouse like game wardens handling an infectious animal.

Harry eventually simmered Ted down and they enjoyed a few more days of relaxation at Shawnee. While they cleared their minds for the Open, Harry was interested to see that rebukes for Johnny McDermott's onslaught quickly filled the local and national sports pages. President Watson issued a press release apologizing to Vardon and Ray for their champion's behavior, labeling his "extreme discourtesy" an outrageous insult to the high standards of the gentlemen's game. Watson also fired off a stern letter to McDermott warning him that because of this unsportsmanlike conduct, his entry in the upcoming Open was now under review, making it abundantly clear the USGA would not tolerate another such outburst from any American professional, let alone the man who currently held their highest trophy. Most of the national press followed Watson's lead and came down hard on the tough jasper from Philly. Tom McNamara and Mike "King" Brady, the two Massachusetts pros who along with McDermott had recently been dubbed "The American Triumvirate," quietly canceled the rest of their scheduled public appearances with Johnny before the Open.

These reactions bewildered and eventually enraged the young champion; Johnny had naively but sincerely believed the public would appreciate his standing up for American golf. The USGA did not make good on their threat and let McDermott's entry to the Open stand—Watson's intent had most likely been to throw a disciplinary scare into him—but as a result of the incident and its fallout, the needle on the pressure gauge inside Johnny's head took up permanent residence in the red zone.

"A prophet is without honor in his own land," he wrote bitterly to a confidant.

Although he didn't know it yet, with a moment's casual thoughtlessness, Johnny McDermott had sown the seeds of his own destruction. Everywhere Johnny looked now he saw enemies, but when the end came, and it would come soon, the forces that tore him apart would attack only from within.

Having assessed what America's top professionals had to offer, as he and Ted resumed their journey northward toward Brookline and the Open, Harry read with interest accounts of the National Amateur Championship taking place that week at Garden City, New York. Ted made a brief detour out to Long Island when they reached Manhattan to catch some of the first day's action in person. He saw enough players teeing off with their irons instead of drivers in order to stay on the course's narrow fairways that he muttered disapprovingly to Bernard Darwin, "That isn't golf." During their tour Harry and Ted had played one of their toughest exhibitions against the tournament's eventual winner, Jerry Travers. They knew that coming so closely on the heels of his victory in the Amateur, Travers would be someone to watch at the Open.

As they rode the train north toward Boston, Harry scanned *The New York Times*'s comprehensive coverage of the National Amateur tournament. He noticed that the only player who had given Travers any real trouble at Garden City was a young unknown from Boston named Francis Ouimet. One column included a quote from USGA president Watson that Ouimet now planned to compete at The Country Club as well. Ted took a quick glance at Francis's smiling photograph.

"No worries there, Harry," said Ted. "He's just a boy."

Harry hesitated, looking a moment longer at that photograph, then turned the page.

"Right," said Harry.

"Jerry Travers and Madman McDermott," said Ted, going back to his section of the paper. "Those are the men to look out for."

PART TWO

THE 1913 U.S. OPEN

Golf is something more than a game, it is a religion.
It reveals a man to himself in all his pristine weakness,
and exposes to others weaknesses which he is ordinarily
at great pains to conceal.
—WALTER J. TRAVIS

Let's play our own game.
—EDDIE LOWERY

PRESIDENT TAFT SHOWS HIS FORM.

(BETTMANN/CORBIS)

1913

WHAT KIND OF world did that year's Open take place in? What sort of America did Harry Vardon and Ted Ray experience as they traversed it in 1913? A better question might be, would you even recognize the place? Chronologically 1913 isn't even a hundred years in the past, but in the broad sweep of history, it looks and feels more like the last year of the nineteenth century.

In 1913, the beating heart of civilization still resided in Europe, but its corrupt, incestuous monarchies were a year away from self-immolation in the Balkans, where the curtain would rise on the twentieth century and its unlimited, destructive exercises. All the groundwork had been laid for the American Century, but it would take the detonation of that European powder keg to kick it off. This was a simpler America, isolated geographically, politically, and culturally. The America of *The Music Man* and *I Remember Mama*. Town squares. Ice cream socials. Porch swings and lemonade. John Philip Sousa playing on the Victrola. Civil War veterans parading on the Fourth of July.

Woodrow Wilson, the fifty-six-year-old first-term governor of New Jersey, had just taken office as the twenty-eighth President of the United States, the first Democrat to win the White House since 1892. Born in Virginia, he was the first elected president from a Southern state since before the Civil War. A former political science professor and president of Princeton, he was also the first and only professional academic to ever hold the job, and with the elevation of the Arizona Territory to statehood in 1912, he was also the first president to govern the forty-eight contiguous United States. Idealistic, high-minded, physically frail, and emotionally brittle, he didn't appear to be a great fit for the horse-trading demands of political hardball. When a hopeless impasse deadlocked the 1912 Democratic convention, he slowly emerged as a compromise candidate and, forty-six ballots later, Wilson captured the nomination. His chances at the polls appeared negligible, until a third-party Republican fracture, between incumbent William Howard Taft and former President Teddy Roosevelt, split the GOP vote and delivered Wilson the election.

It's nearly impossible to imagine today, but before Roosevelt, and between Teddy and his young fifth cousin FDR—with the notable exception of Wilson—presidents tended to be almost ceremonial figures. Greeting visiting dignitaries, presiding over secular celebrations, signing a few checks, they functioned more like directors of some prosperous establishment bank, benign trustees of the local status quo. Wilson vowed to break that pattern and serve as an activist president, spelling out an ambitious, detailed social and political agenda, and he openly acknowledged Teddy Roosevelt as his role model.

People today often wonder what Teddy Roosevelt's face is doing on Mount Rushmore alongside the great triumvirate of Washington, Jefferson, and Lincoln. Here's why: In the first quarter of the twentieth century, Teddy was America's most important citizen and he was one of the most remarkable men in its entire history. Consider this for a résumé: Harvard Phi Beta Kappa, cattle rancher and accomplished horseman, explorer, big-game hunter, state legislator, seminal conservationist, Commissioner of the Civil Service, prolific author, New York City police chief, cavalry field commander, and decorated national war hero holding the rank of colonel, assistant secretary of the U.S. Navy, governor of New York. All by the age of forty. Although out of office in 1913 for over four years, Roosevelt's influence could still be felt in every corner of the land.

A relentless foe of big business and champion of the working man, his instincts for rooting out corruption so concerned Republican party bigwigs they drafted Governor Roosevelt onto the 1900 national ticket as a candidate for the one office where he was powerless to hurt them, incumbent William McKinley's vice president. After easily winning the election, McKinley reneged on his promise to involve Roosevelt in setting policy and shut him out of his inner circle. His dead-end vice presidential chores nearly drove the restless Roosevelt out of his mind, until fate deftly reshuffled the cards. Just six months into his second term, on September 6, 1901, during a glad-handing tour of the Pan-American Exposition in Buffalo, New York, McKinley was shot twice at point-blank range by Leon Czolgosz, an anarchist, and died eight days later.

At forty-two, Theodore Roosevelt became the youngest president in American history and he electrified the office, using it, in his trademark phrase, as a bully pulpit. He renamed the executive mansion the White House, swept out the parasitic party machine hacks, and filled the place with artists, writers, celebrities, and cowboys. He single-handedly took on the country's entrenched industrial and financial monopolies and wrestled them to a standstill. Saving the life of an orphaned bear cub during a 1902 hunting trip, he inspired the creation of a toy that became a nationwide craze, the teddy bear. He was the first president to ride in a car, an airplane, and a submarine. He studied jujitsu for two years. Handily winning reelection in 1904, two years later he was awarded the Nobel Peace Prize for his role in ending the Russian-Japanese War. He doubled the number of national parks, created sixteen national monuments and fifty-one wildlife refuges, and set aside 125 million acres of public land as national forest. After helping Panama gain its independence from Colombia, he pushed through construction of the Panama Canal, and pitched in himself, operating a massive steam shovel for newsreel cameras. Teddy spent seven and a half years in office, and could easily have won an unprecedented third term, not yet prohibited by law, but he abided by an earlier campaign promise and voluntarily stepped aside in 1908. The day he left office, without fear of contradiction, he was able to declare, "I do not believe any President has ever had as thoroughly good a time as I have had, or has ever enjoyed himself so much."

Teddy Roosevelt single-handedly ignited the engines that propelled America's transformation into a world power, dragging a sleepy, self-satisfied country behind him by the hair. Demanding that Americans buck up and march toward their collective destiny as caretakers of a grand political experiment wasn't ideological posturing on his part, but a pure expression of this human dynamo's faith in the democratic idea. There's no question his relentless vigor was fueled in part by a gargantuan ego—as his oldest son said of Teddy, "He always wants to be the bride at every wedding and the corpse at every funeral"—but in the deepest reaches of the man he was a rare leader—good, decent, and honorable. As the saying went in vaudeville, a very tough act to follow. When Roosevelt's secretary of war, William Howard Taft, succeeded him in 1909, the role of chief executive instantly reverted to its inert, pre-Teddy form, in a big way.

William Taft suffered from what we would more sympathetically diagnose today as an eating disorder. In the parlance of 1913, he was just plain fat; 355 pounds piled onto a five-foot-ten-inch frame. Unrestrained by political correctness, the national press savaged Taft about his weight with undisguised glee. (A typical Washington column item from the day: *"I hear President Taft is the politest man in Washington. The other day he gave up his seat on a streetcar to three women."*) Taft didn't help his own cause by getting stuck in the White House bathtub the first time he tried to use it. After six staff members dislodged him, he immediately installed a custom jumbo model the size of a small duck pond. He was by all accounts a wise and genial character who loved to ponder every side of an argument and despised the phony, flesh-pressing demands of elected office; Roosevelt called him "a man who means well, feebly." This reluctance manifested in an alarming tendency to go on vacation to Massachusetts in July and not return to Washington until October. Taft's idea of a productive day in office was to down a twelve-inch steak, a bag of oranges, six pieces of toast, and two pots of coffee for breakfast, nap through a few meetings, wolf down a big lunch, then sneak out for a round of golf in the afternoon. Whenever Taft was unhappy, he ate, and he was unhappy at least twelve times a day. He was also notorious for falling asleep every time he sat down to anything but a meal, with narcoleptic suddenness; at cabinet meetings, state dinners, once in the middle of a speech, and most visibly to the public in the back of his roomy, custom-built White Sewing Machine Company steamer car. (Taft was the first presidential car nut; he converted the White House's horse barn to a four-car garage.) Every time his car cornered sharply, the somnambulant but still upright Taft could be observed gliding back and forth on the rear seat, an unconscious human counterweight. Historians have been no kinder to Taft than his contemporary press; today his single term as twenty-seventh president is viewed as one of the most disastrous on record.

Woodrow Wilson assumed office in March of 1913 and immediately replaced Taft's bathtub with a less Brobdingnagian model. A slender, upright man of principle and little means, Wilson had to borrow money to buy a suit for his own inaugural. The office's $75,000 salary represented by far the biggest paycheck he would earn in his lifetime. Wilson presided over a broad-shouldered country in robust adolescence, still relatively unsophisticated by European standards, avidly seeking definition and a global identity. In fifty years the country had transformed itself from a sleepy rural republic to an accelerating urban empire. Ninety-seven million people lived here, one-third today's number, ninety percent of them east of the Mississippi. Over sixty percent of Americans didn't yet have the right to vote. When early in the year an immigration law mandating English literacy as a condition of citizenship was struck down, America's doors stood as open as they would ever be to the tired and poor seeking refuge, the melting pot at full boil. Fueled by this surplus of cheap immigrant labor, American industrial output in 1913 provided forty percent of the world's gross production, but at a staggering human cost. Only ten percent of America's thirty-seven million workers belonged to a union. Workplaces were so hazardous, thirty thousand people were killed on the job every year. Half a million more were injured, the free world's highest rate, without the safety net of any mandatory compensation. Child labor remained unregulated and routinely abused. The tyranny of company stores in remote one-industry towns enabled big business to own its workers as if they were feudal serfs. Whenever work actions threatened to erupt, the establishment bosses dispatched private armies of club-wielding goons around the country to wage open warfare on strikers and dissidents.

That establishment had been the life work of a group of men scarred by the privations of Civil War, who subsequently engineered a wealthy nation with unprecedented speed and vision. Nineteenth-century European gentry looked down their noses at the American obsession with making money; Carnegie, Morgan, Rockefeller, and Vanderbilt had other fish to fry. This startling new breed of egomaniacal titans rolled the dice on huge financial gambles and delivered Herculean accomplishments: the intercontinental railroad, mass production and manufacturing, a unified banking system, electrified cities, national telegraph and telephone networks. Forging prototypes of the modern corporation, they built the backbone for America's twentieth century almost entirely without government interference or regulation, and with even less regard for individual human lives. The resulting Midas-like riches they hoarded exclusively for members of their own class, and greeted protests they should do otherwise with sneering contempt. By the turn of the century, through the influence of their various "trusts"—i.e., strangleholds—the super-rich controlled virtually every level of the country's financial and political life. All that was about to change.

Inspired by Teddy Roosevelt's presidential activism and led by a crusading younger generation of reformers, during the new century's first decade the growing labor movement mounted a stand against robber baron capitalism. A war for the hearts and minds of the nation's middle class ensued. Newspapers owned by the bosses presented money's side of the argument to a complacent public conditioned to believe what they were told. The Dickensian realities of the sweatshop and slaughterhouse, the mine and the mill, wouldn't be given a national voice until the intellectual muckrakers of Greenwich Village found theirs. Through the novels of Upton Sinclair, Theodore Dreiser, and Frank Norris the horrors of the workplace gradually filtered into bourgeois consciousness, and the nineteenth-century monopolies began to lose their grip on America's pocketbook. Late in 1913, in recognition of the sharpening battle lines, the federal government split the Department of Commerce and Labor into two separate bureaus. If this was the country's "Age of Innocence," by 1913 it had entered its final days.

How was the middle class doing in 1913? Average per capita income: $1,200. Twenty-six of those dollars would have been worth one hundred today. The economy was at the beginning of a two-year recession. Inflation, or rather deflation, stood at negative two percent for the year; goods and services were for the moment getting cheaper. Unemployment was 4.3 percent. The sixteen-year-old Dow Jones Industrial Average hit a high of eighty-nine, and a low of seventy-two; considerably less than one percent of the population owned any publicly traded stocks. Twenty-three percent of American homes owned a telephone. Less than half of them lived in homes wired for electricity. A pair of men's Florsheim dress shoes cost six dollars. A woman's velvet evening gown from Saks Fifth Avenue cost thirty-five dollars. If you invited this upscale couple for an evening of shared song and music, one of the day's social staples, that baby grand piano around which your smart set gathered set you back $600.

In the last ten years the motorcar had rapidly supplanted the horse and buggy as the upper class's favorite means of local transportation. Over fifty companies produced commercial models, but after only five years on the market, one of every two cars on the road was a Henry Ford Model T. When in 1913 Ford implemented his revolutionary assembly line, cutting costs in half and quadrupling production, the automobile fell within reach of the middle-class pocketbook. The woeful condition of American roads discouraged long-distance car travel; eighty percent of the country's 2.5 million miles of road were nothing more than unimproved dirt. Enter Carl Fisher, the entrepreneur behind the three-year-old Indianapolis Motor Speedway, father of the Indy 500 and visionary developer of a malarial South Florida swamp that would soon be known as Miami Beach. In March of 1913 Fisher announced a grand design for America's first paved intercontinental road, the Lincoln Highway. The idea of a single artery uniting the continent struck a powerful chord in communities across the country. The excitement was short-lived; plans for the highway fell apart over local squabbling about preferred routes in nearly every one of those communities along the route, but Fisher's failed exercise paved the way for the formation of the Federal Highway System in 1925. Fearing that an America on wheels would destroy the unspoiled wilds, in 1913 Teddy Roosevelt opened his pet project, the National Park Service, for business.

Weeks after taking office, Woodrow Wilson addressed Congress in April 1913, the first president to make the trip to Capitol Hill since John Adams in 1801. A gifted orator, Wilson delivered the first modern "State of the Union" address, reaching Lincoln-esque flights of rhetoric. To the surprise of many, he quickly proved to be a masterful politician, forging progressive alliances on both sides of the aisle. He proposed that tariffs on foreign trade be reduced in order to encourage competition and open the United States to world trade markets. Congress enacted the bill, but the consequent loss of revenue provoked the advent later that year of the Sixteenth Amendment. Intended initially to take a bite from the upper-class pocketbook, it eventually gave every American something to complain about, federal income tax. The tax started at income exceeding $20,000 a year, but it wouldn't be long before everybody felt its teeth. For the first time in American history, citizens were working for Uncle Sam instead of the other way around. In the year's most farsighted legislation, Wilson prompted Congress to create the Federal Reserve Bank. The Fed forever removed control of credit, and the ability to manipulate interest rates to their advantage, from private banking trusts and placed it in the hands of government. Perhaps from shock, uber-banker J. P. Morgan up and died at the age of seventy-six.

Women hadn't secured the right to vote—the Nineteenth Amendment was seven years off—but in the last decade a group of political activists calling themselves "feminists" had stirred national debate. After six years of obstetric nursing, bearing witness to the horrors of poverty and infant mortality on New York's Lower East Side, in 1913 Margaret Sanger began her pioneering work as an advocate of birth control. Alice Paul, a brilliant twenty-eight-year-old suffragette, conducted daily protests outside Wilson's White House, went to prison for it, and from there waged a successful hunger strike to win her release, focusing national interest on the issue. In Britain that year, militant feminists, attempting to draw attention to their cause, vandalized a number of all-male golf courses.

Voting rights for African Americans wouldn't make it into law for over forty years. Harriet Tubman, patron saint of the Civil War's Underground Railroad, died in 1913. Booker T. Washington's long tenure as spokesman for his people, and his policy of nonconfrontational accommodation, came under attack from a new generation of black voices emerging from the Harlem Renaissance. W. E. B. DuBois and the recently chartered NAACP advocated a more active political opposition to institutionalized racism, signaling the birth of the modern civil rights movement. In Spartanburg, South Carolina, citizens saw fit to arrest and put on trial their own sheriff for preventing the lynching of a black man falsely accused of raping a white woman. In a localized outburst of moral sanity, the sheriff was acquitted. African-American voices expressed themselves more immediately through jazz, a mainstream crossover phenomenon rising from New Orleans and the black exodus in Chicago. Jazz would in the near future propel black entertainers for the first time onto a national stage. In 1913 black pianist and composer James P. Johnson, a seminal figure in the transition between ragtime and jazz, wrote a nostalgic dance number for African-American dockworkers, recently moved north from South Carolina in the black diaspora, who pined for their old home. An up-tempo version of Johnson's tune would soon achieve immortality as an anthem for the white Jazz Age Generation. He called it "The Charleston."

By 1913, the phonograph had become America's home entertainment of choice. It had been available commercially since the 1890s, and record sales were dominated throughout the century's first decade by classical music, particularly opera and its original superstar tenor, Enrico Caruso. Aimed at a more genteel market that could afford the expensive technology, the first full orchestral recording of Beethoven's Fifth Symphony arrived in 1913. As phonographs got cheaper, the appearance on disc of Irving Berlin's "Alexander's Ragtime Band" changed forever the way the music business operates. For the first time a popular recording of a contemporary song, with an attending dance craze, connected with a nationwide audience. Phonograph, record, and sheet music sales allowing people to play along at home went through the roof. The other big hit of 1913 was the haunting Irish ballad "Danny Boy." Tin Pan Alley, the generic, mythical plane where the gears of popular American songwriting still gyrate, was the nickname of an actual location in 1913; West Twenty-eighth Street in

New York between Broadway and Sixth Avenue, home to every musical publishing house of the day. "Tin Pan" alluded to the constant banging of multiple pianos flowing from their windows, as songwriters up and down the street attempted to peddle their wares.

For the first time, in 1913 movie studios in California outnumbered those on the East Coast. Programs of ten-minute one-reelers were their most common fare, rudimentary slapstick comedies featuring performers like early mogul Mack Sennett's Keystone Kops, Mabel Normand, and Fatty Arbuckle. In 1913, Sennett signed a newly arrived English music-hall entertainer named Charlie Chaplin to a contract for $150 a week. The first serialized drama, a thirteen-episode cliffhanger called *The Adventures of Kathlyn*, appeared on screens that year. A better remembered clone, *The Perils of Pauline*, showed up within six months, coining the old adage that imitation is the sincerest form of Hollywood. Controversy raged within the industry in 1913 when actors had the audacity to demand that their names actually appear on screen in the credits. The actors brought an ironclad bargaining point to the table: Secular, democratic Americans, having sworn off gods and royalty, were already demonstrating an insatiable appetite for movie stars. Formerly frowned on as a primitive form of entertainment fit only for the immigrant masses, in 1913 guardians of the cultural gates began to take the movies seriously. The boffo debut of an eighty-minute Italian version of the best-selling novel *Quo Vadis* demonstrated that audiences had the patience to sit still for more complicated pictures, as long as they offered extravagant sets, battle scenes, and scantily-clad slave girls. Reflecting the industry's growing sense of respectability, extravagant motion picture palaces began to sprout up around the country, anchoring downtown business districts. Pioneering American filmmaker D. W. Griffith's four-reel Biblical potboiler *Judith of Bethulia* opened later that year, the first homegrown epic. Its success guaranteed directors' heads would never fit their hat size again.

Although the movies were gaining ground, in 1913 the country's most popular light entertainment remained vaudeville. "Vaudeville" is a corruption of the French *vaux-de-vire*, a term for fifteenth-century satirical songs. Because the Comedie Française had obtained a royal French monopoly on anything labeled "theater" within Parisian city limits, the competition advertised themselves as "vaudeville" in order to loophole the restriction. The word eventually became a catchall phrase throughout Europe for any lightweight, non-narrative theatrical performance. The American variation descended directly from the old English music-hall tradition, and since the death of *The Ed Sullivan Show* it is without parallel in contemporary America. An evening of vaudeville consisted of ten to fifteen unrelated performers: singers, comedians, magicians, animal acts and acrobats, a live orchestra, and a star headliner. By the 1890s the vaudeville chains, which owned groups of theaters and block-booked acts across the country, solidified their position as dominant providers of affordable, lowbrow entertainment.

In 1913, the owner of the largest vaudeville organization, the Orpheum Circuit, erected a spectacular new centerpiece, the Palace Theater in New York City. The Palace struggled initially, as customers resisted the unprecedented two-dollar admission price, until they paired legendary sixty-nine-year-old classical French actress Sarah Bernhardt, performing a one-woman show of her greatest hits, with an eccentric, alcoholic thirty-three-year-old juggler named William Claude Dukenfield, better known as W. C. Fields. A former child performer who grew up on the road, Fields began drinking at the age of twelve to steady his nerves before performing. The odd, reclusive Fields had knocked around for years, even headlined royal performances in Europe, but the big time had eluded him, and the ups and downs hadn't tempered his fondness for whiskey. Sarah Bernhardt, a histrionic diva renowned for eccentricities like sleeping in a coffin, wouldn't even let the loss of her right leg get in the way of her basking in an audience's adoration. Customers at the Palace couldn't get enough of these two on the same bill; one can only dream how sublime their backstage interactions must have been. When later in the season magician Harry Houdini packed 'em in with his death-defying escape from the deadly Chinese Water Torture Cell, the Palace was on its way. For the next twenty years, playing the Palace represented the pinnacle of show business achievement, showcasing every major entertainer of the era, from Will Rogers and Burns & Allen, to Bob Hope and "Funny Girl" Fanny Brice.

The glory was short-lived. Crippled by the 1927 appearance of talking pictures, within five years the Palace became a full-time movie theater. Vaudeville was as dead as Marley's ghost.

Fashion designers in 1913 for the first time displayed their showroom creations on live "models." New York society women, as suggestible then as they are now to misogynistic notions of taste, decked themselves out in the latest trendsetting rags; that year it was turbans and harem pants. Until then considered too indelicate a subject for public advertisement, maternity clothes made their first appearance in stores. In February, the debut of Marcel Duchamp's abstract canvas, *Nude Descending a Staircase, No. 2,* created a scandal at an exhibition of modern art at the New York Armory Show. Critics who couldn't locate either a nude or a staircase, and considered any deviance from pictorial realism an assault on human decency, generated most of the fuss. Teddy Roosevelt compared the painting, unfavorably, to the design of a Navajo rug. Just to prove a little scandal never hurt anybody's box office, over half a million customers paid to see the damn thing when the exhibition toured Boston and Chicago.

Centerpiece of a national beautification movement designed to inspire greatness in her citizens, the heroic main terminal of New York's glorious Grand Central Station welcomed its first visitors in 1913. Thirty blocks south, so did the world's tallest skyscraper, the $13.5 million, sixty-story Woolworth Building. On the West Coast, visionary civil engineer and water bureau superintendent William Mulholland opened the 250-mile aqueduct that brought water from the Owens Valley to the Los Angeles basin. (His single, surly comment to the crowd of Angelenos as the first wave cascaded down the aquifer: "There it is. Take it.") Six months later L.A. opened its first deepwater port at San Pedro. When the Panama Canal began operations later that year, these milestones sparked the metastasizing of the Southern California dream. General Electric introduced the electric fan in 1913, just in time for a long, hot summer. Camel cigarettes made a first appearance in the marketplace—their once controversial trademark character, Joe Camel, was inspired by a famous dromedary in Barnum & Bailey's circus—along with the buffalo head nickel, peppermint Life Savers, Quaker Puffed Rice, and the drive-in service station. The *Mona Lisa,* stolen from the Louvre in 1911, turned up in Florence, Italy, where she'd been hiding for the last two years, apparently homesick.

Donerail won the 1913 Kentucky Derby. Detroit Tiger Ty Cobb won his seventh straight batting title in 1913. That spring the Brooklyn Dodgers opened a new ballpark called Ebbets Field, seating capacity 30,000, built at a cost of $750,000. Cleveland Indian third baseman Frank "Home Run" Baker set a new major league mark for dingers in a season, shattering his previous record of ten with a grand total of twelve. In 1913, the Boston Red Sox began their second season of play in their new field, Fenway Park. George Herman Ruth was a year away from the start of his professional career, as a pitcher, with a Baltimore farm club; later in the 1914 season they sold him to Boston. Quickly emerging as the most dominant southpaw in the league, the Babe led the Red Sox to three World Series wins in the next four years, until the team realized he could wreak more havoc on a daily basis with a bat in his hands. Strapped for cash, the next year Boston peddled Ruth to the New York Yankees for $125,000. The Babe swatted a record twenty-nine homers that year and the formerly hapless Yankees began their rapid ascent to the pantheon of sport, while the legendary Curse of the Bambino slowly settled over shiny new Fenway Park like a shroud.

Navy won the college basketball title. Harvard (!) was America's national college football champion. A small Catholic college from South Bend, Indiana, called Notre Dame accepted $1,000 to lie down for a powerful Army team, and then won headlines with a 35–13 upset. Led by a twenty-five-year-old receiver named Knute Rockne, they relied on a stunning innovation called "the forward pass." Professional football, although played throughout the country at a barnstorming, grass-roots level, still carried about it a whiff of roughneck illegitimacy—helped no doubt by President Roosevelt's 1908 attempts to outlaw it after a rash of serious injuries—and would not pull itself into an organized league under Papa Bear George Halas for seven more years. During the spring and summer of the previous year, three young men of modest circumstance were born in the South: Byron Nelson, Ben Hogan, and Samuel Jackson Snead.

Outgoing President William Howard Taft continued an enduring tradition he began during his administration by throwing out the first ball at the Washington Senators' opening home baseball game. An avid sportsman despite his enormous girth, Taft possessed that pleasing gift occasionally given to oversized men—picture Jackie Gleason—of being light on his feet. Nimble, an exceptional dancer, he was also the first president to enjoy recreational golf, a hobby that became an obsession soon after he took office. Self-taught, employing a baseball grip and a short, choppy swing, Taft played to a twenty handicap but regularly broke 90. His game improved considerably whenever money was on the line, and he was shrewd about using the privilege of office to select whom he teed off with; Old Man Walter Travis became Taft's frequent playing partner at Chevy Chase. The president was accompanied by a single Secret Service agent, but the only other security measure clubs enforced was a one-hole cushion on either side of Taft's group. During the 1908 campaign, Taft traveled with his clubs, played on his off days, and talked frequently to crowds about the game. During one of his endless vacations, he played a round at The Country Club in Brookline; caddie master Dan McNamara carried the president's clubs personally. Taft's interest inspired thousands of Americans to try their hand at golf, but it eventually came between Taft and his old friend and political mentor, Teddy Roosevelt.

Roosevelt heartily disapproved of Taft's fondness for golf and wrote him to complain about it. Golf was an indulgence for the privileged few, snobby and downright undemocratic, not even exercise, an unathletic game for sissies. Never one to mince words, Roosevelt was a tennis player. He had tried golf briefly in his youth and decided he didn't have the patience for it, or much of anything else. Bewildered by Teddy's attack, Taft replied that he found the game ideal exercise since there weren't many games a man his size could play. He added that golf also provided instruction in the development of humility, an area where Americans, Teddy in particular, could stand improvement. This time Teddy retaliated in print, excoriating Taft for his unwillingness to censor photos of himself during his daily round at Chevy Chase Country Club. Roosevelt insisted these images sent the public the wrong message about Taft's dedication to the office. On the contrary, replied Taft—happy to tell anyone within earshot that "politics make me sick"—the photos let people know exactly how he felt about his job. And after thirty-two years of dedicated civil service, Taft went on to say, he'd play golf whenever and wherever he chose, public opinion be damned. Roosevelt, displaying his customary restraint, called him a fathead. The gentle Taft was said to have wept.

After watching the country creep slowly back into the arms of the trusts, Teddy finally decided he had no choice but to bust out of self-imposed retirement and oppose Taft for the Republican nomination in 1912. But the party bosses Roosevelt booted out during his years in office had crept back into power and now lined up behind Taft to exact their revenge; the boys in the smoke-filled rooms cut deals that guaranteed Roosevelt, who had won nearly every primary, would fall short at the convention. Taft retained the nomination, Teddy slouched out of town, and the bosses assumed they'd seen the last of him. Six weeks later, the hastily thrown together Progressive Party convened its first convention in Chicago. Two days later, Teddy accepted the Progressive nomination to run for president. He had pulled one last ace from his sleeve. An immediate groundswell of support for the Bull Moose Party—as it was quickly dubbed, for guess whom?—vaulted Teddy into the thick of the race. While campaigning three weeks before the election in Milwaukee on October 14, 1912, Roosevelt left the Gilpatrick Hotel to give a speech, but couldn't resist standing up in his open car to greet a cheering crowd. Anticipating a later pattern of political terror, a deranged bartender named John Schrank had stalked Roosevelt for months. After dreaming that the ghost of President McKinley had chosen him as an instrument of revenge for his assassination, which it accused Teddy of masterminding, Schrank walked up to Teddy's car, pulled a pistol, and from six feet away, shot him in the chest. The bullet broke a rib and entered his right lung, but only after ricocheting off his glasses case and through a manuscript of the speech in his overcoat pocket, slowing it considerably and saving his life. After rescuing his own assailant from a spontaneous lynching, Roosevelt disregarded his doctors' orders and insisted on delivering his speech before he'd accept any medical attention.

When Teddy walked unsteadily onto the stage of the auditorium, he began his remarks by saying, *"Friends, I shall ask you to be as quiet as possible. [Silence] I don't know whether you fully understand that I have just been shot, but it takes more than that to kill a Bull Moose. [Opened his coat to* reveal his blood-soaked shirt; received five-minute ovation.] *The bullet is in me, so I cannot make a very long speech.* [That prompted boos, all he needed to hear.] *I have altogether too important things to think of to feel any concern over my own death. I am telling you the literal truth when I say that my concern is for many other things. It is not in the least for my own life.*" His advisors gestured for him to finish and at one point a friend laid a hand on his arm; Teddy glared at him ferociously: *"No, sir, I will not stop. You can't stop me nor anybody else."* Teddy proceeded to deliver his entire bullet-riddled text for the next hour and a half, bleeding throughout until his entire shirt turned red, then passed out bloodstained pages of his speech as souvenirs on his way to the hospital. When surgeons decided not to remove the bullet, lodged in a muscle in his chest wall, for fear of causing further damage, Teddy returned home to recuperate. Although he had survived, the attack ended his political comeback; he made only one more campaign appearance before the election.

The presidential contest entered the homestretch, a three-legged race between an egghead, a force of nature, and an immovable object. Pundits declared it too close to call. When America went to the polls, the Elephant and the Bull Moose, former friends, outtallied their Democrat rival by over a million votes, but the schism cost them the White House. Despite capturing only forty-two percent of the popular tally, Woodrow Wilson rode in on an electoral landslide; he took 432 electoral votes, Roosevelt scraped together 88, leaving President Taft a humiliating 8. Teddy's Bull Moose Party turned out to be a one-moose band, born of his disenchantment with Taft. No Progressive candidate was ever a factor in another national election. After a few slow months during which he licked his political wounds, wrote his autobiography, visited the Hopis in Arizona, and won a landmark libel case against a magazine that insanely claimed he was a degenerate drunk, the restless Roosevelt led an expedition up the Amazon, where he discovered a river no white man had ever seen—now known as the *Rio Teodoro*—and there contracted a fatal disease from which he, as you quite rightly suspect, miraculously recovered.

When, in 1918, the United States inevitably entered the European War, Teddy saw red when President Wilson denied his request to let the then fifty-seven-year-old juggernaut personally lead a division of volunteers into battle. All four of his sons immediately enlisted. The two eldest, Ted and Archie, were wounded in combat, but Teddy found cause to rejoice when Quentin, his adored youngest boy, shot down a German plane in a dogfight; he was an ace now, blooded, a war hero like his old man. Within a week a cruel blow followed: Quentin's plane had been shot down over France, his fate unknown. Three agonizing days later, official word confirmed the family's worst fear: Quentin had died in the crash. Although Teddy stoically expressed nothing but public pride in his son's bravery, the loss privately devastated him. His health declining, a shadow fell over him. Teddy had lost both his parents before they turned fifty. Sickly himself as a child, he was forever mindful his own time could be cut short at any moment, and the ideal of "the strenuous life" he extolled and embodied with such supernatural zeal undoubtedly hastened the final curtain. Still wildly popular, proclaiming himself fit and ready to grip the reins of power again, Roosevelt was considered the odds-on favorite to win the Republican nomination in 1920, when he passed away quietly in his sleep three months after his sixtieth birthday. His oldest son, Archie, cabled his brothers and sisters to tell them: "The old lion is dead."

The president who handed Teddy Roosevelt his last political defeat didn't fare much better. Wilson's beloved wife of twenty-nine years died in 1914. To keep up his spirits and delicate health, doctors recommended the president take up golf, a game he'd played fitfully since his days at Princeton. Wilson went on to log more rounds while in office than any president in history. Rising at five, carrying his own bag, Wilson squeezed in nine holes every Monday through Friday before heading to the office, and played a full round on Saturdays, rain or shine. A poor athlete with a damaged right eye that limited his peripheral vision, not only was Wilson the most prolific presidential golfer, he was also the worst; no evidence suggests that he ever once broke 100. He met his second wife, Edith Bolling, in 1915 after returning from the course on a wet day. Trampling mud through the White House hallway he encountered the comely Miss Bolling, who had come to visit at the behest of Wilson's own daughters. As Wilson apologized for his appearance, Edith revealed she was an avid golfer herself; Cupid's arrow nailed Wilson with a kill shot. When they married eight months later, the presidential couple honeymooned at the

Homestead golf resort in Virginia and played thirty-six holes every day. (The second Mrs. Wilson is the only First Lady who ever played the game.) Wary of the criticism Taft received for his golf habit, Wilson played only with his wife or physician, never mixing business with pleasure. When Chevy Chase Country Club in Maryland offered an honorary membership, a courtesy granted to every president after Taft, Wilson refused, creating a strange controversy. A *New York Times* editorial took Wilson to task for hurting the club's feelings; many well-connected Republican members interpreted Wilson's refusal as a political snub. Wilson agreed to accept the membership. And never set foot in the place.

Keeping America out of the European War for its first two years narrowly won Wilson a second term in 1916—he snuck in a round of golf on inauguration day—but his conviction that America must send troops overseas split national opinion and splintered Wilson's popularity. Three years later, disillusioned by the horrors of the war and his inability to realize his idealistic "League of Nations" in its aftermath, the burden of high office precipitated a massive paralytic stroke that led to the worst crisis of presidential disability in American history. Wilson's wife firewalled all access to her stricken husband, and with the cooperation of his doctors masterminded an astonishing cover-up of his condition. The president could not speak, was unable to walk for months, and could barely get out of bed. Whenever he needed to sign a bill, his wife stuck a pen in his hand and guided it along the line in a crude schoolboy parody of his signature. Key senators and legislators, aware of his incapacity but reluctant to take the heat for attempting to remove a sick man from office, lapsed into a paralyzed state of their own. The public never learned the full extent of Wilson's incapacity, and Edith Bolling Wilson, a woman with two years of formal education, effectively ran the executive office during the final year of her husband's elected term. Although after leaving office in 1921 he gradually regained some intellectual and motor function, Woodrow Wilson lived the narrow, sequestered life of an invalid until his death in 1923.

Taft managed to arrange a kinder fate. He greeted his early eviction from the White House with undisguised glee, calling it "the loneliest place on earth." No evidence suggests he had ever really lusted after the job to begin with, and Taft later confided that Teddy and his own socially ambitious wife conspired to push him into it. He would live to see his oldest son elected to Congress; Robert Taft went on to one of the most productive senatorial careers of the century. A former circuit court judge, the elder Taft's most enduring passion remained jurisprudence. Eight years later he was given an opportunity to practice it to his heart's content when newly elected President Warren Harding appointed Taft as tenth Chief Justice of the United States Supreme Court, the only ex-president to ever occupy both offices. As if finding the right job was all he needed to regain his health, while on the bench Taft whittled himself down by a hundred pounds and played more golf than ever before. Taft led the Supreme Court with distinction until retirement and, shortly thereafter, his death from heart disease in 1930.

William Howard Taft makes one last appearance in our story. After leaving the White House in March of 1913, he accepted an offer to become Professor of Constitutional Law at Yale University. Later that summer, in mid-September, Taft fired up his customized White Sewing Machine Company steamer and made the drive from New Haven up to Brookline, Massachusetts, to watch the first day of competition in the 1913 United States Open Championship.

He was there as an enthusiastic amateur golfer, he told a reporter, to see "how the big professionals play the game."

FOR THE NATIONAL GOLF CHAMPIONSHIP.

Tournament Starting at Country Club Tuesday, Has 164 Players Entered—Three Foreign Nations Represented.

LOCAL SPORTS PAGE.

THE STARTING LINE

THE UNITED STATES Golf Association's Open Championship is older than the Super Bowl, the NBA Championship, the NCAA Final Four, the Stanley Cup, the World Series, and the Indianapolis 500. The Open is the second oldest championship contested by human beings in the history of American sports; the Kentucky Derby preceded the Open by twenty years, but horses do most of the heavy lifting in the Sport of Kings. The United States Tennis Association began sponsoring men's championship play in 1881, but their tournament didn't assume anything close to its current form until well into the twentieth century. The America's Cup yacht races also predate the U.S. Open; however, the event began in Britain and wasn't conducted on a regular basis until the 1920s, although one of its erratic meets caused a month delay of the inaugural U.S. Open at the playground of the ruling class, Newport, Rhode Island, in 1895.

Newport's resident professional, a young immigrant Englishman named Horace Rawlins, won that first event, a thirty-six-hole, one-day tournament played on October 4. The original Open came about as an

afterthought; the ten pros who competed had traveled to Newport to caddie for their gentlemen employers who were entered in the National
Amateur—a match play event first held the year before—which had
played out over the preceding few days. Largely for their own sporting
pleasure, the thirty-two big shots in the Amateur decided to give the
working stiffs their own go-around. Horace Rawlins took home $150 in
prize money, a gold medal worth another fifty, and the Open cup—the
same handsome trophy still awarded today, an angel holding aloft a laurel
wreath of victory atop a sterling silver cup, engraved with an image of a
mixed upper-class foursome, circa 1895. (Mysteriously, its original
designer and provenance are now lost in the caverns of time.) As had
happened in Britain with the original Challenge Belt, the USGA immediately asked Horace to give back the trophy. A vestigial custom indicating the profound class difference between gentleman amateur and
working-class professional has carried over to the modern game; in all
paperwork or reportage issued by major tournaments to this day, professionals' names are simply listed, while all amateurs' names are preceded
by the honorific "Mr."

Mr. Francis Ouimet returned to Brookline after his success at Garden
City walking on air and came crashing back to earth. His name was
splashed all over the Boston papers after his fine showing, but Francis was
still living at home and his father didn't see this damn fool game putting
bread on the family table. There was no triumphal homecoming; the
moment Francis walked through the door, Arthur let him have it. Reaching
the quarterfinals of some amateur amusement with no money in it meant
nothing as far as Arthur was concerned; it was high time the boy got serious and faced the hard reality of making a future for himself. While his
mother and sister looked on, Francis absorbed the browbeating silently;
there was no longer anything to gain by arguing.

When they were alone later that night, Francis's mother Mary
offered him quieter words of encouragement; she was starting to come
around on this golf obsession. The appeal of the game itself still eluded
her, but she didn't see how getting written up with your picture in the
newspapers could do any harm to his prospects in the Boston business

world. More important, she could see how happy it made her favorite son to succeed at something he so clearly loved. He appreciated her support, but after playing head-to-head with champion Jerry Travers on a national stage, going back to work in sales at Wright & Ditson Sporting Goods for fifteen dollars a week still felt like quite a comedown. As he contemplated his deeply uncertain future, it occurred to him that maybe loss and disappointment were all he could expect from life. In the war for the heart and mind of Francis, his father had momentarily gained the upper hand.

In the meantime, unbeknownst to Francis, USGA president Robert Watson had gone ahead and entered his new favorite amateur into the tournament. While at work on Thursday September 12, the week before the Open, when the *Boston Globe* published pairings for the upcoming qualifying rounds, Francis was stunned to discover his name listed among the entrants. Before long the news had become the talk of the entire store, which Francis tried his best to downplay and discourage, claiming this had to be the result of some inexplicable clerical error. When, later that morning, George Wright asked to see Francis in his office, his mounting anxiety turned to panic.

From behind his desk, a stern Wright waved him right in. To Francis's dismay, a copy of the *Globe* lay open in front of his employer.

"Well, Francis," said Wright. "I see you are going to be playing in the Open Championship."

"No, sir. Absolutely not. This is some kind of terrible mistake."

"Really? How do you mean?"

"I've already taken my week's vacation to play in the Amateur, and I had a fine time doing it, too, sir, but it would be irresponsible of me to ask for another week off now seeing as how I've only just returned. As I believe I've told you, I have no interest in the professional game—it's going to be the business world for me, and you see, I think they entered me in this thing somehow automatically, without my asking, as a kind of courtesy, and in fact I told Mr. Watson that I couldn't do it when he asked me about it directly, and I'm ever so grateful for this chance to explain it to you so I can clear up this misunderstanding."

"So now let me be sure I understand you, Francis: You're entered in the Open but you're not going to play in it?"

"No, sir, like I said, I think there's been some mistake because I wouldn't ever want to presume on your generosity after letting me go to New York—"

"You know Harry Vardon and Ted Ray are going to be playing, don't you?"

"I do, sir, and may I say that Mr. Vardon has no greater admirer. And now that you happen to mention it, I was going to ask you for some time off during the tournament—not the whole week, mind you—but just a single day, so I could perhaps wander out there and watch Mr. Vardon play."

"So now you want some time off to watch Harry Vardon play."

"Yes, sir, if it's not too much trouble; just a day or even an afternoon, and I'd be ever so grateful."

Wright tapped his fingers on the desk, deliberating. "Here's what you're going to do, Francis." Wright leaned forward with a gleam in his eye, and the slightest smile crossed his lips. "It seems to me that as long as you're entered in the Open tournament, you had better plan to play."

Francis was speechless. Wright's smile widened. "And you can consider that an order," he added.

"Yes, sir." Francis turned and headed for the door, his head in the clouds.

"I'll be taking a few days off to come out and see you play myself, along with a few of the other fellas," said Wright. "You don't want to disappoint the company now, do you, Francis?"

Francis stopped and turned at the door. "No, sir, absolutely not."

"So I guess you'd better take the rest of this week off to practice and sharpen up your game then, hadn't you?"

"Yes, sir." Francis stood in the open doorway, frozen in disbelief.

Wright waited. Francis didn't move. "That's all, Francis."

Also unbeknownst to Francis, Robert Watson had written his old friend George Wright about his plans for Boston's favorite young amateur. Wright, the godfather of Boston golf and Francis's biggest local supporter, had been on board for over a week. George Wright's blessing shook Francis out of his earlier reluctance and he accepted the challenge. For some time he had been planning to play that weekend in his home course Woodland's invitational tournament, an amateur event that attracted players from all over the Boston area; he had already qualified for the match play segment by shooting the lowest score in a day of qualifying. After calling his home club Thursday morning to inform them that he would have to reluctantly withdraw from their event—there were no hard feelings once they heard the reason why—Francis caught the trolley back to Brookline in time for a practice round that afternoon, shooting a fine 76. He spent the rest of the day practicing until dusk, then played another round on Friday and twice on Saturday, sharing the course with over 100 of the other players entered in the Open.

HARRY AND TED arrived in Boston amid considerable fanfare on the afternoon of Wednesday, September 3. Although golf had a long way to go to replace the Red Sox or Harvard football in the hearts of New England sports fans, the two champions carried enough cachet to land them on at least one front page of the city's six daily newspapers. They checked into the Copley Square Hotel, a twenty-two-year-old hostelry offering the city's "most deluxe accommodations in the heart of its upscale Back Bay," a mile west of the Boston Common.

Many of the better-heeled out-of-town players entered in the tournament had also chosen to stay at the Copley Square Hotel; arriving that same day was Louis Tellier, an established French professional and former colleague of Wilfred Reid's at La Boulie in Paris. Although much was made in the local press about Tellier's foreign credentials, his actual résumé distinctly lacked high professional accomplishment, a third-place finish in the previous year's French Open being the best he could offer. A small, natty, personable character, with a delightful tendency to mangle his English, Tellier had recently married Wilfred Reid's sister and the newlyweds had sailed over specifically to hook up with Reid, hustle up some big-money exhibitions, and compete in the Open. Tellier had gone to the trouble of corresponding with a number of New England courses before he sailed, slightly overselling himself as a "French champion," and had arranged a half dozen cash challenge matches for himself before the Open tournament began. Whether the brothers-in-law were working as a team is uncertain; what is clear is that both men hoped creating a big splash in 1913's national championship would allow them to make America their permanent home.

As they walked down to dinner that night, Ted and Harry ran into Wilfred Reid in the hotel lobby. Trailing his English compatriots like a pilot fish, Reid had traveled up from Shawnee to New York, then to Boston and had checked into the Copley Square Hotel that same afternoon. Reid immediately invited himself to join his more distinguished countrymen for dinner. The unfailingly polite Harry agreed before Ted had a chance to object.

"Great," muttered Ted. "Another tax seminar."

The next day all four foreign players made the eight-mile trek out to Brookline for their first look at The Country Club. Leaving no angle unworked, Louis Tellier arrived near dawn in time for a solo round, and was personally shown the "shortest and most correct way" around the course by resident pro Alec "Nipper" Campbell. Ray and Vardon showed up three hours later, leaving time to get in only a few leisurely holes before lunch. Afterward, Tellier and Ray squared off against Vardon and a local amateur in a four-ball match that attracted a sizeable crowd; perhaps at Ted's insistence, Reid was not invited to join them. Alec Campbell made certain Dan McNamara assigned the club's finest caddies to their foreign dignitaries; Tellier's morning briefing from Campbell on how to play the course appeared to make a difference, as he and Ray won the match and split sixty dollars in prize money.

Signaling the seriousness of their intent to win the Open, Vardon and Ray followed the same diligent routine throughout the week, playing The Country Club course twice a day in a number of different formats against a variety of opponents. On September 8, Harry tied the club's scoring record with a flawless 71. During that same week, Louis Tellier, more intent on finance and ingratiating himself to potential employers in his new country, showed up at six private clubs throughout the Boston area for the exhibitions he had previously arranged, even traveling as far as Vermont for one outing. A flaw quickly appeared in Louis's plan to establish himself in America: He lost every single match.

Johnny McDermott arrived in Brookline on Thursday, September 11, in time to watch Vardon and Ray defeat "Nipper" Campbell and Louis Tellier in another exhibition at The Country Club. After walking the first few holes along with a crowd of nearly three hundred onlookers, Johnny waited until Vardon and Ray noticed him in the gallery, slowly tipped his cap to them, then pointedly turned and walked back to the clubhouse to start his own practice round. Unamused by McDermott's latest bit of gamesmanship, Vardon and Ray made quick work of Campbell and Tellier, winning 5 and 3, and splitting $300. The two champions left for Boston immediately afterward to catch a night train to New Jersey; the next day they were obligated to fulfill the last commitment of their pre-Open tour with a final tune-up at Baltusrol Golf Club in New Jersey.

Built in 1895, Baltusrol had hosted the 1903 U.S. Open—won by the late, great Willie Anderson—and already enjoyed a reputation as one of the country's finest private courses. The next morning, fresh off the train, Harry and Ted faced two tough professionals in a thirty-six-hole exhibition: Alex Smith, Jerry Travers's private instructor and two-time U.S. Open champ, and George Low, another son of Carnoustie, now the resident pro at Baltusrol and best known as the man who had taught President Taft how to swing his weight around. The Saturday event attracted an enormous crowd; one estimate numbered the gallery at over seven thousand. An unidentified reporter who covered the match for *American Golfer* expressed amazement that, since they were playing a best-ball match, neither Harry nor Ted exhibited the slightest interest in keeping their own score; best-ball is a team game where individual scores mean nothing, but with typical American interest in numbers and individual achievement, this reporter tallied their scores on his own: Ted shot 70–72, Harry 71–75. And, for the record, the Englishmen won their match easily, 7 and 6.

The reporter found a lot to admire in Harry's classic swing ("He is the same great master, tremendous in length from the tee and just as deadly in the accuracy of his approaches.") and in Ted Ray's entire game, where his prose turned an impressive shade of purple. ("Another magnificent player; more virile, almost bordering on the brutal. And his putting! A short, concentrated glance back of the ball toward the hole, a soft, stealthy, panther-like movement toward it, an unstudied stance, a low, smooth withdrawal of the club, a correspondingly unhurried forward movement full of rhythm, and lo! The ball disappears, quite as one expects.")

Unaware of Harry's physical infirmity—he never mentioned his damaged hand to a member of the press in his lifetime, unwilling to ever appear as though he was making excuses—the writer expressed serious reservations about Vardon's performance on the greens, and went on at some length about them. "It seems to be a compensation of Nature. In her most benign mood she gifted him to an extraordinary degree with the ability to drive both far and sure, and to make his second shots so close to the pin that only mediocre skill is necessary to hole. But there she halted . . . perhaps wisely. For no living man could stand up against that sort of thing. So out of compassion for the rest of golfing mankind she injected into his mentality a whole family of germs of irresolution, of doubt, of timidity—so that the instant a putting implement of any kind passed into his hands he became possessed of an obsession that it was physically impossible to hole those ordinary length putts that the rest of us look upon as comparatively simple affairs; to see the club twitched back and a spasmodic pass made at the ball—truly, it is nerve-racking."

In plainer English, on the very eve of the Open, Harry's yips had returned with a vengeance.

Harry excused himself early from dinner and stayed up until after midnight, putting a ball back and forth across the carpet of his hotel room, patiently trying to regain control of his treacherous right hand. The two Englishmen woke before dawn the next morning and rode the train back to Boston. Dominating headlines in New York that day, pushing news of their celebrated match at Baltusrol to the back pages, was the sudden death of the city's mayor, William Jay Gaynor. Three years after surviving a political assassination attempt, the popular sixty-five-year-old Gaynor collapsed and died a day out at sea on the ocean liner *Baltic*; a coughing fit, prompted by the assassin's bullet that surgeons had been unable to safely remove from his throat, brought on a heart attack.

THAT SAME LAST Sunday before the tournament, with qualifying rounds scheduled to begin on Tuesday, his old friend and school days' rival

Frank Hoyt invited Francis to play his final tune-up at Wellesley Country Club, a short, woodsy course a few miles to the west. Francis had established a course record of 66 at Wellesley earlier in the summer and agreed this familiar ground would provide the perfect track to peak his confidence going into the Open. Francis and Hoyt played two complete eighteen-hole rounds on the relatively easy course that day. During the morning, Francis couldn't find a grip on any part of his game and shot a dismal 88. Hoping to shake it off as an understandable case of pre-tournament jitters, after a quick lunch they immediately went out to play a second round. Francis shot another wretched 88. Afterward Frank Hoyt was inconsolable, convinced the outing had ruined Francis's game and any chance he might have in the championship. Eager to relieve his friend's anxiety, Francis assured him he didn't share those feelings.

"Don't you worry," he told Frank. "A day like this was exactly what I needed. I probably got all the bad shots out of my system."

When he got home and tried to sleep that night, staring out his bedroom window as a muggy late summer night settled over The Country Club's fairways, Francis felt considerably less certain about his prospects.

THE TOWN OF Brookline began life as allotment farmland between the Charles and Muddy rivers parceled out to citizens of Boston in the 1630s. Within seventy years, the locals had built a schoolhouse, laid out three major thoroughfares, and formed a small settlement they inelegantly called Muddy River Hamlet. In 1705, on their third attempt, they were granted permission by the Massachusetts General Court to incorporate as the Township of Brookline. The town's first clerk was a man named Samuel Sewall, son of the hanging judge who had presided over Salem's infamous witch trials. A brook that formed the eastern border of the Sewall family's land, the largest single holding in the tract, gave the town its name, Brookline. On April 19, 1775, Brookline contributed three companies of volunteers to the rout of the British forces at Lexington and Concord; the original "shots heard round the world" were fired less than twenty miles from the fields and forests that would eventually know new life as The Country Club's fairways. A young Brookline resident named Issac

Gardner was the only Harvard graduate to lose his life in the fighting on that first day of America's Revolution.

During the nineteenth century, Boston's wealthy merchant class began building summer homes in the area, signaling the start of Brookline's shift from a rural, agricultural community to residential village. Turnpikes and plank roads extending out from Boston gradually brought the town ever closer. By the time Francis Ouimet entered the world, an electrified trolley car connected Boston to Brookline, which by then had grown into Boston's largest and most prosperous commuter suburb. The Country Club provided the center of Brookline's social existence, and constituted a sizeable chunk of the southwest corner of its real estate. Among those seeking a respite from the steamy Boston summers was a clannish, lace-curtain Irish Catholic family clawing its way toward respectability. Their patriarch, a 1912 Harvard graduate, was a few years away from making his first fortune running bootleg whiskey down from Canada during Prohibition. A few decades into the future, the town of Brookline would gain worldwide recognition as the birthplace of his sons, John and Robert Kennedy.

The U.S. Open, with few exceptions, has traditionally been played at the height of summer. When the USGA conducted their annual executive meeting in January of 1913, they awarded that year's Open to The Country Club and dates for the championship were originally set for June 4–5. Two months later, The Country Club received an inquiry from England—their swift and agreeable response encouraged by seeing Lord Northcliffe's name on the letterhead—wondering whether the added presence of Harry Vardon and Ted Ray might persuade them to postpone the tournament until the third week of September, when the two visiting champions would be able to fit it into their complex traveling schedule. After The Country Club's executive committee approved the change, for the first and only time in its history the USGA agreed to move the date of its championship to accommodate two individual golfers.

As had happened recently in the Amateur Championship at Garden City, the size of the field in the 1913 Open necessitated two preliminary days of double-round qualifying play. Officials split the roster down the middle; the first flight would play thirty-six holes on Tuesday, the second group the same on Wednesday. Laying the foundation for the modern Open tournament model—in which sectional and regional qualifying rounds winnow down applicants over a period of weeks at selected courses around the country—only the low sixty-four players, and ties, would advance into the four rounds of the U.S. Open proper—thirty-six holes a day to be played on Thursday and Friday. (The USGA would not change the Open's format to a four-day tournament until 1965, following Ken Venturi's near fatal bout of heatstroke during the final thirty-six holes of his win at Congressional.) As they had for the last four years, the USGA offered a total purse of $900 for the tournament—$300 awarded for first place, the rest doled out on a sharply descending scale to a tenth-place finish, worth exactly twenty dollars.

On Monday, September 15, the day before qualifying began, The Country Club again opened its course for practice rounds to all tournament entrants. By this final day, the number of players accepted into competition had reached 168—145 professionals and 23 invited amateurs—the largest number ever in a U.S. Open by a considerable margin. Representing five countries and twenty-two states, this field ensured that 1913's tournament would be the first truly international U.S. Open. More than 150 of those contestants played practice rounds at The Country Club course that Monday.

Bernard Darwin arrived in Boston on Sunday, September 14, after taking part himself—and reaching the semifinals—in an amateur match play tournament at the National Links on Long Island. Darwin walked The Country Club course during Monday's practice rounds and filed this report: "It is a very pretty spot and the course is good and picturesque with valleys and wooded hills and rocky promontories in one or two places. If it is not a 'big' course, it is yet a very sound one and quite difficult enough for any reasonable being." Darwin had distinguished company as he explored the course for the first time; eager to see how his investment was paying off, Lord Northcliffe himself had followed Darwin over on another liner from England. In a derby and Bond Street Edwardian finery, he cut an imposing figure as they strode The Country Club fairways. With the impatient zeal of a mogul, Northcliffe had skipped the body of Vardon and Ray's tour, showing up only at the eleventh hour to watch them compete for the pay-off he'd dispatched them to capture, the U.S. Open trophy.

The Country Club course in 1913 measured 6,245 yards, the front longer than the back, which played to an even 3,000. Although this was after the relatively recent concept of "par" golf had been introduced in America, national adoption of par as a benchmark measurement for scoring remained a few years away, so the exact par figure for the course is slightly difficult to determine. The 1913 Country Club scorecard lists the bogey figures on all its holes, for a total of eighty, but at the time bogey was in the middle of a complex transition from the word that used to mean "one's expected score" to "one over the expected score." The evolution of the bogey concept itself is interesting enough to warrant a brief detour.

During the eighteenth and throughout the early nineteenth centuries, match play was the only method of scoring known to the sport. Stroke or medal play first became popular at St. Andrews in the 1840s, during the era of Alan Robertson, and its rising prevalence necessitated the development of a handicap system, a way to level the playing field between players of differing skill. Early attempts divided a club's roster of players, according to ability, into six different groups. When players from different groups competed, a set number of strokes were awarded to the less gifted competitor, doled out in fractions throughout the round. This kept the peace at home, but golf's increasing popularity brought inter-club events into fashion, and the disparity of playing standards at different clubs made fair handicapping between their memberships impossible. Some way of calculating baseline scores on different courses had to be established before an equitable, standardized handicap system could regulate the game nationwide. The introduction of the "bogey" score made that possible, courtesy of England's Coventry Club.

In 1890 Coventry hosted a tournament in which each golfer played a match, with the benefit of their established player's group handicap, against an imaginary opponent who automatically posted what was considered an error-free round, a score they called "scratch." This format quickly caught on at Coventry and spread to other English clubs. A wildly popular music-hall song that same year included an oft-repeated chorus of "Hush! Hush! Hush! Here comes the bogey man!" The club secretary at Yarmouth, one of the clubs using the new scratch format, began jokingly referring to their tournament's imaginary opponent as the "bogey man." The idea was a big hit at Yarmouth, and before long players all over the country started referring to their club's scratch standard as the "bogey" score. Not long afterward, a club in Gosport, England, took the joke a step further and installed the hypothetical "Mr. Bogey" in their club as an honorary member. Because Gosport included numerous military officers in their roster, the local custom was to award every civilian newcomer an honorary service rank. Their secretary decided that a "player" as steady and accomplished as "Mr. Bogey" deserved nothing less than the rank of colonel. This bit of whimsy took the English club scene by storm and within a few years the imaginary figure of Colonel Bogey stepped off the golf course and into British cultural mythology as a stiff-upper-lipped icon of discipline and courage for England's armed forces throughout the next century. You may remember the catchy little tune whistled by British prisoners of war in the classic film *The Bridge on the River Kwai*. This wasn't a theme written for the movie, it was a long-established military standard called "Colonel Bogey's March."

So how did the "bogey," born as a standard of excellence, come to represent niggling, consistent failure on the modern golf course? When playing standards were first established on British courses, bogey represented the score on each hole that a course expected of only its finest golfers. As equipment, player skill, and course maintenance rapidly improved through the boom years of the 1890s, actual scores fell slightly faster than course ratings systems could keep up with. As a result, by the early twentieth century most British courses included a handful of holes where bogey remained a stroke above the newer standard for an error-free score. At this exact moment, after Vardon's first tour, American golf began to soar, eagerly adopting Britain's customs of the game wholesale, but this particular ball got fumbled somewhere out in the Atlantic. By 1920, "par" replaced bogey in America as the score to shoot for on a golf hole, consigning the colonel to an undeserved fate: Not so long ago an achievement of pride for the British golfer, Americans and consequently the rest of the world, now play the game with the mistaken understanding that bogey represents nothing better than ho-hum mediocrity.

Since this bogey-par transition was still very much midstream, contemporary experts calculate The Country Club's par figure in 1913 to be 74. (To avoid confusion, those figures and the appropriate contemporary terms will be the ones cited in this book.) Having played the course over a dozen times, Harry and Ted matched that score frequently but bested it only once, and found a lot to admire about The Country Club. Harry singled out in particular the eleventh and fifteenth holes, and he ranked the layout near the top of the courses he'd played across the country. Although he still privately felt two or three holes needed a good deal of improvement in order to achieve true greatness, in his typically diplomatic, understated way he told Darwin on Monday it represented "a nice test of the game, with a number of pitfalls; it will be necessary for all players who wish to contend to be always on the line." Ted Ray, typically less politic, bluntly ranked it only fourth among American courses he had played. Harry went on to predict to Darwin that, weather permitting, four rounds of 75—for an aggregate score of 300—should be sufficient to win the title, but only if the player stayed accurate throughout; "no deviation from the line could be allowed."

Johnny McDermott's defiant confrontation after his win at the Shawnee Open had sent up a sizeable stink, but his decisive victory there over Vardon and Ray had also raised levels of optimism within the American camp that the two English champions, despite their unblemished tour record, were not the invincible gods everyone made them out to be. They were mortal men who could be beaten on a golf course, and Johnny had showed them how to do it. However, after incurring the wrath of the national press and a USGA reprimand, the man who'd led the charge at Shawnee arrived at The Country Club with clipped wings. Clinging to the conviction he'd done nothing wrong at the Shawnee trophy presentation, and been demonized for it by an unsympathetic press, Johnny McDermott showed up in Brookline determined to keep his mouth shut and let his clubs do the talking. More than one reporter remarked on how chastened and subdued the usually truculent champ appeared in public. Slamming the brakes on his nonstop motor adversely affected Johnny on the course; his play during his practice rounds didn't encourage anyone to believe he could repeat his overpowering performance at Shawnee, but McDermott had climbed up off the canvas to pull out miraculous wins before. On this last Monday before qualifying began, he gave his supporters renewed reason to hope; Johnny went out and shot a blistering 73, aside from Vardon's 71 the best score turned in during the entire week of practice at The Country Club.

Immediately upon their return from Baltusrol, Harry and Ted again availed themselves of the crowded Country Club course during the last days prior to the tournament. Rounding into championship form, Harry drove so straight, so long, and with so little apparent effort, that Francis's friend John Anderson observed Harry Vardon couldn't have played better if his ball was made of steel and a giant magnet had been buried down the center of the fairways. Ted demonstrated surprising restraint by reining in his raw muscle in favor of accuracy to stay on the course's tight fairways; but ever the showman, whenever their gallery swelled, Ted couldn't resist winding up and knocking one out of sight, which brought cheers from the crowd. As the day went on, more and more of the American pros snuck glances their way whenever the two Jerseymen came into view. More than a few even followed them around the back nine when their own rounds were complete, so eager were they to witness Ted's power and Harry's legendary finesse. What they saw put a chill in their blood; the men who'd made such a mediocre showing at Shawnee bore no resemblance to these two evident masters of the game. Their superb practice rounds bled dry any reservoir of confidence the Americans had amassed since Shawnee.

A reunion with his brother Tom provided the emotional highlight of Harry's last days before the tournament. Tom Vardon had sent in his application for the Open weeks before and traveled east from his new job as professional at the Onwentsia Club near Chicago, checking into the Copley Square Hotel on the day Harry returned from New Jersey. As Tom had hoped, the luster of the Vardon name had created a red-carpet welcome in his new country; he was already enjoying the benefits of what would become the most rewarding stretch of his forty-year career. Freed from the constraints of the British caste system, Tom's open, cheerful personality clearly thrived in the egalitarian American heartland. Harry could see the happiness apparent in Tom's every gesture. While watching his brother closely, Harry caught a glimpse of a fascinating what-might-have-been, had he followed through with that powerful, fleeting impulse to make America his home in 1900.

Although he would never admit it to Harry, living out from under the shade of his brother's towering reputation had for the first time opened up room for Tom Vardon to become his own man. With his on-course business thriving and a promising new love in his life, Tom had finally made peace with any past disappointments. All his lean years in Britain counted for nothing now; the hours the brothers spent together in Brookline were warm, happy, and affectionate. Tom and Ted Ray had also become great friends during Tom's time on the English circuit. With a large gallery of American fans walking beside them, the three Jerseymen played their final practice round on Monday afternoon together, each man marveling at how far the primitive childhood game they used to play on the Jersey shore, with clubs hand-carved from a hawthorn tree, had brought them in the world. Afterward they returned to the Copley Square Hotel and attended a convivial public dinner with many of their rivals, every man among them looking forward with great anticipation to what was truly the first international U.S. Open. Harry told a reporter from the *Boston Globe* during the gathering that night he felt in good shape, fit to play, and was confident of doing well. The subject of his putting did not arise.

On the eve of the tournament, a fascinating confluence of complex rivalries met in The Country Club's locker room. The most obvious division pitted American players versus the foreign delegation: Vardon, Ray, Wilfred Reid, Frenchman Louis Tellier, and top Canadian pros Karl Keffer and George Cumming. Within the American contingent lay many smaller competing subsets: the semi-Americans—transplanted Scotsmen like Alex, Willie and Mac Smith, former champs "Wee Freddie" McLeod and Alec Ross, and The Country Club's resident pro Alec Campbell—versus the homebreds, led by Johnny McDermott, and from nearby Wollaston Golf Club, Tom McNamara and Mike "King" Brady, the best pros ever produced by New England. Then there were the country's Western golfers—centered around the Chicago area, which had not yet produced a national champion—versus the to-date more successful Eastern establishment players. Chick Evans represented the Westerners' best hopes, but pressing business had kept him in Chicago that week, so Tom Vardon now carried that standard, figuring in as both a semi-American and a Westerner.

Within the semi-American group, there was even some tension between ex-Scotsmen and expatriate Brits, represented by Tom Vardon, 1909 U.S. Open champ George Sargent, and a tall, lean, big-hitting twenty-five-year-old just starting to make a name for himself off a second-place finish in the Canadian Open, James "Long Jim" Barnes. In his long, distinguished career, Barnes would go on to win four American majors and is somewhat harder to categorize. Although he emigrated to the United States through Canada, played out of a club in Tacoma, Washington, and subsequently worked in the United States for nearly forty years, Barnes always thought of himself as an Englishman and never relinquished his British citizenship. The tournament's most convoluted résumé belonged to Alex and Mac Smith's middle brother, Willie—1899's U.S. Open champ, a semi-American ex-Scotsman from Carnoustie, longtime citizen of the United States, Willie was now working as the professional at the first golf club ever built in Mexico City.

The final, least obvious, and, surprisingly, most bitter rivalry existed between professionals and amateurs, a distinction that cut more deeply than any national or international loyalties. Twenty-three amateurs had been accepted into the field at Brookline, led by Jerry Travers, his runner-up at Garden City John G. Anderson—also on hand to cover the tournament for the *Boston Transcript* and *Golf Magazine*—1910's U.S. Amateur champion William C. Fownes, and runner-up in the 1911 U.S. Amateur

Fred Herreshoff. Although they were warmly welcomed in the pro shop and locker room, all professionals at the 1913 Open, including Harry and Ted, were still denied entry to The Country Club's clubhouse. The amateur players, Francis among them, were allowed free run of all the club's facilities. For their part, top amateurs accepted and admired the pros as seasoned practitioners of the game they all loved. On the other side of the fence the hedge grew a little more thorny; lingering resentments about "gentlemen golfers" who could afford to play the game for kicks and not for a living percolated under the surface of every professional tournament where the two classes mingled, particularly the national championship. No amateur had ever won the U.S. Open and the hard-knock pros who were making their living in the game after struggling up through the caddie ranks didn't cotton to the idea of some pretty-boy amateur playboy like Jerry Travers waltzing in and taking their title.

Francis presented an unprecedented exception. A former caddie himself from a working-class background, he didn't harbor professional aspirations and had no plans to rely on the game for any future employment; after years of his father's hectoring, Francis had his eye fixed on trying to succeed in the business world. Nor was he, like many of the top amateurs, a man who looked confidently ahead to a life with no worries about where his next paycheck was coming from. Francis played golf because his passion for the game exceeded any other considerations about who he thought he was or what he did to put food on his table. Although no one had identified him as such yet, for the first time in memory a golfer had come along who could represent both sides of the game's delicate territorial balance without violating either's proprietary feelings about their half of the map. He not only appeared to have the talent, he also innately possessed exactly the sort of open, generous, and winning personality that could finally lay all such differences to rest. Whether Francis could do anything on the course at Brookline to bring these factions of the American game together remained to be seen; in their analysis of the field the day before the Open began, no one in the huge press corps covering the event, outside of his friends John Anderson and Bernard Darwin, gave Francis even a ghost of a chance.

As the players came off the course at the end of Monday's round, a late entry made his first appearance at The Country Club. He'd talked his bosses into giving him a week off to take his first shot at the title, although they'd refused to pay him for the time away or kick in any money for expenses. He'd ridden the day coach into Boston on Sunday from Rochester and, having heard that was where all the "first-class players" were staying, had checked into the Copley Square Hotel that night, even though the room rate was well beyond his meager budget. The next morning he caught an early streetcar out to Brookline in time to get in a few practice holes. When he entered the locker room on Monday at the end of his round, twenty-one-year-old Walter Hagen, the new head pro at the Rochester Country Club, spotted a small fellow at a nearby locker pulling on a bright sweater, recognized him instantly, went right up to him, and stuck out his hand.

"Say, you're Johnny McDermott, aren't you?" said Hagen.

"That's right," said McDermott, eyeing him warily as he shook Hagen's hand. He eyed everyone warily these days.

"Well, I'm glad to know you, Johnny," he said loudly. "I'm W. C. Hagen from Rochester and I've come over to help you boys take care of Vardon and Ray."

That brought a smile to McDermott's face, and outright laughter from a lot of the veterans who were near enough to hear him. Just what they needed; another wise guy. Walter caught a lot of flak for his intro, and like everything else in his life, it rolled right off his back. Not a soul in the room knew who he was yet—"Nobody gave me a tumble," he said later—but in Hagen's mind, that was just a temporary oversight. Walter had done a lot of thinking about his golf since watching last year's U.S. Open in Buffalo, and even more after suffering his most recent disappointment at the Shawnee. The result: Hagen believed he'd put his finger on why he hadn't come close to winning a tournament yet—he wasn't being himself.

Walter Martin Christian Hagen entered life on December 21, 1892, with a phenomenal set of genetic attributes that translated to tremendous advantage in the sport of golf; uncanny hand-eye coordination, exceptional vision and distance perception, wiry sinuous strength, cat-quick reflexes. His touch was so sensitive, it was said he could guess a club's weight inside of an ounce simply by holding it in his hands. His swing was a long way from Vardon-like perfection; in fact, it more closely resembled Ted Ray's ungainly swat. Starting from an exceptionally wide stance, Hagen himself described his move as starting with a sway and ending with a lunge. But it hardly mattered what his swing looked like; his other talents more than made up for what he lacked in classic form. And on those fairly frequent occasions when he sent one flying toward damnation, his uncanny ability to recover and save par almost never failed to provide redemption.

Walter's psychological makeup suited the nature of the game even more exactly. He possessed every ounce of Johnny McDermott's cheeky self-assurance, but in sharp contrast to the tortured champion, Hagen came equipped with the copper-bottomed, cast-iron nervous system to consistently back up his brassy confidence without stripping his gears. McDermott's polar opposite, Walter Hagen thrived on pressure, especially of the financial variety; the thinner his bankroll, the better he played. Although it seldom happened in his own country, he actually preferred a crowd that rooted against him because winning gave him greater satisfaction. Although he often claimed it later in life, it may not be strictly true that Hagen never worried about anything, but you'd never have known it by looking at him. His monumental indifference to the slings and arrows of outrageous fortune bordered on the supernatural. Tommy Armour later said of Hagen that he could relax sitting on a hot stove. When he officially blew onto the scene of professional golf at The Country Club on Monday, September 15, 1913, Walter Hagen brought with him a personal style as breezy and refreshing as a gin and tonic on a cool porch after a hot day in the sun. No one who saw Hagen in the locker room that day ever forgot their first impression of him; what he did afterward made that impossible.

Align Walter Hagen's background against Francis Ouimet's, and their outlines become eerily indistinguishable: youngest son of a lower-middle-class family, one parent an immigrant; raised in semirural surroundings by a hard-nosed, unsympathetic working-class father and a doting, adoring mother; exposure to the game of golf before the age of five followed by countless hours of practice on a homemade three-hole course cut out of open fields behind the family house; caddying by the age of nine, capping an entire childhood spent in the company of talented golfers; a gifted mimic who could imitate any swing he saw after a single glance. A year's difference in age, Hagen's professional status, and a stark difference in personality are the three factors that prevent the two men from appearing like twins separated at birth; whereas Francis radiated goodness, Walter throughout his life always came off as a bit of a rogue. Not in a dishonest sense; more in the style of an adored, risqué uncle who'd spin tall tales about exotic ports of call while he dazzled you with effortless sleight-of-hand magic tricks, the tang of peppermint on his breath not quite camouflaging the three whiskey sours he'd downed at lunch. In almost every other way, at this point in their lives Walter Hagen appeared to be Francis Ouimet's doppelganger.

The two men even shared scavenging instincts; Walter also collected lost golf balls as a boy, but at the age of ten he traded his collection in for a new first baseman's mitt. Baseball was Hagen's other ruling passion, and until 1914 the two games held equal purchase on his heart; he had professional-level ability and, according to Hagen, that winter the Philadelphia Phillies were about to nearly steal him away from golf. Whichever path he followed, Walter needed sports to make a living because his academic career had ended abruptly at twelve; during one glorious spring afternoon in a terminally boring seventh grade class he spotted some golfers playing across the street. The next time the teacher turned her back on the room, Walter jumped out the window, ran off to join them, and never went back.

By the age of fourteen, so he claimed later, Walter could beat anyone at golf within the Rochester city limits. After serving a five-year apprenticeship to Andrew Christy at the Rochester Country Club, learning the professional's trade from the ground up, Walter took over Christy's job in late 1912 when his boss moved on to greener pastures. When Walter visited the 1912 Open in Buffalo, the sight on the course of a pro named Tom Anderson—the late Willie's youngest brother—struck him with the force of a Biblical revelation. While most golfers still wore the rumpled trousers, ties, and tweeds of the old Scottish guard, Anderson decked himself out in a pure white silk shirt adorned with red, blue, yellow, and black stripes, a natty bow tie, pleated white flannel pants with the cuffs rolled up—just one turn—a bright red bandana looped casually around his neck, a blinding plaid cap, and gleaming white buckskin shoes with thick red rubber soles and wide white laces.

"Now this," said Walter to himself, "is an outfit that screams class."

When he went north the next month to play in the 1912 Canadian Open, his first pro tournament, Hagen finished eleventh in a field of over a hundred. When asked how he'd done when he returned, he replied with typical diffidence: "I lost." Walter tried to duplicate Tom Anderson's finery for his professional debut, but at that point all he could afford was the bandana, and when he tried to order one of those, the company didn't have any in stock. By the time he got to Brookline in 1913, Hagen had put the whole ensemble together—minus the cap. No one in those days played golf without some kind of head cover; Walter greased down his luxuriant head of jet black hair with pomade and plastered it to his scalp like a silent movie star. With his hair styled this way, in some photographs he bears a surprising resemblance to Bela Lugosi's Dracula.

So here comes Hagen traipsing into The Country Club locker room, nearly six feet tall, trim as a light heavyweight at 175 pounds, a large round head with the broad, pronounced features of a budding sensualist, in that wild outfit, with that gigolo-vampire hairdo, and his world-beater's personality. After charming McDermott with his brash opener, he instantly befriended every other man in the room he chatted up; as he proved for the next half a century, no matter what you thought about Walter Hagen from a distance, once you got to know him, he was impossible to dislike. He was a one-man jazz age. Even if the new guy couldn't play the game at their level, his fellow pros at The Country Club probably wouldn't have been able to get this delightful dandy out of their minds. As they were all about to discover, "the Haig" could flat out bring it.

With the largest field ever playing in the Open and the star British attractions on hand, the USGA also anticipated the biggest galleries they'd ever experienced would turn out for the event. Admission would not be charged to an Open until 1922. The ruling organization and The Country

Club took extra precautions to make certain that those crowds didn't over-
whelm their course. They planned to rope off all the fairways and placed
ads in the Boston papers weeks in advance, securing over two hundred
volunteers to mind the lines and to work as flagmen; whenever a player
prepared to make a shot, the flagmen along either side of the gallery were
instructed to raise their red "danger" flags, the signal for silence. So unfamiliar was proper golf etiquette during tournament competition to the
majority of people expected to attend that the *Boston Globe* saw fit to publish a detailed primer on how its citizens should behave during a championship tournament:

> It is quite likely that many persons who are somewhat unfamiliar
> with the etiquette of golf will be attracted to the play. It will be an
> act of kindness to the players if those who are conversant with the
> etiquette demanded will tell the less informed spectators how to
> conduct themselves.

Judging by the behavior that followed, not many of the newcomers to
the sport took the time to read it. A squadron of experienced marshals,
many of them Country Club members, were equipped with megaphones,
then planted around the course to direct traffic and supervise the rope
handlers and flagmen. Others were appointed to serve as "markers"; a custom no longer observed, markers were experienced volunteers assigned to
each player, who walked the course with them and independently kept
their scorecard.

The postponement from June to September created a crisis in The
Country Club's caddie ranks. Although enough boys would normally have
been on hand at midsummer to handle even the overwhelming demands of
a championship, the school year had started by the time the Open began
and cut the number of available working caddies in half. Anticipating an
attendance problem at local schools while the tournament was on, school
district officials deployed extra truant officers to patrol area high schools
and prevent younger caddies from skipping out on class. A plea had gone
out in the press the week before for more recruits, and by the eve of the
tournament the Club had enough loopers on hand to cover the field, but

many of them had never carried clubs before. That necessitated last-minute emergency instruction from caddie master Dan McNamara to his new charges on the finer points of the game's rules; no one wanted a green caddie to cost his player a penalty. They received their crash course from McNamara, but the basics were the same then as they've always been for the boys on the bags: show up, keep up, and shut up.

Francis experienced a last-minute caddie crisis of his own. In the locker room before Francis's final practice round on Monday, his regular caddie, a fellow he'd known for years and used to work alongside at The Country Club, informed Francis he'd received an eleventh-hour offer to carry for Louis Tellier. After losing all his exhibition matches, the Open now represented Tellier's last and only chance to make good on his American dream. The crafty Frenchman had seduced Francis's lad with visions of victory and a share of the spoils, which only a professional like himself would be allowed to collect. With deep regrets, the boy felt financially obliged to take Tellier up on his tantalizing offer. After working with his caddie all weekend, counting on his support, and knowing full well no experienced loopers were left, a crestfallen Francis walked downstairs prepared to carry his own clubs.

Francis looked out at the milling crowds and spotted a couple of local kids he knew from his home club, Woodland: twelve-year-old Jack Lowery and his tiny little ten-year-old brother, Eddie. Jack had caddied for Francis at Woodland a few times in the last year. Francis waved Jack over.

"Hello, Jack," said Francis. "What are you doing here?"

"Me and Eddie decided to hook school and take a look at Vardon and Ray," said Jack.

"Is that right? Well, how would you feel about going out on the course? I just lost my caddie."

"Yeah? What happened to your guy?"

"He's going out with Tellier, and I can't say as I blame him; they say he's a real crack with a good chance to win the championship."

"If you believe what you read in the papers," said Eddie.

Noticing Eddie for the first time, Francis thought: *Quite the wise guy for such a little fella.*

"So how about it," said Francis, turning back to Jack, "you want to carry my bag?"

"Well, I don't know. Can Eddie come, too?" asked Jack.

"Can't have more than one man on the bag, Jack. It's against the rules."

Jack looked a little uncertain but Eddie appeared devastated, almost instantly near tears. Rethinking his hard-boiled assessment of the boy, and nothing if not a soft touch, Francis decided to sweeten the deal.

"But I guess nobody'd complain if he kept score and walked along with us," said Francis.

The Lowerys huddled briefly, then agreed to Francis's offer. An aspiring golfer himself, young Eddie had seen Francis play many times at Woodland and had been reading about him in the Boston papers since Garden City. The brothers had recently put together a two-hole homemade course in the vacant lot behind their house; they were so hooked on the game that before they got their hands on their own clubs, they used to play with umbrellas and crab apples. Both were already trying to imitate Francis's swing. They had come out to see Vardon and Ray, but this was hope unlooked for; Eddie looked up to Francis like a local deity.

Francis led the brothers to the first tee, where he began a four-ball match with Vince Lawrence, a fellow golfer from Woodland, against fellow amateurs John Anderson and Heinrich Schmidt. Jack worked Francis's bag throughout the practice round while Eddie tagged along and kept his scorecard. A sizeable crowd was drawn by all the big names out on the course that day, but not another soul followed them. Shaking off his doldrums from the day before at Wellesley, Francis found some of the sharpness of vision he'd been missing return to his game on the old familiar course. He played a strong round, shooting 77, but he and Lawrence lost to Schmidt and Anderson 3 and 2. Francis made it into the locker room afterward just in time to witness Hagen's memorable entrance, then walked home across Clyde Street, ate a quiet supper with his mother, brother, and sister, and turned in early. He was scheduled to play in the first qualifying flight on Tuesday morning.

The Lowery brothers caught the last streetcar that evening back to their house on Beacon Street in Lower Newton Falls, a smaller suburb eight miles to the west. Both felt ecstatic about their good fortune; his

THE GREATEST GAME EVER PLAYED | 212

practice round had gone so well, Francis had asked Jack to stay on his bag during the next day's qualifying round. When they walked into the house, they found their mother waiting with a local truant officer, making the rounds of all the houses of the school's known caddies, most of whom had mysteriously turned up missing from school that Monday. A recent Massachusetts state law forbade anyone under the age of sixteen from caddying while the school year was in session. The brothers got an earful from the truant officer and after the man left, Jack received the brunt of their mother's anger. Raising seven children alone—her husband had been killed in an accident three years earlier and she had not remarried—she counted on Jack, a straight arrow with a good reputation at school, to set a better example for his brothers and sisters. And she voiced considerable concern for Eddie, who had not a week ago required treatment at the hospital after suffering a severe cut on his foot from a broken bottle.

"Eddie Lowery, you had no business walking all that distance on a bad foot," she said.

"Aw, Ma, it's fine—"

"No it is not fine, you're still wearing a bandage and the doctor told you to take it easy until he sees you again. Jack, you promise me you'll have Eddie back in class with you first thing tomorrow morning."

"Okay, Ma, I promise."

Assuming Jack had dragged little Eddie along with him to Brookline, and that tomorrow the younger boy would follow Jack back to school, their mother seemed satisfied with his answer. With seven children running around underfoot, and no husband to help keep them on the straight and narrow, Mrs. Lowery can be excused for not knowing her youngest son better; playing hooky and heading out to The Country Club that morning had been Eddie's idea from the get-go.

As punishment Mrs. Lowery sent her sons up to their room that night immediately after supper. As soon as their door was closed, and their mother out of earshot, Eddie lit into his big brother.

"Jack, you can't go to school, you promised Francis you'd be on his bag tomorrow," Eddie whispered harshly.

"I know I did—"

"You can't do that to him, he's counting on you."

"They caught me fair and square, Eddie, what am I supposed to do?"

"You're supposed to live up to your promises."

"I can't do it, Eddie," said Jack. "Francis'll catch on with somebody else, you'll see. He'll be all right."

Eddie remained unconvinced, but nothing he said could change Jack's mind. Before he went to bed, Eddie changed the bandage on his foot; there was a fair amount of blood soaked into it. He examined the wound and decided it would stand up to what he was about to put it through. It would have to. As he lay there restlessly trying to sleep that night, Eddie Lowery, tough and tenacious beyond his size and years, had already made up his mind that it didn't matter what his brother decided to do.

Both Lowery brothers weren't going to let down Francis Ouimet.

TAFT, SECOND FROM LEFT, NEXT TO HERBERT JAQUES,
PRESIDENT OF THE COUNTRY CLUB,
HOLDING THE SCORE SHEET.

TUESDAY: FIRST DAY QUALIFYING

SEPTEMBER 16. SUNRISE ushered in a picture-perfect morning. Blue skies, scattered clouds. Moderate temperatures, a slight, refreshing breeze from the east. Activity stirred early that morning all over Boston's western suburbs. Greenkeepers and their crews administered a final grooming to The Country Club course at first light. Drivers hitched their horses or started up their "tin lizzies" and headed toward the Back Bay hotels in town, a long line of them standing ready to ferry visiting players out to Brookline for their tee times.

In the sleepy village of Lower Newton Falls, as they had promised their mother they would do the night before, the Lowery brothers rose early, ate their breakfast, packed their books, and headed straight for school. When a mile later they reached the turn in the lane that led to their schoolhouse, only Jack Lowery took it; Eddie stopped and handed Jack his book bag.

"I'm not going," said Eddie.

"What are you talking about?"

THE GREATEST GAME EVER PLAYED | 216

"I'm going to the club," said Eddie. "If you had any guts you'd come with me."

Eddie waited a beat. No response. Then, ignoring the warnings of dire consequences Jack shouted after him, Eddie kept right on walking to the trolley stop. When he reached the station, Eddie eluded the truant officer patrolling the platform and hopped on the last car to Brookline.

According to the *Boston Herald* that Tuesday morning, "The prediction is for an exhibition of golf never equaled in the United States." The *Boston Post* crawled further out on that hyperbolic limb: "What will prove to be the greatest open golf championship in the history of the game in the United States starts today at the Country Club in Brookline." *The New York Times* ran a front-page feature about the tournament, featuring photographs of all the favorites—including that unproven little P.R. genius Louis Tellier—and posing the provocative question: "Will an American amateur golfer win the national open championship?" *The Times's* money was riding on four-time amateur champ Jerry Travers.

In order to handle the crush of reporters at The Country Club who had requested access to the event, for the first time at an Open, USGA officials erected a separate press tent between the first and eighteenth tees. A section of the tent was reserved for Western Union; ten telegraph lines went up to keep the world connected to events on the course, shot by shot.

Francis didn't read the papers that morning, or on any other day during the week; after his exposure at Garden City he had already decided that there were worse things in life than people knowing who you were, but not many. Beyond the novelty of seeing his name in print, Garden City had taught Francis the valuable lesson that notoriety meant nothing to him. He had taken enormous pleasure in proving himself under pressure and earning the respect of his fellow athletes, but all the rest of the attention and fuss from total strangers made him uneasy. Finding this native reticence in the modern sporting world has become next to impossible; generally speaking, the only modesty athletes and celebrities in the public eye exhibit today trends toward the false variety. Francis possessed the genuine article; born, not dyed, in the wool.

He arose just after dawn to the sight and sound of a ground crew mowing and rolling the seventeenth green. After an early breakfast Francis

walked across the street and up the shaded lane that traversed the fifteenth fairway to The Country Club carrying his own bag; Clyde Street
was already congested with carriages and automobiles bringing players and
spectators to the course. Starting times were posted on a placard near the
clubhouse; eighty-four players paired as twosomes, teeing off every five
minutes beginning sharply at 8:00 A.M. First on the tee that morning were
Nicholas de Mane of New York City, professional, unattached to a club,
and H. C. Lagerblade, pro at Youngstown Country Club in Ohio. They
were to shoot 87 and 81, respectively, in the morning, didn't even finish
their afternoon rounds, and quickly faded from view.

Francis changed his shoes in the locker room and went directly to the
edge of the tenth fairway to warm up for his 9:45 start time by hitting a
few old balls into the trees. As he turned a corner taking him away from
the crowd, for the first time Francis came upon Harry Vardon, hitting balls
alone at the edge of the fairway, preoccupied, self-contained, wearing his
customary knickers, dark tie, white shirt, and tailored Norfolk jacket.
Francis's memory of the fluid swing that had so inspired him years before
meshed perfectly with the silky perfection the man still clearly possessed.
The sight of Vardon in the flesh initially froze Francis in his tracks—

*This isn't a fantasy or a dream, this is the first day of the U.S. Open and
that, so help me God, is Harry Vardon.*

—until he realized a small crowd had gathered just to watch Harry
loosen up, among them Bernard Darwin and an elegantly upholstered figure
Francis later learned was Lord Northcliffe. When Harry moved off toward
the putting green, his followers hovered around him; unnoticed, Francis
stepped aside to let them pass. Vardon was scheduled to tee off at 9:25, four
groups ahead of Francis; he watched Harry move through a swarm of admirers flashing his slight Vardonic smile, friendly all the while but as remote and
dignified as a king walking among his subjects. Harry's caddie followed close
behind, hauling his custom-fitted clubs in a deluxe handcrafted leather bag.
Francis looked down at his own simple canvas bag, his motley assortment of
ten well-worn clubs, his plain white twill pants, and his hobnail boots.
Attempting to ignore the beehive of activity around Vardon as he neared the
first tee, Francis put his head down, determined to stick to his own established warm-up routine. He shanked his first shot into the bushes.

Francis stopped, took a deep breath, and tried to center himself. The only antidote he could find to the deep-seated sense of inadequacy that overwhelmed him had been written by the same man whose sudden appearance had inspired the feelings to begin with.

"Do not reflect upon the possibilities of defeat; you become too anxious and lose your freedom of style."

As his muscles loosened, he began to hit one pleasing shot after another; Francis began to relax. A burst of applause and cheering in the near distance broke his reverie; Vardon had just teed off with 1908 Open champion, five four "Wee" Freddie McLeod. A wave of spectators over a thousand strong headed off down the first fairway with the championship twosome, emptying out the area around the tee. Francis went back to work. Keeping his anxiety in check became more difficult when by 9:30 Jack Lowery had still failed to show; only fifteen minutes to tee time. Sticking to his set schedule, trying hard to maintain his equilibrium, Francis picked up his bag and walked toward the putting green.

As Francis worked on the green, smoothing out his putting stroke, out of the corner of his eye he glimpsed little Eddie Lowery running toward him through the crowd around the clubhouse.

"Mr. Ouimet . . . Mr. Ouimet . . ." Eddie arrived at the putting green, out of breath.

"Eddie, where's Jack? For goodness' sake, I tee off in ten minutes."

"Truant officer caught him when we got home last night. He had to go to school."

"Well, that's a piece of rotten luck, isn't it? Did he get into any trouble?"

"Nah, he's just chicken," said Eddie.

"Is that right?" said Francis, amused. "So why aren't you in school, Eddie?"

"Ah, they can't do anything to you. Besides, this is the U.S. Open."

Francis glanced at the clock on the locker-room wall—9:40—put away his putter, and shouldered his bag.

"Thanks for coming to tell me, Eddie," he said. "I might've worried otherwise."

"That's okay, happy to do it."

Francis started walking intently toward the first tee. Eddie tagged along after him, hesitant to intrude.

"Mr. Ouimet?"

"Yes, Eddie?"

"I could caddie for you."

Francis realized the boy was serious, stopped, and looked down at Eddie Lowery. All four feet of him.

"Eddie, I appreciate the offer, but you're too small. My bag's as big as you are."

"But I carry my own bag all the time. I can do it, I carry for the fellas at Woodland and I'm good at it, you can ask any of the guys—"

"Eddie—"

"See, I came out here to make good on what Jack promised to you—"

"Eddie—"

"—and I hooked school and I'm going to get in big trouble for this and I am big enough to carry that bag, I'm in sixth grade and I want to caddie for you."

Tears sprang into Eddie's eyes—genuine or not, his instant access to emotion approached a level of genius—and that did it; Francis couldn't bring himself to further bruise the little kid's feelings.

"Okay, listen now, Eddie, enough of that, why don't I carry the bag, and you walk along with me and watch the ball."

"No, Mr. Ouimet."

"Please, call me Francis—"

"I can do it, Mr. Ouimet, really I can. I can help you out there. I know your game, I've seen you play plenty of times. I can carry this bag."

Francis looked around; their animated discussion was drawing a few snickering glances from other players and their older, established caddies around the putting green.

The heck with them, thought Francis.

Francis took the bag off his shoulder and handed it to Eddie.

"All right then, Eddie. Let's go. Just please call me Francis."

"Okay, Francis."

With a single move, Eddie expertly slung the bag sideways across his back over his right shoulder, steadying the club heads with his right hand as if he'd been looping his whole life; if he'd carried it in the conventional style, up and down, the bottom would have dragged on the ground. He wiped away his tears. His grin nearly broke out of either side of his round little face. Francis turned, put his chin up, and continued toward the tee. Eddie hustled closely behind.

At the tee box, Francis greeted his partner for the day, lanky six four "Long" Jim Barnes, the Englishman playing out of Tacoma. Barnes shook Francis's hand, then looked down at Eddie.

"This is Eddie. My caddie," said Francis.

"Pleased to meet ya," said Eddie, offering up his hand.

Amused, Barnes leaned down and shook Eddie's hand.

At 9:45 sharp the starter stepped forward to announce their twosome: "Professional from Tacoma, Washington, James Barnes."

The charming old Scottish custom of referring to golf holes by descriptive names instead of numbers still applied at The Country Club. Because its fairway involved a carry over the infield of the old Clyde Park racetrack, used now only occasionally by the Club's polo team, the opening hole is called Polo Field. A slight dogleg left, with bunkers guarding the right side, listed on the scorecard as a five. For long hitters, if they could clear the edge of the racetrack cutting through the fairway in front of the green, a relatively easy 430-yard opportunity for birdie.

Jim Barnes teed up his ball, stepped right to it, and with his long, flowing swing ripped it down the middle.

The starter stepped forward again: "From Brookline, the reigning Massachusetts State Amateur champion, Francis Ouimet." Enthusiastic applause from the twenty or so people gathered around the tee box.

Eddie filled an iron tee mold with moist dirt from the sandbox beside the green, then set it down on the tee box. Francis wasn't the only one with first-tee jitters; as Eddie removed the mold, he accidentally knocked the little mound of sand into a loose pile and had to repeat the entire procedure. This time the tee remained standing. Pocketing the mold Eddie stepped back, briskly whipped out the driver, and handed it to Francis. His heart pounding, Francis teed up his ball, took his stance—*This is it, this is it*—then lashed at it out of rhythm, came over the top, and hooked it into the high grass about a hundred yards down the left side off the fairway.

Out of bounds came into play only a few yards farther to the left but Francis's ball stopped just short of the white stakes.

Francis handed his driver back to Eddie. Neither said a word and the group started walking, Barnes and his caddie taking the lead down the center of the fairway, the older man's long strides eating up big chunks of yardage. Francis was pleased and relieved to see that not a single person from the crowd around the first tee had walked after them; they were waiting for local favorite Tom McNamara, scheduled to tee off twenty minutes later. When Francis and Eddie reached his ball, well short of where Barnes had landed, they found it buried in a three-inch rough, their line toward the green obstructed by a large chestnut tree.

Eddie stared at the ball without comment, waiting for Francis to call the shot. Francis asked for his mashie; all he could hope to do was punch the ball out into the fairway with a slight hook and advance it a short way forward. He executed the recovery shot perfectly, landing the ball forty yards ahead on the right side of the fairway, still well short of Barnes's original tee shot.

Francis and Eddie walked forward to the ball and assessed their situation; 220 yards out, a semiblind shot over the far edge of the racetrack to a small, elevated green tucked in a corner of the course, surrounded by trees and bunkers, sloped severely from back to front, nothing but trouble around and beyond it. As Francis weighed the variables—gamble and go for the green, lay up and play it safe—he appeared to momentarily freeze; Eddie instantly deciphered the indecision on his face.

"Whatever you decide to do, Francis," said Eddie, "you keep your head down and I'll watch the ball. I've never lost a ball yet."

Francis turned back to Eddie; the utter confidence the little boy exuded seemed to settle his mind. He reached for his favorite club, the brassie, and prepared this early in his first round to gamble. Francis made an easy, relaxed swing and sent the ball soaring right on line. It landed on the front of the green, pitched forward, kept rolling, and settled twenty-five feet above the flag.

Francis turned to Eddie, handed back his brassie, and smiled.

"Eddie, I think you and I are going to be good friends."

Francis made his par five. Barnes made birdie. They moved on.

Up ahead, most of the early field was finding that The Country Club course, after yielding a number of low scores during the practice rounds, was showing no inclination to roll over and play dead. The tees had been moved back to their absolute limits, significantly increasing the length of many fairways and bringing a greater number of hazards into play. Traffic from the preceding practice rounds had already trampled the grass on the putting surfaces to the speed and consistency of billiard table felt, particularly around the cups; and then this morning the grounds crew had close cut and double-rolled them. Many of the pin positions on the small, slanting greens made a close approach shot nearly impossible; three-putts, or worse, became the usual penalty for the slightest inaccuracy. As the morning progressed, the east wind gradually increased, gusting on occasion to two-club levels. The players' consensus: The course was playing four strokes tougher than the day before and at least two shots harder than par.

Welcome to the U.S. Open.

Francis's friend and current holder of the Massachusetts Professional title, Tom McNamara, paid a penalty of a different sort, as a result of his partner's inexperienced caddie. Tom had come of age as a player at The Country Club and he knew the golf course every bit as well as Francis. After two second-place finishes in the last four U.S. Opens, including last year's at Buffalo only two strokes behind McDermott, Tom harbored legitimate hopes of finally breaking through so close to home. On the second hole, a 300-yard par four called Cottage, Tom's second shot found a yawning bunker to the front left of the green; it was so deep that when he took his stance over the ball, he couldn't see the putting surface. As Tom dug in to attempt his save, his partner's caddie ran onto the green, misguidedly believing the circumstance required someone to tend the pin. Before his golfer could correct him, Tom made his swing, skulled it slightly, and the ball came out hot. The caddie tried but failed to get out of its way and the ball hit the bag he was carrying over his shoulder, a violation of Rule 13, Article 1. Caddie master Dan McNamara's premonitory concerns about the new caddies' ignorance of the rules damaging a player's chances only came home to roost once during the entire tournament; when it did, it would cost his own brother two precious strokes.

The biggest crisis on the course that morning concerned crowd management, and all because of one man: Harry Vardon. The Greyhound set a furious pace over the front nine and soon attracted to his twosome the rest of the gallery on the course that hadn't begun by following them. Estimates of Harry's crowd ran as high as five thousand people; the marshals and rope-holders were simply overwhelmed. Many of these onlookers had never watched competitive golf before and it showed. Every time Harry advanced down a fairway, a mad scramble ensued as the gallery tried to keep up with him, ignoring the ropes, dashing up and down hills and through the woods that flanked his route. They even bulldozed through any bunkers in their path, leaving a parade of footprints that drove the players who followed to distraction. Harry was used to this kind of mass insanity; The Country Club was not. Marshals shouted through megaphones trying to control their stampedes but did little to dampen the crowd's infectious enthusiasm; they did, however, succeed in distracting and annoying other golfers on adjacent fairways and greens. The only direction the crowd seemed prepared to pay attention to came whenever Vardon was poised to swing and the flagmen raised their red flags aloft; then there was pin-drop silence.

None of them left disappointed; the spectators tracking him that morning watched Harry put on a clinic of power and precision from tee to green. He hit every fairway and reached every putting surface in regula-tion, but then his Achilles heel flared up; he three-putted the third, fifth, and seventh holes, and missed a makeable three-footer for birdie on the second. The *Boston Globe*'s beat writer described his efforts on the greens that morning as "timorous and slack." As always Harry held his disappoint-ment in check. Normally he was a remote, godlike figure on the course, but in a strange way Harry's putting problems humanized him to this gallery, engendering enormous sympathy among the hundreds of amateurs on hand; poor Harry Vardon, the world's greatest golfer, couldn't seem to sink the short ones any better than the average hacker.

Harry kept up his fine shot-making throughout the back nine, despite a double bogey three-putt on the short sixteen, and came home in 38, for a total of 75. The crowd surrounding the green cheered him when he parred eighteen, and a smiling Harry doffed his cap. Officials posted Harry's num-ber on the scoreboard near the clubhouse to another round of applause. His demonstrative following throughout the day had a less salutary effect on Harry's playing partner, Fred McLeod, who shot an 81. Harry walked down to the players' locker room to eat lunch with Lord Northcliffe, who'd followed him on the course during the morning round. Ted Ray soon joined them; he'd wandered out from town to see how Harry was getting on. Ted was scheduled to play in the second flight of qualifying on Wednesday and decided to hang around for the afternoon; the sociable giant wasn't about to spend the whole day alone back at the hotel and pass up a chance to sign autographs and chat up the pretty girls.

The USGA's attempt to toughen up The Country Club succeeded admirably. As they came in after him, two by two, none of the morning qualifiers bested Harry's score; only six of the other sixty-seven men on the course that day even broke 80. Frenchman Louis Tellier, with Francis's former caddie on his bag, attracted the morning's second biggest gallery and shot 80 on the mark. Tom McNamara, despite his oddball two-stroke penalty at "Cottage"—which wasn't assessed until after he finished the round and brought up the incident himself with a USGA official—came in with a 78 to fall into second place. The rule McNamara violated—Rule 13, Article 1—as worded then, read as follows: "When a competitor's ball which lies within 20 yards of the hole is played and strikes either the flag stick or a person standing at the hole, the penalty shall be two strokes." Unsure of how to rule, the official and McNamara had to walk back out to the second hole with a tape measure and determine how far Tom had been standing from the hole when the offending stroke was played. It turned out to be forty-eight feet, well inside the penalty area, so the two strokes were added to his score.

Tom Vardon managed an 85 that morning, as did Fred Herreshoff, the day's top-ranked amateur, keeping their hopes for advancing alive; even before noon, 170 was already being talked about as the cut line for the day's two rounds. The Country Club's own professional Alec "Nipper" Campbell, complaining afterward that all his pre-tournament obligations had prevented him from adequately preparing for actual competition, turned in the morning's most disappointing score, at 84. Mac Smith, the youngest and most talented of the Carnoustie brothers, just coming into his own, carded a 77 to slip in ahead of Tom McNamara. Then in the late morning, 1907's U.S. Open champ Alec Ross, from nearby Brae Burn Country Club, shot a 76 to edge closest to Vardon.

Despite these homebreds' encouraging morning efforts, the cognoscenti around the clubhouse were already spreading a cloud of gloom about the long-term prospects of the American brigade. Those who had watched Vardon play, most for the first time, found his game so effortless and masterful, they harbored no doubts he could go out all week in his sleep and turn in a string of 75s. Former President Taft, who had arrived that morning in time to watch Vardon play his last few holes, joined in the spirited discussion, scrutinizing scores in front of the clubhouse with Herbert Jaques, The Country Club's president. Taft affirmed the growing general assessment that Harry would be very tough to beat. And this forecast was made in spite of Vardon's putting woes, which all the pundits agreed had to be aberrational, a result of his unfamiliarity with the course's challenging greens. Just wait until he found his bearings and started dropping those short putts, warned the wise; then you'll see the Harry Vardon of legend lay waste to the field.

Then a quiet rumor reached the clubhouse that the local boy—*What was his name again? The amateur from Woodland, Ouimet? That former caddie, the kid who lived across the street*—had a splendid round going; he'd made the trip out in 40 and was heating it up again on the back nine. A few people wandered out to the short par three sixteenth—the one named after the street it bordered, Clyde, its green less than a hundred yards from Francis's front door—to confirm the rumors, and sure enough, Ouimet had birdied both eleven and fourteen. News leaped around the course quickly: All the local favorite needed to do to shoot an even par 74 and come in ahead of Harry Vardon was par the last two holes. Francis had cashed in his obvious home field advantage, but he had another edge on the rest of the men on the course; he not only knew how to putt fast greens, he actually preferred them.

By the time he got his routine four at seventeen and reached the eighteenth tee, Francis's gallery had grown to over 200 people; others hurried out to watch, spreading out along the final fairway. So intent were they on completing their morning's work that Francis and Eddie had no idea where he stood in relation to the field. Francis didn't even notice the larger crowd, concentrating on his final tee shot: Four hundred and ten yards, called Home, back across the racetrack—running alongside and opposite the first fairway—to an elevated green, its steep front embankment ready to capture any timid approaches in its heavy beard of rough or send them skidding back down onto the racetrack below. Francis nailed his drive, then stuck a solid approach up onto the green, twenty feet past the hole.

The crowd loitering around the clubhouse edged forward to gather around eighteen and watch him walk in. Francis's long, confident strides now exceeded those of "Long" Jim Barnes; Barnes's tee shot had gone wild to the left and he ended up scrambling to make seven, marring an otherwise fine round and finishing with 82.

Word spread through the crowd now at telegraphic speed; another four at eighteen would bring Francis in with 74, one ahead of Harry Vardon. He needed only to get down in two. As he approached, Ouimet appeared cool, contained. Smiling, unconcerned, talking to some friends in the gallery. And who was that tiny little figure carrying Ouimet's bag, huffing and puffing up the embankment to the green? This was starting to get interesting.

Content to settle for his four, Francis lagged his slippery downhill putt within inches of the hole and tapped in for his par, and just like that he'd done it, shot 74, the low round of the morning; halfway through the first day of qualifying, the unheralded amateur had grabbed the lead from the great Harry Vardon by a single stroke. Francis grinned broadly, shook Eddie's hand, then Jim Barnes's, then took off his cap and shyly acknowledged the crowd's sustained applause. American hopes, close to dashed only an hour ago by Harry's routine brilliance, had in an instant pinned themselves to the most unlikely star.

Vardon, Ray, and Lord Northcliffe heard the commotion outside and stepped out of the locker room, joining Bernard Darwin in time to watch the scene develop around Francis on the eighteenth green. When Darwin told them what Francis had just done, Harry greeted the news without reaction. He sized up Francis for the first time, watching him shake a sea of offered hands as he walked off the green toward the locker room, grinning like a schoolboy.

"That's the lad you were telling me about," said Vardon, lighting his pipe.

"Yes. The amateur, down at Garden City. Marvelous performance," said Darwin, not without a hint of affection. "Fought Jerry Travers down to the bitter end. Nearly had him, too."

"What the devil is that carrying his bag?" said Ray.

"So is this anyone to worry about?" asked Northcliffe, cold and pragmatic.

"Shouldn't think so," said Darwin, backpedaling slightly. "Iron play's a bit loose yet, I'd say. Awfully green. And only the first round of qualifying, isn't it? Early days." An involuntary smile broke out on his face. "But he's a fine boy."

Northcliffe looked askance at Darwin, who slammed the brakes on his admiration and headed toward the Western Union tent, mumbling something about "getting off a dispatch to London."

"I swear, Harry, he's got a bleedin' pygmy caddying for him," said Ray.

Vardon's cool, appraising eyes never left Francis.

"We'll see how he holds up this afternoon," he said quietly to Ray. "Playing with the lead."

Francis enjoyed the kudos of fellow players and members between rounds so much, he forgot to walk home for lunch, as he'd promised his mother he would do; the older pros in the locker room insisted he sit down and eat with them. Mary never left the house to look for Francis, but Louise, his eighteen-year-old sister, wandered over to the course to investigate and returned with the startling news of Francis's early success. Not willing to risk upsetting Francis by showing up in his gallery unannounced, Mary declined to accompany Louise when she hurried back over to the course for his afternoon round. Trying to busy herself with chores, and spending an inordinate amount of time sweeping her front porch, Mary kept an anxious eye on the course across the street for the rest of the day.

When at a little after one o'clock Francis came out to the tee for his second round, he found a crowd of over a thousand people waiting to watch him, balancing his gallery nearly equally with Vardon's, who again teed off four groups ahead of him. Francis's following now included a sizeable contingent of Boston reporters; the "local boy/former caddie" angle had the potential to strike sports page gold; if Francis held up under pressure, they planned to mine it for all the ink it was worth. Eddie's eyes nearly bugged out of his head when they walked between the walls of their gallery, but he steadied himself by keeping his mind on the task at hand, repeating the phrase that was about to become his mantra. There wasn't going to be any flubbed tee shot on the first hole this time around if Eddie had anything to say about it.

"Keep your head down, Francis," he said. "Keep your eye on the ball. I'll watch it for you."

His drive flew straight and true and Francis managed a four on Polo Field this time around; he felt that strong vision and concentration flood through his veins from the moment he stepped to the tee. The increased size of their audience rattled his playing partner Jim Barnes more than it did the young American: With the National Amateur experience under his belt Francis felt comfortable playing in front of a crowd now, and this was his hometown; he appeared to draw strength from their collective good-will. To everyone's surprise, playing a few holes ahead, Harry Vardon was the first to stumble, taking fives at Polo Field and on the difficult, winding third hole, called Pond. He steadied with a birdie two at the seventh, Plateau—the only par three on the outward nine—but faltered again with back-to-back fives at the eighth and ninth. Harry finished with an indifferent 40 for the front nine, nowhere near the result he'd hoped for, but once again his troubled putter let him down within six feet of the hole. As Harry continued to struggle, more and more people deserted Vardon's gallery to drop back and keep an eye on the young American.

Francis played steadily throughout the front, dropping a brilliant twenty-foot putt on Pond for birdie. Sharply focused, he remained indifferent to what was happening ahead or behind him, blithely unaware that as he came to the ninth hole, his lead over Vardon had grown to three strokes. The *New York Times* reporter covering the play observed that Francis appeared to be "going along as if he were merely out for a little holiday." While they waited to tee off at the ninth, Francis caught the eye of Bernard Darwin in the gallery, who waved sheepishly. Standing next to Lord Northcliffe, who'd walked back from Vardon's group with Darwin to check out the American challenger, Francis's English friend didn't want to appear too demonstrative.

Moments later, Eddie nodded toward an impressive, rotund man watching from the gallery nearby, a circle of local dignitaries gravitating in attentive orbit around him.

"Who's the big fat guy?" he asked Francis.

"You don't know who that is, Eddie?"

"I don't know, he looks kinda familiar, doesn't he?"

"That's President Taft."

"Get out."

"I'm telling you, Eddie, that's President Taft."

"President Taft, of the United States, is watching us play."

"That's right."

Eddie chewed on that for a moment, looked Taft up and down, then nodded. "Okay. Let 'em watch." Then, moments later, as they walked to the tee, under his breath: "Wait'll Jack hears about this."

President watching or not, Francis got his par five at number nine—the course's longest and toughest hole, called "Himalaya"—for an outstanding 38 on the front nine, maintaining his three-stroke lead over Vardon.

The strangest turn of the afternoon occurred to a local pro named Fred Brand on the second hole, playing just ahead of Harry. After an excellent drive on the short par four to within 100 yards of the green, Brand knocked his second shot into a tree; it bounced back hard and landed near where he'd just played it from. He made another pass, hit the same tree, and the ball shot backward even farther, this time landing well behind him. On the verge of blowing up, he used the same mashie to play his fourth shot . . . and holed it for a ridiculous par. His one moment of glory; Fred Brand faded down the stretch and didn't make the cut.

Only an hour into the afternoon and the qualifying round had already become a two-man race; nobody else on the course was within five strokes of them, and both men would clearly qualify even if they coasted the rest of the way. But Harry wasn't ready to concede the day's best score to any man on earth, regardless of circumstance. Playing three holes ahead, Harry changed his grip on the putter slightly, locking in his right hand to immobilize the tremor, and finally got it going. Back-to-back birdies at ten and eleven cut Francis's lead down to one. Still blissfully unaware of his lead over Vardon, Francis answered back with a birdie of his own on thirteen. When he holed that putt, for the first time during his afternoon round a loud cheer went up from the crowd around them, startling Eddie and snapping Francis out of his concentrated groove; it was as if someone had woken him from a dream. As he glanced over to respond and shyly tip his cap, Francis's eye fell on President Taft clapping and shouting along with them. The sight of a former president of the United States cheering him on from less than fifty feet away—for him, for Francis Ouimet, from the wrong side of Clyde Street—snapped his ability to tune out all the distractions; it was just too much for his mind to deal with. Moments later, as Francis and Eddie walked over to the fourteenth tee, Frank Hoyt, his old friend from his home club at Woodland who was following Vardon, having heard the yell at thirteen when Francis birdied, came running back to them.

"Francis, Francis; you're three up on Vardon," said Frank.

"I am?"

This was the first he'd heard of it; with that disquieting information compounding his unnerving epiphany about the ex-president, Francis stepped to the tee of the difficult par five fourteenth, called "Quarry," his confidence buffeted by swift and heavy weather.

"Don't listen to 'em, Francis," said Eddie, reading the suddenly uncertain look on his face. "Head down, eye on the ball."

But the self-assurance had sprung a leak and began rapidly taking on water. The fourteenth's elevated tee required a lengthy carry over a nasty trap, against the wind, to a narrow, slanted landing area that tended to bounce the ball left, toward trouble. Francis tried to steer his tee shot, overswung, and duck-hooked it into the waste bunker, short and left of the fairway. Reaching the ball, they found it sitting up in a decent lie in the center of the sand; the low leading edge at the front of the trap should allow for a decent recovery shot. Par was by no means out of reach yet; he had been in that bunker before and managed it countless times. He nestled his feet into the sand, choked down, and nailed his brassie over 200 yards straight down the fairway, but just past the neck of the dogleg, the ball kicked right and hopped into a second bunker. His prospects for par looked dimmer; the ball lay close to the lip, forcing him to blast out sideways onto the fairway, advancing the ball only a few yards. Lying three, it was still 110 yards out from a severely sloped and elevated green. Eager to stick it close to the pin to erase his two mistakes, Francis gave his mashie too much gas and sent his approach skidding just off the back of the green into the first cut of rough. The crowd groaned with him. Eddie tried to settle him down as they walked toward the green.

"Up and down from back there for six is still a decent score," said Eddie. "Nothing to worry about. Let's play our game, let the other guys worry about theirs."

Francis looked over the line of his putt until he saw its path to the cup, then stroked the ball smoothly, but his putter got hung up in the denser grass on the fringe—in those days called the "frog's hair"—and the ball trickled to a stop two and a half feet above the hole, a ticklish leave. Then for the only time that day Francis missed a putt of three feet or less and had to tap in for a double bogey seven.

Two strokes lost. Only one up on Vardon.

Harry had already reached the eighteenth tee before word filtered back to him that young Ouimet had faltered on fourteen. The Vardonic smile appeared, ever so faintly. He hit a perfect tee shot on the long hole Home, then flew his second with a mid-iron right over the flag to the back of the elevated green, thirty-five feet past the hole. A double break and a difficult ridge to negotiate between ball and cup made this one of the toughest putts on the entire course, a three-putt seemed a distinct possibility, but long putts had never been Harry's downfall, only the twitchy four-footers. On this occasion his touch was flawless; Harry vividly remembered the feel of this putt coming off the club for the rest of his life. The ball ran up to the crest of the ridge, nearly stopped dead, turned over once, then again, then slowly picked up speed as it fell down the slope, taking both breaks as if it were running on tracks, but as it neared its target, the ball appeared to be at least six inches off line, until at the last it turned straight for the cup, where it dove like a mouse into its hole for a wondrous birdie three. Miraculous. The crowd, at this point already rooting for Francis, groaned collectively, then remembered its manners and applauded politely. Harry's expression never changed, but he knew full well he had reclaimed a share of the lead while his untested challenger was still out on the course, with four tough holes left to play.

A few other qualifiers picked up their pace late in the afternoon. Young Mac Smith finished strong, adding an identical 77 to his morning round to finish three strokes in back of Harry. Alec Ross came in three behind Smith and Tom McNamara was four shots down. Louis Tellier qualified comfortably, as did Vardon's playing partner Freddie McLeod. The Country Club's resident pro "Nipper" Campbell remembered enough of his game to shoot 77 and make the cut. After a trying afternoon, Tom Vardon righted his ship in time to slip in under the cut line with only three strokes to spare. By day's end, the trial by qualifying had neatly done its job, trimming away the dead wood from the crowded field, while none of the established favorites had failed to be counted among the thirty-two survivors who would advance into the final four rounds.

Jim Barnes caught some of the breeze that had becalmed Francis's sails at fourteen and came on with a strong 34 on the back nine; he finished with 76 to tie Tom McNamara in fifth place. After his miscue at fourteen, Francis regained enough composure to par fifteen and sixteen, but then found himself facing a slippery seven-foot putt to save par on seventeen. The closest green to his home, Francis had been practicing putting on the "Elbow's" delicate contours since he was seven years old, and he knew this putt backward and forward. Today it refused to fall, teetering just off line on a spike mark as it neared the hole and darting to the right. Bogey five.

Francis walked the fifty yards to the eighteenth tee box trailing Vardon by a single stroke. The crowd rallied around him as he teed it up, and after he hit a picture-perfect drive, they cheered him all along the fairway as he walked up to his ball. One hundred and fifty yards out, Francis caught his approach shot the slightest bit heavy, came up short, and landed on the protective rampart in front of the green; the ball bounced to the right into greenside rough, a lucky break considering it might have fallen straight back into a thick grass bunker or even the cinder racetrack below, but it still left him with a difficult lie and stance for his chip up to the hole. Francis took his stance, got his club cleanly on the ball, and made solid contact. It flew six feet onto the green, started rolling on line straight for the cup—the crowd held its breath; if it dropped, he'd match Harry's birdie for the tie—but the ball ducked left at the last and scooted three feet past the jar. No unsteadiness here; his youthful nerves stood up to home hole pressure and he drained the putt for par and a second round 78. The crowd rewarded Francis with an ovation easily exceeding the one he'd earned after his morning effort.

Quietly watching from the steps of the locker room, Harry smiled, turned, and went in to change his shoes.

The first day of qualifying leaders' final numbers went up on the clubhouse scoreboard like this:

Harry Vardon	75–76—151
Mr. Francis Ouimet	74–78—152
Macdonald Smith	77–77—154
Alec Ross	76–81—157
Tom McNamara	78–80—158
James Barnes	82–76—158
Louis Tellier	80–81—161
Alec Campbell	84–77—161

Harry voiced concerns to a few reporters afterward that he still had serious reservations about the qualifying format; if the number of entries meant the trial would take place over two days anyway, why not have the entire field play eighteen holes on each day? Which sounds suspiciously like a forty-two-year-old man worried about his stamina being pressed by a younger player who nearly caught him down the stretch. A sizeable number of players, Vardon included, also complained to the press after concluding their rounds that the club had overdone slicking up the greens; five and eight particularly, they said, felt like putting on a glass tabletop. The Country Club and the USGA, giving birth to a perennial back-and-forth early-round championship tradition, responded by saying, in effect: If it was easy, it wouldn't be the U.S. Open.

President Taft shook the hands of both Vardon and Francis and wished them well before departing that evening; with regrets, obligations at Yale would keep him from watching any more of this year's action. As he left, Taft did mention to a high-roller friend about a cable he'd received from London that Ladbrooke's, the legal betting bureau, was offering two-to-one odds on their English favorites, Vardon and Ray, against the field. Minimum bet: $5,000.

After watching Francis duel Harry down to the wire that afternoon, knowing his friend liked a taste of high-end wagering, Taft advised him he might want to try his hand at that bet.

"On Vardon and Ray?" his friend asked.

"No, no, no," Taft whispered. "Take the field."

ALFRED HARMSWORTH,
LORD NORTHCLIFFE.

TED RAY AT THE
COUNTRY CLUB.

WEDNESDAY:
SECOND DAY QUALIFYING

THE PRESS DINED out on Francis's run at Harry Vardon in their early Wednesday editions, with all six Boston papers trumpeting the local hero's efforts in bold headlines; half of them used Francis as their front-page lead.

Over breakfast that morning, Arthur Ouimet pointedly ignored his son's presence in the *Boston Globe*, which was easier said than done; his name and photograph could be found plastered all over the paper. For his part, Francis pointedly avoided his father, ducking out of the house early to slip next door and watch the day's early action. In his own hard-hearted way, Arthur clearly wished for his son the sustaining dream of every immigrant American father—a better life than his own. His inability to articulate and express that ambition to his boy, perplexed as he was by Francis's mysteriously joyful spirit, resulted in rough words and perpetually bruised feelings. That this happiness radiating from Francis found its most soulful expression in the exercise of a game that represented to Arthur the wretched excess of a spoiled wealthy class, created a gulf wider than any primal paternal affection could span.

Francis played golf. Francis walked a false path. Arthur despaired.

After Arthur left for work that morning, Mary and Louise retrieved all the local editions they could find, cut out every story mentioning Francis, and saved them for a scrapbook they'd started after Garden City. Among those they clipped was an interesting sidebar the *Globe* ran on the appearance at Brookline of former President Taft. A reporter had noticed that Taft had lost a substantial amount of weight since last seen in Boston the previous summer—he was down to a svelte 240 pounds—and queried him on his dietary secrets.

"Before breakfast, cultivate a big appetite through outdoor exercise with a round of golf," said Taft, "and then fool the appetite."

When asked what he then ate for his breakfast, Taft replied: "One egg. Two slices of dry toast. One cup of unsweetened coffee. That is the tragedy of my menu. Obvious, isn't it? My only moments of happiness are spent on the scales. But as you can see, my too, too solid flesh has melted."

WEDNESDAY'S SKIES REMAINED bright and clear but yesterday's steady breeze had vanished; pundits predicted lower scores. The USGA had divided the qualifying field with a careful eye toward spreading the talent equally between the two days. Harry had been yesterday's unquestioned top attraction, with Francis's out-of-nowhere charge providing the day's most dramatic development. On Wednesday, even bigger crowds turned out, primarily to watch Ted Ray square off with the reigning American champions, Jerry Travers and Johnny McDermott.

Jerry Travers went off in the day's eleventh twosome, at 8:55, and he gathered the first substantial gallery of the day. Many of them appeared to be Boston society types, often husbands and wives walking together, who obviously preferred following a star gentleman amateur to an equally accomplished roughneck pro. Jerry's playing partner was Tom Anderson, a well-liked pro whose flashy outfit in the previous year's Open had provided such fashion inspiration to young Walter Hagen. Jerry's preference for match play over the Open's emphasis on consistency in the stroke format showed right from the start; his drives found every kind of terrain but short grass, while his usually surefire methods of recovery were inhibited by a mysteriously erratic putter. After a brilliant bunker shot, Travers missed a gimme three-footer to save par on the first hole. Unquestionably the finest putter in the field, after that first miscue, Jerry appeared to lose his confidence; as his front nine progressed, he found the greased lightning greens increasingly hard to read and even harder to master.

Half an hour later, Johnny McDermott teed off with Henry Wilder, a popular local amateur, and drew the day's second sizeable crowd. From the start it was clear free-swinging Johnny Mac didn't have his "A" game; what's even stranger is that it may have been intentional. Tight and visibly tense, he played every shot cautiously, abandoning his reckless attacking style. No cutting dogleg corners, no blasting it through the trees, no bold runs at the flag. Johnny's legion of working-class fans, accustomed to swashbuckling feats of daring, looked on with increasing confusion. Bernard Darwin soon surmised that after all the turmoil he'd been through since Shawnee, McDermott had modified his strategy to fit a simple formula: eliminate risk, qualify at any cost, and save his heavy ammunition for the actual tournament. A sound approach, unexpectedly farsighted for the take-no-prisoners champ, but it ran counter to his basic nature and seemed to drain the fire from his game.

Fifteen minutes later Ted Ray stepped to the first tee. Ted's soaring, majestic drives during his numerous Country Club practice rounds had acquired among the locals a must-see, circus-sideshow reputation. In a clever bit of pairing, Ted's partner that morning was Jack Hobens, a physically short, long-hitting American from Englewood, New Jersey, with Popeye forearms. When they both launched towering tee shots over and past the elbow of the dogleg on Polo Field, the crowd erupted in appreciation. The two men walked off down the first fairway trailed by the largest gallery of the day—over a thousand people, Bernard Darwin and Lord Northcliffe among them.

Two figures soon followed them off the first tee that morning and attracted no attention whatsoever. The little Englishman Wilfred Reid had no one in his gallery but his own sister and her husband, Louis Tellier, showing up on his day off in support of the family concern. Reid announced he had come to play from the start, sinking a twelve-footer for birdie on the Polo Field's testing green. Teeing off in even deeper obscurity not long after Reid, Walter Hagen had only one person walking behind him, his caddie, a kid he'd known for a total of fifteen minutes. Aside from a few snickers about his fancy golfing ensemble, Hagen was so thoroughly neglected during his first day at Brookline, he couldn't even get the papers to spell his name right; in every single account of Wednesday's play, reporters identified him as "W. Hagin." A few stories insisted his first name was William; no less than the *New York Times* referred to him, as if by generic default, as "Willie." One observational genius in the press corps identified him as "Ned Dagin." Later that day, after he'd stirred up a little attention, the *Boston Record* described him as "someone whom few people knew, even by sight." Guess what? None of it bothered Walter.

Francis bounced back and forth between the three star pairings, the most relaxed human being on the grounds, congratulated everywhere he went for yesterday's achievement. He walked part of the front nine with his boss George Wright and then stationed himself at the course's prime viewing spot, a thatched hut adjacent to the tenth tee that offered a clear view of no less than five fairways and greens. Temporarily shaking himself loose from his demanding employer Lord Northcliffe, Bernard Darwin ran into Francis there, and found a moment to offer his warmest congratulations. Then Darwin beckoned him aside, drawing him to the edge of the hut.

"You've got the ability to contend with anyone on this course, Francis," said Darwin quietly, hoping no Englishmen were near enough to hear this heresy. "And you've got the local knowledge. I must tell you I like your chances."

"I don't know about that, Mr. Darwin—"

"Well now, listen, I do; you keep your eyes forward, pay no mind to whatever anyone else says, and play your own game."

"I never asked you, Mr. Darwin, do you play?"

Glancing past Francis, Darwin spotted Lord Northcliffe approaching the ninth green, walking along with Ray's twosome. For the first time that day Ted Ray looked a little stormy; he was, in fact, halfway to his only double bogey of the morning. Darwin read the looks on both Ted's and Northcliffe's faces and smelled trouble.

"I scrape it around from time to time," he said. "Must go. London awaits. All the best." Darwin patted Francis's arm, winked at him, and quickly walked back toward his boss.

Ted Ray had a talk with himself early that morning. To qualify, that was the thing, risk-taking be damned. He manfully took his six at the ninth, kept the cap on his volcanic temper, and his play throughout his first round remained sound and steady. But more often than not he left the driver in his bag. The rough had sprouted up four inches high and Ted had spent enough time during his practice rounds among the "monarchs of the forest" skirting the fairways to know they promised disaster for anyone who ventured past their line of defense. The crowd felt the slightest bit let down that Ted wasn't murdering every tee shot like an unchained gorilla; today his drives were "only" flying an average of 260 yards. Many of his followers deserted Ted's gallery during his back nine to look up Jerry Travers, who if nothing else made every hole an adventure with his wacky drives and madcap recoveries.

Maintaining the same cautious approach as Ted Ray, Johnny McDermott found the going a little tougher, perhaps because to begin with he had less game to rein in; to excel at the level demanded by U.S. Open conditions Johnny needed to play past his limits, not within them. When his putter failed to make up for mistakes, his margin for error grew razor thin. On the difficult fourteenth hole that morning, Quarry, McDermott hooked his tee shot toward a massive elm on the left edge of the fairway; it settled just short of the big tree, in thick gnarled rough. When he found his ball, Johnny discovered that it rested directly on top of another ball, one that had been lost by an earlier player and never found. No one in his group knew exactly how the situation should be treated within the rules, and a call went out to summon USGA president Robert Watson to the scene.

Watson arrived within minutes, leaned down, and looked the ball over carefully; the tension between them from Johnny's behavior at Shawnee and Watson's harsh reprimand to him had never been resolved. This didn't help.

"Play it," said Watson finally, "as it lays."

McDermott protested. Watson wouldn't relent. McDermott fumed, staring down at his ball wide-eyed with anger. Given the recent paranoid drift of his mind, Johnny must have suspected the USGA had lain in wait until they saw him coming and then planted this derelict ball below his like a land mine. Watson and his entourage stepped back and waited for Johnny to make the play as he'd been instructed. The knowing crowd around them braced for a meltdown. McDermott finally turned to his caddie and asked for his niblick; he'd decided the only chance he had was to blast out the lower ball like a plugged bunker shot and hope his own carried out with it. He raised the club and chopped down into the grass as if it were an axe splitting firewood; the stray ball on the bottom flew forty yards straight out onto the fairway, but his own ball squirted dead sideways, only six feet, and settled right back down into the punitive rough. McDermott stared holes at the ugly scar his stroke had left in the turf and somehow kept himself from blowing his stack. Watson turned his back and walked away. McDermott played on and took a double bogey six on the hole.

Maintaining his steadfast pace through the back nine, Ted Ray finished with an even par 74, matching Francis's low round from Tuesday. Ray's playing partner, Jack Hobens, missed a putt by an inch at eighteen to finish one stroke behind him at 75. Ray's lead appeared as if it was going to stand up; Jerry Travers limped home in 82, chastened and full of articulate self-recrimination. Four putts at the seventh. The same again on ten. "I am," Jerry declared solemnly, "the worst putter in America." Overstated in a moment of despair, but unless he found an answer in his afternoon round, making the cut looked a doubtful proposition. Johnny McDermott, bushwhacked by his eerie mishap at fourteen, finished well back in the pack with 81. Boston favorite Mike "King" Brady returned with a workmanlike 80. Two-time Open champ Alex Smith needed fifteen putts on the first five holes and blew up with an 84; the other former champ in the Smith clan, his younger brother Willie, shot 83.

Francis's friend John G. Anderson led the morning's amateur contenders with 81. Taking advantage of an inexplicable loophole in the USGA's airtight seal on amateur status, Anderson was also drawing a paycheck from both *Golf Magazine* and the *Boston Transcript* to write about the Open at the same time he was competing in it as an amateur. For inexplicable reasons the USGA had decided caddying for four bits a round constituted "professionalism," while turning out columns for cold cash for newspapers and magazines kept a golfer pure as the driven snow. Anderson's fellow Massachusetts amateur Heinrich Schmidt, performing identical player-journalist duties for the *Boston Traveler*, shot an 81 as well. One of the last to finish that morning, still flying under the radar of anyone's attention, imperturbable Walter Hagen carded a 78 to slide neatly into third place. Only a triple bogey, Quarry—a hole that would later come back to haunt him—prevented Hagen from dominating Wednesday's headlines.

In jacket and tie and a jaunty cap, looking as suave and collected as if he'd just stepped out from one of his many magazine ads, Harry Vardon showed up to join stablemate Ted Ray just as he finished his morning's work. The crowd at eighteen greeted the completion of Ted's outstanding 74 with sustained applause; he took his pipe from his mouth, smiled broadly, and swept the green with his bucket hat in a self-mockingly grand reply. Tournament galleries then and now have an unerring instinct for reading a player's innate character and responding in kind. That morning Ted showed them nothing but Rabelaisian good humor under fire while radiating the common touch. If Harry had an element of the divine that elevated him beyond the reach of mortal men, Ted was unmistakably the salt of the earth rubbing elbows with you at the neighborhood bar. The no-nonsense New England crowd's unanimous verdict on Ted Ray: How can you not love this guy?

The two Jerseymen took seats with Lord Northcliffe on the patio outside the locker room, looking down on the eighteenth green, and talked shop about Ted's round. It appeared likely that Ted's morning lead would stand up, as Harry's had the day before, until down the stretch, after playing in a near vacuum, their fellow Englishman abroad, welterweight Wilfred Reid, made a bold move along the rail. He holed a long putt for birdie at the tough fifteenth, Liverpool. A fifteen-footer for birdie dropped at the par three sixteenth, Clyde. Solid pars at seventeen and eighteen and, shockingly, Reid came in to the clubhouse with the morning's best score, 72, the lowest by two strokes recorded in either day of qualifying.

As the euphoric little Reid made his way toward the locker room, receiving what was for him an unprecedented amount of acclaim—he later said he had made up his mind to remain in America, no matter what happened in the tournament, right then and there—Ted Ray's mood drooped lower than his mustache.

"Anyone but him," muttered Ted darkly.

Harry exchanged a sly conspiratorial glance with Northcliffe. "Come along now, Ted," said Harry, straight-faced, enjoying his friend's sour turn. "All for England."

"That's right, Ted," said Northcliffe, winding him up even further. "All for England."

" 'All for Wilfred's' more like it," said Ted, rising abruptly. "He's half a bloody Frenchman anyway."

Ted stalked off in search of a beer. Northcliffe and Harry stood up and offered Reid some polite applause as he passed by; he looked up in surprise, smiled, waved back gallantly, and tipped his little plum-colored beret, a twin to Louis Tellier's.

"He's not even on the bleeding payroll," said Northcliffe through his smile. "Hope you're not going to let him beat you."

"Alfred. The day I lose to Wilfred Reid," said Harry as he got to his feet, "you'll be running my obituary."

As Harry descended the locker-room steps, he came face-to-face with a familiar face emerging from the crowd.

"Mr. Vardon, sir," said Francis, extending his hand.

"Mr. Ouimet," said Harry, shaking the young man's hand, his smile friendly and approving. They regarded each other for a moment, Harry gently amused that Francis appeared momentarily overcome by the presence of his idol. "Enjoying a day off, are you?" asked Harry.

"I am, indeed. Yes."

"Fine play yesterday."

"Thank you. Thank you very much," said Francis. "You, too."

Harry's smile widened slightly. "You nearly had me there, at the last."

"Just dumb luck, I think."

"A little more than that at work, I'd say. I've seen your swing."

"You have? I mean, you have."

Harry leaned in slightly. "Some people have a talent for luck. It's a skill, you see, like any other. Maybe the most useful of them all."

"I think I know what you mean," said Francis.

"And so. The best of luck to you, then."

Harry patted Francis on the arm and continued on. As Francis stood there watching Harry walk away, Walter Hagen walked up and joined him. "What'd the old boy say to you?" asked Hagen.

"He wished me luck," said Francis.

"Don't let that act fool you," said Hagen. "He wants to beat our brains in." Hagen stuck his hand out and introduced himself. "Ouimet, right?"

"Call me Francis."

"Glad to know you. You get a load of the hands on Vardon? They're like catcher's mitts."

"I did notice, yes."

"Guy knows more tricks out there than Houdini. Ever see him play before?"

"Just once. A long time ago," Francis answered.

"He can make it dance. I was screwing around a little in practice trying to imitate his swing, and you know what? It's gangbusters. You're an amateur, right?"

"That's right."

"So, tell me, how is it in the clubhouse? Looks pretty sweet from here."

"It's very nice," Francis agreed.

"Someday maybe I'll get to take a look," said Hagen, gazing a little wistfully at the big yellow clubhouse. "Here's the thing, though, Francis. About that trophy; what do you say we keep it on this side of the pond?"

"I'm all for it."

"Deal," said Hagen, shaking hands again. "See you round the campus, kid."

The afternoon rounds began promptly at twelve, before the last golfers who'd gone off in the morning had even finished their work. As on the previous day, the order of play and the pairings remained the same. Fine weather had drawn a steady stream of spectators out to The Country Club throughout the morning, and galleries of equal four-figure size now followed the same three star attractions; Ted Ray, Johnny McDermott, and Jerry Travers. His first-round success also earned Wilfred Reid a healthy crowd and their jostling, boisterous presence appeared to unsettle him; he pulled his tee shot at the difficult third hole, Pond, and took a seven.

His pipe going full blast, trailing a stream of smoke worthy of a tramp steamer, Ted Ray picked up right where he left off, with a rainbow drive that led to an easy birdie at the first hole. His ungainly lumbering gait, ready smile, and crowd-pleasing interactions after almost every shot earned him back any of the gallery that he'd lost earlier in the day. Ted played in this comfort zone all afternoon, but despite his easygoing manner, he possessed an unerring instinct for knowing exactly where he stood in relation to the rest of the field. When after a birdie at thirteen it became clear that he would finish more than comfortably inside the cut line, and probably capture the qualifying medal, Ted unsheathed the driver and let slip the dogs of war, thrilling his audience with a succession of rocket-shots.

Boom! Three hundred yards plus on the par five fourteenth, on the green in two, two-putt for a routine bird. Hundreds of newcomers flocked to his gallery now. An entrance road leading to the clubhouse from Clyde Street cuts directly across the fairway of the 370-yard fifteenth hole, Liverpool, at about the 260-yard mark. The average player lays up well short of that road, leaving a long-iron second shot into the green. Ted blew his drive over the road by fifty yards and inspired a chorus of gasps and wild approval; he could nearly putt it to the green from there. A party atmosphere prevailed around Ted over the last few holes, and no one enjoyed it more than the affable big man marching at the head of the pack. Ted killed another drive at eighteen and made an easy par to match his morning score with a second 74, establishing a new Country Club record for a thirty-six-hole single-day outing. Ted had played himself into the Open three strokes ahead of Harry's Tuesday benchmark, delivering the tournament's best qualifying number.

Few others enjoyed such a frisky afternoon. Wilfred Reid managed to hold himself together after his early triple bogey to finish with 79, as did journeyman Robert McDonald; they tied for second at 151, matching Vardon's total. To the continued bewilderment of his supporters, Johnny McDermott maintained his guarded, commonsensical line of attack and carded an 80, improving on his morning exertions by only a single stroke. Ahead of him, Jerry Travers's stomach-churning roller-coaster ride continued: in the trees, out of the trees; six bunkers, four saves for par; six three-putts, two four-putts, five single putts. After he finished with 83, looking as haggard as a lost explorer returning from six months in the bush, Travers paced anxiously around the clubhouse to see if his 165 total for the day would survive the cut. More tongues started wagging about that impertinent young hotshot from Rochester, when Walter Hagen followed his solid morning round with a 79; the Haig had lived up to his mouth and made it into the Open. He was observed shortly thereafter outside the locker room, bending the ear of a local reporter: "It's Hagen, with an *e*: H-a-g-e-n."

Francis spent the afternoon watching his friends from the Massachusetts contingent work their way around, and they made a fine showing; Heinrich Schmidt and Mike Brady both ended the day even with McDermott at 161, tied for fourteenth. John Anderson shot 79, once again the round's top amateur and the last man to break 80 on the day. Immediately putting on their reporters' hats, Anderson and Schmidt had enough fuel left in the tank afterward to hunker down in the press tent and grind out twelve inches of ink for the readers of their Boston newspapers. Confirming the press's general pessimism, both men were forced to reluctantly conclude that the British invasion of the U.S. Open, now prominently including Wilfred Reid among its number, looked almost certain to succeed.

The day's leaders and qualifiers included:

Edward Ray	74–74—148
Wilfred Reid	72–79—151
Robert McDonald	72–79—151
Walter Hagen	78–79—157
Jack Hobens	75–84—159
Mr. John Anderson	81–79—160
Mr. Heinrich Schmidt	81–80—161
J. J. McDermott	81–80—161
Mike Brady	80–81—161
Alex Smith	84–79—163

And there, dangerously near the bottom of the list, appeared Mr. Jerome Travers: 82–83—165.

The cut line fell at 166, four strokes below Tuesday's deadline. Jerry Travers had walked another tightrope and made it into the Open by a single stroke.

The tournament's first gauntlet had been run and the surviving field was set: sixty-one battle-tested professionals, led by Vardon, Ray, and Reid, and eight gentlemen amateurs, Francis posting the best score among them. The skirmishing was done. The bodies were quickly buried and forgotten; 100 defeated men lowered their heads, packed up their sticks, and hurried back to catch late trains out of Boston.

In every major tournament one expects that some of the game's top names will be making an early exit; the biggest eye-opener of the 1913 Open was that all but one of them made it through. The only real surprise among those casualties who'd had their ticket punched: 1899's U.S. Open champion, late of Carnoustie, Scotland, playing now out of Mexico City, thirty-seven-year-old Willie Smith, who finished well out of the running at 171. Later that night, Willie hopped on a midnight train to begin the long trip back down south of the border, where a bizarre and tragic fate awaited him. His brothers, Alex and Mac, would never see him alive again.

FRANCIS WADED INTO the mob that swarmed around the clubhouse scoreboard posting tomorrow's pairing for the Open's first official rounds. The first group, Wilfred Reid and C. R. Murray, a Canadian from Royal Montreal, was slated to go off at 8:15 the next morning. When he finally worked his way close to the board, Francis found his name listed in Thursday's twenty-eighth twosome, scheduled for 10:30, paired with another Canadian, Karl Keffer.

Low dappled sunlight burnished the fairways a warm coppery green. The day's buzzing crowds dispersed back out the gates. The Country Club's members lingered, filling the clubhouse porch and bar, laying odds, making their bets, high on the thick excitement in the air; after his trying day, Mr. Jerry Travers joined them for a couple of gin and tonics. The surviving professionals changed their shoes in the players' locker room, grabbed their kit bags, and hitched rides back to their lodgings in town, making plans for the evening, hastily arranging transport back out to Brookline in the morning.

Lord Northcliffe's car and driver waited outside in the club's circular drive for Harry and Ted, then escorted them back to the Copley Square Hotel, along with their patron, and an ink-stained Bernard Darwin.

Leaving the crowd behind, Francis took his well-worn shortcut past the sixteenth hole, across the seventeenth fairway, waiting for the heavy traffic on Clyde to part before he crossed the street; the U.S. Open's only entry who walked home that night. His younger sister Louise and brother Raymond had already helped Mary prepare the family's supper, sparing Francis his usual evening chores. Mary waited to serve until Arthur came home; he stormed in the door complaining loudly and angrily that tournament traffic had held him up for over half an hour. An awkward, silent dinner followed, broken only by Louise's enthusiastic questions to Francis about what he'd seen that day; of all his children, only his daughter refused to be cowed by Arthur's menacing glower. Francis answered her questions plainly and simply—yes, it had been a fine day out there, yes, some very good golf had been played—not eager to test his father's patience on this of all nights. Francis excused himself right after he finished eating and went outside to roll some balls around on his old putting green in the backyard.

As Raymond and Louise cleaned up the kitchen, Arthur and Mary sat in the dining room, in silence. Mary poured coffee. Arthur paged through his evening paper.

"How did he play today?" Arthur asked finally.

"He didn't play today, Arthur," said Mary. "He plays tomorrow. And he played yesterday, for that matter."

Arthur grunted. Silence.

Mary set her coffee cup down on the saucer, with a little more force than usual. Arthur looked up in surprise. Mary got up, walked into the parlor, and returned with the scrapbook she and Louise had put together. She slapped it down on the table in front of her husband.

"You can see for yourself," she said, the slightest quiver in her voice.

Mary walked quickly out of the room. Raymond and Louise peered in from the kitchen. Arthur lowered his paper and stared at the cover of the scrapbook: a photograph of Francis from Garden City, smiling, holding a club high at the finish of his swing.

Arthur raised his newspaper again, and went back to reading.

WILFRED REID.

THURSDAY: DAY ONE

BUNKER HILL. LEXINGTON and Concord. Trenton and Valley
Forge.

Headline writers for Thursday morning's Boston papers couldn't
restrain themselves, invoking one rallying American battle cliché after
another, but a thinly veiled desperation lay just beneath the surface of their
rampant boosterism. There was no denying the fact that Harry Vardon, Ted
Ray, and Wilfred Reid had dominated the Open's qualifying rounds,
although some consoled themselves with the possibility that McDermott,
McNamara, Brady, and Travers had coolly held their best effort in reserve
for when it counted most. The blood, sweat, and tears the homebreds had
all left out on the course just to survive to this point begged to differ.

Regardless of how many times local scribes reminded their readers
that every one of the sixty-nine players would break from Thursday's starting gate with the same score, each acknowledged that an American victory
required feats of skill and fortitude none of their boys had yet demonstrated they had in their bags. Except Ouimet, of course, when he had
slugged it out toe-to-toe with Vardon on Tuesday, but Francis was a fledg-

ling amateur who'd clearly played out of his head, beginner's luck. The press seemed loath to heap too many additional expectations on the youngster's shoulders—he was green as spring corn. No one in his right mind expected the local kid to duplicate that performance under the weight of actual U.S. Open competition.

Although most papers reported front-page forecasts for afternoon rain, as morning broke, the weather looked as if it would hold; another perfect late summer day, low seventies, mostly sunny, light to moderate winds. The United States Weather Bureau had been operating as a division of the Department of Agriculture for over twenty years. In recent years the bureau had advanced the coordinated collection of information by sending up balloons across the country with meteorological instruments on board, but their forecasting skills remained spotty, at best. *The Farmer's Almanac*, published annually, sported a better predictive record, but it had only been about fifty years since scientists first penetrated the mysteries of why storms occurred, let alone being able to predict when and where they would strike. When Thursday dawned bright and clear, Boston's seven dailies immediately revised the weather sections of their afternoon editions, pushing back the arrival of an expected storm front until early Friday morning.

After dutifully returning to school in West Newton on Wednesday, Eddie Lowery sweet-talked his brother Jack into providing a cover story for him Thursday morning: that he'd taken ill on the way to school and had to return home. Eddie again evaded the neighborhood's patrolling truant officer, stepping up his efforts to nail serial offenders during the Open, and hopped an early train to Brookline. Eddie was determined there would be no repeat of Tuesday's last-minute arrival; he wanted his man sound of mind and free of worry as his tee time approached. When Francis left his house on Clyde Street at a little after eight that morning, he found Eddie waiting for him just outside the gate. They hadn't spoken since Tuesday evening; Francis had spent the last thirty-six hours with no way to be sure he'd ever see Eddie again. The sight of his resolute little squire brought an immediate smile to his face.

"Morning, Eddie."

"You sleep okay, Francis?"

"I did, thank you."

Eddie immediately gestured for his golf bag, Francis handed it to him, and Eddie slung it over his shoulder. They walked over to The Country Club together, a quick pace but a somber purpose in their step, Francis leading the way over his old familiar shortcut.

"You're going to shoot seventy-two today, Francis," said Eddie.

"Now Eddie, let's have no talk like that this morning—"

"No, I saw it, like in a dream. You're going to shoot seventy-two."

"Well, we'll just have to go out there and see, won't we?"

"Okay, so maybe it won't be today," said Eddie. "But I'm telling you that sometime during this tournament you're going to shoot seventy-two."

Francis realized there was no point in arguing with him. "That's fine then, Eddie."

They arrived at the clubhouse just in time to see the first twosome officially begin play at the 1913 U.S. Open; C. R. Murray of Royal Montreal and Englishman Wilfred Reid teed off at exactly 8:15. Pale and nervous, up since an hour before dawn, the pudding-faced Reid had secretly been delighted by his early draw. The day's anticipated crowds from Boston had not yet found their way out to Brookline, allowing him to avoid the klieg light of public scrutiny he'd found blinding the previous afternoon. Although attended only by an early-bird gallery of a few dozen people, Reid didn't entirely avoid first-tee jitters; he bogeyed the first hole.

Francis walked into the locker room to change his shoes and immediately sensed a change in mood. The week's casual camaraderie among the Americans had given way to silent, tense determination. Vardon and Ray hadn't arrived at the club yet and Reid had just teed off; the home team had the locker room to themselves. Jim Barnes, Alec Ross, Tom McNamara, Mike Brady, Jerry Travers, they all had their game faces on, exchanging tight nods, few words, hard, quick handshakes. Johnny McDermott, as was his custom before big matches, spent a few private minutes vomiting in a toilet stall. No one there stated the underlying objective in so many words, even McDermott, but every man knew the time had come to do on the course what had preoccupied them all ever since Vardon and Ray first set foot in New York: Keep the cup in America.

Only Walter Hagen showed up loose, and late. He confided in Francis, whose locker was down the same row, that he'd been lured out of the Copley Square Hotel by the attractions of Boston's nightlife and stayed out carousing until the early morning hours. Slapping backs, shaking hands, and wishing all the boys around the room good luck, Hagen carefully tied the wide white laces of his red-rubber-soled shoes into fancy loops and ambled casually out to the first tee just moments before his scheduled time at 8:25.

When Hagen teed off on Thursday morning, he stuck his drive in the middle of the first fairway, acknowledged the polite applause he received, and walked off the tee whistling like a man on his way to the barbershop. At least three dozen of the growing crowd loitering around the clubhouse, undecided about whom to follow, threw in their lot with Hagen and headed off after him. During Wednesday afternoon's qualifying round, people on the course had begun to notice and appreciate Hagen's rose-colored nonchalance. As true then as it is now, any display of untroubled exuberance and colorful personality among the dour, rigid practitioners of the world's most exacting sport attracts waves of popular affection. Instead of trudging around like a bloodless mortician working a funeral procession, Hagen played with the exuberant swagger of a frat boy at his first kegger, a couple of snorts under his belt, who's just realized he's the life of the party. He relaxed between every shot, joked with his gallery, flirted with the prettiest girls; the only thing missing was card tricks. Despite the pressurized atmosphere, he never deviated from this easygoing routine. More people flocked to him as if magnetized by some primitive homing instinct for fun, and as Hagen sauntered around The Country Club's fairways that Thursday, the curtain went up on one of the greatest long-running hit shows in the history of sports. In the decades to come, along with Babe Ruth and Jack Dempsey, Walter Hagen would virtually invent the now familiar role of the playboy pro athlete, self-made from the poorest clay, adding an indelible icon to the pantheon of quintessentially American heroes. For his opening number, all Walter Hagen did was march out in the initial nine holes of his first U.S. Open and shoot a one under par 37.

As Francis left the locker room to warm up, Lord Northcliffe's custom rented steamer car pulled into the circular drive, delivering Harry Vardon and Ted Ray to The Country Club. Their caddies hustled out to meet them, collecting and carrying their clubs and shoes into the locker room.

The two men were greeted warmly by tournament officials and a circle of affluent well-wishers from the club gathered around them.

Eddie stopped with Francis on their way to practice to watch the spectacle. Eddie's eyes narrowed.

"Who do they think they are?" said Eddie. "The kings of England?"

"Well, that *is* who they are, Eddie, more or less," said Francis.

"This is America," he said, and continued on.

America's National Amateur champion Jerry Travers stepped to the first tee for his 8:35 starting time as Francis passed the nearby practice green. A warm round of applause from his own upper-class constituency greeted Jerry's introduction. Francis was interested to see that Jerry had his driver in hand, not the ominous black driving iron.

Maybe Jerry's pulled his swing back together, thought Francis. *Good news for our side if he has.*

Moments later Jerry snap-hooked his tee shot into the deep rough and another manic-depressive Travers round was under way; he would bogey the first three holes, birdie the fourth, settle down to par the next four, only to three-putt the ninth for an outward 41. Tom Vardon and his playing partner quietly followed Jerry Travers's twosome off the tee, completely ignored, just as his illustrious brother reached the practice green, surrounded by an adoring crowd.

Six hundred automobiles occupied every spare inch of free space on the grounds by the time Harry teed off at 9:05, paired with a pro from South Carolina named Tom Bonnar. Thanks to the budding international rivalry made possible by Harry and Ted Ray's presence, Boston had embraced this U.S. Open; thousands poured out of the city toward Brookline by bus, car, train, and on foot. With the tournament's full field of players all on the course to choose from, Thursday's crowd opted for the sure thing; over half of the 9,000 spectators on hand decided to follow the King of Clubs. Shepherded by platoons of megaphoned marshals, a sea of straw boaters and sun bonnets bobbed along after Harry down the first fairway. Notepad in hand, Bernard Darwin dutifully trundled off in their wake. Lord Northcliffe followed Harry inside the ropes, wearing the agitated distraction of an owner watching his prize Thoroughbred head for the first turn.

He needn't have worried. Fine-tuning his concentration now that the championship was on the line, through the front nine Harry hit every fairway and every green in regulation. Executing a flawless tactical attack, on each of those approach shots, he landed the ball well below the hole, avoiding the dizzying breaks of the downhill slants. Then his personal war with his crippled putting hand began.

As long as he could lag longer putts to within a foot of the hole, Harry had no trouble tapping in for par. Only when he found himself within that volatile three- to six-foot range would even the most observant witness have noticed the tightening of the grip, the clenched brow, the slight arrhythmia in his setup as he worked through his routine over the ball. He avoided leaving himself in that awkward position until the fifth hole, a testing 420-yard par four called Newton; on its right to left slanting green he faced a sharply breaking ten-footer. When for the first time in the day his right forearm jumped on his backswing, Harry ran the ball four feet long. Sweat greased his forehead. He addressed the comebacker, made a balky pass at it, and missed the hole completely. Bogey five. The crowd groaned. Harry never changed expression, picked up his ball, and walked on.

On the short par four sixth, Baker—ordinarily a birdie opportunity for Harry—another textbook drive and approach landed him six feet below the hole, putting straight uphill. But the genie had slipped out of the bottle. The nerve jumped again; his ball slid three feet past. The slippery downhill return he'd left himself stayed up on the grass as well. Tap in; bogey five. No one on that course looking at Harry could have guessed at the torment it caused him. Although in Harry's case his troubles began as a physical problem, over the years they had wormed their way into his mind. The yips, as they're now commonly called, have recently been under extensive study by psychologists and physiologists, who categorize the symptoms as specific expression of a diagnosable anxiety disorder. At their worst, the brain literally ceases to function; the ability to focus evaporates, inappropriate thoughts light up the mind like firecrackers, small-muscle motor control vanishes. For people who've never fallen into their grip, it's difficult to comprehend the unholy terror the yips inspire. Psyches crumble. Strong men weep. Some decide to give up the game rather than continue to face the furies that descend upon them. That's just among amateurs; imagine what it's like when you depend on making those putts for a living. No one in his lifetime ever knew the private hell into which Harry stared when confronted with such an innocent tableau; a ball and a hole, separated by thirty-six inches of grass.

John McDermott kept his cold hawk's eye on Harry throughout the morning; he began his round at 9:05, directly behind Vardon's twosome. The spillover from Vardon's gallery blending with his own legion of fans sent Johnny off the tee with a massive following. Today, at last, he didn't disappoint them. Only drawing Harry as his playing partner would have made McDermott happier, but keeping his main target in the crosshairs ahead of him stoked a steady supply of fuel into the chambers of Johnny's angry core. He shook off the caution and self-imposed restraints of his qualifying rounds and played his crowd-pleasing fearless, slashing style again. The great strength of McDermott's game had always been his precision with long-irons, and whenever he landed within range of the green, he relentlessly attacked the flagstick, regardless of where it was planted on the green. On his off days he paid for that recklessness with bunker shots and chips from heavy rough; on Thursday morning he dropped every one of his approaches close enough to throw a picnic blanket over the ball and the hole. He didn't stop there; McDermott canned three of those early birdie chances, giving his crowd plenty to cheer about. When they obliged, Johnny raised a fist to egg them on, trying to whip up as much noise and mayhem as possible and get into the head of the man ahead of him. The American hopefuls needed no other volunteers to lead their brigade today; just as he had been for the last two years, McDermott appeared to be up to the task. After only six holes the two-time defending champ had jumped out to lead the tournament at three under par.

Following his custom, Francis made his way out to a remote corner of the tenth fairway to warm up by knocking a few derelict balls into the woods. He saw Brae Burn's 1907 U.S. Open champ Alec Ross tee off at 9:40, then watched his friends Mike "King" Brady and Country Club pro Alec Campbell follow at 9:50. Francis had eaten a full breakfast—his mother had insisted on it—and after a surprisingly sound night's sleep, he felt rested and strong. Eddie fed him a low, steady patter of reassurance keeping Francis focused on his routine. But as the minutes ticked down and he looked back at the clubhouse, at the swarming crowds, the stacks of players lining up to make their starts, Francis felt something huge and overwhelming barreling down on him. Butterflies the size of barn owls fluttered in his stomach

At 10:10, Long Jim Barnes went off. At 10:15, Tom McNamara.

Francis and Eddie walked back to the practice green near the clubhouse. Francis spotted Ted Ray near the locker room, pipe going full steam, twirling a club in his hand, and laughing as he entertained a circle of admiring young ladies. Scheduled to go off second to last that morning, Ray looked like a man without a care in the world. *Why can't I feel that way?* Francis asked himself. He dropped two balls on the green, tried to fend off the encircling doubts by finding his putting stroke. No use. Every sound, every sight, every unwelcome thought thrust into his jumbled hypersensitive awareness like a bayonet, a cacophony of outcomes, all bad, crowded his mind: *What if? What if this? What if that?* His hands trembled. Eddie watched him miss one putt after another with silent concern.

What am I doing here? I'm in over my head.

The 10:25 pairing teed off. It was time.

Francis and Eddie moved to the first tee along a tight corridor of well-wishers, a wall of vivid faces urging him on, patting him on the back. Francis didn't see or hear a single one of them. He shook hands with his playing partner Karl Keffer as they waited for the fairway to clear. Keffer mentioned that Francis had caddied for him once years before, during one of The Country Club's annual matches with Royal Montreal. Francis vaguely remembered Keffer; he might have been someone he'd once seen in a dream. Sounds and voices reached him as if muffled through a stack of mattresses. He heard his own name introduced by the starter and had trouble connecting the words to himself. *Who is this person stepping up to the ball? Is it me?* As he took his stance and the crowd around them hushed, even Eddie's familiar voice barely got through.

"Keep your head down," said Eddie, "and keep your eye on the ball."

No guiding thoughts. No words of wisdom from Vardon. Blank. An alien stick in his hands. A white sphere on a small mound of dirt sticking out of the ground. *What do I do now?*

He swung. The ball whipped out low, turned over, and immediately started to hook toward the out of bounds on the left, ripping through the tall grass and stopping just short of the white stakes. It had traveled less than forty yards and stopped nearly dead behind a tree. A truly wretched first shot. Francis's boosters in the crowd offered applause, not for his foozled drive but to encourage and support the poor kid—poor thing, he looked a nervous wreck—as they sent him on his way.

Francis felt as if he'd been slapped in the face, the first blow struck in a prizefight, but instead of the shock waking him out of his torpor and pulling him into the action, he felt stunned. Aimless. Helpless to defend himself. Francis and Eddie waited as Karl Keffer drove his first ball down the fairway, then started walking.

"That's okay, Francis," said Eddie, hustling to keep up. "We can still make four from there."

Francis picked up his pace and tried to walk it off, but he was back on his heels. There was grit in his eyes. His mouth felt as if he'd been chewing cotton. His hands looked as though they'd been screwed incorrectly to his arms. No conditions he'd ever played in before, not qualifying, not even the match with Travers at the Amateur, had prepared him for this. You needed a whole new panel of instruments to register the overwhelming barometric burden of U.S. Open pressure.

Eddie found the ball nestled down in high grass under the spreading branches of an immature pine. They sized up their unpromising options; Eddie did most of the talking.

"Hit a low runner," he said. "Keep it under the tree, try to advance a little. Get it back on the fairway."

Francis nodded, half-hearing, distracted, still not present. "Jigger," he said.

Eddie handed Francis his jigger, a low-lofted trouble club. He carefully assumed a contorted stance, folding himself in among the branches of the pine. A few rehearsals, backswing attenuated by the tree. Lacking confidence he could make this shot work, Francis pulled the trigger. In his anxiety to follow its flight, he looked up a fraction of a second too soon; half-topped, the ball skittered out from under the tree and settled just off the fairway in the first cut of rough. In two shots he'd advanced the ball a total of sixty yards off the tee.

"You hit that one on the forehead, Francis," said Eddie. "You gotta keep your head down."

"I know," said Francis.

They had over 300 yards left to the green and still had a long poke just to reach the elbow of the Polo Field's dogleg. Francis asked for his brassie and clobbered it, but the ball tailed right at the last and jackknifed into a bunker. A groan from the crowd. Francis heard them this time but he still wasn't completely back in his body. Keffer had reached the green in two, waiting patiently for Francis to catch up. He dug in his feet and blasted the ball out of the bunker and onto the front of the green, more than twenty feet from the hole. His first putt came up a foot short; Francis tapped in for a slack bogey six. Jaw tightening, he quietly handed the ball to Eddie as they walked toward the second tee.

"Let's try another one," said Francis.

Francis teed up the new ball Eddie gave him at the second, the short par four, Cottage. Eddie offered the mid-iron, trying to emphasize accuracy over distance, but Francis asked for his brassie. Eddie hesitated, considered insubordination, then handed over the brassie without comment; he still didn't like the remote, sunken look in Francis's eyes but chose not to say anything rash, hoping he wouldn't have to before Francis came back to himself.

He wasn't there yet. His brassie tee shot flew wide right, missing the fairway by twenty feet, caught a bad bounce, and careened to the right, putting a stand of trees between the ball and the green. His punched recovery shot came up short in a deep greenside bunker and his explosion out of the sand left him thirty-five feet from the cup, and then he three-putted. Double bogey six.

Disaster. Back-to-back brain lock. Two holes into the Open and Francis was already six strokes behind leader Johnny McDermott.

Francis's eyes flashed with anger at himself as they walked to the third tee. *Wake up, Francis!*

Okay; what is it I'm supposed to remember at times like this?

That damned soprano. Losing herself in the music. Letting it flow through her. Without trying.

Right; like there's some faucet in your head you just turn off and on . . .

Francis looked like a man having a hell of an argument with himself. "You want another ball?" asked Eddie.

"It's not the ball, Eddie," he said sharply. "It's me."

Now that he'd identified the guilty party, as he stood over his ball at the serpentine third, Francis felt sensation flow back into his hands and arms; he could feel again. Instead of stepping up and flailing away at the ball indiscriminately, this time his eyes selected a specific target—a small patch of fairway, barely visible, threaded between two tall, dangerous mounds—and once fixed there didn't wander, his mind remembering how to focus again. He made his best swing of the morning and found the short grass he'd been aiming for.

Better.

Two hundred and twenty yards left to the green, but instead of bouncing and running onto the green as he intended his long-iron approach to do, the ball took a bad hop into thick greenside rough. Francis chipped up from there to within ten feet and burned the edge of the hole with his par effort, then tapped in for a five—hardly a disaster on the difficult third, where par was probably closer to four and a half. Not exactly cause for rejoicing yet—he was four strokes over par after only three holes—but he sensed the spell of evil nerves had been broken. Francis felt his feet touching the grass, his thoughts cleared as if a storm had passed, the jitters vanished from his hands. The Open's trial by fire had scorched his mind and burned a hole in his confidence, but Francis knew he could play again. And if he wanted to climb out of this early grave he'd dug for himself and survive the tournament's first morning, he knew he had to start right now.

He would have to answer the question: What was he capable of?

Two-time Open champ Alex Smith followed Francis off the tee, then Louis Tellier began his quest for asylum in America at 10:40. Francis's old friend John Anderson followed two groups later, and the last large gallery of Thursday morning lined up around Ted Ray at 10:55. Unlike the gallant swagger he'd walked around with during his record round on Wednesday, Ted appeared tight and uncomfortable as he stepped to the tee. At Lord Northcliffe's urging, Bernard Darwin had doubled back from Vardon's gallery to watch Ray begin his morning's work. Ted thrilled his crowd by crushing his tee shot, but as he walked down the fairway inside the ropes alongside Darwin, he confided that he'd spent what was, for him, an unaccountably sleepless night.

"I'm afraid I played too much good golf yesterday," he said.

"You'll come around," said Darwin.

"No; I'm out of sorts."

His easy par at the testing Polo Field disputed that assessment, but he followed it with two straight bogeys. By then it was clear to anyone watching that Ted's customary trust in his driver, the master key to his whole game, had left town under cover of darkness. As one after another of his tee shots stubbornly refused to stay on the course, Ted's morning round would become a taut, trying ordeal, relying on guile and his deft touch to repair the damage done off the tee. The old pro had weathered the mysterious desertion of his big stick on countless occasions; Ted hunkered down and prepared to grind out a score until his stroke came home.

By the time Ted Ray reached the first green, little Wilfred Reid was already deep into his back nine. He made the turn at even par 38, playing the same watertight, low-risk game he'd exhibited during yesterday's late qualifying round. With a tenacity and resolve greater than any he'd displayed before in his professional career, Reid kept up his faultless quality of play throughout the back side as well. After a brief stumble, he strung together five straight pars at the finish to card 37 for his trip back in. Wilfred Reid, first player on and off the course on Thursday morning, established the early first-round lead with an outstanding 75.

Two groups later, the first dark horse hit the finish line. Walter Hagen concluded an action-packed even par back nine—three birdies, three pars, three bogeys—to pull two strokes ahead of Reid with a 73. When he stepped off the Home green and reporters abandoned Reid to flutter around the tournament's new first-round leader, Hagen followed the philosophy he'd developed to face any unfamiliar situation: *Act like you've been there before.* The press quickly realized that the fresh young swain from Rochester spewed quotable copy like the Tivoli fountain.

How did you put together such an outstanding round on such a difficult course? *It was either the course or me today, boys, and the course just sits there; I bet on me.* Did luck play much of a part in your score today? *Hey, without the breaks, a golfer is lost. With 'em, and the good Lord helping, he's damn near unbeatable.* (All deleted the *damn* for publication.)

His interview session turned out to be one of the longest of the morning. The spotlight had at last picked Walter Hagen out of the crowd and it liked what it saw, although every single reporter covering the event persisted in misspelling his name for at least one more day.

The day's first casualties began to hobble their way in: Jerry Travers, America's match play king, had staggered around in 78. His driver had forsaken him again with the predictability of a wayward lover in a delta blues standard. After running through more trees than a sawmill blade on the front nine, Jerry finally turned to his driving iron on the back. Only dropping a few putts from deep downtown had kept him from blowing up completely. Despite his impeccable Park Avenue outfit, Travers looked haggard and worn, gamely trying to order up a smile for the wall of reporters that faced him as he came off the eighteenth. Asked to explain his trials at The Country Club after recording such an easy victory at Garden City, Jerry politely went right to the heart of the matter. "This course is harder," he said.

Tom Vardon came in next with an 85, already dead, embalmed, and entombed. The kindest thing reporters could find to say about Tom, who over the years had become every bit the fashion plate as his older brother, was that when he came into the press tent after his round he looked "as fresh as if he'd stepped out of a bandbox." He smiled throughout his brief interview; no one had much to ask him except how he felt about his brother's chances, but he answered every question cheerfully. Vintage Tom Vardon; he shoots himself out of the first round of the Open, and he's still happy just to be there.

As he reached the turn in what had been, at best for him, an indifferent 39, Harry Vardon knew from the cheers he heard erupting behind him that John McDermott was making a run at him; through seven holes John had taken only twenty-seven strokes, three strokes ahead of Vardon's pace. Harry glanced back and caught a glimpse of McDermott from time to time, chin thrust out, strutting around to the cheers and delight of his home field boosters. Vardon looked over and caught a worried glance from Lord Northcliffe in his gallery—*Come on, then, time to get down to busi-*

ness, Harry. Vardonic smile. A reassuring, low-key shake of the hand from Harry.

Not to worry.

Harry had predicted to Ted Ray over breakfast that morning that McDermott would start hard and mount an early charge. Forget the way he'd played in qualifying, Harry said, this tough kid from Philly was a front-runner by hardwired nature. Harry had seen that in him at Shawnee when they were partnered together and knew his presence one group ahead would provide all the motivation McDermott needed to come out swinging.

Although his supreme self-containment made it seem as though Harry played only the course and his own ball, oblivious to what any opponents might be doing, no one in the game ever maintained a more acute awareness of where his opposition stood and how to answer. John McDermott was a one-speed sprinter, an intimidator who fed off his own success, but if he got knocked off his stride, Harry sensed he'd find it almost impossible to recover from a stumble. He also knew that all morning Johnny had been sending a platoon of young scouts ahead to keep him apprised of Harry's score, betraying his anxious preoccupation with how one other player was doing. The nine holes they were about to play made it clear that the long-range meta-strategist in Harry had allowed McDermott to run away with the Shawnee Open three weeks earlier for a reason, encouraging in him an overblown bubble of blind-eyed arrogance. McDermott's headlong sprint from the starting gate played perfectly into the scenario Harry had envisioned; no one could have been happier than Harry to have the man he considered his most dangerous adversary in the tournament playing directly behind him. McDermott had unknowingly run himself right into the teeth of a trap. As Harry stepped to the tenth tee, it was time to snare him and show the unstable young American champ exactly whom he was dealing with.

Harry had been able to draw on this ability throughout his prime, the singular skill that separated him from every other player in the world; when championship pressure began to mount, he could dig deeper into himself and mine pure gold. During practice rounds he had calculated that The Country Club's back nine not only played at least three strokes easier than the front, it was better suited to his game; now it was time to make his own first-round run. Harry held par at ten, made birdie at eleven, then recorded three straight pars over the side's most difficult stretch. He watched the message boys running back to McDermott with his score as he completed every hole, then heard from an excited Lord Northcliffe as he walked to fifteen that America's champion had begun to falter. A three-putt on ten. A double bogey on eleven. Harry poured it on—another birdie at fifteen, two more pars—while McDermott continued to deteriorate behind him; par, bogey, double bogey.

By the time Harry reached the final tee, McDermott's commanding early lead had shrunk from six shots down to two; now to administer the *coup de grace*. Just as Harry stepped up to hit his drive at eighteen, a flock of chickens ran across the tee; they may even have belonged to the Ouimets across the street. Harry stopped, doffed his hat, and waved them through with a bow; his relaxed, spontaneous response drew a big laugh from the crowd. His playing partner Tom Bonnar, who'd grown up on a farm, shooed the birds off the tee box while Harry waited. When the poultry cleared out, Harry crushed a sterling drive at eighteen, then stuck his approach twenty feet below the hole. Harry lined up that putt, gave it a solid thwack, and watched it run dead into the hole for a stiletto-thrust round-ending birdie. When the large crowd erupted and surged toward him, Harry immediately stepped forward and raised his hands to stop them in their tracks. Ever mindful of proper sportsmanship, he knew that Tom Bonnar, who had paradoxically faced the largest crowd of his life that morning while playing in complete obscurity, owed a two-foot putt to close out his round. Only when Bonnar had put it home—for a see-you-later 86; Bonnar would go on to finish next to last in the tournament—did Harry allow the crowd to resume their ovation. Harry had shot 36 on the home half of his morning round, equaling Hagen's low score on the back nine, for a total of 75, matching his best qualifying score and tying Wilfred Reid in second place behind the upstart Hagen.

McDermott struggled in right after him, running on fumes now, his face pinched and drawn by the ragged, ripsaw effort he'd expended. Johnny managed to save par at Home by sinking a fifteen-footer and he salvaged a 38 on the back, for a total of 74. He slipped into second place a shot ahead of Vardon and Reid, but the cost of his phenomenal 36 on the front to his nerves appeared damaging. John hurried through the mob of reporters toward the refuge of the locker room, avoiding the press tent and offering only monosyllabic responses to their barrage of questions. Harry, just starting his own gracious interviews outside the press tent, watched closely as McDermott retreated, pain and confusion bleeding through the defending champion's stone-faced mask.

The Vardonic smile appeared; Harry's trap had sunk its teeth into John McDermott with ruthless efficiency.

There was a good deal more than disappointment with his golf behind Johnny's high-strung, antisocial behavior that day. America's paranoid champ had not shared the bad news he harbored with anyone, not even his parents with whom he still lived. Over the course of the previous few weeks McDermott had suffered devastating losses in the stock market; his entire savings from the last two years had nearly been erased. Johnny needed a third straight win in the U.S. Open for reasons a lot more pragmatic than national pride. After escaping a lifetime of poverty, and two years spent at the pinnacle of success, McDermott once again found himself back down at square one, in a struggle just to survive.

As the middle of the pack completed their first rounds, two transplanted Scotsmen with immortal pedigrees tossed their hats into the ring. Thirty-two-year-old Alec Ross, the son of a stonemason from the remote northern Highlands of Scotland, had emigrated to the States in 1904 with his older brother Donald, former pro and greenkeeper at the legendary Royal Dornoch links and a protégé of Old Tom Morris. While Alec found immediate success as a playing professional, winning the 1907 U.S. Open, Donald's indifferent record as a player led him to abandon his playing career early. The game profited: Donald Ross would go on to become arguably America's greatest course architect, designing over 300 courses, Pinehurst, Interlachen, and Oak Hill among them. One of his earliest designs, Brae Burn in suburban Boston, had by 1910 become his brother Alec's employer and home course. On Thursday morning, after a nothing-special 39 on the front side, Alec Ross ate The Country Club's back nine for breakfast. He missed a hole in one by inches on the par three tenth, settling for a kick-in birdie. After parring the treacherous eleventh, he nailed his approach shot on the 415-yard twelfth within six feet and drained the putt for a second birdie, and then followed it with a third at the thirteenth. A bogey at the short sixteenth was his only misstep en route to a phenomenal 32 on his trip back in, at which point Alec Ross had wrested the lead from Hagen and tied The Country Club's four-year-old scoring record by shooting 71.

Following him shortly thereafter, Macdonald Smith, twenty-two, youngest of the accomplished Carnoustie clan and last to reach the United States, completed his first round with an equally brilliant, albeit more balanced 71. Mac Smith had recently settled in Westchester, New York, after beginning his career in California, and he possessed the most admired swing this side of Harry Vardon. Even at his tender age, he had already experienced the rarefied air of championship altitudes, finishing third in the 1910 Open's three-way play-off to his older brother Alex and Johnny McDermott. Great achievements had been predicted for Mac ever since; his appearance at the top of the first-round leader board elicited no surprise from any savvy student of the game. (Years later no less an authority and lifelong student of the game than Bing Crosby, himself an exceptional amateur player, voiced his opinion that Macdonald Smith owned the greatest swing of all time.)

Nor had the last of the homebreds been heard from. Determined on his home turf to close out the Open win that had so narrowly eluded him during the last few years, Boston native Tom McNamara had an equally effective first round going through the front nine. A solid, steady player who always managed to hang around in big tournaments until something strange happened to him, he had only just started his bad luck in majors with the heatstroke that ruined his chances in the last nine holes of the 1909 Open. After being penalized by the bizarre rules infraction involving his partner's caddie during Tuesday's qualifying round, Tom felt certain he'd already put this year's misfortune behind him. Wrong.

On the par three tenth, Tom sent a gorgeous iron shot tracking dead for the pin; it landed two feet away. And plugged, buried almost below ground level. Believe it or not, in 1913 no rule providing any relief for his dilemma was on the USGA's books, nor would there be for another forty-seven years. Forced to disinter it as it lay, Tom wasted a stroke excavating the ball, using his mashie like a clam digger. He played an amazing shot

THE GREATEST GAME EVER PLAYED | 266

under the circumstances, his ball now sitting neatly on the green a mere eighteen inches below the hole, but it was half-encrusted in a thick capsule of mud. However, the USGA rule allowing him to lift, clean, and replace his ball didn't exist yet either. Tom tried to bang it into the hole to save his par, but its nimbus of muck sent the ball lurching off line like a lush on a moving sidewalk. Instead of the birdie that would and should have been his score, Tom wrote down a bogey four.

If McNamara wasn't yet 100 percent certain he'd been cursed, the short par four thirteenth, Maiden, settled the matter. After a perfect drive, Tom sent another sensational iron shot high and straight at the flagstick. It landed heavily just short of the hole, kicked up a massive pitch mark, then promptly spun a foot backward. McNamara had left himself a gimme three-foot putt, straight uphill, for his birdie three. But the sizeable crater his ball had created on landing lay directly between the ball and the hole. And you guessed it—no rule yet existed allowing him to repair that massive divot before attempting his putt. After determining he couldn't avoid the pitch mark with his putter, Tom creatively decided to chip the ball over his own divot into the hole. He missed, settling for par instead of the sure-thing birdie he deserved. Despite this uncanny string of mishaps that might have broken a weaker man, Tom kept up his outstanding play and finished his morning round in 73, pulling into a tie with Walter Hagen for third place. Played under the more compassionate USGA rules in place today, tough-luck Tom McNamara would have been in first place, alone, having broken The Country Club's scoring record with a 70.

IN HIS SHORT life Eddie Lowery had watched Francis play a total of two complete rounds of golf and one sixth of a third—some good, some indifferent, today's first three holes appalling—but he'd never seen him catch fire. By 11:30 on Thursday morning, word filtered back to them through the gallery grapevine that a number of players ahead were posting lower scores than those seen through either day of qualifying. Eddie realized that if Francis maintained this current level of ineptitude, it wouldn't be long before the entire field lapped him and Eddie would be right back in West Newton Falls Elementary School. He rummaged through his limited catalog of life experience for the right piece of advice.

"Okay, we just gotta settle down now, Francis," he said. "What are we gonna do to turn this around?"

In every competitive round, in every tournament that begins to slip away, a player finds himself at a final point of no return; he either reverses course or kisses his chances good-bye. Francis Ouimet had just felt his back bump against that wall, and he didn't have to turn around to read the writing on it. The way he responded now would determine the course of the rest of his life.

Francis looked at Eddie and smiled. "I guess I'm just going to have to play better," he said.

"That'd be a good place to start," said Eddie.

As they reached the fourth hole, Eddie noticed a change come over Francis. He walked to the next tee up on his toes again. An outgoing intensity in his eyes replaced the hollow reserve with which he'd started the day. He set up to the ball with a more upright angle to his spine. The difference was subtle, unnoticeable to anyone who hadn't been watching him acutely, but profound. To Eddie's eyes, Francis looked like a different man.

And then he killed his tee shot. Stuck his approach on the green. Two-putted for par, his first of the day. The same at five, then six, picking up momentum as his pace of play increased. The forward lean came back into his stride. He smiled again and radiated purpose. The wise words of Vardon echoed through him; Francis wasted no energy in the niceties of social lubrication with playing partner Karl Keffer. Eddie hardly said a word to him beyond his mantric "keep your head down," sensing anything more wouldn't even penetrate the force field Francis had around him now.

Francis's swing still hadn't fallen into the effortless free-swinging ease he'd found when at his best that summer, but there were more ways to get around a golf course than sheer unconscious brilliance. To survive the morning he would have to play a blue-collar grinder's round, working for every shot, each par a product of sweat, desire, and tenacity. The crowd adored him for it. His younger sister Louise and brother Raymond had been part of the gallery all morning. They found watching Francis in his element out here an eye-opener, deeply thrilling in a way they could hardly comprehend; apparently the guileless, happy boy they'd known all their lives possessed a secret, heroic identity. Many of the people around them, even those without a clue about the game of golf, sensed something special at work in the air. They watched Francis execute a crisp up and down for a par three at the short seventh, the same at eight, then another workingman's par at nine. He made the turn in 41, without wasting a single stroke beyond those three he'd squandered at the start.

As Francis scrambled to stay in the game, his concentration and poise remained absolute. If he didn't have command of his complete repertoire, there was no question Francis had the right look. Vardon had just finished his round when Francis moved to the tenth tee. As word that young Ouimet had it going again shot through the crowd, people eager for an American favorite to follow were drawn out from the clubhouse. Eddie estimated that their crowd had increased by at least 300 people since they started. Francis didn't notice.

Like most of the men in the field, Francis played better at a brisk pace. The era's prevailing style differed wildly from the calculated, plodding rate of play of today's pro tour. Players reached their ball, sized up their situation almost at a glance, and took a swing at it. Club selection was more intuitive than mechanical, less dependent on precise distance calculation, which was often just a rough guess back then. They trusted their eyes, not a yardage book. Players only rarely analyzed putts from every conceivable angle. The average round in 1913's U.S. Open lasted three and a half hours. Impatient players like Ted Ray got around in less than three.

Francis's steady march continued through the back nine. He regained one of the shots he'd wasted at the start with a birdie at the par five fourteenth, but gave it away again with his only slip of the inward journey; at the par three sixteenth his tee shot caught the high lip of the front bunker. On in two from there, two putts for a bogey four. Instead of berating himself, Francis took a series of deep breaths as they strode over to the seventeenth tee. They stopped and waited for the fairway ahead to clear; Eddie noticed Francis staring through the stand of beech trees toward his house across Clyde Street. Whatever Francis saw or thought about appeared to center him back in his diligent, economic sense of purpose.

Without a word Francis smashed his tee shot past the treacherous bunker guarding the dogleg on the left, leaving a short-iron into the two-tiered green, in the opinion of many the most difficult on the course. Two putts for par. One hole to go. When Francis reached the eighteenth, he encountered the largest gallery he'd seen in his life stretched out along the fairway nearly all the way to the green.

"That," said Eddie, "is a big crowd."

Francis didn't even look at them. He put his drive in the fairway, found the green with his approach, and took two putts for his four. The crowd saluted him; Francis basked in it, with relief and exhilaration. After a careening, spendthrift start, in his first official U.S. Open round, Francis had played the last fifteen holes at dead-even par to finish with 77. Posting the second best round of the morning among the field's twenty-three amateurs—New York's Fred Herreshoff bested him by two—Francis was still six strokes off the lead, but definitely back in the hunt.

Shortly after Francis turned in his score at the USGA's tent, Frenchman Louis Tellier reached the first quarter pole of his American dream in promising fashion. Playing the same cautious, shotmaker's style favored by his brother-in-law Wilfred Reid—a style often rewarded by cramped U.S. Open layouts—the little Frenchman came in at 76. His work didn't stop when he left the golf course. Even more important to his long-term ambitions, Louis's clever, ingratiating personality had already gained him a number of fans among The Country Club's elite.

As the first round drew toward its close, the exertions of McDermott, McNamara, Mac Smith, Alec Ross, Walter Hagen, and Francis Ouimet gave the resurgent American cause renewed reason for hope. A strong 74 from Long Jim Barnes, a 75 from 1909's Open champion George Sargent, and a 72 from unknown homebred pro Jack Croke added late reinforcement. By one o'clock, when Wilfred Reid once again stepped to the tee to lead off the day's second round, all eyes had shifted to the last British ship afloat in the first, and found another reason to like America's chances.

Ted Ray's early prophecy to Darwin about having used all his good shots the day before had become self-fulfilling. Missing fairways and putts with equal abandon, he ended up playing the worst golf of his entire stay in Boston. Out of sorts and struggling with his emotions, the big man's habitually fair mood turned foul. The heat bothered him. Inept marshals shouted through their megaphones during his backswing. The rowdy partisan crowd got under his skin. His less than accomplished American playing partner's painfully deliberate pace compounded all the other irritations. The Jerseyman's temper sent up a darker plume of smoke than his ever-present pipe when he double bogeyed the ninth and missed a three-footer at eleven and a two-footer at twelve. He threw away an easy chance for birdie at fifteen, bogeyed sixteen, then finally scraped together a couple of pars at the finish. Instead of mixing with the crowd as he had after Wednesday's finish, Ted stormed away from the eighteenth green, toweled off in the locker room, and grabbed a beer and a sandwich at the players' complimentary concession stand. A reporter who had found him a cooperative interview throughout the week, eager to ask about his effort between rounds, steered clear after Ted growled he wasn't interested in rehashing what he'd just been through. "What's done is done," he said. Another writer caught him as he left the locker room and made the mistake of telling Ted that his 79 had placed him eight strokes behind the leaders.

"Then I'll just have to shoot seventy now to make up for it, won't I?" said Ted. "Maybe I'll just bow down to the ball whenever it won't go where I want it to, try to win back its respect that way. What do you think?"

The writer stammered, wilted, and withdrew. Bernard Darwin passed the man as he approached to conduct his own interview, sized up the stormy weather swirling around Ted, and knew well enough to give him a wide berth; Darwin made a quick course correction toward a lemonade stand. Even a hand-wringing Lord Northcliffe, hovering nearby, dying to offer some unsolicited inspiration to his discouraged star, chose the better part of valor and left Ted alone to brood.

The morning's last player, Herbert Strong, a thirty-four-year-old expatriate English professional from Inwood Country Club in Far Rockaway, New York, forced to play alone because of the odd number of men in the field, didn't finish his first round until just before three o'clock. Posting a solid 75, Strong added an exclamation point to the Americans' early assault on The Country Club. Of the homebred favorites, only Mike Brady, the third leg of the American triumvirate, had failed to answer the bell, shooting a messy 83.

Joy abounded; Americans dominated the first-round leader board, not a

British challenger in sight until Reid and Vardon, tied for seventh. Ted Ray, tied for twenty-ninth way back in the pack, might have shot himself out of the running already. The Country Club crowd sizzled with patriotic fervor. The goal that only last night had seemed impossible now appeared shockingly within reach. As they passed one another going in and out to refresh and prepare during the idle hour before their second rounds, the home-breds huddled in the locker room, quietly congratulating each other. Francis beamed his megawatt smile, ecstatic to discover his fellow players felt he was holding up his end. Hagen worked the room like an alderman at an ice cream social, pumping everyone up, exhorting them to do it again that afternoon, keep the pressure on. For practitioners of a lonely sport, not one of them could remember experiencing such powerful feelings of solidarity. Even gloomy John McDermott got caught up in the excitement; he whispered to someone that this might shape up to be Shawnee all over again. Yankee expectations had reached their high-water mark.

Reality was about to come calling. By evening the soaring afternoon spirits of The Country Club locker room would be a distant memory. Wilfred Reid doused the first cold water on the Americans' prospects. While most of them were still congratulating themselves in the locker room, Reid was already back out on the course, restating his own case for the championship. The pudding-faced little man many had dismissed as a fop earlier in the week showed unexpected backbone on Thursday afternoon. When Lord Northcliffe heard of Reid's success later that day, he grabbed Bernard Darwin to say: "England is damn lucky to have Wilfred in the field." Darwin chose not to share with his boss what he already knew about Reid's plans; that he was playing strictly for personal ambition, not national pride, and that if he did pull off a victory, chances were the trophy would be staying in America with him.

In both of Thursday's rounds Reid took on the role of the "rabbit" to perfection, running out to an early lead and posting numbers that tested the resolve of the players behind him. Never a long driver, he recognized his limits and kept the ball in play off the tee, relying on a deadly short game to offset his shortcomings. Sinking six putts of over ten feet in length kept him out of trouble, and he didn't miss a short one all afternoon. In other words, he followed the now familiar formula for modern success in an Open. A model of plodding consistency, Wilfred Reid shot 36–36 for a two under par 72, and a total of 147 on the day, putting up the first score everyone else would have to shoot for.

With few notable exceptions, one of sports' ugliest words sums up the collective American effort on Thursday afternoon: *choke*. Compound the game's inherent difficulty with testing championship conditions and it usually guarantees any given player in a major tournament will turn in one lackluster performance out of four. During the noon hour on Thursday no one at The Country Club in their worst imagining would have bet that nearly every single American contender was about to play his lousiest round on the same afternoon. The reasons are hard to decipher but some group psychology may have been at work. More comfortable in the role of the underdog, too much early success seemed to rob the homebreds of their daring. As if playing to protect a first-round lead they didn't fully believe they deserved, like shoplifters caught red-handed, one after another they went out for their second round and handed it right back.

Nearing the conclusion of a sturdy front nine, Walter Hagen stumbled first, set off by an uncharacteristic loss of nerve. After a great drive he had a chance to go for the green on the 520-yard ninth in two, but elected to lay up short and pulled his timid approach into the woods. He recovered for a bogey six, finishing the front nine only one over par, but self-doubt had corkscrewed its way into the bank vault that served as his brain. Hagen didn't suffer any spectacular meltdowns, but his confidence bled slowly out of him during the back nine as if he'd opened a vein, resulting in a string of careless late bogeys. Walter limped home with a four over par 40 and followed his brilliant morning 73 with a disappointing 78, landing him four strokes in back of Wilfred Reid. He may have affected the easy manner of a riverboat gambler, but inside Hagen beat the competitive heart of a lion. Even at this stage in his career, as far as Walter was concerned there was no such thing as second place. After putting a carefree spin on his lackluster round for the press ("It's the same course for everybody, boys; we'll get 'em tomorrow"), Hagen retreated to the locker room and nearly put his fist through a wall.

The weather added another complication, gradually heating up throughout the afternoon, humidity rising steadily along with the mercury.

The air turned as oppressive as the developing tension. The second round now became a test of stamina as well as nerve. National amateur champion Jerry Travers headed into his second consecutive eighteen holes of stroke play with all the eagerness of a condemned man facing the gallows. Despite leading another fervent, loyal gallery, Jerry played an identically hapless afternoon of golf, matching his mediocre first-round 78. Only two rounds into the Open and America's early favorite trailed Wilfred Reid by nine shots.

The three brightest surprises of America's big morning turned in equally sour second efforts; Mac Smith blew out all four tires with a horrendous 44 on the front. After slapping himself around at the turn, he recorded a flawless 35 on the back. Smith's line: 71–79, for 150, three strokes behind Reid. Following the same pattern, Alec Ross went Smith one blown shot better; 45 on the front, 35 on the back for an 80, four strokes back. To no one's surprise, after he jumped in front with his out-of-left-field 72 Thursday morning, unknown early contender Jack Croke sank back into obscurity with an 83. He would not be heard from again. At the midway point of Thursday afternoon's round, half of the first-round's American leaders had already fallen by the wayside.

Sandwiched between that flailing trio of Americans, Harry Vardon put in a routinely splendid afternoon's work at the office. Far too seasoned to believe any of the glowing assessments people continually wrote or said about him, Harry remained equally disinterested by predictions of his imminent demise. The name of the game was golf and they awarded trophies and prize money after four rounds, not one. Harry played the same unruffled, Olympian style he'd been turning out professionally since most of these upstart Americans were wearing short pants at school. Despite two more butchered three-foot putts on the back, Harry shot 37–35 for 72. By the end of his day he had leapfrogged the six Americans ahead of him and pulled even with Wilfred Reid at 147 for the halfway lead.

Following in Harry's wake for the second time that day produced a starkly different effect on young John McDermott. Vardon had stood directly in front of Johnny that morning, absorbed his best knockout punch, and never flinched. Although he began the second round with a one-stroke lead over the focus of his wrath, McDermott knew his usual style of blitzkrieg and bullying had failed. This Harry Vardon was not the same man he'd beaten three weeks ago at Shawnee, and as Thursday afternoon unfolded, it become clear Johnny didn't have a Plan B.

After playing even through the first four holes, at the par four fifth Johnny reached the green in two, fifteen feet from the flag, then needed four putts to get down, the last two from inside a foot. From that point onward, Johnny's vitriol reversed course; instead of raging against Harry, the English, and the world, it splashed back on himself. No one living with his precarious emotional balance could be expected to muster such a demanding game under that kind of strain. As his round slipped away from him, McDermott felt compelled to take more chances. When they didn't pay off, the anger pick-axed deeper into his mind, affecting his judgment. He barked at himself after errant shots, slammed clubs into the ground, tossed one at a tree, anything to shock himself out of his restive agitation. His tee shots still flew off line and the putts wouldn't drop. He finished the afternoon with back-to-back bogeys for an ugly 79, leaving him six strokes in back of Vardon and Reid.

Mentally and emotionally spent as he walked off the eighteenth green, McDermott caught a glimpse of the elegant, immaculately groomed Harry, pipe in hand, addressing a cluster of reporters near the press tent; the sight drove Johnny straight to the locker room. He refused to be interviewed for the second time that day and wouldn't even speak to the other players. McDermott sat slumped in front of his locker for half an hour, motionless, hands pressed to his forehead, as if trying to prevent the unthinkable from bursting out of his skull. Shortly afterward he left The Country Club for his hotel in Boston without having said a word about his day to anyone.

Amateur champion Jerry Travers dragged himself back to the clubhouse after another sweaty 78. Nine strokes behind the leaders after two rounds of an Open is still considered within reach, but Jerry knew by now he didn't have his swing this week; his hopes had been transferred to the critical ward. Massachusetts's top pro Mike Brady gamely mounted a second-round comeback, shooting a 74, and pulled himself onto the outer shores of those within striking distance, ten strokes off the lead. On the way up, Brady passed compatriot Tom McNamara, who was taking the express elevator down. His level of play finally matching his rotten luck, Tom shot a disastrous 86 and walked off to pack his championship ambitions into mothballs for another year. Soon afterward, one of the only American pros to answer the call to arms Thursday afternoon flashed a preview of the championship form he would show in years to come; Long Jim Barnes posted a 76 to join Mac Smith in second place. George Sargent, 1909's Open champion, also came in with 76, a stroke behind Barnes and Smith, to tie Alec Ross for third.

Francis's fellow Massachusetts amateurs both saw their hopes short-circuited by day's end. Heinrich Schmidt trailed the leaders by nineteen after the second round; he would not survive the cut. Schmidt spent the rest of the Open fulfilling his journalistic obligations full-time. Although Anderson would easily have made the final day's field, after finishing his second round thirteen strokes in back of the lead, John chose to withdraw from the tournament, citing pressing business reasons. Those reasons become apparent under scrutiny: After realizing he had no realistic chance to win, his reporter's instincts told him a story might be in the offing that deserved his complete attention. Playing two groups behind Francis Ouimet, John had watched his young friend play a remarkable second round.

After his lunch break in the locker room, Francis moved to the first tee box again shortly after three o'clock. No final second-round scores had yet been posted at the clubhouse; he and Eddie went off unaware that so many Americans ahead of them had jumped off the rails. Intent on nothing other than avoiding a repeat of the morning's early stumble, Francis stepped up to his ball and felt that lightness and ease of vision come over him. As he made his practice swing, he already knew where the shot was going. It landed within a foot of the spot he'd seen in his mind.

This is going to be good, thought Francis.

This is the round, thought Eddie, *when he shoots 72*.

This was the same Francis who had emerged that summer, the one who'd torn Wollaston apart on his way to winning the Massachusetts Amateur, the one who'd battled Travers toe-to-toe at Garden City. Francis birdied Polo Field, recorded an easy par at the second, then birdied the third and fourth. Over the first four holes he had improved on his first-round performance by six strokes. It didn't stop there; he ripped through the next four holes in one over, then completed the treacherous front nine with another birdie for a two under par 36. Lightning in a bottle.

"This kid's for real," Eddie heard someone in the gallery say after he sank a ten-footer at nine.

"You bet he is," said Eddie under his breath.

As players ahead began to wrap up the day's work, their caddies refrained from the usual after-round caddie shack imbibements to rush out to the back nine and join Francis's gallery. The Country Club boys moved as a pack, the savviest fans on the course, almost all of them his former colleagues. As Francis kept up his inspired performance, they led the cheers. For a group of struggling blue-collar kids and rootless young men kicking around the margins of the game, Francis's quest meant more than a fantasy come true; for the first time in its history one of their own was holding his own in their national championship. They meant just as much to Francis, too; he knew how bleak life looked from that dead end of the street. Caddies were the game's lowest caste, some of them little more than pack animals, beasts of burden often abused by their masters. Most had come from nothing and were going nowhere, despite their big talk and fancy pipe dreams. If he did nothing else in this tournament, maybe he could give them something to believe in, show them there was a way out if you worked hard enough. Hope personified, Francis led them down the back nine's fairways as proudly as the Pied Piper. He negotiated the side's most fearsome stretch—twelve through fifteen—in one over par. He came to the course's easiest hole, the short par three sixteenth, trailing Vardon and Reid by only two strokes, the closest any American had been to the British leaders in the last two hours.

The sixteenth hole, Clyde, tucks into a corner near the Clyde Street entrance, tee pointed away from the clubhouse. One hundred and twenty-five yards, par three, the least demanding hole on the entire course. A large bunker front and right protects a forward flag, but on this day the pin was middle left, the most accessible position on the green. The only real danger lay beyond the green; out of bounds five steps off the dance floor. Waiting for the group ahead to putt out, Frances noticed his brother and sister in the gallery, who both called out to him, urging him on. Then as he stood on the tee, his eye drifted beyond the green toward his house, visible through the beech trees to the right. There a less comforting sight caught his eye; the small figure of his father arriving home from work across the street, 200 yards away. Standing on the front porch, Arthur turned and looked toward the sixteenth. Francis couldn't be sure if his father knew he was there—he was too far away to read any expression on his face. No matter. Eddie didn't see Arthur, didn't know the first thing about the intimate damage Francis's father was capable of inflicting, but he noticed a lapse in concentration. The sun had gone behind the clouds. Francis's eyes dulled. Eddie pulled the mashie from the bag and offered it to him.

"Keep your head down," said Eddie. "I'll watch the ball."

Francis took longer than usual settling over the ball, the footwork and rhythm of his pre-shot routine looked ragged to Eddie, disjointed. Francis paused, looked down at the club in his hand as if second-guessing the choice, then made the swing with nowhere near the necessary full commitment. The ball arced high and looked for a moment as if it would land softly on the front of the green; then, just as his tee shot had that morning, the ball caught the high banked front corner of the bunker. This time it plugged in its entry point, nosing down into the sand nearly out of sight.

Francis inspected his lie. This was twenty years before the invention of the dedicated sand wedge, tooled to smoothly slice through and under sand. The only solution for a buried sand lie like this was to hood closed a mashie, blast down at the ball, and pray it popped out, a shot almost impossible to control. Francis tried this now. The ball did emerge from its tomb but hit the high lip of the trap and dribbled back into the sand again. Now desperate to get the ball close to the pin and salvage a bogey, he opened up the blade of the mashie, laid it flat, and hit a conventional explosion shot in the sand two inches behind the ball. The ball flew high out of the bunker, too high, and settled twelve feet short of the pin. Francis took his time lining it up, but the putt refused to fall. Double bogey five. Four strokes in back of the leaders.

"Forget that now, it's over with," said Eddie to Francis as they walked to the next tee.

"That's right," said Francis.

"Two holes to go," said Eddie. "Champions finish strong." He'd read that somewhere.

"One shot at a time, Eddie," said Francis.

"You said it," said Eddie, taking out the driver.

Francis resisted the impulse to look over at his house again, even closer in view now at the seventeenth tee, trying to find a way back to his swing: *Think, Francis, think. What do you do when your emotions run away with you? What do you focus on?*

I know this course. Better than anyone out here. I know the correct way to play every hole. I know the bounces and rolls of the fairways, the tricks the wind plays as it dives through the trees. I've watched this hole out my bedroom window since I was four years old.

"Driver here," said Francis.

Eddie handed him the club he was already holding.

"Right side, away from the trap," said Francis.

"That sounds good," said Eddie.

Francis slowed down his swing as he practiced on the tee, then placed his drive exactly in the fairway's right center, avoiding the deep trap protecting the dogleg. They walked out to the ball, a good lie, 170 yards from the green.

"Mashie," said Francis as they looked it over.

"Keep it below the hole," said Eddie.

Francis stood over the ball, saw the shot in his mind, then made it happen; a solid long-iron approach that landed just short, ran up onto the green, and stopped well below the hole. Mindful of not running his first putt past the hole for a downhill leave, he lagged up just short, then tapped in for his par. His gallery cheered long and loud. He followed this steady formula at eighteen for another safe and sure par four, and moved into the crowd's welcoming embrace. Francis ended his second round with an even par 74, tying Alec Ross, Walter Hagen, and George Sargent in fifth place at 151.

"Sorry, Eddie," said Francis, after they cleared the crowd. "If I hadn't slipped up at sixteen, I would have had your seventy-two."

"Don't worry," said Eddie. "We'll get it tomorrow."

Of the few contenders left on the course, Louis Tellier kept France's and his own hopes very much alive with a 76 to match his morning effort. His sturdy second round once again passed all but unnoticed. Shrieks and hollers had been issuing from the trees behind him for hours, attracting all the spectators within earshot. They were being treated to quite a show; three groups behind Tellier a freight train named Ted Ray had been tearing up the course all afternoon.

After fulminating for an hour between rounds, Ted walked to the first tee loaded for bear. A scowl on his face, pipe smoking hot, when Ted killed his first drive and set out down the fairway, he took along a gallery that some observers estimated at over 6,000 people. With the burning look in his eye of a mad visionary leading his flock to the promised land, Ted slipped off the gloves and punched The Country Club in the face. He hit the Polo Field's green in two and two-putted for birdie. He nearly drove the green at the inviting second, chipped on, and then sank a thirty-footer for birdie. At the sixth he chipped into the cup from the light rough off the fringe for his third birdie of the second round, and missed a fourth by a fraction of an inch at seven. Six pars, three birdies; Ted Ray made the turn in 35, the lowest score anyone had posted on the course's front nine in its twenty-year history.

As word spread around The Country Club, people peeled away from every player still out on the course and rushed to see what the giant Jerseyman was doing to the U.S. Open. They would not be disappointed. Ted parred ten and eleven and then launched a skyrocket drive on the 415-yard twelfth that flew over the crowd, the dogleg, the bunkers, and the trees, leaving him in the middle of the fairway only 110 yards from the green. His niblick shot flew straight at the flag and settled ten feet away. He walked up to his ball, took one quick look, and drilled the putt for an eagle three.

Talk crackled through the crowd that Ted looked like a safe bet to break the course record of 71—he might even break 70 while he was at it; unheard of! During the course of his assault, along with his game Ted also retrieved his sense of humor. Whenever a makeable putt refused to fall, as he'd sarcastically suggested to the reporter between his rounds, Ted took off his hat and bowed down to the ball. He played so brilliantly, it only happened twice, but each time the crowd loved it. As Ted reached the thirteenth tee, Harry Vardon walked out to join Northcliffe and Bernard Darwin in his gallery. After watching Ted slaughter his drive and chase after it as if he were still mad at the ball, Harry said dryly: "I see Ted's woken up."

Would he break the record? Ted secured his par at thirteen, jumped all over another drive at the reachable par five fourteenth, but came up just short on his approach. After a bump and run chip ran through the green, he had to settle for an up and down par. He gave himself another chance for birdie at fifteen but ran a twenty-footer four feet by the hole and then missed the comebacker, his first and only unforced mistake of the entire afternoon. Ted didn't blow up; he took his hat off again and offered another mock salute to the ball, then tapped for bogey, which earned him his biggest ovation of the day. With three holes left to play, Ted needed one more birdie to break 70. He wouldn't give himself another reasonable opportunity, after two more pars, until the eighteenth.

Four hundred and ten yards of rope packed with spectators lined the last fairway. They exploded when another tape-measure drive and pinpoint approach left Ted five feet directly below the hole, in perfect position to record an unprecedented 69. Members crammed the porches and balconies of the clubhouse looking down on the Home hole. The crowd surged forward to surround the green ten people deep. Ted let his partner hole out, then took what for him seemed like an eternity—nearly a minute—examining the line. He settled over the ball and finally made his stroke. The putt tracked right for the hole, wobbled at the end, and missed by a hairsbreadth to the right, hanging on the lip. Ted waited for it to fall; it didn't. He tapped in with genuine disgust.

Ted Ray had just broken The Country Club's scoring record, under U.S. Open pressure, and in one great leap vaulted from also-ran twenty-ninth into sole second place, trailing Harry and Wilfred Reid by only two strokes. And he was fighting mad about it. If "Never despair" was Harry's motto, Ted's might be best summed up as "Never satisfied." In the interviews he granted afterward, all Ted wanted to talk about was how poorly he played in his morning round or his deep disappointment at missing that easy last putt and failing to break 70; as usual, he'd known exactly where his score stood. For the discouraged Americans who had fallen by the wayside that afternoon he offered a priceless demonstration of what it was going to take to win this or any championship. Most of the players who had finished earlier had already left the grounds for the day; they missed the lesson. Francis, watching Ted's final putt and its aftermath from the clubhouse porch with Jerry Travers and John Anderson, grasped it instantly.

"He's mad at himself," said Francis. "For shooting seventy."

"Hell of a player," said Anderson.

"He's not going to be easy to beat," said Travers.

"From what I'm gathering here, Jerry," said Francis, "I don't think it's supposed to be easy."

Former American amateur champion Fred Herreshoff came in just after Ray, shooting 78 to finish the day at 153, leaving Francis as the low amateur in the Open. Then a solitary figure followed five minutes later, without a soul in the greater Boston area paying him the slightest attention: Herbert Strong from Inwood Country Club in New York, once again playing alone as the last man in the field, followed his morning 75 with an outstanding even par 74. Once Strong turned in his card to the recorder's tent, here is how the first day's final results were posted outside the clubhouse:

Wilfred Reid	75–72—147	
Harry Vardon	75–72—147	
Edward Ray	79–70—149	
Herbert Strong	75–74—149	
Mac Smith	71–79—150	
Jim Barnes	74–76—150	
Francis Ouimet	77–74—151	
Alec Ross	71–80—151	
George Sargent	75–76—151	
Walter Hagen	73–78—151	
Louis Tellier	76–76—152	
John McDermott	74–79—153	

After huddling in the scorer's tent, USGA president Robert Watson and his senior committee members announced that they had decided once again to trim the field before the final day's action. Any player more than fifteen strokes removed from tenth place—the cut line falling just where it had during qualifying, at 165—would not be invited to take part on Friday. Twelve more men banished. Six additional players near the back of the pack withdrew, John Anderson among them. On the tournament's final day only 49 out of the 169 who began on Tuesday would compete for the U.S. Open trophy.

Although Jerry Travers, Mike Brady, Alex Smith, and Tom McNamara had survived the final cut, few now expected them to be there at the end. In their private exchanges, not many fans or journalists realistically believed any players in the group from Herbert Strong to John McDermott would be much of a factor either. Class was beginning to tell, and the three British invaders had risen to the top with a chilling aura of inevitability. Judging by their headlong retreat back down the leader board, the Americans appeared to have already surrendered the field to them.

As their last official act of the day the USGA announced their random pairings for Friday's final two rounds. After nearly bringing up the rear on Thursday, Ted Ray would lead off at 8:45 with Mike Brady. Harry was slated to play in the day's fifth twosome at 9:05, with Walter Hagen to follow immediately after. John McDermott drew the eighth group. Barnes, Tellier, and Reid would go out in the middle of the pack; Tellier drew Tom Vardon as his partner. Mac Smith and Alec Ross had been paired together at 10:15. Francis once again found his name deep in the field, the fourth twosome from the last, at 11:00 sharp, paired with fellow contender and former Open champ George Sargent. Against all odds, Herbert Strong again drew the short straw; he would tee off as the last man and play alone for the second consecutive day at 11:15.

After Francis changed his shoes and prepared to walk home with Eddie, a senior Country Club member approached him outside the locker room.

"Congratulations, Francis," the man said. "You played marvelously today. We've so enjoyed watching you."

"Thank you, sir." Francis used to caddie for the man.

"Wonderful display," he said, then lowered his voice. "And you've made your point. We were thinking that perhaps it would be best to quit now."

"Excuse me?"

"You've shown everyone how well you can play. The sporting thing to do now is step aside, don't you think? Let the pros have a go at it for the money. It's their game after all."

"I'm only four strokes behind," said Francis.

"All the better. Leave the field with honor. Dignity intact, if you get my meaning."

Francis felt his face flush red. He couldn't believe what he was hearing, but the last thing he wanted now was to lose his temper.

"Are you drunk?" Eddie asked the man.

"Excuse me, sonny?"

Francis held up a hand, silencing his little caddie, then turned to the man himself.

"I don't think you understand," said Francis. "I'm in this to the end. As far as I can go. I made a promise. To Mr. Watson and the USGA. That's what I said I was going to do when they asked me—"

"Fine, fine," said the man, equally eager to avoid a confrontation.

"And as far as honor goes, I honor my promises—"

"Indeed. As well you should, as well you should," said the man, backing away now, with a wave of the hand. "Just a suggestion."

"Thank you for your concern, sir," said Francis.

"Not at all. All the best to you." The man turned and hurried away.

"The nerve of that guy," said Eddie, watching him with slits for eyes.

"Let's go," said Francis.

Francis and Eddie cut across the fifteenth fairway toward Clyde Street, avoiding the departing crowds. Francis tried to walk off his anger, thoughts firing through his head. Had the man spoken for The Country Club, or only for himself? How could anyone who knew him expect him to come this far only to quit? He walked so fast, Eddie struggled to keep up with him, balancing the golf bag on his back.

"The guy's a big, fat, stupid dope, Francis," said Eddie. "Don't let that bunk bother you."

By the time they crossed Clyde Street, Francis felt the anger draining away, replaced by the dread of facing his father. Only when they had reached the front yard would Eddie relinquish the golf bag.

"I cleaned 'em good," said Eddie. "Wiped down the grips, too."

"You did fine out there today, Eddie. Just fine."

"You, too."

"Are you going to skip school again tomorrow?" asked Francis.

Eddie looked straight at him and nodded solemnly. He didn't need to tell Francis anything more about promises.

"I guess I'll see you in the morning, then," said Francis.

"You didn't shoot a seventy-two yet, but you will. Probably tomorrow, I think."

"That'd be a very good round if I did."

Eddie hesitated. He wanted to offer some reassurance. "Get some rest, Francis. Don't worry about nothing. It's going to be okay."

Francis smiled. "Are you going to get home all right?"

"Don't you worry about me."

Eddie smiled, gave a little wave, and walked away. Francis climbed the steps to his front door. He lingered on the porch before going inside, turned back to look at The Country Club one last time. A tower of dark clouds bloomed above the horizon.

BERNARD DARWIN REMAINED in The Country Club's press tent until nearly ten o'clock Thursday night, writing his copy for the day and cabling it off to England, where Northcliffe's editors stood by on twenty-four-hour alert. Papers trumpeting the British players' first-day triumph at the Open would be on London's newsstands by dawn.

At seven-thirty Lord Northcliffe himself rode back in his touring car with Harry and Ted to the Copley Square Hotel. Exhilarated by the afternoon's stirring reversal, he offered to treat his two prize charges to oysters, champagne, and an extravagant dinner. Harry politely declined. As had become his disciplined custom during two-day tournaments, he would take only a light supper in his room before retiring early. Although his own competitive hunger remained as ravenous as ever, he had privately begun to tire of Northcliffe's relentless, bombastic obsession with winning the Open as revenge for England. More pragmatically, at forty-two Harry also knew he needed to reserve all the energy he could spare for the demands of the tournament's final day.

Still coming down from the high of his adrenalized afternoon round, Ted said he needed a stiff drink and a bath, in that order, and then he'd see about joining Northcliffe for a quick meal, emphasis on quick. The morning's first tee time required he report back at The Country Club in less than twelve hours.

Ted walked into the bar at the Copley Square Hotel and ordered a double whiskey to go. The bar adjoined a popular bistro that offered Hungarian food, an exotic cuisine just catching on in America. The dining room was crowded with players staying at the hotel and locals who'd spent the day in Brookline watching the tournament. Ted's arrival stirred up considerable attention throughout the room. As he picked up his drink, he heard a familiar voice.

"Ted! Ted! Over here, old boy!"

Ted turned. Wilfred Reid was sitting at a nearby table over drinks with Tom Vardon and two men Ted didn't recognize. In deference to Tom, Ted accepted the invitation and sat down with them. The other men turned out to be prominent members of The Country Club, eagerly soaking up an insider's blow-by-blow of the day's action, which Reid was only too eager to provide. Ted listened quietly, paying more attention to his whiskey than the voluble Reid, occasionally contributing brief, modest responses about his record-breaking second round in response to the members' polite questions. Just as well; Reid hardly let him get a word in edgewise.

"All I can tell you, gentlemen, is that when the day began, I scarcely imagined I would find myself tied with good old Harry Vardon for the lead," said Reid. "Let alone two strokes ahead of the great Ted Ray."

Ted rewarded that prize piece of fawning with a pained smile. Tom Vardon had to turn away and stifle a laugh. Ted ordered another drink. The two Americans, certain by now Wilfred had exhausted the subject of his own heroics, shifted the conversation to their distinguished visitors' home country; both men planned to visit London in the near future. The discussion soon turned to the current political climate. Inevitably, this provided Reid with an opening to launch into another withering critique of the British taxation system.

"I've lived the last four years abroad, you see," said Reid. "In Paris. My own small form of protest. In England, the workingman stands at the absolute mercy of the Inland Revenue."

"If you loved Paris so damn much, Wilfred," said Ted, finishing his second whiskey, "why'd you come back, then?"

"Truth be told, I was offered a better job at a club near London," said Reid to the Americans. "Been there just shy of a year now. Much to my regret when I realized the high price I'd be forced to pay for it."

"The British tax system," said Ted, reaching a low boil, "treats both rich and poor alike. You won't find a more equitable arrangement anywhere else in the free world."

"I daresay you have a fairer system here in your country," said Reid to the Americans again, who were beginning to sense this might be an ongoing dispute they didn't necessarily want to wade into.

"We've only just started the income tax here this last year," said one of them.

"Yes, and I'm given to understand it's a far cry from the punitive levy we face in Britain," said Reid.

"At this point it affects only the well-to-do," said the American.

"Then it's a safe bet Wilfred here will be knocking on the door of your Immigration Service within a matter of months," said Ray, also to the Americans. "He'd be well in the clear."

"As I understand it," said Reid, ignoring him, "America welcomes all manner and variety of the oppressed and downtrodden to her shores. Isn't that right, Tom?"

Tom Vardon looked stricken. He had witnessed the volcanic fire of Ted's temper many times, sensed an eruption was brewing, and had no more desire to get caught in the crossfire than the two Americans did. On the other hand he felt fairly certain that Reid had just insulted him. Ted jumped back in before he had time to figure out his response.

"Well, I guess that just goes to show how geography can adversely affect your point of view," said Ted.

"I'm afraid I don't know what you mean by that," said Reid, addressing Ted directly for the first time.

"What I mean is," said Ted pointedly, at last turning to Reid, "you've spent so much time in Paris breathing in that daffy Socialist atmosphere, it's warped your tiny little mind—"

"I'll have you know I'm originally from Surrey," said Reid, his face reddening brightly, "and damn proud of it."

"You've made my point for me, then," said Ted. "It's a well-known fact that men from Surrey lack the proper mentality to grasp any of the larger issues—taxation, for instance—"

"Is that right?"

"Yes, as a matter of fact it is."

"Well, you know what I say: better from Surrey, better anywhere than Jersey—"

"What about Jersey, then?"

"It's a well-known fact, isn't it, that regardless of what they think—and they think damn little about anything—men from Jersey don't amount to very much at all—"

Ted stood up abruptly, his chair skittering to the floor behind him. He reached across the table and slapped Reid right across the face.

"What about that, then?" said Ted. "What does Surrey think about that?"

Momentarily astonished, Reid froze in his seat. The two Americans at the table thought that surely Ted must have been joking. Then Reid jumped forward and took a flying leap at Ted, who reared back and socked him right in the nose, hard. Reid crumpled to the floor in a heap, blood gushing out of his nose, then immediately popped back to his feet and tried to go after Ted again. The restaurant's headwaiter rushed over and threw himself between them, followed by Tom Vardon and the Americans. Somehow they prevented the two men from reaching each other.

"You'd better go," said Tom quietly to Ted after taking him aside, then added: "Well done for Jersey, though."

Ted bolted for the door, left the restaurant, and took the stairs up to his fourth-floor room. The sudden melee, which had brought the busy restaurant to a dead stop, was over as quickly as it had begun. Reid, still hopping mad, threatened to go after Ted, forcing the others to restrain him repeatedly. Finally, Tom gripped him firmly around the shoulder, held him tight, and whispered into Reid's ear.

"He outweighs you by a good eighty pounds, man. Are you trying to get yourself killed?"

Reid heard that line of reasoning and finally settled down. He wiped away the blood still trickling over his mouth and chin and ordered another drink. A flock of waiters descended to right overturned chairs and clear spilled drinks from the table. Holding a napkin to his nose, Wilfred offered profuse apologies to the two Americans; they offered their regrets and hastily left the restaurant. Wilfred and Tom sat back down. Reid appeared stunned, withdrawn.

"How do I look?" Reid asked Tom quietly, removing the napkin.

"To be perfectly honest, Wilfred," said Tom, "you look like a man who's lost a fight."

An agitated murmur ran through the restaurant about what they'd just witnessed. Someone hurried out to fetch a reporter they knew. Wilfred Reid felt every eye in the place staring his way. A waiter set a fresh drink in front of him. Tears quietly welled in Wilfred's eyes. He sat with Tom for another five minutes, sipped his drink with a trembling hand, then quietly gathered the remnants of his dignity like a tattered skirt, rose, and walked slowly out of the room.

When reporters showed up at the Copley Square Hotel, neither Reid nor Ray would agree to come downstairs and discuss what had happened between them. After repeated calls to their rooms went unanswered, both men finally sent down word that they had retired for the night in order to properly prepare for tomorrow's work out on the course. Neither wished to talk about the incident. Reporters went to work on the people in the room who'd seen it happen.

FRANCIS AVOIDED HIS father that night. His father returned the favor. A provisional truce had kept the peace; Mary had strong words with Arthur when he returned from work and extracted a promise from him to leave Francis alone. The family had already eaten supper at Arthur's insistence by the time Francis returned home. Mary prepared a plate for Francis and he ate alone in the family kitchen, relishing the familiar peace and quiet after his tumultuous day. When they sat around the dining room table afterward, Louise and his younger brother Raymond couldn't stop talking about all the excitement they'd seen at The Country Club. As much as he liked and appreciated their support, Francis quietly suggested they not discuss it too much in front of their father. Louise and Mary spent the rest of the evening cutting out clippings about Francis and the tournament, and there were many, from the evening newspapers for their growing scrapbook. His father, as was his custom, sat alone in the front parlor reading his paper.

Francis went up to bed at ten o'clock. He lay awake for over two hours, replaying the day's two rounds over and over again in his mind, identifying his mistakes, determining how he would avoid repeating them tomorrow. The pin positions would all be moved overnight; they'd be set up much tougher than today's. He visualized the probable changes—he knew them all, on every green—then played the ideal way around the course to each of those positions in his mind.

Placement. Accuracy. Discipline. And then, just maybe, if the vision came to him as it had at Wollaston or Garden City . . . *No, don't you dare think about that now. One shot at a time.*

Sometime after midnight, he drifted off to sleep.

At two o'clock that morning, it began to rain.

WALTER HAGEN AT THE COUNTRY CLUB.

FRIDAY: DAY TWO

DREAMLESS SLEEP. DEEP, motionless, restful. No sudden
starts, no wayward thoughts or intrusive sensations.

What was that sound?

Francis woke slowly. Looked at his pocket watch, sitting open on the
bedside table: 6:45. He turned toward the window.

Rain. That's rain.

Francis opened the curtains, then the window. A dark, wet, gray-green
world outside, cloaked in a steady soaking downpour. Francis looked at
it all for a moment in disbelief. A cold storm, he recognized the sights
and smells at once, come down from Canada. Slow moving. Heavy cloud
cover parked over Boston. The sun had disappeared. It would rain like this
all day.

Francis looked down at the road. Puddles clogged the length of Clyde
Street already. He looked across at The Country Club; the fairways draining well, as usual. No standing water. The greens would be the same,
maybe even more playable than they'd been all week. An uncommon happiness bloomed in him.

I've played the course in weather like this a hundred times.

HARRY, AWAKE SINCE dawn, ate breakfast before six, alone, in the hotel restaurant downstairs. He gazed calmly out the window at the driving rain.

English weather, he thought.

He lifted the pot to pour more tea. His right hand shook, almost uncontrollably. The plunging barometric pressure affected the damaged nerve. *No one will know. Just as it's been for the last ten years.* He set down the pot, kept his right hand below the table clenched in a fist, and lifted his cup to drink with his left.

Ted walked into the room, dressed in the same light seersucker coat and rough corduroy pants he'd worn the day before. He wore a felt hat with the brim rakishly angled down on one side. He sat down, stuck his pipe in his mouth and bunched his hands in his pockets fishing for matches, looking restless, distracted.

"Sleep well?" asked Harry.

"Like a baby," said Ted. "Woke up every two hours and cried."

Harry smiled, handed Ted a match. He filled and lit his pipe. Tom had told Harry all about the fight with Reid. Ted didn't mention it.

"Seen Reid?" asked Ted, once the bowl was going.

"Not a peep."

Ted puffed on his pipe, looked out at the rain. "Bloody English weather," he said, and ordered breakfast.

EDDIE LOWERY STOOD just inside his front door beside his brother Jack. His mother knelt down in front of them, somber and earnest.

"You have to promise me you'll go to school today," she said. "I don't want that truant officer over here again, what would I tell him?"

"Tell him to go fry an egg," said Eddie.

"Eddie—"

"All right, I'm going."

7:30 A.M. They trudged through the rain toward school, two miles away, huddled under one umbrella.

"She's gonna stop believing you if you take off again," said Jack.

"Too bad. I'm going anyway."

"That truant officer's got it out for you."

"He's got to catch me first."

Eddie handed Jack his book bag, grabbed their umbrella—"I'm gonna need this today, Jack"—and took off running toward the West Newton train station.

"What do you want me to tell 'em at school?" Jack yelled after him.

"I don't care anymore!"

ARTHUR SAT IN the kitchen, reading his morning paper, sneaking looks at Francis as he prepared to leave the house. Dressed in boots, white twill trousers, white shirt, tie carefully knotted. Two-button dark cloth coat. Knit cap. No rain gear today; real players didn't wear that stuff in competition. A spare dry coat bundled under his arm for the day's second round. He collected his sticks from the closet in the front hall beside the door.

"Playing in the rain," said Arthur, to no one in particular.

His sister, Louise, dressed for the rain and her stenography school in Brookline, wished Francis luck with a bear hug. She planned to leave work early that afternoon to come watch him play. His younger brother, Raymond, had already informed Francis that he planned to skip out from school and follow him all day. His mother, Mary, stood on her toes and kissed him at the door. She didn't care if Arthur saw her encourage him.

"Good luck, Francis," said Mary, beaming.

"Thank you, Mother."

Francis glanced back at his father and stepped outside. Arthur turned the page he was reading. His son's name was on it.

Shortly after 8:00 A.M. and cars filled Clyde Street from one end to the other. Every available parking space on either side had already been seized. As he left the house, in the front yard at the bottom of the stairs, a huge black umbrella swung around toward Francis; Eddie huddled beneath it, nearly swallowed by its span. He hurried to Francis before he stepped off the porch into the rain and grabbed his golf bag, slinging it over his right shoulder, under the umbrella he held over his left.

"Can't let those sticks get wet," said Eddie.

Francis pulled down his cap, turned up his collar, looked out at the rain.

"Those greens aren't gonna be too fast today," said Eddie.

"We'll take what the course gives us."

"It ain't going to be easy to shoot seventy-two today," said Eddie. "But I think you'll do it anyway."

"Eddie," said Francis. "It's a fine day for golf. Let's have some fun."

Eddie gave him a skeptical look, not sure if he was serious. But Francis was smiling. "Okay," said Eddie.

They walked across the street, dodging cars and puddles.

"LITTLE LEFT BUT Hope," said the *Boston Globe*. "Vardon and Ray Versus Very Few Americans," read the *Herald* that morning. McNamara, Travers, and Brady were done, most agreed. McDermott had yet to show his real form, and might not still. This Hagin, or Dagin, or was it Hagen kid showed some promise, but he was green as grass; he needed seasoning before much more could be expected of him. Who did that leave? Mac Smith, maybe this new guy Jim Barnes, or 1909's Open champ George Sargent. None of the local beat writers gave Francis a chance, although at least most of them had stopped referring to him as a boy. Halfheartedly trying to stir up some patriotic excitement while deriding every remaining American contender, the columns rambled on in this divided, anxious manner, all of them grasping at straws. Alone among these local front-page doomsayers only John Anderson saw a ray of light:

"And now for the man—who many yesterday called boy—who will have the best wishes of over 10,000 spectators today. I mean Francis Ouimet, the brilliant young player from the Woodland Golf Club. He is only four strokes behind the leaders and it begins to look, most decidedly, as if he were destined to finish in the money. No matter whether it were even in tenth place, that would be an accomplishment the most brilliant of any ever recorded by an amateur in this country in medal play, taking into consideration the strength of the present field."

Arthur Ouimet finished reading Anderson's entire feature column in the *Boston Transcript*—the first he'd ever read about Francis all the way through. He folded his paper neatly, as was his custom, and set it down on the corner of the kitchen table. He put on his rain gear, left the house, and walked off to work, cursing the traffic on Clyde Street.

NO AMERICAN TEAM spirit emanated from the players' locker room that morning; Ray and Vardon had been among the first to arrive, well before 8:00. Thursday's performance, the inexorable steadiness with which they'd risen to the lead, had only confirmed their daunting reputations. Their quiet, confident presence stilled the room around them, homebred players unconsciously lowering their voices and averting their eyes. The Englishmen appeared not to notice; they were of course supremely aware of their effect on the competition, and took their time getting ready. Both Harry and Ted had brought along a change of dry clothes and a spare set of boots, setting them carefully in their lockers.

English weather, went the whispers around the room. *They're used to playing in this. Just what we need now; another reason to like their chances.*

The American players avoided the Jerseymen at every turn, as if they'd already conceded defeat. Only Walter Hagen chatted up Vardon and Ray on his way out the door; a little light patter about the weather. "How about this stuff, huh? Pea soup out there. My caddie's gonna need a paddle." Both men seemed to enjoy his chatterbox routine; what wasn't to like?

No one braved the rain to practice. They lingered inside, shaking off the cobwebs, stretching out, waiting for their times. Uneasiness as cloying and clotted as the air outside. McDermott lost his breakfast again. Most players only went out to putt for a few minutes on the way to the tee before their names were called.

Francis came into the room only minutes before Ted Ray went out to kick things off. The big man steamed past him without a glance or a word. Harry gave Francis only the vaguest of nods as he passed by, as if they'd never met before; he was in game mode, and gamesmanship was part of it. Mike Brady, following Ted out for their start, stopped to shake Francis's hand. "Best of luck out there," he said quietly. "You, too," said Francis.

Moments later Francis passed Hagen, applying the finishing touch to the knot on his red bandana. They instantly recognized something in each other; they were the only two Americans enjoying themselves in the room.

"Hey kid, what do you say?" said Walter. "Let's go get these big shots."

They shook hands; Hagen went out into the rain. Francis had two hours to kill. He lay down on the bench in front of his locker, pulled his cap over his eyes, and visualized the round he hoped to play.

During a stop at the scorer's tent on his way to the tee that morning, Walter Hagen solved a mystery. The USGA's secretary had misread the spelling of his name on the original application he'd mailed in—his signature already incorporated a few stylish flairs that may have hindered interpretation—and as a result "Hagin" had made its way into print on all official tournament documentation. That's where the reporters drew all their information—leaving whoever had called him "Dagin" with no excuse whatsoever. Too late to fix now, the secretary told him, with apologies. "Tell you what; I'll bet they get it right if I win," said Hagen, and walked off toward the tee.

8:45. TED RAY and Mike "King" Brady at the first tee. Not too early for the crowd to gather, in spite of the heavy driving rain. Ninety-one percent humidity. Wind from the northeast at twelve miles per hour. Fifty-seven degrees, already the warmest it would get all day; with the steady wind, it felt more like forty. New England residents call these storms "nor'easters"; this was fall's calling card, announcing the change of season. A wet sodden cold felt deep in the bones embraced the grounds with rain, mist, fog; the slick, lambent fairways ahead slipped in and out of sight. Only twenty-four hours ago a sylvan sun-drenched retreat, today the Brookline woods looked like forest primeval. From a distance, mounds and hillocks of wet black umbrellas surrounded the first tee; a thousand die-hard Bostonians in black raincoats, slickers, galoshes. As golfers stepped up to the tee, they were each offered a small, single-shot bottle of whiskey to ward off the chill, an old Scottish custom in foul weather championships. Many accepted. A few asked for a second tot to see them through their back nine.

At Lord Northcliffe's insistence he and Bernard Darwin disdained umbrellas. Northcliffe's greatcoat appeared as if it could accommodate a party of five; Darwin looked less sanguine about the arrangement. Northcliffe was in an ebullient mood as he and Darwin left the clubhouse and surveyed the crowd surrounding Ted on the first tee. The three-month delay he had arranged in the Open had brought them good fortune, and he was quick to claim credit for it.

"Real English weather," said Northcliffe. "Just like the last day at Hoylake this year. Jolly good for our boys, I'd say, wouldn't you?"

On the last day of the British Open two months before, at Hoylake near Liverpool, a day of equally foul weather had thrown the tournament up for grabs. Darwin had been out in it all day covering the action. He'd caught a bad cold.

"We'll soon see," said Darwin. Already he looked drenched and miserable.

Ted sliced his tee shot into the rough. Rain slopped off the rim of his bucket hat. He shoved his hands into the pockets of his coat and set off. His caddie held their only umbrella over the golf bag, keeping the grips dry, while Ted marched ahead, leaning into the downpour. Real players braved the elements unprotected; that was the English way.

Brady's tee shot was in the fairway. Ted sliced again, his second shot flying into the woods twenty yards to the right of the hole. Brady cleared the racetrack and landed just short of the green. Ted threaded a delicate pitch back through the trees, trickling the ball onto the front of the green. Brady pitched up and made his putt for birdie four. Ted needed two putts for a five, and looked mad about it.

Both parred the second hole. At the third, Pond, Ted again hit a high, wicked slice that landed short behind a tall mound guarding the right side of the fairway. Brady crushed his tee shot but hooked his approach into a bunker short of the green. Ted's second shot skimmed the top of the hill, lost steam, and came up sixty yards shy. He chunked his third, sending up a soggy divot the size of a toupee, and fell short again. Brady tried to blast out of the bunker; his club skidded on the soaked, compacted sand, caught the ball thin, and sent it flying over the back of the green toward the pond that gave the hole its name. Only the wet, tall rough stopped it short of the water. Both men chipped on. Both needed two putts for double bogey six.

When Ray had to scramble after another woeful tee shot to sink a six-footer for par, it would have been clear to a blind man that Ted's rhythm had deserted him. Swaying, lurching, he had no feel of the tee and Brady knew it: This was the opening he'd hoped for. Now within striking distance of Ted he looked poised to make a run at him. To hold him off, Ted would have to grind.

By the time Ray and Brady reached the third tee, Darwin and North-cliffe had circled back to the first hole to watch Harry Vardon step to the tee at 9:05. While the crowd huddled under the pelting assault of the storm, Harry stood tall. He wore no rain gear, only his traditional knickers, Norfolk jacket, and tie. Already soaked, only the bill of his cap keeping the water from his eyes, he radiated such calm and self-possession, the rain didn't seem to touch him.

Walter Hagen walked over to the tee five minutes early to watch Harry put his drive in the first fairway; the image of that pure swing lingered in Walter's mind. Harry and his partner Elmer Loving, a pro from Arcola, left the first tee trailing a crowd of over 3,000 people. Not a single one of them had come to watch Elmer Loving.

As Harry's massive gallery disappeared down the fairway, Hagen stepped to the tee before a tidy little crowd of his own; frat boys, cute girls, guys on the make, gamblers, horse players, the ragtag crowd he'd attracted over the last two days, made to order for him. Walter's handsome golf ensemble didn't look quite so stunning in the rain; the silks drooped, his razor-sharp cuffs dragged in the mud, his red bandana hung limply around his neck. The red-rubber-soled shoes that gripped dry ground so effectively tended to slip and slide in wet grass. Still, Walter smiled broadly when he reached the tee. Come to Boston on a dare and look where he'd ended up, a contender on the last day in the U.S. Open. He made some crack about the rain, got a laugh from the crowd, and aced his tee shot. Hagen's improbable chase after the title was under way and he had leader Harry Vardon right in front of him.

John McDermott stepped onto the first tee ten minutes later, grim determination stamped on him like a coin. Johnny had discarded his coat and tie in the locker room, stripped down to his shirt, and rolled up his sleeves. The already drenched thin white cotton plastered his wiry frame, defining ribs and sinewy lean muscle. Six strokes behind Vardon and the lead, four in back of Ted Ray for second. John looked possessed with fury, jaw thrust out, every fiber in him taut with purpose. Now or never. The morning's third large gallery followed America's defending champ off the tee, marching into the mist and fog now swirling around the trees.

FRANCIS GOT UP off the locker-room bench at 9:30. He heard Mac Smith and Alec Ross talking softly nearby about Wilfred Reid. Only half an hour to co-leader Reid's tee time and he still hadn't shown up at The Country Club. They discussed a rumor making the rounds—something had gone sideways at the Englishmen's hotel in Copley Square last night, some bad blood between Reid and Ted Ray. When Reid's brother-in-law, little Louis Tellier, had arrived earlier that morning, he refused to talk about it.

Wilfred Reid walked into the room a few minutes later. Head down, eyes forward, cap pulled low on his head. He went straight to his locker without saying a word to anyone. A social animal, always glad-handing his way around, this morning he looked like another person altogether. Through a gap between lockers, Francis caught a glimpse of Reid sitting one row over, pale and shaky, eyes crimson with fatigue. A mouse under his right eye, swollen nose, discolored bruising on that side of his face. Louis Tellier walked over and sat next to Reid, they spoke quietly, in French. Francis didn't understand the words but got the gist; Tellier trying to prop him up. Reid looked lost, shaking his head, wringing his hands. What was wrong with him?

None of my business, thought Francis, feeling like an intruder. He got up and moved away to stretch his legs.

BRADY AND RAY kept their duel going; dead even through six. Both bogeyed seven. Ray was dropping strokes at an alarming rate, tumbling back toward the rest of the field. At the par four eighth Ted caught a break; after his first good drive of the day he half-topped a mashie that skittered through heavy wet rough toward disaster, then stopped on the edge of a cavernous bunker. From there Ted clipped a perfect recovery shot to within three feet and made the saving putt for par. They came to the ninth dead even on the round. Another wayward tee shot for Ted cost him bogey six. Brady logged another steady par.

Maybe the lack of a meaningful warm-up had hurt him, although practice time meant less to ever-ready Ted than most. Perhaps the weather or some psychological hangover from the altercation with Reid had thrown his complicated swing off its axis. Ted Ray had gone out in 41 and opened the door for the Americans chasing him; Brady had shot 40 and trailed Ted now by seven. As they reached the cover of the thatched hut near the tenth tee, coming in from the relentless deluge for the first time in over an hour, the worry that Ted had worn all morning drained from his face. He relit his pipe, took off his bucket hat, mangled the water out of it, and smiled at Brady, who thought this odd behavior to say the least. The front nine, the side Ted had grown to despise, was behind him again. He felt like a brace of wet sandbags had just slipped off his shoulders.

DAMP, INSINUATING COLD. Raining so hard, every step became an effort. A swirling, intermittent mist made distances impossible to judge. The dense atmosphere leaned on the ascent of every tee shot. Rain pounded rising golf balls back toward the ground where the heavy, swollen turf deprived them of roll. Harry calculated that these conditions translated to a four-stroke handicap for everyone in the field, but he and Ted paid a stiffer price; their superior talents off the tee were penalized more than most.

Harry realized he was in trouble on the first hole. He had slept well, eaten a big breakfast, stretched his muscles, followed his disciplined monastic routine to the letter. But when the time came to start his round, his swing wasn't there. His right hand felt numb on the club. He hit the fairway with his tee shot, but his second shot at Polo Field sliced badly. He missed the green coming back, then missed a short saving putt. A bad bogey six.

Harry tried to walk it off. He'd played through weather far worse than this, time and again. Just two months ago, at Hoylake in the last day of the British Open, he'd mounted a closing charge and nearly stole his unprecedented sixth title. Brutal weather was part of the game, just another obstacle to overcome. Harry's tee shot at the second felt smoother; he reached the green and took an easy par. But then at three, a wild, unruly slice off the tee. A recovery that flew disturbingly off line. Another botched chip. Another bogey six. The same again at the fifth; no control with the driver. Inadequate recovery. Indifferent putting. Bogey five. Three shots of his lead gone in only five holes; Harry had fallen right into Ted's staggering footsteps.

Walking along with Harry's twosome, Lord Northcliffe nearly popped the buttons off his overcoat after Harry's bad drive at five. Both his champions in trouble now. Going red in the face, Northcliffe looked as if he were about to turn to Darwin and shout: "Do something!" To avoid that conversation, Darwin quickly walked back to see how Hagen was doing; at least that was the excuse he used on his boss.

Walter started out smoothly, collecting easy pars at one and two. You didn't grow up playing the game near Lake Ontario without becoming a veteran of foul weather. His only concern now were the rubber soles of his snappy new shoes. Hagen employed an exceptionally wide stance; whenever he wound up to hit one hard and overdid his unorthodox weight shift, his shoes hydroplaned through the casual water collecting underfoot. And, damn it, a slave to fashion, he'd left his weather shoes, a pair of reliable hobnail boots, back in his locker at Rochester Country Club. At 435 yards, the third hole, Pond, demanded an exceptionally long and accurate tee shot. Walter tried to knock the cover off the ball, his right foot slid out from under him, and he popped it straight up, less than 100 yards down the fairway. Angry at himself, he tried to make up for the miscue with one swing and yanked a brassie second shot into the trees to the left. After a four-minute search Hagen was astonished to find his ball resting upright directly on top of an old rotten tree stump, slivers of wood as sharp as needles jutting upward all around it. A lie so improbable, a leprechaun must have left it there.

Walter weighed his options; the ball was actually teed up rather nicely and since the stump sat out in the open, he could assume a stance. He decided against declaring the ball unplayable, which would cost him a stroke, choked down on an iron, and chopped sideways at the ball. As it flew off, it caught some of the slivers, ricocheted off the trunk of an elm, and fell into a tangled, soggy lie just short of the fairway. Hacking it out of the rough he advanced it far enough to crawl onto the front edge of the green, lying four. The pin was cut at the back. Tense and rattled, he needed three putts to get down for a double bogey seven.

No whistling between holes, no jokes to the crowd this time. Hagen walked to the 275-yard par four sixth, called Baker, quiet and mad. Narrowing his stance and holding the image of Vardon's balanced swing in his mind—feet planted firmly on the ground this time, no slipping—he hit a solid drive with his brassie to the middle of the fairway, leaving 140 yards to an elevated green concealed by a hillock; a completely blind shot. He walked forward to look over the ground and saw a young boy dashing out of the woods behind the green. Thinking nothing of it, Walter walked back, took his mashie from the bag. He sent his caddie to stand on top of the hillock to line him up on the pin, then waved him away. Hagen wiped the rain from his face and swung easy.

Silence. Beat. Beat. Hearing nothing, Hagen ran forward up the hill to see what the hell had happened. His caddie was already up on the green, looking around in vain. Hagen knew he'd hit a crack shot but didn't see his ball anywhere; his first thought was the kid he'd seen running toward the green had picked it up. He looked left and saw the same boy loping down the next fairway.

"Get after that kid," he yelled to his caddie. "Search him, I think he grabbed my ball."

The caddie sprinted after the kid. Hagen started beating through the rough beyond the green; maybe he'd gone long after all. This was crazy. Then his playing partner called him back onto the green. When Walter got there, the man pointed at the cup. Walter looked down and smiled.

"Hello, beautiful," he said.

He'd holed his shot from the fairway. For a two. Double bogey on three, eagle on six.

Walter lifted the ball out of the hole and kissed it. His gallery ate it up. With the single most amazing shot played in the entire tournament, Hagen was back at even par for his round. (Tellingly, in his colorful and completely unreliable autobiography, Hagen transferred this encounter with the stump and subsequent eagle to Friday's more dramatically suitable final round, sandwiched between two heartbreaking bogeys and a death-defying birdie, none of which ever occurred.)

Harry heard the cheer for Hagen's eagle behind him. As he walked to the sixth hole, Darwin came back with the news: Walter Hagen had just passed Ted Ray and drawn within one of Harry's lead. Equipped with this new clarity of how the game stood, Harry felt calmer than he had all morning.

He parred the next four holes.

FRANCIS TIED HIS shoes, looked at his watch, ticked off the starting times in his head. Long Jim Barnes had gone out at 9:30. Louis Tellier and Tom Vardon four groups later, 9:50. Mac Smith and Alec Ross at 10:00. He watched Wilfred Reid finally leave the locker room, at the last possible minute, for his 10:05 start.

Eyes lifeless, moving like a sleepwalker, Wilfred Reid reached the first tee to begin his third round of the U.S. Open with a three-stroke lead. Drawn by yesterday's heroics, a large, eager gallery of over 1,500 people awaited him. Reid hadn't slept a wink all night. He'd been unable to eat a single bite of food, last night or this morning. His spirit and confidence, so essential to golf and fragile in his case to begin with, had collapsed with one punch to the nose. Unsteady on his feet, a stranger in a strange land, Wilfred didn't even acknowledge the applause that greeted his introduction. Convinced last night's public humiliation was already common knowledge, certain his dreams of success in America had been shattered by Ted Ray's right hand, Reid had nothing left in him to combat the challenging course, the dreadful conditions, or the world's best competition. He pull-hooked his first tee shot into the weeds, then stubbed his recovery.

An astonishing full-speed retreat was under way. Reid double bogeyed two of the first three holes, then bogeyed the fourth; less than an hour into the round, five shots and his share of the lead was gone for good. Retreat soon turned into full-scale rout. There was no sustained drama to his breakdown, he looked too helpless to mount any discernible struggle against it. Painfully evident even to non-golfers, Reid was a man just going through the motions, an act of pure capitulation, his tournament over and done with the moment he teed it up.

In over twenty rounds played during nearly three weeks at The Country Club, Reid had never finished a full eighteen in more than 76. Friday morning he completed his front nine in a devastating 46 strokes. Slowly at first, in ones and twos, then in ever-larger numbers his gallery deserted him, like reluctant eyewitnesses slinking away from the scene of a suicide. By the time he finished his third round in 85, less than half a dozen people had stayed to watch, his poor wife among them, openly in tears. His playing partner, 1910 U.S. Amateur champ Bill Fownes, felt so bad for the pathetic figure Reid presented by the finish that he wanted to hug him. Reduced instantly to an also-ran, caught and swallowed by the pack, in the press tent, clubhouse, and galleries Wilfred Reid's utter collapse became the biggest mystery of the morning. The explanation for it, which he soon became only too eager to offer, was about to become the biggest scandal of the Open.

FRANCIS WALKED OUT of the locker room at 10:30. Waiting for him under the eaves of the caddie shack, stamping his feet and drinking hot chocolate to keep warm, Eddie spotted Francis as soon as he emerged and scurried over to join him. Eddie had collected a couple of towels, wore one around his neck, and folded the second over the mouth of the bag to shelter the clubs. He tried to lift his big umbrella to keep Francis dry but couldn't reach that high without a stepladder. Francis told him not to bother, grabbed his putter from the bag, and headed for the practice green.

"What have you heard, Eddie?" he asked as they walked.

"The boys say Ray and Vardon aren't going so good. That wise guy Hagen's doing all right. Reid's blown up sky-high."

If all that were true, with a shock Francis realized it would put him close to the lead. He dropped two balls on the practice green, sending up a splash.

"I don't know about the other fellas; McDermott and that Frenchman might still be in it, maybe that tall guy Barnes—"

"Okay, good. Once we're out there, let's not pay any more attention to all that, shall we?" said Francis.

Eddie nodded, somber as a judge. "Let's play our own game."

JOHNNY MCDERMOTT WAS indeed still in it. He'd competed in enough Opens by now to know the third round of any championship usually proved to be decisive. The last chance for trailing contenders to take reasonable risks and make a move up the board, before caution and dwindling opportunities tightened the final round into a chess match endgame. Johnny knew the course well enough by now to know where those risks should be assayed, and he was close enough to the lead for them to matter; six behind Vardon, four behind Ray. Another bonus; he even found himself paired with a recent English expatriate, H. H. Barker, which helped whip up his xenophobic antipathies. Despite his similarly frail appearance, and facing personal hardships off the course even more dire, on the inside John McDermott was no Wilfred Reid. America's best professional player had one last run left in him.

As Johnny teed off two groups after Hagen at 9:20, the steady rain became a monsoon. The wind whipped around, turning bitter cold. McDermott's discarding of his coat may have been similar to an ascetic's act of self-negation, as if only by subjecting himself to their worst could he will himself to ignore the elements. Johnny played the front nine as well as anyone in the field that morning, and better than most. Nothing spectacular, nothing disastrous, he took what the conditions gave him, gambled only twice, and came out unscathed. Through nine holes McDermott shot an even par 38, picking up three strokes on Vardon, cutting his advantage in half, streaking past the plummeting Reid, and drawing within one shot of Ted Ray and the lead.

But well ahead of him by the time McDermott made the turn, Ted had turned his game around. As poorly as he had performed on the front nine, he played just as brilliantly on the back, another inspired Jekyll and Hyde job. Instead of loose drives, off-line approaches, and muffed putts, now every shot combined power and precision, his coattails flapping in the wind as he cracked it off the tee. What had changed? The weather hadn't let up; it had grown steadily worse all morning. It's tempting to speculate Ted had finally shaken off some lingering effect of the altercation with Reid, but the theory doesn't stand up. He'd always had a touch of the brawler in him; if anything a fight tended to clear Ted's mind, not cloud it. A simpler explanation is more likely; Ted just hated The Country Club's front nine. When he came off the course that morning, something Ted said to Bernard Darwin cleared up the reason behind his wild ride. "I like the back nine so much better than the front, I'd like to carry them around with me and use them again instead of the first nine."

One of the most amazing facts about Ted Ray is that he never carried more than seven clubs: driver, brassie, four irons, and his putter. He often played entire rounds using no more than four of them: driver, brassie, putter, and his favorite club, an iron he called a "Snieler" niblick—whatever "Snieler" signified to him has since been lost in time. Although it carried no more loft than a contemporary nine-iron, because of Ted's immense strength, he used that niblick for everything from shots 200 yards out to the most delicate chip shot. On most days when he drove the ball long and straight, his "Snieler" took him the rest of the way to the green; no other clubs need apply. Friday morning's back nine was one of those occasions. He chipped in for a birdie with the "Snieler" on twelve and went on to par the next six holes on the side: 41–35 for 76. First man on the course, first man off it, Ted Ray had recovered himself in time to establish the early third-round lead at 225.

His playing partner Mike Brady fought a game fight but couldn't match Ted's finishing kick. Brady left three more putts hanging on the lip down the stretch and finished the morning with 78, giving back the early stroke he'd gained on Ray and one more. Now ten shots in back of Ted's lead, Mike Brady's Open was effectively over. Shortly afterward, recording a sensational 32 on the back nine, Tom McNamara came in with an outstanding 75, but it was too late for him as well; Tom had already given up the ghost with his disastrous second-round 86. Tommy Mac stood three strokes behind his friend "King" Brady. At the tournament's three-quarter mark, two thirds of the American triumvirate were officially out of the running.

NOT LONG BEFORE Ted Ray finished his third round, Francis stepped to the first tee to begin his. Bursts of ghostly fog wrapped around the rocks and slipped between the trees ahead. He could barely make out his target. A gallery of over 3,000 gathered to see him off, among them many friendly faces; his brother, Raymond, George Wright, and a dozen others from Wright & Ditson, Frank Hoyt leading a whole contingent from Woodland, his old Country Club patron Mr. Hastings, and caddie master Dan McNamara. When Francis was introduced, their applause went on for nearly a minute; he had to raise his hand to acknowledge them before they'd let up. Surprising that he even noticed them at all, because somewhere between the locker room, the practice green, and the first tee, Francis felt that clear, enveloping, unearthly sense of calm settle around him. As always its arrival came unpredicted, but he had prepared himself for this round with care and precision, mentally, emotionally, physically. He had allowed none of a thousand possible distractions to wedge their way between him and the work at hand. He felt warm inside, in spite of the rain and piercing cold, holding no thought in his mind except to play steadily and surely. *One shot at a time.*

Francis teed up the ball, Eddie handed him the driver.

"Keep your head down," said Eddie. "I'll watch the ball."

Francis smiled. He knew he had it today. Eddie smiled back; somehow he knew it, too. Time stood still. The crowd went silent; all you could hear was the soft hammering of rain on a thousand umbrellas. A pause: Francis addressed the ball, then the swing; in rhythm, perfectly timed, killed. Ripped through the rain, dead center of the fairway, 240 yards away. The gallery erupted. Francis and Eddie marched off; marshals barked through their megaphones, rope handlers scrambled to keep the crowd outside their lines.

Of all the hopefuls and notables walking in his gallery that morning, no one knew better than John Anderson what that joyously engaged and solemn look on Francis's face signified. He'd experienced it firsthand only two months ago, during those miraculous six holes at Wollaston in the state championship. He'd seen it again early on in Francis's match with Jerry Travers at Garden City in the Amateur. Anderson felt a chill run up his spine, goose bumps on his arms, and he knew it wasn't because of the weather.

This, thought John, could be good.

A few hundred yards away, at 246 Clyde Street, Francis's mother, Mary, was working in the kitchen when she heard the echoing cheer that greeted his first drive. She looked at her kitchen clock: 11:00. She knew that was his tee time; that cheer had been for Francis. She walked outside and pulled up a chair on the porch, wrapped a shawl around her shoulders against the cold, and sat down facing the golf course. She fingered a string of rosary beads in the pocket of her skirt. Every time she heard another cheer from the club, and there would be more than a few, she whispered a Hail Mary. Aside from her busy fingers, she wouldn't move for the next two hours.

In the first fairway, Francis used his brassie from 210 yards out, sailed over the racetrack, and landed just short of the Polo Field green. He pitched up to within eight feet of the cup and dropped the putt for an opening birdie. Francis carried ten clubs in his bag: a driver, then two nearly identical brassies, one slightly more lofted than the other that he called a spoon, today's three-wood. A wooden cleek, similar to a modern five-wood. A rounded-back utility club he called a "sammy." A low-lofted iron jigger for bump-and-run shots; a mid-iron, a mashie, a mashie niblick, a niblick (three-, five-, seven-, and nine-iron), and his putter. All had fragile, flexible hickory shafts; steel shafts had been introduced some years before but were considered illegal by the USGA until 1924. Hold Francis's putter in your hands and you can hardly reconcile it with the clubs used on greens today. The head, a thin tapered blade of steel with surprisingly little mass, measures less than an inch in height, barely reaching the midpoint of a ball on the ground. To strike a ball consistently on the blade's sweet spot would require extraordinary precision. The hickory shaft is supple and whippy, but the club as a whole possesses superb balance and feel. In

Francis's experienced hands, who had held and worked with that club for years, it must have felt as light and expressive as a conductor's baton.

At the short second hole, Cottage, Francis teed off with his favorite brassie to within sixty yards of the elevated green. He softly coaxed a niblick to within eight feet of the stick. With that soulful putter in his hand, he dropped the putt for a second straight birdie. The crowd cheered again, louder this time. Driver off the third tee; long and booming. Two hundred and twenty yards remaining, a blind shot to the Pond green with nothing but trouble in every direction except straight down the line, he hit a brassie to the front of the green. Two putts from there and Francis had birdied his third hole in a row. This time the crowd went crazy.

Eddie and Francis walked together to the next tee. Francis nodded and smiled to the gallery; he might have been the most relaxed man in Massachusetts. Hurrying to keep up, Eddie couldn't keep the smile off his face. People in the crowd were patting him on the back as much as they were Francis. Eddie didn't dare say a word, afraid he might put a jinx on what Francis had going. The crowd felt electrified, boys scattered all around the course to spread the news of his spectacular start, and brought back word about where the leaders stood. Word of Reid's collapse had already reached them and they knew Ted Ray had finished his third round at 225; after three holes Francis had already surpassed him by a shot. The big question remained unanswered: Where was Vardon?

Harry had reached the fifteenth by the time Francis made his opening run. His back nine started poorly with a bad luck bogey at the par three tenth. He'd struck his best shot of the day off the tee, a beautiful, sweeping long-iron that landed a yard short of the hole. But then it rolled and settled into a deep, unrepaired pitch mark left by an earlier ball; nearly half of it lay below the surface of the green. Although it was against the rules to fix divot marks on the green until your ball was in the hole, players were absolutely expected to repair them afterward. Outright negligence. Bad luck, thought Harry, and he didn't linger on it. He used his niblick to dig the ball up out of the putting surface but he ran it past the hole, leaving him a dicey downhill five-footer for par. His right hand jumped on the downswing, the putt lipped out violently, and he took an undeserved four.

Four strokes over for the day through ten holes. Certain this had cost him his lead, Harry might have been excused a moment of despair, but he perceived the ebb and flow of fortune in a round more by means of intuition than numbers. For reasons he couldn't quite explain, but trusted explicitly, Harry felt certain the worst was over. He was back in control of his game. Never despair. Once again he ran off a string of four straight pars.

When he reached fifteen, Harry's strategy for the rest of the round came to him, confident and fully formed; he'd found his swing and could afford to coast in at this measured pace through the rest of the third round; the beastly weather would eliminate at least half the contenders chasing him. Then he'd see where everyone stood.

The fifteenth tee placed him at the remotest corner of the course from the front nine, but he could hear a series of distant roars echoing eerily through the mist and fog. He knew that meant someone on the front side must be closing on his lead, or had perhaps already caught him. A local favorite judging by the sound of it; it had to be McDermott or the youngster Ouimet. He guessed McDermott; no worries there, he knew he had Johnny's number.

But what if it wasn't? There was something more to this Ouimet that worried him. Harry had been top dog in the game for so long, he'd watched a hundred pretenders come gunning for him. Hotshots like McDermott with their exaggerated swagger and that lean and hungry look. He'd stood his ground for twenty years and beaten every one of these fresh-faced killers. Because they lacked the forged strength of his championship experience, he knew their hard-bitten confidence was still brittle where it counted most, in the mind. Most split wide open under the bone-breaking jaws of Open pressure in the final hours. Harry had learned just how to play these Young Turks along, too; bring them close, let them wear themselves out with a strenuous charge, and then break their hearts with a blinding run for the finish. He'd done it to McDermott just yesterday. Today's U.S. Open would follow that pattern; whichever young buck came charging at him out of the pack would go down to defeat like all the others, just another notch on Harry's holster. He prepared to hit his drive.

And yet . . . the way that young boy smiled as he played. He didn't walk around in a half-mad trance, he relaxed between shots, laughed and joked with his little caddie, letting off some steam. He didn't need to work himself into a sustained fury like McDermott or shut down his emotions like those twin automatons, Jerry Travers and Old Man Travis. The truth was Harry had never seen any top homebred American behave this way on a golf course, pro or amateur. His conclusion was unlikely but inescapable: *Ouimet liked it out here.*

Harry heard an involuntary question in his head: *Who does he remind you of?* And the answer he got back disquieted him.

It's you, Harry. He reminds you of your younger self.

This was a game won and lost between the ears. Over the years Harry had watched more than a few players with physical skills superior to his own come and go; his illness had made sure of that. It had also given him an advantage no one could counter: Harry had fallen straight down into hell and clawed his way back. He'd never met any man with the tenacity of will to endure what he'd gone through and still compete in this game at the highest level. He'd never imagined it was possible. This had always been the secret knowledge that held him up as he worked his way back to the top, the final ace up Harry Vardon's sleeve: *No one can match my nerve.*

He looked down at the driver in his hand. Both hands trembling slightly. *What is this?* He took a deep breath, willed them to stop. All these intrusive thoughts he stuffed into a box, draped it in chains, and dropped it into deep, dark water. There was work to be done.

The tremor disappeared. Without another wasted breath, each shot and putt struck with absolute economy and clarity of purpose, Harry parred the last four holes. He walked off the course with a 78, four over par for his round, just where he'd stood after the first disappointing ten holes. His total through three rounds: 225. Harry and Ted were tied for first place.

Lord Northcliffe and Ted Ray waited for him in the shelter of the locker room as Harry came in after fulfilling his obligations in the press tent. Although Northcliffe expressed enormous relief and pride that his two men had come through the morning's ordeal in front, neither player felt anywhere near satisfied with their slender lead. Although they had already heard of Reid's demise—and as far as Ted was concerned, the less said about that entire subject, the better—too many Americans remained with a chance to close the gap.

Hagen came home first. After his double bogey at three and eagle at four, Walter eliminated the extremes and settled into a sure and steady pace. He finished his front nine in 39, making up two shots on the Jerseymen. To keep his wild weight shift under control in the slippery conditions, Hagen found himself relying on the image of Vardon's flawless rhythm more and more frequently. Walter played a back nine as smooth as his silk shirt, for a one under par 37. The longest of long shots from Rochester had crafted a clutch 76. Hagen trailed the Englishmen by two shots, alone in second place, at 227.

John McDermott followed shortly thereafter. After inching inside an arm's length of the lead through nine holes, he had Vardon and Ray well within his reach through fourteen until a three-putt double bogey six at fifteen spiked his momentum. Although he parred in from there for 77, on the round John had made up only a single stroke on the Englishmen.

The press tent opened the McDermott question for lively debate: Had the champ done enough to set himself up for a closing kick to matter in the final round? He'd followed this exact scenario before, some believers argued, citing chapter and verse; three strokes in back of the lead going into the Open's final round in 1910 he'd closed the gap to force a play-off. He'd also come from behind in the last round of the championship the following year to grab a share of the lead he eventually took home. Heinrich Schmidt offered a minority dissent, on the strength of three points: McDermott didn't start either of those last rounds from quite so far behind; it hadn't been pissing down rain like the Great Flood on either occasion; in neither instance had he been chasing Ted Ray and Harry Vardon.

Although he refused to answer questions between rounds, anyone who caught a glimpse of McDermott's haggard face as he studied the leader board outside the clubhouse could tell John leaned in Schmidt's direction; privately the champ felt he had missed his main chance and let Vardon and Ray off the hook. Shivering from the cold, soaked as a drowned rat, McDermott left the grounds for the warmth of the locker room. Five shots in back of his hated nemesis, in conditions that hadn't yielded a sub-par round all day, he knew his hopes for retaining his title had been reduced to an unlikely outside shot.

Two groups behind McDermott, the focus of the crowd irised down on

Long Jim Barnes. The lanky Englishman/American from Tacoma had hung tough all morning; his drives, typically long, low, and boring into the wind, appeared less affected by the congealed air than anyone else's out there. His scoring pattern throughout the tournament resembled Ted Ray's; Barnes threw away strokes like a sinner on the front nine, then made a convert's atonements on the back. After a front side 41 he birdied eleven, twelve, and fifteen. With three holes to go, all Jim Barnes needed to do was par his way home and he would seize the lead. After someone made him aware of his opportunity on the next tee, Barnes slipped back into his unrepentant ways; a bogey four at the easy sixteen.

That's just fine, went the impassioned analysis in the gallery. *Two pars still buy him a three-way tie with Vardon and Ray.*

Too much prosperity; Barnes took bogey five at seventeen.

Okay, what's done is done. A par at eighteen and Barnes grabs second place alone, one stroke back.

Except that after a sensational drive at eighteen, his second shot flew the green and bounced over the road behind it, coming to rest sixty yards from the hole. His exquisite recovery shot from there traced a lazy rainbow through the air, landed softly on the green, and trickled down to within six feet of the pin, leaving him a straight uphill putt to save his par four. Concerned journalists and American players who'd already finished their rounds and knew the homebreds' chances were running thin now spilled into the gallery and pressed closer around the green.

Surely Barnes will come through. Even if he doesn't make it, at worst he gets down in two to tie Hagen for second.

Their confidence had been misplaced; Barnes pushed his first putt, running it two feet past, then he yanked the simple comebacker. Double bogey six. Barnes grabbed his ball out of the cup and angrily swiped a silver-dollar-sized chunk of mud off the back; bad luck had found him at the end. Jim Barnes turned in a card of 78 to the scorer's tent, one behind Hagen, in third place, three strokes shy of the lead.

RAYMOND OUIMET MADE good on his promise to skip out of Brookline High School that morning and journey to The Country Club to join his brother's gallery. He arrived in time to see Francis sink a sinuous twenty-foot putt for his fourth birdie of the morning at the sixth hole; another mighty shout rolled and rumbled down along the tree-lined corridors. Attracted by the steady cheers, people came sloshing in from all around the soggy grounds. Ten minutes later, when he confidently rammed a five-footer home for a solid three on the tough par three seventh, Francis had amassed the largest gallery left on the course.

In spite of the tension and expectations weighing down on him, Francis remained friendly and approachable between holes. Among the many who came up to him on his way to the eighth tee was his old friend from Woodland, Frank Hoyt. Francis liked Frank enormously; a fine player in his own right, Frank had been competing with Francis for years. At Woodland Francis had coined a fond nickname for Frank—"Stealthy Steve." But "Steve" was also the same well-intentioned fellow who had invited Francis out to play his disastrous tune-up rounds the Sunday before the tournament at Wellesley, the same eager beaver who'd come rushing up to tell him he'd grabbed the lead against Vardon halfway through Tuesday's qualifying round, snapping his concentration like a twig. Given his sensational start Friday morning, when he saw Frank Hoyt rushing his way, Francis's first impulse was to turn and run.

"Francis, Francis," said Hoyt, out of breath.

Oh no, thought Eddie. *Not this joker again*.

"You won't believe it: Vardon just came in with seventy-eight. Ray shot seventy-six, and Reid's gone completely, blown up sky-high—"

"Thanks, Frank, that's good to know."

"But you know what this means, don't you?"

"Yeah, we've got a pretty good idea," said Eddie, trying to cut him off.

"You should see what's going on back at the clubhouse. Pandemonium!" said Frank, ignoring the little caddie. "Everybody's talking about it, what are you now, four under?"

"Three," said Eddie quickly.

"Bogeyed five," said Francis, picking up his pace.

"Well then let me think a second . . ." said Frank, taking out a scorecard on which he'd written some notes. "That puts you three under for the day, even par for the tournament—good Lord, you're two strokes clear of Ray, you're four ahead of Vardon. You've passed them both, Francis. You've got a two-shot lead."

"Thanks for coming by to tell me, Frank," said Francis, politely trying to disengage.

They reached the eighth tee box and the crowd parted like a curtain to let Francis pass. Eddie stepped into Frank's path so he couldn't follow any farther, then turned to face him.

"Yeah, Frank," said Eddie. "Thanks for coming by."

Eddie waited until the crowd closed in front of him, blocking Frank out, then he joined Francis on the tee. Eddie dried the grip with his towel and handed Francis his driver.

"Don't pay any attention to that stuff, Francis," he said. "Just keep doing what you're doing."

"Play our own game," said Francis.

"That's right. No matter what they say."

Francis went through his pre-shot routine exactly as he had all morning. But Eddie could see some splinter of doubt had perforated Francis's perfect sphere of concentration. Punctured, even this slightly, his confidence was about to spring a leak, just as it had on Tuesday. The rain had soaked into the hickory in the shaft of his driver, rendering it even whippier than usual; that would mean trouble if he swung too hard or out of rhythm. Rising anxiety prompted him to do so now; his drive at eight hooked way left into a bunker. His recovery fell well short of the green. A chip and three putts later he had a double bogey six.

Eddie tried to steady him between holes. "Take the bad with the good, Francis," he said. "Everyone gets a tough break once in a while."

Francis nodded as if he heard him, but at the long par five ninth, more of the same; a foozled drive, an inadequate second that barely cleared the brook that split the fairway, onto the front of the green in three. After lagging to ten feet, his putt to save par turned left at the hole; bogey six. In only two holes, Francis had surrendered his short-lived lead. For the first time Francis fell into a flat-footed three-way tie with both Vardon and Ray.

As they walked to the tenth tee, Eddie spotted a rough-and-tumble friend of his outside the ropes and waved him over. He quietly pointed out

Frank Hoyt, still walking along with the gallery, scribbling away on his scorecard.

"If you ever see that guy come running up to us again," said Eddie, "tackle him."

AS NOON APPROACHED, the real contenders left on the course dwindled to a handful. After staying up half the night at the Copley Square Hotel tending to the wounded psyche of his brother-in-law Wilfred Reid, the little Frenchman Louis Tellier fought valiantly to stay alive all morning. He played with Tom Vardon, who'd witnessed last night's altercation and offered him the first objective report of it Louis had heard. Hearing an objective point of view uncolored by Wilfred's self-pity helped settle him down. That their twosome passed the entire morning completely unnoticed among all the swarming galleries didn't hurt, either. Valiantly picking up the family standard surrendered by Reid, Tellier toughed out a 79 to finish his third round six strokes out of the lead.

Playing together just behind Tellier and Tom came good friends Mac Smith and Alec Ross. Despite his Scottish Highland roots, Ross found the relentlessly rotten weather tough sledding; he carded a calamitous 93 and shot himself out of the tournament. Mac Smith played the front in a similarly hapless 42, then once again turned himself around on the back and finished with 80. Mac kept his chances alive, slipping ahead of Louis Tellier to join John McDermott in fifth place.

Now only Francis remained. His playing partner, George Sargent, in contention when the day began, headed due south in the lousy conditions from the first and had already dropped from sight. As he waited for the fairway ahead to clear, Francis grabbed hold of himself at the tenth tee. If his perfect feel and vision had left him for the moment—there was no use pretending otherwise; it had vanished—he'd just have to buckle down again and grind his way home.

Think it through, Francis. No one expected you to be this close in the first place; be honest with yourself, not even you did. And if that's the case, what are you afraid of?

That simple shift in perspective calmed him immediately. Francis had happened upon an emotional resource miraculous in its common sense; all he had to do was change the way he looked at his situation: *This is golf. It's a game. It's supposed to be fun.*

The tenth hole yielded par to him after he placed his mid-iron tee shot on the green, but more trouble lay ahead. After a good drive in the fairway his approach at eleven found the rough, a bogey five resulted. News rippled quickly through the crowd and grounds now: Francis trailed Vardon and Ray again by one.

Ted heard about Francis catching them while he stood on the practice green, preparing to tee off at 12:15 and open the final round. He'd downed a hot meal in the locker room, chugged a shot of rye, and changed into his spare dry clothes. Surprised to learn the lead had fallen back into his lap, Ted felt fortified and ready to face his last trip through the front nine he dreaded. He was equally surprised to see that significantly fewer people were lining up around the tee to follow him. Before long he would be less pleasantly surprised to find out why.

The rain fell continually harder, slanting down sideways when the wind gusted. Dark glowering clouds appeared to bear right down on the treetops, making manifest the mounting pressure. Francis squandered another chance to retrieve any lost strokes at the par five twelfth; he bunkered his tee shot, had to pitch out sideways, then came up short of the green in three. Only a sound chip and a sure putt saved par. At thirteen and fourteen he took no chances, played the odds, and walked away with par. His drive at the long fifteenth nearly reached the road. Francis studied this approach shot long and hard; only 120 yards to the green but dead into the wind. He and Eddie quietly conferred about which iron to go with. His gallery had by now accumulated over 4,000 people, but his concentration remained absolute. They decided on the mashie; five-iron. Francis made a perfect pass at the ball; it landed softly on the green and settled ten feet below the pin.

The crowd drew nearer, ringing the fifteenth green as Francis and Eddie looked for the line from every angle. Francis employed a less than orthodox putting style, although contemporary students of the game would recognize a decidedly modern stroke; more shoulders involved than wrists, elbows extended out to either side, less of a pop than a smooth stroke through the ball. Francis found the line he liked and Eddie stepped away. He settled into his stance, momentarily set the slender putter down in front of the ball for a final check of the line, then replaced it behind, turned his head to the right, and made the stroke. The ball rolled straight and true on the line right into the heart. Birdie three. Another roar. Nourished by the crowd's encouragement, Francis and Eddie walked to the sixteenth tee.

Ted stood on the first tee, already addressing his ball when he heard that last roar. He knew exactly what it meant—Ouimet had caught them again. Ted stepped away, lined himself up again behind the ball, regrouped.

That's just fine, he thought. *Let junior catch us now. Then he'll find out what final rounds are for.*

Ray stepped to the ball again and annihilated his tee shot; 260 yards into the teeth of the wind straight down the fairway. The final round was under way.

Across the street, that last shout after Francis's birdie at fifteen proved too much for Mary Ouimet; the closest one she'd heard to home all day, it lifted her straight out of her chair on the porch of 246 Clyde. She pulled her umbrella from the stand by the door, marched down the stairs, and walked right across the street as if summoned by the voice of God, heading for the largest mass of people in sight. Francis's gallery, although she didn't know it, bunched up now around the sixteenth green, stacked ten people deep—but at only five foot two, Mary couldn't see a thing. When the crowd clapped and cheered again, she asked a taller man next to her what was going on; he stood on his toes, peered in, and told her Ouimet had just landed his tee shot on the green.

Louise and Raymond Ouimet had found each other in their brother's gallery on the way to sixteen; they watched Francis make his par three— the first he'd scored there all week—then quickly stepped around to grab an open spot on the rope lines guarding the seventeenth fairways. Megaphones swung this way and that, marshals shouted their lungs out trying to control the masses stampeding around them. Mary bobbed in the flow like a cork in heavy surf, but she quickly grasped the fundamentals: Grab a section of rope and hold on. She purchased herself a place on the line in time to see Francis hit his drive long and straight into the fairway. She tried to call out to him as he walked past, but her voice was drowned out in the tumult. Mary didn't know much about golf; she'd picked up a little reading about Francis here and there, but she knew enough to know it was good when Francis landed his second shot on the mowed oval of short grass they called the green. The crowd seemed to like it even more when it only took him two more hits to put his ball in the hole. She cheered right along with them.

"That's my son," she tried to tell the man next to her, as people rushed off to the next tee. He didn't hear her.

A rush of feeling overwhelmed her. Her eyes filled with tears. She'd never seen such a crowd, such excitement, all these people hurrying after Francis. She pulled up short and stopped where she stood, well shy of the next tee, and couldn't bring herself to continue. The crowd rushed past her in a wave and just like that she was standing alone; the twosome playing the seventeenth behind Francis had no one watching them. She saw a great black line amass ahead of her on either side of the eighteenth fairway, spreading all the way to the clubhouse. Chattering with excitement until a group of men wearing white armbands lifted megaphones to their mouths and shouted for silence. Other men stabbed tall red rods straight up toward the sky; the air around her reverberated with sudden silence. No one moved. All she could hear was the sound of the pouring rain. Francis stood somewhere in the middle of that human sea, the object of every eye. She followed their line of vision and there, just rising above the broken profile of black hats and shoulders, she saw a golf club lift into sight, then the sound of a solid thwack, wood meeting ball.

Like a single massive creature, they all gave voice at once and rushed forward along the ropes. He was walking among them now, she felt sure of it; she could see the ripple of his progress in the way the crowd reacted, waving, calling out his name.

That's him. That's Francis.

Moments later they erupted again; he'd taken another shot and they liked this one, too, they liked it very much. The big black crowd poured itself in around an elevated, circular plateau to the left of the big yellow clubhouse.

Too much. Too much. And then looking down, Mary realized she was wearing only her simple housedress. Good heavens, what had she been thinking? She shouldn't be seen in public dressed like this. Mary wiped the tears from her eyes and immediately turned for home. She'd wait for Raymond or Louise to come and tell her exactly what had happened.

But it has to be good, she thought. *It has to be good.*

FRANCIS WALKED UP the face of the embankment leading to the eighteenth green. He stopped to lean back and offer a hand to Eddie so he didn't slip coming up the soggy slope. Eddie waved him off and picked his way up the hill to join him, bag on one shoulder, umbrella over the other, as surefooted as a billy goat.

Out on the course, already into their final rounds, Harry and Ted had heard the ascending string of cheers. After the latest one, Lord Northcliffe stepped up to fall in alongside Harry as they walked toward his ball in the second fairway.

"What's all this about, then?" asked Northcliffe.

"It's Ouimet," said Harry. "I expect he's come close. Maybe about to tie us."

"That green boy?" said Northcliffe. "Nonsense."

"He'll do it, too," said Harry.

"Rubbish. He's still wet behind the ears," said Northcliffe.

"You watch," said Harry. He reached his ball in the fairway, selected a club, and focused on the shot ahead.

On the Home green, George Sargent offered to putt out first and clear the green. Francis acknowledged his gracious gesture with a tip of his cap. Sargent got down in two for a round of 79; the crowd applauded dutifully. Sargent retrieved his ball and stepped aside. Bernard Darwin had doubled back to the eighteenth in time to see this unfold. Standing near the clubhouse, grateful for the moment that Northcliffe was elsewhere, Darwin tried to keep a persistent smile from his face as he looked down at Francis, but it kept climbing back on. *The lad I met at Coney Island. The one I noticed in that crowded field at Garden City—was it only three weeks ago? Just look at him now.*

The ball rested twenty feet to the right of the hole, slightly downhill left. Eddie handed Francis his putter. They were completely alone, in one of the odd intimacies of major tournament golf, inside a circle of 6,000 people.

"What do you see?" asked Francis, almost as a courtesy. He knew this putt as well as the sight of his face in the mirror.

"It has to go left," said Eddie. "Down the hill."

"Left it is," said Francis.

"If you don't sink this one, be sure of the next."

Francis stepped up, took one last look, and then the ball was running, tracking straight for the hole. Riding the break to the left, it appeared to be on line—the crowd let out a rising gasp—but at the last he'd given it too much speed. It passed by on the high side and ran four feet long. The crowd sighed and then applauded, relief mixing with excitement that began to build again; Francis had just this putt left to tie the Englishmen for the third-round lead.

They looked it over briefly, Eddie crouched behind Francis, peeking through his legs. His injured foot had started to hurt something awful but he willed himself to ignore it.

"Straight in," said Eddie.

No hesitation: Francis knocked it in the center of the cup.

Out on the course, Vardon heard the roar, followed by a chorus of shouts from what sounded like a single voice, the loudest, most sustained cheers they'd heard all week. Harry turned to Northcliffe and nodded matter-of-factly: *See? He's done it*. Irritated, Northcliffe huffed and hurried ahead to check on Ted.

Walter Hagen, on the first hole behind Vardon, just reaching the Polo Field green, said to no one in particular: "Well, hot dog; the kid's come through."

Mary heard the yell from her seat back on her front porch. She gripped her rosary, giving thanks where thanks were due: another answered prayer.

Near the clubhouse, Raymond Ouimet ran forward to try to reach his brother. The crowd wouldn't let him through. Louise hurried back to the house to tell Mary the news.

On the clubhouse steps Bernard Darwin nearly punched a fist into the air, then remembered his native sympathies and smothered the gesture before it got away from him. He jotted in his notebook—*Marvelous. Marvelous!*—and hurried back out onto the course to find Vardon and Northcliffe.

Standing to the right of the scorer's tent under umbrellas in the pouring rain, as Francis passed by them with a happy wave to turn in his card, USGA president Robert Watson and his old friend George Wright shook hands.

Ten minutes later a solitary figure trudged up the last fairway. Herbert Strong, the third round's last player, had this time suffered from playing alone. After beginning the day tied with Ted Ray in second place, with an 82 Strong had tumbled all the way down into a tie with Louis Tellier for eighth place. Moments later the final figures through the third round were posted on the scoreboard:

Francis Ouimet	74–225
Ted Ray	76–225
Harry Vardon	78–225
Walter Hagen	76–227
Jim Barnes	78–228
Mac Smith	80–228
John McDermott	77–230
Louis Tellier	79–231
Herbert Strong	82–231

Under conditions that permitted only seventeen of the top fifty players in the world to break 80, Francis had shot Friday's lowest round and picked up four strokes on the best two players in the world. Scholars of the game agree that, although there have been rare exceptions, only players within five shots of the lead going into a major's final round remain legitimate contenders. That left seven men inside the fall line, with Tellier and Herbert Strong on the outside looking in.

Pundits laid odds about America's chances in the press tent; McDermott looked spent, and although they couldn't count him out, most didn't like his chances. Mac Smith remained a solid possibility—he'd lost in a play-off for the title before and both his brothers had won Opens in the past; championship golf was in his blood. Not many knew much about Jim Barnes, coming from as far out west as Tacoma—few had ever seen him play before, but they liked the way he'd finished strong in the first two rounds; many felt he might be the best American contender still standing. Reporters were in the first blush of their thirty-year love affair with Walter Hagen, but even though he stood only two strokes back in second place, expecting the young dandy to shoulder past Vardon and Ray in his first Open seemed too much to hope for.

That left Francis. He spent a few dutiful minutes in the press tent after his third round, most of the time apologizing for the wretched shots he'd made at the eighth and ninth holes. Whenever a reporter tried to rile up his patriotism and extort a prediction of victory from him, Francis refused to rise to the bait.

"Fortune has to deal kindly with any golfer," he said, "to win a championship against such a field, and in such conditions as these."

The kid from across the street. He wasn't even supposed to be here. It seemed clear by now that fate had plucked him from obscurity, but after he left the tent, opinion differed on what that signified. Lifted by some unknown inspiration and the goodwill of his hometown fans, was he an overachiever who had hit the ceiling of his talent, or did destiny have bigger things in store for him? The cynics and wise guys, types not unknown to sports journalism, had done the math and figured his bubble was about to burst. The boy had come from out of nowhere and soared as high as any man could go. Did the name Icarus ring a bell? In the fourth round his inexperience had to bring him crashing back to earth. Tied for the lead, with the U.S. Open on the line, Vardon and Ray would crush him.

Not everyone in the tent shared that feeling. The opposite number to these jaded skeptics, the shameless sentimentalists—both extremes are flip sides in almost every sports reporter—weren't ready to write Francis off just yet. Not because they genuinely felt he could pull it off. They were tantalized by the mouthwatering prospect of all those juicy hometown headlines; the stories would practically write themselves.

For far less mercenary reasons, only John Anderson among the press corps stood up and stuck to his guns. "Don't give up on Francis," he told the naysayers. "Not even he knows what he's capable of out there. Didn't he come in a shot ahead of Vardon during Tuesday's qualifying? Hadn't he just slapped them both silly that morning to pull dead even?" But how can you account for it, they argued. They're top pros, the best in the world, he's just a nobody. Some wag from New York made a crack about how Francis's ears stuck out and got a cheap laugh.

"I'll tell you how he did it," said John, getting angry. "He played better than they did."

His tin-hearted colleagues remained unconvinced. Only Anderson and, secretly, Bernard Darwin kept the flame. Francis's legion of local supporters in the crowd outside, voting with their hearts, not their heads, almost didn't dare to hope. The singular sound hanging over The Country Club was of 10,000 people holding their breath.

Francis never told a soul what his thoughts were in that hour before his final tee time. He sat in front of his locker with his back to the room, eyes fixed, staring straight ahead. Visualizing the round to come, perhaps. Remembering how he'd gotten here, the lean years, all the disappointments. He changed into dry clothes, cleaned his shoes. Coming and going out of the room for their own tee times, other players left him alone, like a pitcher in the dugout halfway through a no-hitter.

Eddie waited for Francis out back in the caddie shack. Soaked to the skin, he hadn't brought a change of clothes that morning. When caddie master Dan McNamara saw him shivering, his lips blue with cold, he invited him into the pro shop and let Eddie sit in the back by the potbelly stove. Eddie took off his coat and hung it up to dry near the fire. Someone brought him a cup of hot chocolate.

"Keep him going out there, kid," said Dan.

"I'll do my best, sir," said Eddie.

As he sat by the fire, Eddie cleaned every club in Francis's bag, checked and rechecked his supply of balls and tee molds. When no one was watching, he untied his right shoe and peered down at his foot. He saw blood seeping through the bandage. He spotted a small display of American flag ribbons for sale on the pro shop counter.

"How much for one of those?" asked Eddie.

"No charge," said Dan.

Eddie thought that over. "How much for two?"

. . .

WHEN WILFRED REID came off the course after his third round, his wife and sister sought out a reporter they'd met in the press tent to tell him what had happened the night before between Wilfred and Ted Ray at the Copley Square Hotel. The dam of what the two women had been holding back burst; frequently in tears, they both blamed Ray for the stunning collapse Reid had suffered that morning. Their confirmation of the rumored fight quickly spread through the press corps. After turning in his card, Wilfred stepped into the press tent and finally offered his version of events for public consumption.

He tried to pass the incident off as a spirited political disagreement between friends that simply got out of hand, refusing to suggest any underlying animosity between the men might have been responsible. In every account he gave, Wilfred cast himself as a bewildered, innocent party, the subject of an unprovoked attack who had manfully tried to respond before others stepped in to prevent him from taking his satisfaction. He didn't whine or complain about being on the short end of the fight's outcome, although that was physically self-evident. Nor did he in so many words ever directly attribute his poor play that morning to the fight's emotional consequences. He didn't need to; reporters drew their own conclusions. When Reid went out on Friday afternoon and followed his dismal third round with an equally pathetic final round 86—finishing out of the money in a tie for sixteenth place—the idea that his tournament had been ruined by what had happened the night before gained even greater currency.

To Reid's credit he didn't refer the matter to the police. He filed no assault charges, initiated no lawsuits, sought no punitive damages from Ted for lost wages, a reaction nearly unimaginable today. Clearly no lawyers were on hand to counsel him, but he may have rebuffed them in any case. An age-old behavioral code was at work here, he seemed by his reaction to suggest; English gentlemen settled their differences between themselves, sometimes with their fists. If one of them walked away with a busted nose and bruised feelings, so be it. In many ways, considering that the fight had clearly just cost him a legitimate chance to win the U.S.

Open, this willingness to confine the matter to the realm of the purely personal may have been Wilfred Reid's finest hour.

For reasons of his own, Ted Ray never discussed the run-in with Reid publicly. "No one else's damn business" would undoubtedly have been his explanation. He regretted the punches he'd thrown—he said at least that much to Harry—but the incident was over and done with as far as he was concerned and should never have found its way into the papers at all. He seemed baffled by the Americans' interest in it, feeling certain that the more discreet members of the British press would have left the thing alone; Bernard Darwin, for all the ink he spilled about the Open, never wrote a single word about it. This blind spot in Ted about the essential differences in how the egalitarian American press operated created an unforeseen problem for him on Friday afternoon. As details of Reid's account filtered out unchallenged by Ted's point of view, from the press tent down and throughout The Country Club grounds, sentiment slowly but perceptibly turned against the man who all week had been the crowd's great favorite. For the first time in his life, Ted had suddenly and unexpectedly found himself cast in the role of the bully.

MORE RAIN. MORE cold. There had been brief periods between downpours earlier in the morning when the rain lightened up, but it never stopped altogether. By early afternoon it seemed as if the skies had opened over Brookline permanently. With the ground reaching saturation levels, shallow puddles formed all over the fairways. Only the superior drainage systems of the greens, most of them elevated and slanted for just this reason, prevented them from becoming unplayable. Just after noon USGA officials ruled that the tournament would continue; fourth-round play would proceed as scheduled.

When Ted Ray and Mike Brady walked back out to the first tee at 12:15 to begin the final round, the air looked as thick as chocolate milk. Unaware yet of Wilfred Reid's comments to the press or the crowd's negative reaction, Ted attributed his smaller gallery to the increasing severity of the weather. When they greeted his introduction this time with a bare smattering of applause, he paid it little mind. Ted had anticipated weeks ago that down the stretch Americans would find it hard to generate much sympathy for "the big Brit"; nobody cheered for Goliath. But despite his sophisticated emotional defenses, Ted felt beleaguered and weary. The road had worn him down; he'd been away from home for close to three months, the longest hiatus of his life. He liked America well enough, but felt no resonant affinity for the country as a whole; nowhere near as much as Harry. He also shared Harry's growing feeling that in the last few days Lord Northcliffe's need to capture this U.S. Open had revealed itself to be more egocentrically obsessive than sporting; revenge might be Northcliffe's motive but it was his alone. They still had to put the ball in the hole, and by Friday afternoon, even after fifteen years of slogging through British weather, these were the worst conditions Ted had ever played in.

One more round to finish and he could put all of that behind him. Skill. Forbearance. Professional pride. Playing at the front of the field, Ted faced an empty course; he could set a blistering pace, the way he preferred to play. Maybe this damnable front nine would finally yield to him his last time around it. He sent his first drive soaring; it scraped the overhanging clouds. As Ted moved out to his ball in the Polo Field fairway, there was Northcliffe again, marching in step with him.

It's a wonder he doesn't carry a whip, thought Ted.

Ted's second shot sliced off line to the right into the rough, spoiling his chance for birdie. He pitched up to the green, two-putted for his par, and moved on. He reached the second green in two but putted hastily, and poorly, three times, and walked away with bogey. At the par five Pond, a hole that had bedeviled him all week, he hit one of his signature drives, then reached the green in two with his brassie and two-putted for a brilliant birdie. Back to even par.

The fourth hole, Hospital, was only 300 yards long, and on a normal day Ted could reach its green on the fly eight times out of ten. Hospital was about to inflict more damage than it healed. Ted nailed his drive but the wet ground stopped it at the top of the hill that looked down at the green, less than fifty yards away. Pulling out his reliable "Snieler," he chunked the ball fat and it pitched only twenty yards ahead into a deep pot bunker. Using the same club, he played his next out onto the edge of the green. Once again he needed three putts to get down, missing a one-footer.

Ted fumed; nothing made him feel more like an idiot than missing a twelve-inch putt in front of a crowd of people. Double bogey six. Two over par on his round.

As Ted walked off the green, Bernard Darwin came trotting up to join his gallery, just arriving from the clubhouse where he'd seen Francis finish.

"Where have you been?" demanded Northcliffe.

"Watching Ouimet. He's caught them," said Darwin, out of breath.

"No he hasn't," said Northcliffe. "He's gone ahead; Ted's cracking."

Darwin watched Ted moving through the crowd to the fifth tee. He looked beset, under siege. Northcliffe snapped opened his pocket watch and checked the time. "I'm going back to watch Harry. You stick with Ray. Don't let him let me down."

Northcliffe stalked away. He missed seeing Ted put together his best three shots of the day at the fifth, a hole he'd parred once in the tournament. Confronting a blind tee shot over mounds with a slight dogleg right hugging a stand of deep woods, Ted split the fairway. Deep traps protected the green on the left, high rough on the right; Ted put a "Snieler" shot in the middle of the green. After six tentative putts in a row, he dropped this fifteen-footer for a birdie three. One over through five holes. He'd played them like a man in pursuit of the land speed record, in three-quarters of an hour.

Ted got his par at the sixth, then ran into trouble again at the seventh, the longest and most difficult one-shot hole on the course. Ted's tee shot fell short and right, and after pitching up onto the green, he once again needed three putts to finish. Double bogey five. Three over par.

Now his Jersey temper got the better of him; as he stormed away, he kicked the ground, flinging his putter off into the grass so his caddie had to walk ten yards to retrieve it. Northcliffe had been right about him, thought Darwin, only two holes too soon; he looked ready to blow sky-high. The death march continued; Ted bogeyed eight after another criminally wasted tee shot. He reached the side's last hole four over par, desperate now to stop the bleeding. The 520-yard ninth, Himalaya, should have played as a relatively easy par five for a man of Ted's prodigious length; nevertheless he had butchered it all week. He needed a birdie.

The rain pounded him as he stood up to his ball. His white bucket hat, having lost all its shape, appeared to melt into the sides of his head. He rallied long enough to hit another vintage Ted Ray drive and followed it with an equally sharp brassie off the fairway. That left him ninety blind yards to the elevated green. His Snieler niblick in hand, he looked up too soon and flobbed the shot thirty yards short. It landed on the steep slope leading to the green; only the saturated ground prevented it from rolling all the way back down to where he stood. Darwin felt convinced at this point that his furious pace made possible by the open course in front of him was actually hurting Ted's play; he seemed to be rushing every shot he took, particularly on the greens.

When he hit that fat niblick approach to nine, for the first time that morning a few American partisans in the crowd cheered one of his mistakes. Marshals chased down the offenders and barked through their megaphones for quiet. Ted did a slow burn at the egregious lapse of etiquette—"It's not a bloody football game," he muttered—and refused to take his next shot until the gallery fell completely silent. He had no way of knowing that by now Reid's account of their run-in had spread all over the course and accounted for most of this unsportsmanlike reaction. The remainder had everything to do with the fact that Ted's meltdown left an opening for the Americans trying to catch him.

Whatever their reason for turning on him, Ted reacted badly. He chipped up shy of the green and came up short again on another par-saving putt for bogey six. That gave him 43 on the front nine, five strokes over par. Catastrophic by his or anyone else's standards. The front nine had extracted one last pound of Ted Ray's ample flesh. At a little after 1:30 that afternoon, the U.S. Open was officially up for grabs. And not just because of what Ted was doing.

Harry didn't have to worry about the crowd turning against him; that had never happened, never would. People don't boo the Rock of Gibraltar or the Statue of Liberty. His spotless reputation, his presence and poise under pressure commanded too much respect. Even if these novice American fans didn't understand the game and knew little about him, they sensed that Harry Vardon stood for something honest and decent: hard work, independence, self-reliance, and fair play. Beyond his evident genius for golf, this may have been the secret of his appeal to so many people in the United States; Harry embodied something close to the idealized American character. That his dreadful short putting scratched a ragged flaw across the face of such a paragon only increased their affection when they saw him deal with his Achilles heel so gracefully. Never a club thrown or a word spoken in anger. Never an expression of reproach or self-pity. On Friday afternoon the only enemy Harry had to confront at The Country Club was himself.

After parring the first hole Harry found himself growing unaccountably nervous while he waited at the second tee. He knew by then that Ouimet had drawn even with them as the third round ended, and had also been told that Ted was stumbling badly ahead. This time around the Greyhound wasn't thundering up on the field from behind, passing exhausted minor talents with ease as they staggered toward the finish. He was in a dead heat with a younger man who worried him as no other player had for years. With the weather equalizing almost every inherent advantage he might bring to bear, it was coming down to a simple case of whose nerves could stand the strain. For the first time since he'd recovered from his illness and climbed back to the top of the mountain, Harry feared he might not be up to the task. There comes a moment in every champion's life when he has to step aside for someone faster, stronger, younger. Was today that day?

As Harry played the second hole, he knew something was amiss; he felt as if his ability to command both mind and body had broken loose from its moorings. The tremor he'd experienced briefly at the fifteenth tee that morning had returned, and not just in his damaged right hand; both hands now were shaking. Although he could still swing the longer clubs and keep the ball in play, he couldn't putt to save his life. Helpless as a babe in a storm, Harry bogeyed the next four holes.

Walking in Harry's gallery, Lord Northcliffe watched in horror, living a worst-case nightmare; in the final hour, with the victory he'd waited nine years to taste nearly in hand, both his champions appeared to be going down in flames. Their scores through the front nine: 43 for Ted, 42 for Harry. The worst nine holes either man had played during their entire time at Brookline.

The first American with a chance to capitalize was Walter Hagen. With no spare dry outfit to change into, Walter stepped to the tee after Harry's group at 12:40 in the same wet and soiled silks he'd worn that morning. In the hour since he'd finished his third round, the footing on the tee ground had turned to mud; in order to keep from sliding around he had to dig in his slippery red-soled shoes like a baseball player in the batter's box. His biggest gallery of the tournament surrounded him now, and this time, Walter didn't throw winks at the girls or joke with the kids. Even he had to acknowledge this situation qualified as serious business. For the first time all week the devil-may-care young pro felt the steely pincer-grip of U.S. Open pressure compress his brain in its skull.

Walter pushed his tee shot toward the trees on the right. From a damp lie in the rough he couldn't quite get home in two at Polo Field. He chipped up and took his par. At the second hole his approach shot flew the shallow green into a backside bunker. Trying to chop out of the wet sand, he caught the ball thin and sent it trickling off the green's opposite side. After a weak chip he needed two putts to get down for double bogey six on a hole he considered the easiest on the course. *Come on, Hagen, what was that about?*

Although he knew where he stood in relation to the leaders at the start of the round, Walter was unaware of how badly Vardon and Ray were doing ahead; he had decided he didn't want to be told and wasn't going to ask. Walking to the third tee, Hagen had a little chat with himself.

One more screwup like that, kiddo, and you can kiss your chances good-bye right on the lips. And what'll they think of you in Rochester then, Mr. Fast Talker, when you come crawling back home without the trophy and your tail between your legs? Is that why you bought those fancy clothes and came all this way, just to call it quits in the middle of the biggest game of your life?

His answer was, naturally, no. But Hagen didn't have a clue about how he was going to pull it off. Between the rain-soaked turf and those damn red-soled shoes, his swing just couldn't find its groove. As he reached the elevated third tee, discouraged and not a little desperate, Hagen looked down onto the fairway below and caught a glimpse of Harry Vardon hitting his second shot.

That's it. The Vardon stance and swing.

Walter had been knocked out by Vardon's swing ever since he'd first seen him play in Monday's practice round; he was in awe of Harry's fluid grace. With his native gift for mimicry, just for fun Hagen had been toying around with imitating Vardon's move for days, even trying it out on a shot in his round that morning. But if what he needed now was nothing less than perfection, why not borrow the swing of the best player in the world?

Hagen teed up his ball. Holding the image of Harry in his mind, he stepped back, took three practice swings, and liked the way it felt. He didn't sway or lunge. He stayed in balance. His feet remained firmly rooted to the ground. Before he had a chance to talk himself out of trying it, he stepped up to the ball and, repeating that swing, smacked a beauty, 230 yards straight down the middle of the fairway.

Works like a charm.

Hagen walked out to his ball, channeled Harry again, and lofted a long brassie onto the front of the third green. Using his own putting stroke from there, two strokes later he had a birdie four. One over par for his round.

At the short fourth, he hit another Vardon-like drive and followed with a remarkably Vardon-esque pitch to within six feet of the flag. Bingo, he sank the putt for his second birdie in a row. Back to even par. His Vardon impersonation got him safely home with pars on five and six. At the par three seventh, he stuck his mid-iron tee shot within twelve feet of the hole. As he walked up to the green, he heard a buzz running through his gallery.

"Well, that's fine!" he heard a man say.

"What's so fine about it?" asked Hagen.

A complete stranger ran up to the ropes to tell him: "Ray and Vardon have gone out in forty-two and forty-three."

"You don't say," said Hagen. He felt his heart jump halfway up his throat.

"You're a stroke ahead of them, Hagen," said the man. "You're in the lead!"

"I wish you hadn't told me that," he said. (One has suspicions, but there is unfortunately no way to verify if this unidentified stranger was Francis's friend Frank Hoyt.)

Walter reached the green, but the Vardon half of his Vardon/Hagen combo, perhaps now that he knew the score, refused to tag along; Hagen, alone and squirming, three-putted from twelve feet for a bogey four. Tied with the real Vardon for the lead.

At the eighth hole neither Hagen nor his version of Vardon's swing could find the fairway; he took three shots to reach the green and two-putted for a bogey five. He no longer knew where he stood with the Englishmen ahead of him and liked it better that way, but now he began to worry he was screwing himself up with this copycat routine. His own swing had brought him this far. He would have to trust it to take him home the rest of the way. Going back to the Hagen original, Walter easily parred the long par five ninth to complete his front nine. He'd shot 40. Judging by his rapidly swelling gallery, he guessed he was still in the thick of it. Walter's instincts were as usual on the money; he was still one stroke ahead of Ted Ray and tied with Harry Vardon, the man whose swing Hagen had borrowed to catch him.

RUMORS BLANKETED THE press tent and clubhouse. A steady stream of boys and men came running in with updates from all directions. As the mood rose and fell on every new piece of hearsay, the press tent began to look and sound like a clinic for bipolar personalities.

"Hagen's gone out in thirty-five!" Cheers.

Minutes later his actual score of 40 was reported. Enthusiasm wavered until . . .

"McDermott's out in thirty-seven!" "He's right back in it!" "In it? He's just taken the lead!" "We knew he'd come through!"

Word soon filtered in: Johnny had actually made the turn at 39. He was still two strokes off the lead.

"Barnes has done it! Out in thirty-six!" "He's up by three!" "Barnes is going to do it, by God, he's got them!"

Another hope dashed, this one by the widest margin; Barnes was actually 41 at the turn. Behind Ray by one and Vardon by two. Mac Smith's announced 37 turned out to be a 38. He had tied Ray but trailed Vardon by a stroke.

This bedlam in the press tent couldn't compare to what the first nine was doing to the front of the field. The Englishmen had both staggered badly. Hagen had barely survived. Barnes was taking a self-administered beating. Courting pneumonia, John McDermott had gone out two groups after Hagen once more without a jacket, in the same soaked shirt he'd worn that morning. But alone among the early leaders he played boldly and brilliantly in the harrowing weather, even par through seven, a bogey on eight resulting from his only loose shot. McDermott played like a man fighting for his life, his country, and his mother. Johnny's gallery felt convinced the heroic charge they'd been waiting for all week was finally under way; people flocked to his twosome when they heard that at last their champ was flying his true colors.

Would it be enough?

WHEN YOU STOP to consider their situation, what did Ted Ray and Harry Vardon have left to prove? Over their last two months in America they had already spanked every top professional and amateur in the country on their own home turf. Both their reputations, even their places in history, had long ago been secured. They were universally liked and admired throughout the golfing world and were financially as secure as any two players had ever been in the history of their game.

On that Friday afternoon they were playing in a foreign land, at the tail end of a backbreaking tour schedule, in front of an unsympathetic if not openly hostile crowd, under conditions that would have caused the cancellation of any other athletic event imaginable and sent a duck flying for cover. The man who'd financed their trip had turned out to be an overbearing zealot on a private crusade to avenge a nine-year-old defeat in an amateur event they'd had nothing to do with. Harry was in acute physical distress. The crowd had turned on Ted, and after what he'd been through in the last twenty-four hours, he had every excuse in the world to emotionally fold his tent. Playing well ahead of the field, Ted reached the tenth tee convinced that his main chance to win the tournament had long since vanished down the drain. He promptly bogeyed the tenth hole to go six over par for the day. Reports from around the course informed him that three Americans had caught or passed him at this point and three more were nipping at his heels.

If you've ever wondered exactly how to measure what separates a champion from the rest of the great and talented players who've come and gone in golf, consider what Ted Ray and Harry Vardon did on the back nine at The Country Club on Friday afternoon in the final round of the 1913 U.S. Open.

Albeit more seamlessly integrated into his personality, Ted's emotional makeup bore a striking resemblance to John McDermott's: Controlled fury and an underdog's resentment of class privilege had always played a huge role in his ability to motivate himself. Beginning at the eleventh hole Ted finally found a way to funnel all the anger and frustration of the last twenty-four hours into his actions on the course. His swing came home. Drives found the fairways. He birdied the eleventh, parred the twelfth, birdied the short thirteenth, and parred the fourteenth. Luck is nothing more than the residue of hard work, Ted had been known to say. At the fifteenth his hard work paid another dividend; he sent a skyrocket drive hooking off line to the left, apparently headed for disaster in the woods when it struck a tree and bounced into the middle of the fairway. Catching a second wind from this good fortune, he parred three of those last four holes, marred only by a three-putt bogey at sixteen, to salvage his back nine with an even par 36. Ted had gone out angry, and he came back in angry. In between he completed play in less than two and a half hours and shot 79 for his final round. His playing partner Mike Brady shot 80 and finished the tournament in fourteenth place, out of the money.

Ted turned in his scorecard, fully prepared to watch a parade of players pass him and claim the title. In the press tent, just as Harry had done before the tournament began, Ted predicted the winning score would be 300; he'd come in at 304. He offered no excuses for his plan, and refused to answer any questions about Wilfred Reid: "I have nothing to say about that." He left minutes later, downed a whiskey, and went out to watch Harry Vardon play in.

Ted Ray had played his round so quickly that by the time he finished,

Francis hadn't even reached the first tee. While he prepared on the practice green, Francis paused to watch Ted par the Home hole. Eddie hurried back from the edge of the crowd to tell him Ted's score.

"Seventy-nine?" said Francis, taken aback. "That's not very low, is it? I mean, even with the rain."

"He's dead," said Eddie.

"I wouldn't go so far as to say that, Eddie—"

"He's dead and gone. Where should we send the flowers?" said Eddie.

"Let's not get ahead of ourselves—"

"It don't matter anyway, Francis, 'cause this is the round you're going to shoot seventy-two, just like I been telling you all along."

For the first time Eddie's predictions were starting to make Francis uneasy. "We'll just have to see about that."

John Anderson walked out from the press tent to join Francis's gallery as he moved to the tee. Whatever else happened, as far as John was concerned, the story of the day and of the tournament began and ended with the kid across the street.

OVER THE PREVIOUS fifteen years Bernard Darwin had watched Harry Vardon play over a hundred rounds of golf all over the world. He had seen him at his zenith and his nadir. As a journalist he had watched him rise and fall, and then charted every step of his return from the dead. As a friend and fellow player, his admiration and appreciation for the depth of Harry's talent ran deeper than just about anyone else's on the planet. But Darwin had never seen Harry look more distracted than he did early Friday afternoon. After recording a par at the tenth, Harry bogeyed the eleventh, a hole he'd handled easily all week. After a birdie at the twelfth, he bogeyed the thirteenth, another hole he'd never faltered on before. Whatever was eating away at him, and Darwin knew him well enough to know something was wrong, Harry had clearly not found a way to right the ship.

When Harry reached the fourteenth tee, his twosome faced a slight delay. While they waited, Harry fumbled around in his pockets, took out his pipe and pouch, filled the bowl, and struck a match under the cover of his caddie's umbrella. As far as Bernard Darwin could remember he'd never seen Harry light up his pipe on a golf course before. He thought it looked as if Harry's hands were trembling.

A runner came streaking out of the press tent to let Darwin know that Ted had just finished his round at 79 for a total of 304. Lord Northcliffe came stomping through the puddles moments later. Harry waved Darwin over. He wanted to know Ted's score as well. Darwin told him. Harry glanced at his scorecard.

"I'll need to par the last five holes to tie Ted for the lead," said Harry.

"That's right, Harry," said Darwin.

As Harry stood on the tee puffing on his pipe looking out at the fairway, Darwin saw a noticeable change come over him; he looked calm and collected again. A slight smile appeared. Maybe giving himself something to do with his hands eased Harry's nerves. Perhaps it was just the soothing blend of tobaccos he favored.

Sure, that was it.

Harry drove the ball deep into the fairway at the par five fourteenth. He played a precise, safe second shot to within a hundred yards. A niblick from there just missed the front of the green. Harry chipped up to within five feet of the pin, short and below the hole. Lying four, he needed this putt for par. He looked at it for a long time, then settled into his stance, moving even more slowly and deliberately than usual. As he took the putter back, Bernard Darwin held his breath—he was tempted to close his eyes—but Harry's hand didn't jump. The ball ran up and into the cup. Par five.

Harry secured a routine four at fifteen and moved to the par three sixteenth. His massive gallery flowed in and around the boundaries of the short hole like mercury on a tabletop. He knew sixteen represented his best remaining chance for birdie and a chance to win the Open outright. Harry decided to gamble and shoot at the flag, tucked in the right front corner. Slightly miscalculating the distance, he planted the shot in the front right bunker. Although there were no overt celebrations from the crowd, as there had been recently with Ted, when Harry made this unforced mistake, the reaction was clearly less than sympathetic.

"He's done for now," someone said, loud enough to hear. "It's all over for him."

Darwin saw the muscles in Harry's jaw tighten as he walked toward the green. He stepped in and carefully examined his lie, half-buried in the muddy waste that now filled the bunker. He had short-sided himself, the pin set only ten feet from the edge of the trap leaving him no green to work with. He would have to somehow slice under the packed and sodden sand and apply enough spin to stop the ball in its tracks. Degree of difficulty: almost impossible. Margin for error: zero.

Harry selected his niblick, laid it flat open, and made a couple of abbreviated practice swings. He stood over the ball, dug in his feet, looked at the target, looked back down at the ball, and made a short, unhurried swing, snapping his wrists as the blade dug under the ball and then abruptly stopped the club at the bottom of its arc. The ball elevated softly out of the trap riding a small scallop of sand, just cleared the lip, landed on the front of the green, and rolled gently forward to within four feet of the flagstick. In spite of their partisan sentiments the crowd felt compelled to applaud his artistry. Smiling slightly—*How quickly they can turn*—he acknowledged them with a tip of his cap as he walked to the green. Harry puffed on his pipe and looked over the line carefully before taking his putter. A patch of mud clung to the side of the ball. After calculating how it would affect the path of the putt he calmly rolled it right into the heart of the hole to save his par.

Ted Ray walked down from the clubhouse to join his gallery as Harry walked to seventeen. Inside the ropes they shared a quiet word.

"It's come to me, Harry," said Ted. "Not a single one of them out here wants to see us win it."

"Is that a fact?" asked Harry.

"Yes. But the thing is, if it is going to happen, old boy, I'd just as soon not do it alone. That is, if you think you can catch me."

That actually made Harry laugh. He had played these last two holes even par in every round that week. As if sinking those saving putts at fourteen and sixteen had cauterized every jangled nerve in his body, he now easily matched the feat again; two fairways, two greens, four putts. Harry tapped in a six-inch gimme for par at eighteen. Just as his countryman had before him, Harry Vardon gathered himself in time to shoot 79 and tie Ted Ray for the lead at 304. The huge gallery that had followed Harry throughout gave him a polite round of applause and then immediately evaporated, rushing away in search of the nearest American contender.

As Harry walked off the green, Ted waited to shake his hand, but a glowering Lord Northcliffe avoided them both, retreating to a corner of the clubhouse to order a drink; for the moment he refused to meet their eye and said nothing to either man.

"You're welcome, Alfred," said Ted to his back as Northcliffe walked away.

Harry turned in his card to the scorer's tent. Bernard Darwin waited for him there and took Harry aside before the other reporters converged on him.

"I don't believe I've ever seen you smoke on the course before, Harry," said Darwin.

"Yes," said Harry with a rueful smile. "I wish I'd started four holes earlier."

The two Jerseymen entered the press tent and faced the reporters together, dejected but presenting themselves with dignity and composure. Northcliffe slipped into the back of the tent to listen.

"You're both tied for the lead; how do you like your chances?"

"It was a game effort but I'm afraid we have no hope of winning now," said Harry.

"But you both played so well all week; why, how did this happen?"

"No excuses, gentlemen. I played rotten," said Ted. "And to make matters worse, Harry went out and did the same thing."

"But how do you account for your poor performances? Was it simply the dreadful conditions?"

"No, the conditions are the same for everyone. We had our chances. I am very sorry," said Harry, "but it was my putting that has let me down again. As I feared it would."

"So what do you think will happen now?"

"It's anyone's tournament," said Ted. "And the best of luck to them."

"Are you saying you think it's possible an American will win the Open?"

"Yes," said Harry. "There are three or four men still out on the course who will beat us." *But there's only one you're truly worried about, Harry, and you know it.*

"Won't be long now," said Ted. "In the meantime, we may as well both go pack."

Hearing that bombshell, people sprinted out of the tent and the word spread like a brushfire: Vardon and Ray had as much as conceded defeat. An American was going to beat them; you could print it! Northcliffe stormed out of the tent. Ted and Harry walked back out to the course, grim-faced, curious to see who would be the man to beat them.

Half an hour later, they'd all be smiling again.

ON THE FIRST tee, Eddie handed Francis his driver.

"Keep your head down," he said. "I'll watch the ball."

Francis hit a beautiful drive. Eddie liked the way he looked; smiling again, focused, and sharp. Play smart, play steady, just as he had all week. Pay no attention to what anyone else is doing. That's what they'd agreed to do in this last round, as they walked to the tee. Francis appeared eager and ready.

"You look pretty happy, Francis," said Eddie.

"We're not supposed to win, are we? No one expects us to, rightfully so," said Francis.

"Don't say that, we've got as good a chance as anybody—"

"So we're not out here playing for anything but fun, Eddie," he said, interrupting again. "Let's not forget that."

In the pouring rain he parred the first four holes.

BY NOW IT had become impossible to play among the galleries swirling around the course and not hear about the action up ahead. As Walter Hagen reached the eleventh tee, he overheard another conversation that told him he was tied again, this time with Ted Ray for the lead. He didn't let it bother him. He had command of his own swing again, he had his native confidence back, and now he had momentum.

Hagen parred the eleventh. At the twelfth tee word came filtering back from the clubhouse that Ted Ray had finished with 79; 304 for the tourney. Walter needed only to finish the back nine with a 37, one over par, to tie him. Even par from this point on in would win it for him outright. Seven holes to go, with a stroke to spare.

Fame, riches, glory. The future he'd always imagined for himself called to him. Hagen listened; was it destiny or sirens luring him toward the rocks?

After two good shots put him on the green he three-putted the twelfth for a bogey. There went his insurance stroke; back into a tie.

The short par four thirteenth. A birdie hole for many, although Walter hadn't managed one yet during the tournament, maybe the best chance for birdie left on the course. Should he play safe—he could still par in to tie for the lead and force a play-off—or take a chance here and go for the win? He'd tried to play it safe on twelve and look where that got him.

Reason won the argument. Walter played it safe again; instead of a driver, he hit a long-iron off the tee into the fairway. Then an exquisite approach to within twelve feet of the hole. *See that, Walter; you play the percentages and your birdie chance comes along in any case.*

Twelve feet for birdie and the lead.

The putt tracked on line, straight for the hole, straight in, the crowd yelled . . . it hit the edge a touch too fast, skidded on the rim, ran around half its circumference . . . and somehow stayed out. A huge groan from the gallery. He tapped in for par.

Steady, Walter, steady; par's a swell score here, all you need. Keep that up; four holes out of the way, only five to go. Play for the tie, not the lead. Don't gamble now and this thing's in your hip pocket.

The fourteenth, Quarry; 470-yard par five. Walter hit a perfect drive, a powerful draw that hugged the curve of the fairway, caught a downward slope as it landed, and gave him twenty extra yards of roll even in the rain. He could see his ball from the tee, sitting up, a good level lie on short grass.

As he walked to the ball, a boy came running back from the green. News from the group directly ahead: With four holes to play, Vardon was now tied with Ray. He'd caught both of them. He could do this.

Hagen looked at his ball. He'd hit his drive so far, it brought the green into play. Two hundred and ten yards. Perfect lie. He could get there in two. This was the last par five on the course; a birdie here could cinch it, might vault him over both Brits for the title. The idea worked on him, starting to win him over. Not only that, a birdie here would give him a cushion for the last four testing holes; he could bogey one of them and still finish tied for the lead.

Walter had walked out onto the razor's edge every contender eventually has to traverse in a championship; do you take the bold gamble that if successful guarantees the win, or is this the one ambitious shot that overreaches, fails, and drives a stake through the heart of your chances?

He looked at his bag. He could lay up with a short-iron, leave himself an easy third shot into the green, maybe still make four. That was the safe play. Par would almost be a certainty then. Pars were all he needed now. On the other hand . . .

Tough green, sloped back to front. Big breaks. Easy to three-putt.

Walter's thoughts doubled back on him. He'd birdied the damn hole on Thursday morning by going for the green in two and getting there easily after a solid drive like the one he'd just hit. But the course had been dry and fast then. Conditions had changed radically. Could he afford to risk that same shot now?

His hand rested on a short-iron, hesitated, then Hagen reached in and defiantly yanked out his brassie. The crowd saw his club selection and a thrill ran through them: *He's going for it!*

Hagen rehearsed the swing, once, twice, three times. Two hundred and ten yards, slightly right to left, slightly uphill. Pin in the back, let it land just short and roll the last few yards onto the green. Nothing but trouble on the left, woods and a wall marking out of bounds, room to bail out on the right. Roll the wrists, not too quick, let the club do the work. *Don't worry about going long; all that water on the grass will act as a brake if you give it too much gas.*

He took his stance—one last thought: *Whose swing will this be, mine or Vardon's?* No answer.

He swung. He swung hard. He gave it everything he had and topped the ball. It skidded along never rising more than a foot off the ground, spinning through the grass, pinwheeling water like an old river paddleboat. It came to rest forty yards ahead, still in the fairway. That miserable sight, the ball rooster-tailing water as it spun away, in spite of all his triumphs to come, would haunt Hagen for the rest of his life.

Now he had no choice. One hundred and seventy yards left to the green. Birdie was gone. He had to get there, had to save this par. He took out a long-iron. Anxious now. He swung hard again and too fast and now those chic, stylish, impractical red-rubber-soled shoes finally did him in; Walter's feet slid out from under him on the soaking turf. His hips whipped through out of sync, his arms jerked around after them, and the ball hooked left off the club face, hard left, headed directly for the wall that marked the out of bounds—if it went over, he was as good as dead . . . but the ball hit the wall and bounced back into play. Settled in tall, wet grass between the wall and fairway, lying three.

Sixty yards to the green with a wide bunker to clear. The ball resting down in very heavy rough. From bad to worse, but at least the wall had saved him; now he needed to get up and down out of this mess to save his par.

He could do this. Land the ball on the edge, just over the bunker, let it roll back gently to the pin. Hagen gripped his niblick and dug the ball out perfectly from the rough. It flew straight for the green and landed just where he'd been aiming, two inches over the lip of the bunker. But the rain had dislodged a strip of black squishy soil on the green's margins; instead of bouncing forward when it plopped softly into this muck, the ball hesitated and then slowly, agonizingly, rolled back down into the sand.

Hagen walked forward to the green. His stomach churning, sick with anger and disappointment. Lying four in a greenside bunker. One last chance: He could still get up and down for bogey. With a birdie somewhere in the last four holes, Ray and Vardon could still be caught. He could do this.

He looked down into the bunker. A good lie, on the uphill slope, plenty of green to work with. The chunk of mud he'd landed it in had attached itself to the ball, but not on the side he had to strike now; surely it would come loose when he hit this shot. Then he'd be able to putt once he was on the green, he was sure of it.

Niblick again. He settled over the ball, opened the face of the club, swung long and lazy. Perfect swing. The ball flew up with the sand, landed, and rolled to within a foot and a half of the cup. The crowd went mad; what a shot! Yes, he would salvage his bogey after all and stay in the thick of the race. Walter took the putter from his caddie, walked up onto the green to tap it in.

That fat dollop of mud attached to his ball had not come off. Worse, the ball had lined up in such a way that the mud sat facing him, directly where his putter would have to make contact.

Lady Luck has left me.

Wait: Hit the ball hard enough and the mud might flatten out. He could still apply a solid strike to the ball and drive it forward on line to the cup. It was only eighteen inches; he could do this. The caddie walked up to quietly suggest that maybe his niblick would work best here, belly it open, blade the ball in with the leading edge.

"No," said Walter. "The putter."

Walter settled; an absurdly easy putt under any other circumstances. Straight uphill. Eighteen inches.

The putter struck mud, the mud failed to compress, and after one roll the ball veered quickly and sharply to the right of the hole. The crowd groaned as if they were in pain.

Not as much as Walter. He tapped in for double bogey seven. He would play solidly from here in and finish three strokes behind them, but Hagen knew it was too late.

The sirens had lured him onto the rocks.

TWO GROUPS BEHIND Hagen, Johnny McDermott continued to rage against the storm. His final charge, gallant and brave, suffered no collapse to compare with what happened to Hagen at fourteen. The crowds didn't desert him, as they did in droves after Walter took his seven; in fact, he inherited most of the people who had fled Hagen at fourteen and they stayed with him right through the end. Small niggling mistakes applied the final blows to McDermott's last stand; a halfhearted chip at ten resulted in bogey. A careless short putt at fifteen gave him another. A drive that hit the fairway and bounced into the rough at eighteen handed him his third bogey at the last, but his championship defense was already well over by then. John shot 78 for his final round and finished at 309, five strokes in back of Vardon and Ray. No one could fault him for the complete committed effort he'd shown them; in the end, he'd begun his charge from too far back. On Friday afternoon McDermott had at last played with all the fury and brilliance his fans expected from him, and when he dropped his last putt at the Home hole, they gave him a sustained ovation. The now former champion took off his sodden cap. He'd left everything he had in him on the course. He stood before them, shivering in the rain, exhausted, scarred, and pale, looking around darkly at the crowd surrounding the green. It was impossible to tell: Did he see friends or enemies?

Two-time U.S. Open champion John J. McDermott, all of twenty-two years old, would never win another tournament, at any level of play, in his lifetime.

Harry and Ted watched McDermott hole out from the shelter of the press tent. They turned to each other, eyebrows raised.

"Unexpected," said Harry.

"Very," said Ted, then added quietly, "but not unwelcome."

America's once shining beacon had been reduced to a flickering flame. Hagen was gone. McDermott was finished. The crowd's attention shifted to Jim Barnes; they'd heard he was going like a streak! Not exactly, as it turned out he'd shot 41 on the front, but had drawn within two of Ray and one of Vardon. He needed 34 on the back, two under par, not an easy assignment under the best of conditions, but he'd done it already during his first round the day before. It quickly became evident that on this rain-soaked Friday afternoon, Jim Barnes wasn't up to the task. Consecutive bogeys at ten and eleven left him three strokes down. His star faded fast; Barnes was done.

Among the American pros, that left only Mac Smith. Despite being five strokes down at the start of the afternoon, for a short while his chances looked the most realistic; his even par 38 on the front was the best turned in by an American contender all afternoon. Mac's gallery grew accordingly as he made the turn, and expanded further when he stayed even par through thirteen. He faced the same situation Hagen had an hour before;

five more pars would tie him with Vardon and Ray. But once again the four-teenth hole jumped up to claim another victim; a loose drive resulted in bogey six. One stroke down. A bogey at seventeen finished Smith for good.

There was only one last unlikely professional still out on the course with a chance to catch the British greats. He played virtually unnoticed among the crowds intent on hustling around to follow the marquee names, in front of only his wife, two caddies, and his playing partner Tom Vardon. Alone in the entire field he flew neither the Stars and Stripes nor the Union Jack. Down to one last roll of the dice to make his mark in America, six strokes in back of the leaders when the final round began, lit-tle Louis Tellier walked out into the tempest that afternoon and nearly pulled off a miracle.

Back-to-back birdies at the first two holes got him going. A string of pars and then the unlikeliest birdie at the imposing eighth. Amidst all the false reports crowding the course that day, no one got this one right. Louis Tellier had shot a three under par 35 on the front nine, at which point he led the tournament by three strokes. All he needed to do now to jump out of the bushes and take the trophy back to Paris with him was shoot a one over par 37 on The Country Club's easier back nine.

Opportunity knocked, the door opened and Louis was halfway through it, when he slipped on a wet tee box at the twelfth hole. Fashion killed the Frenchman; Louis was wearing a pair of the same stylish rubber-soled shoes that had spelled the end for Hagen. His tee shot dove into the woods. His recovery failed. Bogey six. Tellier rallied to par the thirteenth, but then another bogey six at the fourteenth shoved him back out the door and slammed it shut in his face. Still just one stroke off the lead as he reached seventeen, all Louis could manage coming in were back-to-back bogeys. Only his black-eyed brother-in-law Wilfred Reid stood waiting for him at the Home hole green. They embraced, a kiss on each cheek. Tom Vardon shook Louis's hand and congratulated his fine effort, in the broken Jersey French he and his brother had spoken as boys. Louis Tellier finished his tournament at 307, three strokes back, tied with Hagen, Barnes, and Smith for third place.

After quickly scanning the scoreboard, Tom spotted Harry and Ted moving out with the swelling tide toward the front nine.

"Who's made a run at you?" asked Tom.

"No one," said Harry. "So far."

"All come a cropper," said Ted.

"Damndest thing. A bit like that last finish at Prestwick, isn't it?" said Tom, referring to 1911's British Open, where he'd waited with Harry at the eighteenth green expecting a whole squadron of pursuers to beat his early lead, and none had materialized. "All those bright young lads falling down at the end."

"Right," said Ted dryly. "You'll remember I was one of that bunch."

Bernard Darwin came out of the trees to tell them Barnes and Mac Smith had just joined the list of casualties on the back nine.

"You might want to let Northcliffe know," said Harry.

"Where is he?" asked Darwin.

"Back at the clubhouse. In the bar, I suspect."

"Tell him he can take the pistol out of his mouth," said Ted.

The three Jerseymen laughed. Darwin hurried off.

"So who's left?" asked Tom.

"They've got one last hope," said Harry.

ONE LAST HOPE.

As Eddie and Francis moved to the fifth tee, in the distance Eddie saw a great black-clad wave sweeping toward them through the trees, thousands of people, all agitated, some great excitement driving them forward like a stampeding herd. Then he spotted Frank Hoyt in their front rank.

"Here comes trouble," said Eddie.

Try as he might, with the size of that crowd, Eddie couldn't prevent the news from reaching Francis, although he saw to it that Frank Hoyt didn't deliver it personally. The news came to them complete and, for once, accurate in detail: Vardon had finished his round in 79, tying him with Ray at 304. No one else had mounted a successful challenge. All the American pros had failed. Done. The road to victory in front of Francis, even par to this point in his round, stood empty and unimpeded. He had the lead in the final round of the U.S. Open by five strokes.

Eddie glanced at Francis; he wouldn't meet his eye. He looked as if someone had just dropped a safe on him.

Not again, thought Eddie. *Not now.*

The 420-yard par four fifth hole, Newton, features a blind tee shot over a rocky ledge to an elevated landing area. Players line up their drives by choosing a spot on the rocks for their target. Beyond them the fairway doglegs to the right and a long, narrow bunker guards against an approach twenty yards short of the green. Francis sliced his tee shot slightly, clearing the rocks easily, but the ball caught a mound in the fairway and bounced into the right edge of the rough. He had shortened the distance to the hole by cutting the corner, but that brought the long bunker into play on his second shot from a less than perfect lie. Faced with a choice of laying up short and then going for the green in three, Francis decided to try to fly the bunker and reach the green in regulation. One hundred and ninety yards. Eddie handed him his lofted brassie. The swing felt good, but wet grass grabbed at the hosel of his club, the head twisted slightly, and the shot came out short, right, and weak. The ball landed hard in the bunker. They hurried forward.

Buried in mud. A gardening tool might not dig it out of there in a single try. He stared at it hard. Eddie waited. Francis asked for his niblick. He rehearsed the swing, then carved down at the ball. It popped out of its sandy grave but stayed in the bunker. Lying three, in a civilized lie. He eased his next shot onto the green. Twenty feet to salvage a bogey five. The putt came up short. Double bogey six. His lead was down to three.

"That's okay, Francis," said Eddie. "Steady as she goes."

The short par four sixth, Baker, was Francis's favorite hole on the front and he'd handled it easily all week; two pars and then a birdie just that morning. Three bunkers within reach of the tee guard the right side of the fairway; if they can be avoided, the hole offers a relatively easy second shot to a flat, elevated green, bunkered on three sides.

An iron, he thought. *I should hit an iron here.*

He'd hit his driver, and trusted it, in the other three rounds and played the hole one under par. The knowledge of where he now stood in relation to Vardon and Ray had insinuated itself into his mind like a snake. Play safe. Ahead by three strokes. Protect the lead.

Eddie offered the bag. Francis pulled out the one-iron.

"Sure you don't want to hit the driver?" asked Eddie.

Francis nodded. He set up to swing. *How sure are you really, Francis?* asked the snake.

He made the swing with a divided mind; the ball reacted accordingly. Started on line, drifted slightly, landed short of where he would have hit his driver, and kicked dead left into the rough. Still a relatively easy, albeit blind, approach shot to the green. Francis swung hard but pulled the ball left; it landed ten feet from the edge of the green between two bunkers, in heavy rough. The pin was set left and front; he'd short-sided himself. His chip ran long. He needed two putts to get down. Bogey five, another stroke wasted. Ahead by only two.

As he made the lengthy walk to the seventh tee, the ever-swelling sea of people around him overwhelmed the marshals and the rope men. Francis had to fight his way clear at the tee box before the lines were restored, and when he walked into the open, he discovered he was alone. He'd lost Eddie.

"Eddie? Eddie!"

Moments later marshals wedged open a small gap in the rim of the crowd; what looked like a walking umbrella dragging a large bag of clubs squeezed through. As the tiny figure joined Francis on the tee, the crowd gave Eddie a round of applause. Francis smiled, directing the cheers and good-natured laughs toward his caddie.

"Jokers wouldn't let me through," said Eddie as he reached Francis, his face red and hot. "I got the man's clubs here, I'm saying, and they don't move."

"That's fine, Eddie. Let's have the mid-iron here."

Eddie and the laughter lightened Francis's burden for the moment. He parred the par three Plateau without incident.

The 380-yard par four eighth hole, Corner, proceeds from an elevated tee looking down at a sharp dogleg right protected by three bunkers, the farthest and last of these the most dangerous; large, deep, and heavily trafficked. The ideal shot calls for a powerful fade starting down the left side, ending just right of center. A hush as Francis stood at the tee peering down at the fairway; only the muffled pelt of water on thousands of umbrellas and rubber raincoats.

Out of the corner of his eye, Francis caught sight of two tall men standing away from the crowd near the trees on the right side of the tee. Vardon and Ray. They'd come out to watch him. Cool, assessing, pipes in hand. Francis's heart thumped at his ribs, he felt a kick of adrenaline rip through his body.

Harry Vardon. Watching me. Yikes.

Eddie followed his gaze to the Englishmen. Saw the alarm spread across Francis's face.

"Got to stay focused now, Francis," he said. "Keep your eye on the ball."

"Okay, Eddie."

Look around, plenty of other faces in this crowd. Most of them strangers but among them many friends; there's John Anderson, George Wright, Heine Schmidt. My brother Raymond, sister Louise. So many others I've only just met during the last four weeks; Jerry Travers, Robert Watson, Jim Barnes, Walter Hagen. All pulling for me.

But of all those untold thousands surrounding him, Francis could feel only Harry's eyes on him now, as cold and hard as slate. He ran through all his checks to settle himself down as he stepped over the ball: grip, stance, alignment, weight. He selected his target, but the flight of the ball that usually followed didn't come into his mind. Nothing. The vision was gone.

Too fast. He swung too fast, hands and hips out of sync, club face open. The ball went right from the start, slicing away from the target and the fairway, toward the three bunkers, toward the worst of them, the last one, and in it went. As Francis and Eddie hurried down to examine his lie, he could already hear people in the crowd ahead gasping. The ball had drilled into the forward face of the bunker, directly beneath a sheer four-foot embankment, in a cavernous footprint left by a previous visitor who hadn't raked the sand afterward. No hope of advancing the ball ahead. Almost no hope of even getting a club on it, so dense and angled the lie. Disaster. Eddie looked stunned.

"They might as well bury him right along with it," whispered Ted to Harry, not without sympathy.

"It's a bad break," said Harry.

Francis stood stock-still on the edge of the bunker, hands on his hips, staring down into the pit. The crowd waited. Unconsciously copying Francis's stance, Eddie never took his eyes off the milky crown of the ball peeking up through the wet, broken sand.

"You see that, Eddie?" said Francis finally, pointing to the footprint, finding an outlet for his anger. "That's why they put rakes near all the bunkers. Let that be a lesson to us."

Eddie nodded. "What should we do?"

"I'll have to knock it back this way, away from the green. I don't like to do it, but there it is. Let's have the niblick."

Francis dug in as close as he could get to the ball, nearly up to his ankles in the pliant mud, facing back toward the tee box. He rehearsed the swing but could barely clear the front embankment behind him. He paused for a moment, gathered himself, then blasted down at the white dot in the sand. The ball jumped out of the footprint but not the bunker, rolling back down toward its opposite side into a playable lie. Lying two.

Now judging he had enough room to clear the steep front lip, Francis selected a slightly longer iron. He made crisp contact and flew it out sharply, but the ball came up forty yards short of the green. An effective pitch from there left him ten feet from the flagstick, lying four. Unsure of the line, he pushed the putt to the right and tapped in for a double bogey six.

All five shots of his precious lead squandered in three holes. He'd fallen back into a tie with Vardon and Ray.

"That's what I get," said Francis, "for playing safe."

"Those English guys are watching us," said Eddie as they walked to the next tee.

"It's a free country; they can do whatever they like," said Francis.

"It makes me mad."

"Think of it this way, Eddie," said Francis, feeling his spirits take an unexpected lift. "We're still tied with them and now there's nothing they can do about it."

Eddie considered it a moment. "That's pretty good, isn't it?"

"That's pretty good."

A breathless Lord Northcliffe, Darwin in his wake, caught up with Ted and Harry as the gallery followed Francis to the ninth tee. His eyes bright as pearl buttons again, cheeks flushed with excitement or drink, or both, Northcliffe looked like a man who'd just been resurrected from the grave.

"We're all square now," said Northcliffe. "Only the boy left with a chance to catch you, has he got that right?" He gestured back at Darwin, who shrugged and smiled sheepishly at Harry: *What can you do?*

"That's about the size of it," said Harry.

"All square it is," said Ted.

"Bravo. Brilliant work, lads," said Northcliffe. "Well done."

"We haven't 'done' anything for the last hour and a half, Alfred," said Harry.

"Closer to two for me," said Ted.

"Yes, well, you know what I mean. Well done for England."

Ted looked at Harry, shook his head, and kept walking.

For only the second time that afternoon, at the ninth hole Francis waited for George Sargent to hit first off the tee. Francis kept this drive safely in the fairway, then played a solid second shot and reached the par five's green in three. His putt for birdie creased the lip of the hole and spun to the side. Francis reached down and tapped in to complete his front nine in 43, no worse than Ted had done, one better than Harry had managed. All three deadlocked in the same tie with which they'd begun the final round.

It's difficult to pinpoint exactly how large his gallery had grown as Francis made the turn. Estimates run as high as 10,000 people; include the number of people in years to come who claimed they'd been there that day and it could easily reach six figures. Every player and caddie who'd finished up ahead, every tournament official, every jaded hack in the press corps, every member of The Country Club with two good legs was out on his trail now. Rank novices who had come to Brookline on a lark without a clue about the game of golf realized they might be witnessing something extraordinary. For the first time in its four days the entire focus of the 1913 U.S. Open had telescoped down to one single player. As Francis walked among that gallery to the tenth tee, enough electricity flowed through the grounds to run a streetcar all the way to Boston.

Francis's playing partner George Sargent had been reduced to an invisible man; as a former Open champion, he also had the sense to recognize the building drama and get out of its way. He'd started his last round with an outside chance himself, but that had flown away many holes ago. Sargent played quickly when his turns came, and poorly, but he never begrudged the circumstances or made excuses for the last-round 89 that dropped him from contention. A great teacher who would soon become one of the driving forces behind the formation of the American PGA, George Sargent had lasting memories of this day that would more than make up for any disappointment. The back nine on Friday afternoon at The Country Club would offer Francis his moment on the stage alone, if he wanted to seize it.

That would be entirely up to him.

FRANCIS TEEING OFF AT THE 13TH HOLE, FRIDAY AFTERNOON.
(EDDIE, WITH TOWEL, WATCHES FROM LEFT.)

FRIDAY AFTERNOON: THE BACK NINE

"STAND CLEAR!" "QUIET please!" "Silence!" "Trim that line to the right!"

So many tenors, bassos, and baritones shouted at the crowd through their megaphones that they drowned one another out. Rope men scrambled like soldiers called to arms, spreading out down the edge of the fairway to even up their lines. Thousands jostled along the ropes for position, slipping and sliding in the muddy turf; it's a minor miracle no one in the crowd fell underfoot to be trampled.

Francis and George Sargent walked out onto the tenth tee, Redan. The elevated tee box looked down across a narrow vale to a plateaued, slightly less elevated green. Three traps guarding its left-hand side, one long bunker protecting the front. One hundred and forty yards to the pin.

The rain hammered at them. The wind picked up, blowing directly into Francis's face as he stared down at the green. He had parred this hole in all three previous rounds; Eddie offered him the same lofted iron he'd used on each of those occasions. Francis hesitated to accept it.

"What are you thinking?" asked Eddie.

"It's soft as a marsh down there now," said Francis. "A high pitch falling from this angle might bury on the green."

"That's no good."

Francis narrowed his eyes. "I could run a mid-iron up, punch it through the wind. Might keep any mud from collecting on the ball as well."

"Can you hit that shot?"

"I hit it all the time," said Francis.

"Well, okay then," said Eddie, and handed over his mid-iron.

Francis teed the ball low, wiped the rain from his face, rehearsed the swing—shorter going back, hands low coming through, smooth tempo, low finish—and took his stance.

"Keep your eye on the ball," said Eddie.

But for the first and only time that day, Francis failed to follow Eddie's advice. He looked up a fraction of a second before the swing was through, anxious to see how this ambitious shot would fare. He almost missed it entirely. Badly topped, the ball skipped forward no more than fifteen feet, failing to even reach the end of the teeing ground. The crowd reacted as though they'd just witnessed a car wreck. Flushed and embarrassed, Francis walked forward to the ball and handed the mid-iron back to Eddie.

"That wasn't quite what I had in mind," he said.

"You can still make three," said Eddie.

"I'm going to try, Eddie."

Francis asked for the niblick Eddie had originally offered. After smoothing out his stroke, he made a beautiful pass at the ball, lofting it high and right on line; it landed softly, without plugging or accumulating any mud, and rolled to within eight feet of the cup. With their hopes brought back from the brink again, the hometown crowd cheered him all the way to the green.

"That," said Harry to Ted, "was a good shot."

"It'll be an even better putt for three," said Ted.

"He'll never make it," said Northcliffe.

As they walked toward the green, Darwin agreed with his boss but to his surprise found himself secretly hoping that Francis would make that putt. Harry and Ted felt certain he would; that's how pros protected themselves. Always expect your opponent to succeed.

But he didn't. Francis rolled the ball three feet past the hole, and to make matters worse, this left him with a downhill slider coming back. Loud gasps filled the air when he missed that one, too. Three putts from inside eight feet. Double bogey five. A living nightmare. Francis now trailed the Englishmen by two strokes with only eight holes to play.

As the crowd hurried on to line up at the next hole, Harry held his ground for a moment, puffing his pipe, studying the dejection on Francis's face. He read more there than most.

That was it.

"Let's have that drink," said Harry to Ted.

"My thoughts exactly," said Ted.

The two turned and started back toward the clubhouse; to their minds the game was over, but Northcliffe hung back with Darwin, momentarily confused about how to interpret his players' behavior.

"Right, I'm heading back in," said Northcliffe finally. "Our boys'll have their play-off for the cup tomorrow. Maybe this damn New England weather'll be gone by then." He started off. When Darwin didn't immediately follow, Northcliffe stopped and turned back to him. "Coming, Bernard?"

"I'll stay out a while," said Darwin, pad in hand. "You know, see the proper end of it. For the story."

"Suit yourself," said Northcliffe, and set out after Harry and Ted.

A similar conclusion sadly worked its way through the crowd; he'd made a courageous effort but their valiant young man had finally reached his limit. All was lost; the cup would be going to England with Vardon and Ray after all. Ready to finally quit the wretched weather, more than 100 Americans turned and followed the Jerseymen back in. Ninety-nine out of every 100 in the crowd who stayed behind wouldn't have bet a nickel on Francis's chances now.

"That's done it," said one man, a first-time tournament observer, shaking his head, already an expert. "He's finished now."

The two men standing next to him—he didn't know them—voiced their disagreement.

"Oh? And what makes you so sure?" asked the man.

"I've seen him play before," said Jerry Travers.

"He's two shots down with eight to play," said the man, as if explaining it to a small child. "I'm telling you there's no chance." The man turned to go.

"You may be right," said John Anderson. "But if you leave now, you'll regret it."

Francis couldn't help but notice Vardon and Ray walking back toward the clubhouse. He saw the hundreds of others in the crowd giving up on him as well to follow them in. As Francis and Eddie walked off the green, they passed through a narrow lane formed by spectators leading to the eleventh tee. His most loyal supporters, the boys of the Brookline caddie corps, pressed the rope line to get close and pat him on the back, throwing shouts of encouragement his way: *You can do it, Francis! You can do it!* They wouldn't give up until the last dog died. But behind them in the crowd, Francis heard one man turn and say clearly to another: "It's too bad, he's blown up."

The words rocked him. *He means me.*

This triggered a fascinating reaction in Francis; instead of crumbling, allowing his gallery's desertion to encourage any self-pity or resignation, he got steamed. Good and angry. Exactly the state of mind he needed to keep fighting.

"That hole's done with," said Francis to Eddie as they approached the next tee. "Let's forget about it, Eddie."

"Okay."

"The plain fact is we're two strokes down with eight to play."

"That's right."

"There's still a chance," said Francis.

"One shot at a time," said Eddie, the last true believer on the course.

"There'll be no more flubbed tee shots like that. Can't have it."

"I keep telling you you gotta keep your head down, Francis. I'll watch the ball."

Francis smiled. "Okay, Eddie."

The 390-yard par four eleventh demanded a long and accurate drive. Francis hit one. His long-iron approach found the green safely. He two-putted for a par that restored his composure; absolutely crucial now. As they moved ahead to the twelfth, Francis swiftly analyzed the task before them.

"Seven holes left to make up two strokes," said Francis. "I figure our best chances are here at twelve, and sixteen."

"Let's get one," said Eddie.

A short par five at 415 yards, after an elevated tee shot the twelfth fairway ran uphill and right the rest of the way to the green so it played considerably longer. A good drive guaranteed a chance to get home in two; a solid second shot would result in an excellent chance for the birdie four he needed.

Francis met the first half of the challenge with a long, powerful tee shot to the center of the fairway. Less than 200 yards to the hole, the ball rested slightly above his feet on the side of the hill; a hook lie. To reach the green, the ideal shot called for a high fade. He selected his brassie, opened his stance and the club face until it felt right, then rehearsed the swing. The club made perfect contact but the ball stubbornly refused to turn right, drawing slightly, bouncing further left when it landed and rolling into a bunker fifty yards short of the green. The crowd's dwindling optimism reached its lowest ebb; Francis had no chance for birdie now; even saving par looked considerably less than a sure thing. Dozens more packed it in and headed for the clubhouse, a steady exodus.

Facing what many pros consider the toughest shot in golf, a long bunker shot, Francis coolly lofted the ball on the front of the green, lying three. A forty-foot putt for birdie proved too much to hope for, but he canned the next one and salvaged his par five. Still his crowd drained slowly away, two here, three there. One more unforced error would end America's chances with finality; it was almost as if they couldn't bear to see it end. Even John Anderson and Jerry Travers found their faith sorely tested now.

Francis's mind raced ahead with so many calculations, he left himself no time to feel nervous. *Six holes left. Two strokes down. The twelfth is gone, but thirteen can be played in three, and then I'll need one more somewhere . . .* And then it came to him, call it a hunch or a vision, whatever it was he saw it right in front of him, clear as glass; he would get one of those strokes back here, at thirteen, and the second at sixteen . . .

But hold on, Francis, thirteen comes first.

Thirteen. Par four. Three hundred and thirty-nine yards, uphill and right to a bowl-shaped green, its right side protected by a tall, narrow spit of trees jutting sideways from the woods. The pin tucked in behind them on that right-hand side. To get a clear shot up to that flag, his drive had to find the left side of the fairway. He visualized the shot he needed, the vision coming back to him, then Francis landed his tee shot on the left side of the fairway, exactly where he'd just seen it in his mind.

"I'll need the exact yardage to that pin, Eddie," said Francis, as they started down the fairway. "And show me the line while you're up there."

"You got it."

When they reached the ball, Eddie set down the bag and umbrella and stepped off the distance to the top of the slope, then added the yardage across the green. He turned, lined himself up between Francis and the flag, and waved his arms. Francis bookmarked the spot in memory, then waved back. Eddie ran back down the hill to where Francis waited.

"One hundred eighteen yards," said Eddie, out of breath.

Francis pulled his niblick, keeping his eye taut on the line Eddie had given him. *Flag's on the upslope to the right of center. Everything on the sides runs down to the middle of this green. I'll need to land the ball to the right of the flag and let it drift left to get close; that brings the trap on that side into play. A target of no more than six square feet.* He waggled the club until he found the feel he was looking for and then let it go. The ball lifted high, it looked perfect but then . . . *No, no, it's drifting right, too far, it's going to find that trap—*

Francis ran up the hill, as if trying to grab back the ball. Eddie followed him. The crowd behind closed in and raced along with them. Every eye watched that ball rise into the air, crest, and then drop . . .

It landed two feet off target, just off the front right side of the green on a sliver of rough between the edge of the collar and a deep, dangerous bunker. Bounced, with a splash, once and then stopped dead in the rough. The soggy ground had saved him from certain disaster. But for what?

When he reached the green, Francis knew he had come up against another breaking point; four feet off the fringe, thirty feet of green sloping down through the bowl to the flag. Stopping the ball on that slope anywhere near enough to the hole to save his par would be next to impossible.

"We'll have to chip it," said Francis. "Land it on the collar here to slow it down then let it roll on and trickle to the hole. It'll break right to left, almost two feet, depending on the speed."

"Make sure you leave yourself an uphill putt coming back," said Eddie.

"No," said Francis. "I have to make this. Mid-iron, Eddie."

Eddie handed him the club.

He crouched over the ball, swiped the low-lofted iron back and forth through the grass to find the rhythm he wanted, then reached down and flicked the water from the blade. Last chance. He brought the club back and then smoothly through, brushing the top of the grass, making crisp contact with the ball; it hopped forward five feet, landed just on the edge of the collar, bounced once, and rolled onto the green.

Bernard Darwin stepped forward out of the crowd. *That looks like it—*

LORD NORTHCLIFFE HAD ordered in a bottle of Scotch and three glasses from the clubhouse to the locker room. Harry and Ted had shed their wet coats and changed their shoes. Northcliffe was pouring out the scotch.

"Here's to England and victory—"

A roar boomed out of the trees behind them and blew through the locker-room windows. Northcliffe stopped mid-pour.

"What the hell was that?" he asked.

AFTER RETURNING HOME and changing into a more presentable daywear dress, Mary Ouimet had stayed out on her porch all afternoon, afraid to move. She'd been told he would begin his last go-around, or whatever they called it, close to three o'clock. She looked at the clock in the front hall; it was already after five. Raymond and Louise had promised to come back and tell her how Francis was doing, but she hadn't heard a word from them. Not an encouraging sound from the course in over an hour. Despite the shawl she'd wrapped around herself, her hands were so white and stiff from cold, she could hardly work her rosary. Mary stood up to go inside.

The moment she left her chair, the roar that had just rolled through the locker room reached all the way across Clyde Street.

She gasped and sat right back down.

. . .

—*LIKE IT MIGHT just go,* thought Darwin.

"Come on," he whispered.

The ball crawled down across the thirteenth green, painfully slow at first but gathering speed, taking the precise line of the break and turning toward the hole, diving sharply left now nearer the end. Francis walked onto the green to follow it forward, Eddie started after him. Something inevitable about the way it was running . . .

"Yes," said Eddie. "Yes!"

The ball smacked dead into the flagstick, rattled it, and dropped straight down into the hole. For three. Birdie.

The crowd erupted with one voice.

"HE'S GOT A stroke back," said Harry the moment the shout had died away.

Harry and Ted looked at each other—a small, tight, weary nod—then without a word both men stood up and reached into the lockers for their soggy coats.

"But we don't know that," said Northcliffe. "He may have blown up completely by now, I'm telling you they're just grasping at straws."

"Hold that whiskey, Alfred," said Ted.

"It's not over yet," said Harry, already heading for the door.

DARWIN ADDED HIS third stroke to the scorecard and wrote down a three.

"Well done," he whispered. His own hands were trembling now.

Eddie lifted out the pin, Francis pulled the ball from the hole and handed it to Eddie for cleaning. Eddie speared the flagstick back into the cup with an extra flourish.

"That's one," said Eddie.

Hearing that cheer from the thirteenth green, the hundreds of people headed toward the clubhouse halted in their tracks all over the course.

Most of them turned on their heels and hurried back to where the shout had come from. John Anderson shook his head as he watched these deserters pour back into the gallery, firing questions about what they'd missed as they eagerly filled the rope line along the fourteenth fairway. Jerry Travers pulled a silver flask from his pocket and toasted the returnees.

"Here's to thee, o ye of little faith," he said.

Jerry took a healthy chug, then handed the flask to Hagen.

Lady Luck, thought Walter, raising the flask toward Francis. *He's all yours.*

Francis felt a surge inside him; his hunch about making three at thirteen had paid off. Despite the rain and numbing, penetrating cold, his mind felt keen, his entire body reenergized, it was all he could do to keep from running ahead to the fourteenth tee box. Playing ahead of George Sargent from the tee again, his drive found the fairway. He took no chances with his second shot; never his favorite hole, Francis had scored his only seven of the week here in qualifying, then that untimely six yesterday afternoon—and besides, his hunch had told him the second stroke he needed would come at sixteen, not here—so he wisely laid up short instead of trying for the green. Most of the crowd didn't understand or appreciate his caution, but then they didn't have to keep track of their opinions on a scorecard.

"Smart play," said Hagen, reliving his recent demise there.

"Damn right it is," said Travers, and took another nip from his flask.

"He knows exactly what he's doing," said John Anderson.

A simple wedge put Francis on the green in three. The crowd groaned again when he missed the long birdie putt, but he hadn't expected or even particularly tried to sink it, just get it close, and that he did. After which an easy tap-in gained him his par five.

One stroke down. Four holes to play.

Anxiety so thick, you could cut it like cake. The crowd looked halfsick, half-crazy. While they waited briefly on the fifteenth tee for the fairway to clear, a man came toward Francis out of the gallery. A middle-aged businessman he knew from The Country Club, a hack golfer for whom Francis had caddied years ago, and apparently someone whose selfabsorption reached levels reserved for infants and movie stars.

"Francis, can I speak with you a moment?" asked the man.

Expecting another encouraging pat on the back from an old friend, Francis gestured to a marshal to let the man approach.

"Francis," said the man in hushed confidence, "how are you?"

"I'm just fine," said Francis. "How are you?"

"I'm glad you asked," said the man. "The truth is I'm having a terrible time keeping my tee shots in play. I can't seem to stop slicing the ball. I wonder, do you think I'm leaving my hands too open as I come through?" And with that he proceeded to repeatedly demonstrate his utterly misbegotten swing.

Too polite and accommodating by nature to drop-kick him into the woods, Francis watched the man gyrate a few times before offering a simple swing fix. By which time Eddie had sniffed out the situation and immediately inserted himself between them, high as a cat's back and right in the man's face.

"Hey, get lost, mister, can't you see we're busy here?"

"But I was just trying to—"

"Beat it, scram, shove off; go on, get," said Eddie. "Go haunt a house."

Eddie advanced on him like a guard dog backing up a burglar. The gallery in the immediate area of the fifteenth tee laughed as they picked up what was happening. Flustered and red-faced, the man lunged back into the crowd and disappeared. Eddie earned a round of applause. Francis had a good laugh himself.

"Don't let that moron bother you," said Eddie. "You believe the nerve of that guy?"

"No, but it was worth it just to watch you go after him," said Francis.

Without intending to, Eddie had let some steam out of the pressure cooker. Now more relaxed than he'd been since losing the stroke at ten, Francis stepped to the tee, reached back, and ripped one deep, a marvelous drive, long and straight, leaving him the perfect angle from which to approach the green. As Francis moved on, Vardon and Ray rejoined the back of the crowd. Moments later Northcliffe came running out of the trees as if he were being chased by a predator.

"Well, well, look who's back," said Eddie to himself as they walked down toward the fairway.

Francis didn't spot their return, and the gallery around them hardly noticed the Englishmen now; this was not the same funereal mass they'd abandoned four holes earlier. Francis had jolted the faithful back to life. Four holes to go. Harry and Ted kept silent, looking on unobtrusively from the side of the hill. They'd been down this road many times. Nothing more for them to do now but watch.

The fifteenth's two-tiered green offered a generous target for Francis's approach, the largest on the course. One hundred and eighty yards out, the flag back and left; to get close, he needed to land the ball on the upper tier. As Francis took his stance, he realized the ball had settled slightly below his feet, a hanging lie that might send the ball right, but with all the other factors to consider, he neglected to take this detail deep enough into his mind.

Not a bad swing, but the lie immediately affected the ball's flight; it sliced hard right, heading for the severe bunker right of the green. If it landed there, it almost guaranteed bogey and the end of the line, but the ball kept slicing; the shot turned out to be so bad, it was almost good. It flopped down into the rough ten yards to the right of the bunkers, pin high, about forty paces from the cup. The rope men fought a battle after every shot now, struggling to contain the crowd around the ball and target. Living shot to shot with Francis's every effort, the gallery's collective mood swung violently back and forth. Now they were silent again, grave with worry. Francis had reached another breaking point.

"It's all over now," said Northcliffe to Darwin, his own mood rebounding as the crowd's plummeted, like the far end of a teeter-totter. "Nothing to be done from there."

Francis and Eddie looked over the lie. Dreadful. Buried down in the sodden, trampled grass where the gallery had walked all day, surrounded by muddy footprints and small pools of water. Francis lined the shot up, looking repeatedly down at the ball and then back at the pin, fierce as a warrior.

Eddie offered the bag. Francis pulled his wedge.

The shot demands a positive stroke. The slightest hesitation, the tiniest lack of conviction in this swing will kill any chance to hold the line. Firm grip, firm stroke through the ball, let the wrists hinge slightly to get this up in the air . . .

The ball came out of the watery muck cleanly, right on line, and soft. A good landing, on the upper tier, an ever better roll, look at that . . . for a moment it even looked as if the ball might curl in—the crowd's astonishment rose to a piercing crescendo—before it turned just left and settled to a stop. Three inches below the hole. He could blow on it and knock it in from there.

Wild cheers and applause, mood tilting toward the manic once again. Francis smiled and waved his thanks as he walked up to the green.

"How can he do that?" mumbled Northcliffe, to no one in particular.

Harry and Ted looked at each other: *That was a golf shot.*

After George Sargent putted out, Francis took a moment, giving the line of the little tap-in a mock serious once-over. The crowd laughed, relieving more tension, then gave another roar when he knocked the ball home for his par four.

"I don't know how he can keep this up," said Ted to Harry.

Harry didn't answer. *How do any of us do it?*

"He can't keep this up," said Northcliffe to Darwin, clutching him by the arm.

"I shouldn't think so, Alfred," said Darwin. *But maybe he can.* Darwin gently pulled his arm away.

Just as they had that morning, as the cheers drew closer and closer to Clyde Street, they finally pulled Mary Ouimet right down off her porch. She wasn't going to wait for Louise or Raymond any longer; she needed to know what was going on with Francis. Right now.

Umbrella hoisted, she waited for an opening to cross the street but none appeared. Clyde Street was now packed along its entire length with a mass of slowly moving cars; drivers who'd left The Country Club grounds prematurely had heard the recent shouts and were trying to turn around to go back inside. Hundreds of others who'd read about Francis's morning charge in Boston's early afternoon editions had driven out to Brookline on the spur of the moment to see him finish. Dozens of vehicles had bogged down in the unpaved mudslide the street had degenerated into over the course of the stormy day. Anyone with either the skill or authority to sort out the congestion—policemen, tournament volunteers—was already on the course watching Francis, leaving this snarled knot of cars. Tempers frayed, horns blared in anger. Mary finally made herself tall, held up her hand, stopped traffic in either direction, and marched right between cars toward the crowd she saw gathering around the sixteenth green.

"This is the hole," said Eddie, as they walked to the par three sixteenth. "We gotta do it."

"We'll get two here," said Francis. "I haven't made two here all week. I've been making twos at this hole since I was your age."

One hundred and twenty-five yards. Easiest hole on the course. No hesitation. Francis teed his ball, stepped up to it, and swung with utter conviction: His hunch had come through at thirteen and it would again here. This was his hole.

His tee shot flew straight as a plumb line right at the flag—another rising gasp—but he'd hit it too hard, that confidence had pumped him up too much; the ball flew over the flag, pitched down, rolled, and came to a skidding stop at the back edge of the green. The pin was all the way up front; he'd left himself a forty-foot pilgrimage of a putt.

What have I done?

"That takes two out of play," said Ted to Harry quietly.

"Maybe three as well," said Harry.

Francis looked the putt over from back and front. He had an apple in his throat. His heart beat hollowly inside his ribs: *This wasn't supposed to happen. I was supposed to make two here.* He searched for the line to the hole, but no hope of sinking the putt that faced him would emerge from the shadow of his disappointment. With the promise of that hunch dashed, his mind lingered on the opportunity he'd lost a fraction of a moment too long; some near-fatal indecision passed from thought to action, from mind to hand. His stroke wavered, the putter met the ball without the urgency that in the next instant he realized it would need. The ball rolled directly on line, he had gotten that much right, but it stopped nine feet short of the hole.

Another desperate downward swing for the crowd. Another crisis point: How many of these could the kid stomach?

"That putt's no bargain," said Ted. He'd left himself with almost the same one, and missed it for bogey, in his own last round. "That should be the end of it."

Harry didn't answer. *Young nerves*, thought Harry. *There's no substitute for it.*

"He's done for certain now," said Northcliffe to Darwin with odd false cheer. Darwin noticed that under his hat, even in the rain and bitter cold, Northcliffe appeared to be sweating.

Dead silence around the green. Francis stalked the putt from every angle, kneeling down with Eddie to double-check his reckoning.

"Inside left," said Eddie.

"Inside left," said Francis.

"Take your time," said Eddie. "We got all day."

Eddie moved away. Francis stepped to the ball and stared down the entire length of the nine-foot line to the cup.

Just as Mary Ouimet walked up to join the outer suburbs of the crowd, an explosion burst out of them that nearly knocked her backward off her feet. Cheers and whoops of happiness and joy. Strangers embraced. Men and women kissed each other. Kids jumped up and down in the air. The crowd surged in her direction and she hurried toward the rope line to get out of its way.

Francis made the putt.

"I'll be damned," said Ted, involuntarily.

Harry didn't say a word. He'd fully expected Francis to make it. Nothing surprised him about this young doppelganger anymore.

Francis and Eddie splashed along in the mud to the seventeenth tee. Two holes to go, both long, testing par fours. One stroke down; two chances to get even.

"Got any hunches?" asked Eddie.

"No more hunches, Eddie," said Francis. "I don't care where we get it, I just want that three."

Bernard Darwin separated himself from Northcliffe and the Jerseymen as they strode ahead. He wanted to be on that rope line. He needed to see this. He felt dizzy with excitement; a glance around told him he was far from alone. People around him looked half-mad with tension; breathing erratically, eyes wide, some looked lost in prayer while others twitched with jagged energy and bursts of nervous laughter.

A cluster of the Brookline boys who'd grown up with Francis found

Mary Ouimet lost in the gallery. They immediately took her into their keeping, ushered her to the front of the ropes, aggressively clearing out a path—*Let her through! We got his mother here!* She wasn't going to miss a moment if they had anything to say about it.

Seventeen, 370 yards, dogleg left. Bunker at the left elbow.

Keep it right. Keep it right and straight.

As he waited for Francis on the tee, George Sargent caught Harry Vardon's eye in the crowd; he'd worked for three years as Harry's assistant at Ganton, knew him well, had more reason to admire him than most. When Harry left for England, George had stayed and worked another year under Ted Ray before moving on to America.

George looked over at Francis, eyes bright with purpose, efficiently lining up his tee shot. *Incredible,* thought Sargent. *By all rights this boy has no business being here—the pressure should have destroyed him long before now—and yet look at him, fresh as a spring colt.* He glanced back at Ted next to Harry in the crowd. Both men's jaws clamped down so hard on their pipes, it looked as if the stems might snap. *And would you look at Ted and Harry; they've been playing Opens since before the kid was born and you'd think all the pressure's square on them.*

For the first time that day, Eddie crossed his fingers behind his back.

Francis hit a sound drive straight down the right-hand side of the fairway. Not overly long; he'd dialed back his swing, sacrificed some distance for accuracy. Safe. Position A. One hundred and sixty-five yards to the green, two traps to the left, one short and right. An opening between them straight to the pin.

"Jigger," said Francis.

"You want to run it up there?" asked Eddie, remembering the disaster at ten.

"That's right."

They looked at each other. Eddie looked deep into Francis's eyes. He saw that rock confidence. No hesitation.

"Knock it dead," said Eddie, and handed him the club.

Red flags shot up, the marshals barked for silence. Francis made the swing, thousands of heads whipped around to follow the ball's flight. It landed just where he'd asked it to, short of the green, then the ball jumped forward and rolled up onto the second tier past the pin, twenty feet above the hole. Before it had even stopped rolling, Eddie toweled off the putter and handed it to Francis.

A huge shout and a mad scramble forward to reach the green, 20,000 arms and hands pushing and shoving for position, the seventeenth surrounded within seconds, the rope men and marshals tested to their limits. Somehow they contained the unruly mass, and then as Francis reached the green, the air became instantly as hushed as a cathedral. Not a peaceful quiet; a latent charge building in that crowd, a dynamo coiling toward explosion. Whispers whipped around like ghosts: *Can he sink it? Will he sink it? He's got to sink this. He will sink it.*

Soft rain patting the ground. Air hissing with tension, that heavy pregnant stillness before the arrival of a thunderstorm. Francis walked around to look at the putt from in back of the ball. Deathlike silence.

No wasted movements. Businesslike, unhurried, Francis walked around, knelt, and examined the line from each side; gradually his idea of the putt formed—*downhill/sidehill, it would slide right, sharp, and fast as it neared the hole*. He picked out the spot he would aim for, a discolored patch of green, an old hole location, eight inches outside left. Francis walked solemnly back to where Eddie waited for him behind the ball. He knelt again and pointed out his spot to Eddie with a whisper.

"There," he said.

"I like it," said Eddie, and stepped away.

Bernard Darwin settled in at the rope next to Jerry Travers, thirty yards to the right of the green. They acknowledged each other with the barest nod. Travers sipped from his flask, offered it to Darwin; he accepted.

"He's a fine putter," whispered Darwin.

"And won't there be a yell if he holes it?" Travers whispered back, and smiled.

He'll make this, thought John Anderson. *He'll do it.*

As Francis settled over the ball and started his putter back, not fifty feet away from him some impatient fool in the traffic jam on Clyde Street leaned on his car horn. It set off a honking chain reaction of angry replies that rippled all the way down the road. Every single person on the golf course heard them, but one.

Give it a chance, thought Francis. *Get it to the hole.*

The putt felt good the moment he hit it, firm and sure. He waited until the ground appeared below the ball as it departed before he dared look up, and then with his first glance at it, he thought . . .

Traveling fast—no, I've hit it too hard.

"Yes," said Eddie.

The ball held the line, running true, crossed, and took the break exactly at the old cup mark he'd selected—the crowd surged forward all around the green, a silent scream welling up in its chest and throat—

"Yes!" said Eddie.

The ball slammed into the back of the cup with an audible thump, bounced straight up two inches in the air . . . and fell straight down into the heart of the hole.

For three.

You could have heard the shout two miles away in downtown Brookline. Hats, umbrellas, handbags flew into the air. Embraces, arms thrust toward the sky, wild dances of joy, ecstasy, seventh heaven. No celebration like this had ever taken place on an American golf course; no player had ever given anyone a reason until this moment. A longing that only a short while ago these people didn't realize they possessed, awakened by this young man, then answered like a prayer.

Jerry Travers, not the world's most animated character under the loosest of circumstances, leaped three feet into the air. Hagen kissed every girl he could lay his hands on. Bernard Darwin had tears in his eyes, and he was far from alone. Mary Ouimet embraced every adoring caddie around her. The boys danced around as a group, chanting: "Francis holed the putt! Francis holed the putt!" The cheering would not abate, went on for over a minute; it felt like an hour.

"That," said Harry finally, "was a great three."

"That," said Ted, "was a great putt for America."

A short distance away, staring at the ground, Lord Northcliffe said nothing.

In their center, the still eye of the storm, Francis allowed himself a shy grin, offered a wave of thanks in each direction, then walked over and plucked his ball from the hole. Eddie met him there, looked up at him, beaming, no words necessary, as Francis handed him the ball to clean. They wouldn't have been able to hear each other anyway.

"One hole left to play!" shouted John Anderson, trying to restore some order to the marshals as well as the crowd. "He's still got one hole left to play!"

Coming back to their senses, remembering the grave work left to be done, the marshals and rope men and the rest of the crowd stuck a cork in their excitement and rushed toward the eighteenth tee and fairway.

"Now let's go get that four," said Francis to Eddie.

One last hurdle. Tied with Vardon and Ray for the moment, but everything now rested on his parring the hole they called Home. A tin cup stuck in the ground on an elevated circle of grass 410 yards away across the flats of the old racetrack. Three strokes to win it, four to tie and force the playoff. The crowd's elation swung halfway back toward dread and distracted worry when it hit them: This thing was by no means assured. Shouts ran ahead of Francis down the rope line: *He needs a four! A four to tie! Can he do it? Will he do it?* Fortunately for everyone concerned, these final shots would be struck by the coolest, most collected person in sight.

Eyes clear. Hands steady. No distractions. His drive split the fairway with a splash, getting no roll but far enough out to reach the green in two with a well-struck mid-iron. Eddie pulled the club from the bag as they walked on and handed it over before Francis even asked for it.

"Keep your eye on the ball and hit it," said Eddie.

He did just that. Francis looked up in time to see the ball sailing toward the flag, just visible above the grassy twin mounds defending the front of the green. The rain picked up again just as he made the swing, falling into his eyes. Francis saw the ball land and send up a sizeable divot off the top of the final embankment. That meant it must have kicked forward onto the green.

"Eddie, I think I have a putt to win this championship," he said.

They rushed forward along with the crowd. Eddie handed him the putter for this last try at the win. But as they climbed the hill, they realized his ball had not kicked forward onto the putting surface; it had slammed into that embankment just short of its crest and bounced slightly backward. If it had hit three inches higher up, no doubt he would have been left with only a putt to win, but Francis still counted his blessings. Under normal conditions a shot that landed where this one just had would have rolled all the way back down onto the unforgiving cinders of the racetrack below, almost guaranteeing bogey five. The saturated grass had stopped it cold and saved him.

There the ball sat, in a decent lie, on top of the last mound just shy of the green. A few inches of fringe, then nothing but short grass between it and the hole, forty feet away, sheltered in a slight depression. Francis paced off the shot for a precise measurement, then walked back to his ball.

"You got the right club?" asked Eddie.

"Let's putt it," said Francis. "Up and in."

"Lay it dead," said Eddie.

Not an easy putt. Hard to calibrate the effect of those few inches of spiked wet collar, then at least two breaks through a swale before it reached the hole. He meant to strike it firmly but the moisture grabbed at his club, ever so slightly, and as a result he hit it even harder. The ball ran straight down the line through the swale, missed the hole by an inch, and didn't stop until it had run five feet past.

The crowd let out a collective sigh and then immediately pulled in and held its next breath. One last hurdle. Those who'd lingered around the Home green that afternoon had seen a number of players attempt, and miss, this exact same putt he'd left himself. Downhill and straight to the eye, but there was subtle movement in it, a definite break to the left. While they waited for George Sargent to finish, 10,000 pairs of panicky eyes scanned back and forth from Francis's ball to the hole; those five feet may as well have been half a mile. A desperate uncertainty ran through the crowd. Limbs trembling, people grabbed one another, teeth chattering from cold and apprehension. George Sargent putted out quickly and stepped away, Francis moved to his ball. Thousands couldn't take their eyes off him. Thousands more stared straight down, anywhere away from the green, unable to watch, the strain too much.

Darwin thought: *Impossible to believe so many people could produce this much silence.*

Francis wasted no time. He took no more than ten seconds to look it over. Eddie handed him a towel. He dried his hands, then the grip of his club, stepped up, set his putter down in front of the ball to check the line, put it back behind the ball, looked down, and took back the club.

Do you think he ever considered, for one instant, that he would come this far only to miss this putt?

He gently tapped the ball and then stepped back to watch its progress. The ball rolled slowly down to the edge of the hole, crawled around its lip for an inch, and dropped in for the four.

And then the dam burst. Deafening. If the shout at seventeen could be heard in Brookline, this one must have made it all the way to Boston. Whatever authority the USGA's marshals and rope men had held over the crowd all afternoon vanished at that moment; a multitude rushed helter-skelter onto the green from every direction, a solid circle of humanity converging on Francis in their center. Tournament officials gave up any last pretense of impartiality and ran right after them. The Brookline boys who got there first lifted Francis up and put him on their shoulders, and as he was hoisted into sight above the black-coated masses, the shouts and cheers redoubled. His putter still in his hand, Francis let himself relax, smiling and safe in the crowd's arms as it held him high. Eddie got lost in the rippling currents, thoughts of being crushed in that mob briefly entered his mind until another group of friendly arms found him and carried him to safety. The cheers organized themselves, but instead of three cheers for Francis, there would be thirty-three. Girls wanted to marry him, mothers wanted to mother him, fathers wanted him for a son, every boy in that crowd wanted to be him. Naked raw emotions, all the accumulated tension of the entire day released in this magical, visceral elation, tears of joy and astonishment. Bonds of friendship between strangers, indelible memories that would last a lifetime were forged in those delirious moments. A spontaneous procession formed, a triumphal march that conveyed Francis off the green toward the locker room as the thirty-three cheers continued.

As she watched Francis being carried away, Mary stepped back to the edge of the crowd, eyes sparkling with happiness. Raymond and Louise finally found her there, proudly accepting congratulations from people in the crowd she didn't even know. She embraced them both; they'd never seen her so excited.

"Do you think he'll be home for supper?" asked Mary.

They assured her that he would be. Mary gave one more look toward her son riding atop the crowd, then turned for home; she'd put a chicken in the oven, just in case. She wanted his favorite dinner to be waiting for him.

When that last putt found the hole, Harry and Ted looked at each other and nodded their silent approval. They watched the crowd moving off with Francis toward the locker room, looked at each other again with knowing eyes and slight wry smiles, and shook their heads. How great was that. Both knew how poorly they'd played that afternoon, they'd owned up to it already in the press tent. They'd left an opening and he'd made them pay. In a way, this was only fitting. In many ways, they were more able to appreciate what they'd just witnessed than anyone else in that crowd.

The two old friends began walking toward the clubhouse, eager now to get back to their hotel and prepare for the next day's play-off. No sign of Northcliffe. Reporters caught up in the soaring emotion of the aftermath, the same jaded souls who'd tried to write Francis off for the last two days, spotted the Englishmen before they moved out of range and had the wherewithal to ask for a comment about the young American's performance.

"That was the greatest demonstration of skill and nerve I have ever seen in golf," said Ted.

"We must all of us take our hats off to his remarkable achievement," said Harry. "And we greatly look forward to meeting Mr. Ouimet in the play-off tomorrow morning."

What did they think about his putt for three at seventeen?

"Only perfect judgment could have put that ball in the cup," said Ted. "I've never seen a putt more confidently played."

"Coming when it did," said Harry, "I count it as one of the master strokes of golf."

The procession carrying Francis neared the locker room, showing no signs of becoming any less boisterous. Worried the prolonged demonstration might start to wear down its subject, John Anderson stepped into the middle of the fray and shouted at them: "He's got to play again tomorrow! Let him down!" Others like Jerry Travers and Tom McNamara quickly joined in, voices of reason and restraint. The crowd finally heard them, lowered Francis to his feet outside the locker room, and offered one long, last cheer. Francis waved to them again, then turned and went inside. Slowly, reluctant to let the moment end, the crowd began to disperse.

Player after player approached Francis in the locker room. He sat on the bench greeting each man by name as they came by; happy, humble, gracious, and most grateful for their appreciation. Mike Brady, Jim Barnes, Mac Smith, Louis Tellier in his broken English, Tommy McNamara and his brother Dan, a warm and tearful George Wright. John Anderson waited until most of the line had finished, then shook Francis's hand and hugged him.

"I don't know how you made that putt on seventeen," said Anderson. "How did you manage it?"

"I don't know what you mean."

"All those car horns honking, that didn't bother you?"

"I never heard them, John," said Francis. "Honestly. I never heard a single sound."

Anderson soon moved off to the press tent to begin his evening's work. A parade of prominent Country Club members filed through next to offer individual congratulations; among them was the same man who, after Thursday's play, had suggested Francis quit the tournament. Neither of them referred to it in their conversation now. The adrenaline burning off, Francis had begun to weary by the time Walter Hagen stopped by, the only other man left in the room, freshly showered, shaved, and dressed, packed valise in hand, trailing a spicy cologne.

"Hey, hey, you did it, kiddo," said Walter as they shook hands. "You really showed 'em something."

"I hear you didn't do so badly yourself," said Francis.

Hagen shrugged. "I gave it a go, made a dog's breakfast of it down the stretch. But you had the real stuff out there today, brother, that was some kind of playing."

"Thank you."

"Sorry I can't stick around to see you lay a beating on those boys tomorrow, but I got to catch the midnight train. I'm flat busted."

"But I saw the scoreboard. You finished in the money, didn't you?"

Walter shrugged. "Tied for fourth. Sixty-five bucks. Trust me, between here and half a dozen girls back home, most of it's already spoken for."

"Walter, it's been great fun," said Francis.

Walter lowered his voice. "Kind of a kick to find out we can play with the big boys, huh?"

"It's a wonder, isn't it?"

"We'll do it again, Francis, after you put this one away. See you next year."

They shook hands one last time. Hagen started for the door.

"Hit 'em straight tomorrow," he said. "Knock 'em dead."

"Don't spend it all in one place," said Francis.

"Like I always say, kid, I don't plan to be a millionaire. I just want to live like one." Francis heard him whistling after he went out the door.

Alone at last, Francis soaked in a hot bath for fifteen minutes until every trace of the bone-deep cold finally drained away. He dressed in dry clothes his brother had brought over from home. By the time he walked outside, it was after eight o'clock, nearing dark. The rain had finally diminished to an intermittent drizzle. The grounds were by now almost deserted. Lights burned in the clubhouse—members still celebrating the day's great events; they'd invited Francis to stop by, he'd politely declined—and in the press and telegraph tent, from where news of what he'd done that day had already traveled halfway around the world.

When Francis came outside, Eddie stepped forward from where he'd been waiting, under the shelter of the locker room's eaves, golf bag in hand.

"Eddie, you're still here? What are you doing?"

"I done it every other day, Francis, I gotta walk home with you. You know, for luck."

"Did you at least dry off, get something to eat?"

"You bet. They took real good care of me," said Eddie with a grin. He hoisted the umbrella and handed it to Francis. They walked under it together in silence for a while, down past the eighteenth green and across the fairway, dodging the puddles.

"That was some kinda day, huh?" said Eddie.

"Eddie, it was just fine. A wonderful mood."

"You ever heard people screaming and carrying on like that before?"

"You know, I can't say that I have."

They approached the seventeenth green, empty now, glowing faintly in the dwindling daylight. Eddie hesitated on the collar for a moment, then Francis stopped. They turned and looked around at the still and peaceful scene, and without thinking, both took in deep breaths, as if trying to capture one last taste of that exquisite moment from only an hour before.

"Wish you coulda seen the looks on those English boys' faces when that putt dropped in," said Eddie.

"Were they out here?"

"You bet your tea and crumpets they were."

So Harry saw me do it.

"Good," said Francis.

They moved on, stepped carefully across the quagmire of Clyde Street, and arrived outside Francis's house. Francis took the golf bag from Eddie; he knew by now not to ask for it until reaching his front door. He handed Eddie the umbrella.

"Hey, tomorrow's Saturday; no school," said Eddie with a grin. "That truant officer'll probably be looking for me anyway."

"You'll come by and meet me in the morning then?" asked Francis.

"Provided he doesn't find you first."

"Don't you worry about me. That play-off's at ten. I'll be here eight-thirty sharp."

"Eddie. You were a great help to me today. I can't begin to tell you how much. I don't think I could have done it without you."

Looking up, Eddie's eyes shone brightly in the dying light. "Thanks, Francis." They shook hands.

"Go get some rest."

"You, too." Eddie started away down Clyde Street, only his little legs in sight trudging under the span of the umbrella.

Mary, Louise, and Raymond waited for Francis inside, a roast chicken dinner laid out on the dining room table. When Francis came through the front door, Arthur stood up in the front parlor, evening newspaper in hand; he still wore his gardener's clothes. He'd spent much of the day working on the grounds of a man named Alfred Douglas, whose estate was adjacent to The Country Club. He'd heard the shouts and roars issuing from the golf course all day long without knowing who they were for. He did now. They stood still, looked at each other for an awkward moment.

"You did well today," said Arthur. It was a question.

"I did, yes. I did pretty well."

"I heard people talking." He shifted, uncomfortable, looked away. Silence.

"How was your day, Poppa?"

"Mine?" Arthur looked up, surprised. "Too much damn traffic around here. I guess tomorrow will be the same now."

"Do you have to work tomorrow?" asked Francis.

"In the morning."

"I play again tomorrow."

"I know," said Arthur, clearing his throat. "Your mother has dinner on the table."

"That's good. I'm about half-starved."

Arthur held out his arm toward the dining room, the arm with the newspaper; Francis's picture was prominent on the front page. They all sat down at the table together. Arthur said grace. Mary served. While his brother, sister, and mother talked about Francis and his remarkable day all through dinner, Arthur said little, but he listened closely.

OF THE FORTY-SEVEN players who made it through all four rounds at the 1913 U.S. Open, only the top ten finished in the money. First-, second-, and third-place money—300, 150, and 100 dollars, respectively—could not be determined until after Saturday's eighteen-hole play-off. In addition to the U.S. Open Trophy, which John McDermott had turned over to USGA officials before the tournament began, a gold medal would also be awarded to the winner. If Francis won the play-off, as an amateur he was ineligible to receive any cash prize, only the trophy and the medal. No matter what happened on Saturday, either Harry or Ted would be taking home first-place money. The USGA handed out the remainder of the prize money to players before they left The Country Club on Friday night, in these amounts, along with their contemporary equivalent:

Fourth place:	Jim Barnes		
	Walter Hagen		
	Macdonald Smith		
	Louis Tellier	$65	($1,174)
Eighth place:	John J. McDermott	$40	($719)
Ninth place:	Herbert Strong	$30	($539)
Tenth place:	Patrick Doyle	$20	($360)

ALONG WITH TWO dozen other reporters, John Anderson remained in the press tent turning out copy for their morning editions until almost midnight that Friday. This is how Anderson began his dispatch:

How is anyone to sit down in cold blood and attempt to give any lucid comment upon what happened at The Country Club today in the final 36 holes for the National Open golf title? Every thought comes back to the thrilling finish of Francis Ouimet, whereby he tied Harry Vardon and Edward Ray for the title.

We have seen, in other sports, the hero of the day cheered to the echo and hoisted upon the shoulders of his admirers, for a jerky ride of fame. We have seen it on the football field in recognition of the kick that saved the day or won the game, we have seen it on the diamond for the man who has won the game with a homer or the pitcher who has struck out the opposing batsman with three on base and two men out, one run needed to tie the score. But such enthusiasm has been foreign to America's golf links until the modest Woodland boy, Francis Ouimet, carried the gallery completely off its feet at The Country Club and brought about the most enthusiastic demonstration ever accorded a golfer in this country or probably in the world.

Working alongside Anderson, Bernard Darwin described what he'd experienced in the first of his lengthy cables to the London *Times* this way:

After sober reflection I state my conviction that if I lived the length of a dozen lives I should never again be the spectator of such an

amazing, thrilling and magnificent finish to an Open championship. Mr. Ouimet's golf today was astonishing. I do not believe
any golfer has ever been under greater strain, and the strain is of its
kind the greatest test of nerve to which a man can be subjected in
any department of any sport—or anything else, I am very much
tempted to add. He achieved something which was just about as
near to the impossible as anything one could think of. Nobody who
was there will ever forget the wild shouts, the shaking of hands,
the throwing of highly respectable hats into the air, when Mr.
Ouimet holed his three on the seventeenth green. All the most
venerable of Bostonians appeared to have gone simultaneously
mad, and for that matter, although my cheers were more restrained,
I did not feel wholly sane myself. It was a wonderful scene. When
all the rest of the American golfing strength was stiff and cold, as
we say, after its desperate, exhausting and fruitless struggle to stop
the advance of my countrymen, this little cocksparrow of a Ouimet
came out at the very last hour and pulled them up.

The picture that remains to me is of the young hero playing all
those last crucial shots as if he had been playing an ordinary game.
He did not hurry; he did not linger; there was a decisiveness about
every movement, and whatever he may have felt, he did not betray
it by as much as the movement of an eyelash. He was just entirely
calm and entirely natural. When Mr. Ouimet finally succeeded in
making a tie of it, everybody was in a dazed and topsy-turvy frame
of mind. The American crowd let loose and nearly dislocated its
limbs in their joy. They had the full right to be proud of their golfing boy. I am proud myself of the game that can produce such a
display of nervous strength, for he needs a great game as well as
great human stuff to do it.

It really seems impossible to believe that this young gentleman of twenty could hope to beat those two seasoned champions
tomorrow. Even if he plays good enough golf, it seems almost too
much to expect that he should stand the strain, but then he has
shown himself capable of standing so great a strain today. He will
have a night to sleep on the situation in which he suddenly finds

himself, although I know from his phenomenal imperturbability that he really will sleep as most others would not. He will have to play against Vardon and Ray in the flesh, not merely against their scores on paper. He will see their shots and have to follow them; one David against two Goliaths. I am not sure I believe in the possibility of an actual defeat, but I feel that England has already suffered a moral one. It is all very confusing, and personally I have given up all attempts at prophecy and will start out Saturday's round with a completely open mind, prepared for anything. It will be the greatest tie that has ever been played.

THERE WOULD BE no appearances for Ted Ray in the bar of the Copley Square Hotel that night. He took an early dinner in his room alone; just as well since Louis Tellier, Wilfred Reid, and their wives were in the dining room. Tellier's fourth-place check was the largest he'd ever received in his playing career, and even though Reid's hopes had fallen one punch in the nose short of his dreams, the young couples were still in a celebratory mood. Perhaps in sympathy for the way his tournament ended Wilfred had already received some positive interest in him from a few American clubs. That night the two young men finalized their plans to seek work as professionals in the States. With Louis's money as their stake, after a brief visit home to settle their affairs, they would soon be returning to America.

In a private booth across the room, Harry ate a quiet dinner with his brother Tom and Lord Northcliffe, thoughts of the play-off and echoes of championships past swirling in the air around them. Tom's tournament was long over, but once again he'd be there to walk the course alongside Harry tomorrow.

"Setting what he did today aside," said Tom, "between you and Ted you should beat him easily."

"Yes," said Harry. "We should."

"A two-man tournament now," said Northcliffe.

"Give the lad credit," said Tom. "It was a game effort but he'll have left everything he had on the course this afternoon."

"Exactly. How could he possibly manage that sort of thing a second day?" added Northcliffe. "He's an amateur. Have you ever been beaten by an amateur, Harry? I mean in any match, man to man. In your life."

"No," said Harry.

"No amateur's ever won an Open here," Northcliffe went on. "Only one's ever won it back home in sixty years. I tell you it's inconceivable."

Harry flashed his distant, enigmatic smile, barely concealing a steely hint of anger. "If you think the game's so easy, Alfred, maybe you'd like to go out tomorrow and play him yourself."

Northcliffe mumbled a rejoinder but had no real comeback. After an uncomfortable silence, Tom moved the conversation on. Harry excused himself shortly thereafter and was in bed by eleven that night, but he didn't sleep for a long time.

FRANCIS TURNED IN soon after the family finished supper. His sister Louise went to practice on the family piano in the parlor, until Francis overheard Mary ask her to stop so that he could get a good night's rest.

"Don't stop, Louise," he called from upstairs. "I'll go to sleep a good deal easier if you keep playing."

The melodies continued. Francis fell into a dead sleep by 9:30, just as Darwin had predicted, and wouldn't stir again until morning.

HARRY, FRANCIS, AND TED, OUTSIDE THE CLUBHOUSE.

SATURDAY:
THE PLAY-OFF

AN EIGHTEEN-HOLE play-off to settle ties has been the USGA's policy from the inception of its national championship. In the Open's nineteen years, this would be its sixth extra round, and the fourth in the last six years. Leading up to the 1913 Open, Mr. G. Herbert Windeler and Mr. Herbert Jaques, the past and current presidents of The Country Club, respectively, had put in two straight weeks of eighteen-hour workdays. Both were also former presidents of the USGA; no two men in the country knew more about how to run a U.S. Open, and with unfailing foresight they had anticipated every detail of hosting the tournament and handling the enormous crowds that showed up to take it in. Despite the complications created by Friday's dreadful storm, everyone agreed the entire show had still gone off without a hitch. A play-off had been discussed beforehand as a contingency, but its necessity presented a whole new series of last-minute challenges. After only four hours of sleep in the upstairs clubhouse rooms reserved for members, both men were out on the course again by 5:00 A.M. Saturday to see that no task was left undone. To their dismay, they discovered it was still raining.

Windeler and Jaques spent an hour walking the course to consult with greenkeepers and identify problem areas on a number of holes. As the two men made their dawn rounds, they also selected the day's new pin positions. After thirty continuous hours of rain, The Country Club's greens continued to hold up remarkably well and most of the ground was still draining adequately, but additional areas of nearly every fairway had to be declared unplayable.

AS EDDIE LOWERY prepared to leave his house in Lower Newton Falls early that morning, he turned to his mother and said, "Francis is going to shoot seventy-two today. See if he don't."

"You be careful with that foot, Eddie."

"I'll be fine," said Eddie, and he was gone.

HARD RAIN BEATING on his bedroom window woke Francis just before 7:00. He looked out to see the grounds crew cutting today's new hole on the seventeenth green. After a light breakfast and great wishes for success from his mother and siblings—his father had left the house for work before Francis arose—he walked outside to find Eddie waiting for him.

Eddie Lowery didn't look up to Francis Ouimet just because he was two feet taller and ten years older. Eddie had been living without a father for the last three years, and there were recent behavioral signs the tough-minded, self-reliant little kid might be drifting toward trouble. People had always underestimated Eddie; he was smart, the smartest kid in school, and had twice been promoted ahead of the kids his own age. His mother constantly worried about whether he was falling in with the wrong crowd, or how he'd learn the discipline she knew he'd need to channel his intelligence and restless energy. With prescient timing, Francis and Eddie entered each other's lives at precisely the moment each needed someone most like the other. That would never hold more true than on Saturday, September 21, 1913. Whether by conscious design or random chance, Eddie showed up that morning wearing an outfit that matched almost exactly what Francis had chosen to wear: white shirt, black tie, brown jacket, dark knickers, high wool socks, hobnail ankle boots, the only difference being Eddie's white bucket hat. Francis wore a light knit cap.

"I got this for you yesterday," said Eddie. "So much happened I forgot to give it to you."

Eddie handed Francis the spare American flag ribbon Dan McNamara had given him in the pro shop.

"I got one, too. You wear it right here," said Eddie, pointing to the identical flag on his own lapel.

"Thank you, Eddie. I appreciate it." Francis accepted the gift with gratitude but didn't seem to fully grasp the intention behind it.

"Francis, you just got to beat these fellas," said Eddie, feeling the need to explain. "You know you're the last American left."

"I hadn't really thought of it that way."

"Well, you are."

Francis let that sink in, then attached the ribbon to his lapel as they picked their way across the street. "Is this rain going to let up?"

"Doesn't matter," said Eddie.

"Why do you say that?"

" 'Cause today's the day you're going to shoot a seventy-two," said Eddie. "It's your last chance."

"So it is. I'd completely forgotten about that."

"See, so it don't matter whether it's raining or not raining; you're still going to get seventy-two."

"I hope you're right."

"I am. We should just walk up to those other fellas and ask 'em when their boat sails for England. They might as well begin to pack."

Francis stopped in his tracks, struck by some powerful emotion, and he looked at Eddie with such force and determination that it took the younger boy by surprise. "Whatever happens today, Eddie, win or lose, when it's all said and done, I give you my solemn word the one thing they will not be able to say is that my tying them for this championship was a fluke."

Eddie looked at him solemnly, speechless at this burst of intensity. Francis walked on, Eddie followed, wearing a grin.

When they reached the club, Francis received a warm greeting from Mr. Windeler and Mr. Jaques and various USGA officials. While Eddie waited, Francis went into the locker room to change his shoes; empty, no other players on hand today, and the two Englishmen had not yet arrived. As he rose to leave, Francis was startled to feel a steely grip take hold of his arm; he hadn't heard anyone else in the room. He turned, confronted by the spectrally pale and haunted face of John McDermott.

"I watched you yesterday," said McDermott, his voice urgent, hushed, little more than a whisper. "You're hitting the ball well."

"Thank you, Johnny." Francis felt a little spooked. *What does he want?* He waited for Johnny to speak.

"You must go out there and pay no attention whatsoever to Vardon or Ray. Listen to me; at some point Vardon will try to draw you into matching him. That will be a dangerous moment. No one can match him. Don't try. Do you hear me? You've got to play your own game."

McDermott held on to Francis's arm, maintaining intense eye contact. Francis waited until he was sure Johnny had nothing more to say. "That's good advice, Johnny. I promise I'll do my best."

McDermott blinked once or twice. Without another word he let go of Francis's arm and backed away, his footsteps echoing on the wooden plank floor.

When Francis walked out of the locker room, he found his golf bag leaning near the door outside and saw Eddie speaking with Dan McNamara and Frank Hoyt some distance away. He grabbed three clubs and a handful of balls from his bag and walked down onto the empty Polo Field fairway to warm up. A wave of dark clouds had passed by overhead, and the rain had softened to a light and tolerable drizzle. He scattered the balls on a dry patch of grass and began to hit some practice shots, moving back and forth on the fairway. His swing felt sound and solid. Gradually a few early spectators filtered down to watch him. But no Eddie.

Francis didn't feel nervous or even unduly excited. As he thought ahead to the play-off, he succeeded in finding only positive ways to consider it. In at least one respect he felt better about his chances than he had at the start of the tournament; he wasn't going against an entire field. This would be match play, the competitive format he preferred, in the guise of stroke play, and if he was facing two opponents instead of one, they would at least be right in front of him the entire round. He would know exactly where they all stood at every turn. The truth he couldn't or chose not to admit to himself in this moment was that in effect he would be playing against the better ball of the two best players in the world.

At 9:30 Francis walked back up to the practice green. By now the grounds of The Country Club had begun to fill with people. Given that this was Saturday, the weather had slightly improved, and Francis was part of the play-off, today's crowd would easily be the largest of the week. Francis dropped two balls on the putting green and worked to find his stroke, but the fact that Eddie was nowhere to be seen nagged at his mind. This wasn't like him. It wasn't until minutes later, when Frank Hoyt and a small group of Country Club members approached him from across the green, that Francis finally saw Eddie emerge from the crowd behind them, holding on to his golf bag.

"Morning, Frank," said Francis.

"Francis, we've been talking this over between ourselves," said Frank quietly, indicating the others behind him.

"What's that, Frank?"

Hoyt moved closer, turned his back toward Eddie, and lowered his voice. "It's our feeling that you'll need as much help as you can get out there today."

"I certainly appreciate that, Frank—"

"And since the only person who can give you advice legally within the rules is your caddie, we think you ought to have somebody carrying your bag who really knows the game and this course."

Francis felt a sinking feeling in the pit of his stomach. "But Eddie's done a wonderful job for me."

"No one's disputing that, and everyone agrees he's a fine little kid. But this is for the U.S. Open, Francis, not some junior club championship. You need every edge you can get. So what we were thinking is, I should carry for you today."

Eddie had edged closer to them, not quite near enough to hear, still clinging to the bag. Francis glanced over and met his eye. "Have you spoken to Eddie about this?"

"We have. I've been very nice about it," said Frank, slightly exasperated. "I even offered him a couple of extra bucks, then went all the way up to five. He wouldn't take it."

"And so you want me to talk to him," said Francis.

"Exactly. He'll listen to you," said Frank.

Francis nodded, then walked over to where Eddie waited, hanging on to the bag now with a death grip, about ten feet away. He looked up at Francis fearfully.

"Did Frank offer you some money, Eddie?"

"Five bucks," he said.

"You know that's a lot more than I can give you. You could use the money, couldn't you, at home?"

"I wouldn't do it for a hundred." His lip trembled. His eyes filled with tears. "I'm the caddie."

Francis looked down at him for another moment, smiled, then walked back to where Hoyt and the others were waiting.

"I truly do appreciate your offer, Frank," said Francis, "but I've already got the man I want on my bag."

Francis turned back and gestured to Eddie, who hustled to Francis's side, wiping his eyes as he hoisted the bag up onto his shoulder, a few lingering tears still leaking down his cheeks. Frank Hoyt shrugged to the other members—*I tried*—and as a group they turned away. When he saw Eddie still clutching the bag as if he felt someone might snatch his job away, Francis put a gentle hand on the boy's back and helped guide him through the crowd.

"You didn't really think I'd let anybody replace you now, did you?" asked Francis quietly.

Eddie finally managed a smile. "That guy's a jinx anyway. He'd'a found some way to mess things up. You wouldn't stand a chance."

As they made their way through the gallery together, Francis looked ahead up the slight rise to a small tent they'd raised beside the first tee. Harry Vardon and Ted Ray had arrived, they stood waiting for Francis with their caddies outside the tent. It was nearly 10:00.

When Francis reached them, Harry extended his hand. "Congratulations," said Harry. "Well played yesterday."

"Thank you, sir." Francis stilled the urge to say anything more. Vardon himself had put it best: *"Treat your opponent, with all due respect, as a non-entity."*

"And the best of luck to you today," said Harry, mirroring back the same friendly but aloof manner.

"You, too, sir."

After Ted shook Francis's hand and wished him well, he turned to Eddie. "What's your name, little man?"

"Eddie Lowery."

"Eddie, you're not much bigger than a peanut."

"That's okay," said Eddie. "You're big enough for both of us."

Ted laughed heartily, and as often happened when he did, so did everyone else.

Officials summoned the three players into the small canvas tent by the first tee. USGA president Robert Watson, Herbert Windeler, and Herbert Jaques each offered their congratulations. Watson briefly explained the rules of the play-off; if a tie still existed at the end of these first eighteen holes, the survivors would immediately begin a second eighteen later that afternoon. Due to the inclement conditions, the USGA had decided to allow a special exception to their rules; in the event any player's ball became embedded on reaching a green, he would be allowed to summon a referee. If in his judgment a buried lie unfairly affected the player's next shot, the referee would remove the ball from the ground. The player would then be allowed to clean the ball and replace it on the green within three inches of where it landed, no closer to the hole, with no penalty. All three players agreed the ruling sounded eminently fair.

Considering the importance of the round, each player was assigned a personal marker to keep his scorecard. In the interest of fair play, Vardon and Ray were both assigned prominent members of the American press. Bernard Darwin had accepted their invitation to serve as Francis's scorer. With solemn ceremony, the day's date and each player's name were written down on their scorecards in fountain pen ink while they all stood by and watched inside the tent.

Robert Watson showed the players three straws he held in his hand; one long, two short. Whoever drew the long straw would take the honors off the first tee. He mixed the straws up behind his back, then held them out. Harry and Ted gestured for Francis to select first. He pulled the long straw.

"Gentlemen," said Watson, "it's time."

Estimates for the number of people who crowded The Country Club on Saturday are even harder to verify than Friday's figures. The lowest estimate comes in at 8,000 and the highest at 20,000; the actual number undoubtedly falls somewhere in between. What is clear is that almost every single person who had been there to see Friday's thrilling conclusion had returned, men and women alike, and when they did, they brought a lot more people with them. At least 700 automobiles choked every parking place within a mile of the grounds. An atmosphere of portent, of history in the making, could be as concretely felt as the thick and leaden air.

Much of the ground and pathways trampled by the gallery on Friday had been reduced to a muddy paste. Many felt the sodden fairways favored Ted Ray; deprived of any roll, his ball would fly the longest off the tee. Others argued that Vardon's perfect iron play gave him the edge, and the heavy, moisture-laden greens could only help his balky putting. Most of the local press, retreating back to cold hard reason from last night's euphoria, entertained little speculation that Francis would be up to this final challenge, citing all the familiar arguments: untested, over his head, out of luck, emotionally drained from the day before, going head-to-head against two champion professionals, one of them without a doubt the greatest the world had ever known. Vardon and Ray would sort this out between themselves, with Francis as an afterthought, thankful just to be in their company. The Boston betting lines backed up their assessment, although some local sentiment may have prevented the odds from growing even longer: Touts picked Vardon or Ray to win at five to four, Francis at three to one. Twenty would get you ten that Vardon would finish either first or second. That same bet for Francis was even money.

The players exited the tent. The solid throng surrounding the tee box and lining the entire length of the Polo Field fairway saw them emerge and burst into applause. The three men made their final preparations and showed one another the balls they would put into play. Francis had drawn a circle on his, a Spalding with a swirling mesh cover pattern. Ted Ray played the same make, with a different mark on it. Harry used a Wright & Ditson ball with a bumpy raised cover called a bramble, a dimple pattern that closely resembled an old gutta-percha design. The Englishmen moved to the back of the tee and waited.

Drizzle continued to fall. Warmer than Friday by twenty degrees, an almost sultry heaviness in the air, no wind to speak of. Battleship gray clouds overhead bore down on the course from the north with the promise of more heavy rain. Windeler and Jaques had dispensed last-minute instructions to their marshals and rope men. Everyone stood ready. A chorale of silent prayers for Francis went skyward from the gallery and the first of them was this: "Let him make a good start."

John Anderson and Jerry Travers found each other in the gallery; the two men would walk the entire round together.

"It's match play today, in effect, isn't it?" said John.

"That's right. And eighteen holes of match play'll tell you more about who you're up against," said Jerry, "than eighteen years of dealing with him across a desk."

At exactly 10:00 Eddie handed Francis his driver and looked him square in the eye. "Be sure and keep your eye right on the ball."

Francis looked out at the vast crowd skirting the fairway and his heart leaped; he felt an almost crippling excitement course through him. He glanced back at Vardon and Ray. Time stopped. For the first time since last night's final putt the enormity of what he was up against hit him like a punch in the gut.

What would Harry say? thought Francis. *I can't very well ask him myself, can I?*

Another fragment from Vardon's book came back to him: *"Remember that more matches are lost through carelessness at the beginning than through any other cause. Make a point of trying to play the first hole as well as you have ever played a hole in your life."*

All fine and good, but how well was all that going to work when *Harry's* the man he's going up against?

Because I'm going to forget about him now, came the answer. *Vardon and Ray both. I'm going to forget they're even here and play for all I'm worth.*

Francis crushed his drive out long and hot, tailing slightly to the right at the finish. It skidded just a little as it landed, still safely in the fairway. The crowd's explosive cheer echoed all the way down along the fairway and back. Harry followed him off the tee and sent his ball straight down the middle, just shy of Francis's. Ted's drive soared right on line with Francis's, slightly further and a few more yards to the right. More applause as they walked off the tee together, the wall of the crowd immediately pressing in behind them.

"That was a good shot," said Eddie, wiping off the driver, whipping it back around into the bag.

"We can go for it in two from there," said Francis, feeling his heart begin a slow crawl back inside his ribs.

Vardon was judged to be away and played first. After assessing his lie, Harry decided trying to clear the outward curve of the racetrack in front of the green presented more risk than reward; he hit a three-quarter brassie and left himself in perfect position, short of the track, eighty yards out.

Francis watched Vardon's ball land, then pulled his own brassie and went boldly for the green. He cleared the track but caught a bad bounce into a hanging lie on the side of a small mound covered with light rough about twenty-five yards from the flag, set two-thirds of the way to the back of the green. Ted sliced his brassie second shot into high rough ten yards to the right of the green, exactly pin high.

Harry pitched up onto the green with his third, about twenty feet below the hole. Francis followed with an effective chip out of the rough, landing just inside Harry's ball. Attempting a delicate pitch, Ted got his club face caught up in the long grass; it decelerated and the ball landed on the fringe just short of the green. Still away, Ted scooped a near perfect chip within a foot of the flag and tapped in for a par five. Harry lagged his putt up to within inches and secured his par.

Francis left his first putt four feet short.

He took his time looking over the line for his par. He couldn't prevent a wayward thought from forming: *This putt will set the tone for my entire round.* His nerves buzzed.

Although there was a space provided for it on each scorecard, of the three official markers, only Bernard Darwin, with typical conscientiousness, set down a hash mark in the far right-hand column for every stroke Francis played that day. He'd applied four slashes already and stood inside the ropes just off the green with his pencil poised.

Francis turned his head to the right and stroked the ball firmly, straight into the hole. Par five. A huge cheer from the hometown crowd.

All square after one.

Darwin added the fifth stroke—short and firm, slightly apart from the others—and returned the card and pencil to his dry coat pocket. His hands trembled. *Look at me,* he thought. *All this on his plate and the lad's nerves are stouter than mine.* Darwin walked over to double-check the score with Francis, as he would after each hole all day.

"I've got you for five, Francis?" asked Darwin.

"Five it is," said Francis.

Darwin glanced over at Lord Northcliffe, walking in the gallery with Windeler and Jaques. Trying to play the part of the impartial senior sportsman; positively radiating dread and worry.

With the possible exception of the final stroke that secured yesterday's tie, no putt in the entire tournament did Francis more good than dropping that one for par on the first. The moment Francis picked his ball out of the hole, every feeling of nervousness, excitement, and awe he'd experienced on the tee vanished completely. As he exited the green, he looked ahead at the backs of Vardon and Ray, already walking toward the second tee; Harry stooped slightly forward as he struggled with the uncertain footing, Ray with that odd ungainly hitch to his stride.

They're human, thought Francis.

"Good putt there, Francis," said Eddie, taking the ball and putter from him to clean. "That was big. That was real big."

Francis nodded, hardly hearing him. As they walked on, he felt an unearthly calm spreading through his entire body—he described it afterward as if he'd slipped into a coma. Just like that the vision had come over him. Trailing along at his side, eyes on the ground, Eddie didn't notice any change.

"Now we can just play golf," said Eddie.

All three men placed their drives in the fairway on the 300-yard second hole, Cottage—named for a farmer's cottage that had stood near this green long before the course came into being. All three landed their approach shots on the green, leaving them with birdie putts inside twenty-five feet. Vardon and Ray ran theirs close, but each went long. Francis came up short for the second hole in a row. All three secured their pars.

A last line of dark clouds opened overhead and a driving rain fell briefly as they stood on the third tee—435 yards, Pond, named for the artificial lake installed by the club behind the green for ice skating and curling. Still holding the honor, for the first time that day Francis outdrove both Harry and Ted; Harry trailed him by ten yards on the same line down the middle. Ted's drive drifted right again and he found himself with a wicked sidehill lie, his line to the green impeded by a large oak. Playing first, he deftly drew a mid-iron around the tree, but the ball continued to hook, flew over the left front of the green, took a fortuitous kick off a rocky embankment that rose steeply toward the next tee, and landed on the back left corner just off the green. For his second, Harry played a superb long-iron approach up and onto the green.

Worried that Francis might have some difficulty following these two exceptional shots, Eddie toweled off the grip of his mid-iron as he handed it over and said, "Don't worry about what they're doing, just get it close."

Francis smiled, took the club, stepped up, and played the best shot of the three, a 200-yard dart that landed closest to the pin, set toward the front. The crowd rewarded him with their loudest cheer of the morning.

Ted ran a long chip down the length of the green; its back-to-front slant encouraged the ball to run four feet past the cup. Francis and Harry two-putted for outstanding fours. Ray missed his four-footer to match them; Ted Ray had blinked first and taken five, one stroke down to Harry and Francis.

"He looks steady," said John Anderson.

"They're not even paying attention to him yet," said Jerry astutely. "They're only playing each other."

The 300-yard par four fourth hole, Hospital, was named for the Brookline Hospital for Contagious Diseases, at one time a tuberculosis sanatorium that still lay just off the club's property line beyond the green. Next to the hospital stood the one-room Putterham School-house, Francis's old grammar school. Neither reminders of their past occurred to either man as they stepped to the fourth tee. A rocky outcropping a short distance in front of the tee box required a quick rising drive. Since length wasn't a necessity here, Francis asked Eddie for his more lofted driving iron. His tee shot easily cleared the rocks but cut slightly and landed on the first cut of rough in a suspect lie. For the fourth time that day, Harry landed his drive in the dead center of the fairway. Trying to atone for his three-putt at the last, and less than delighted about the three sliced tee shots he'd delivered so far, Ted pulled a sailing drive into the left rough at the top of the hill that looked down at the green, only fifty yards away.

One hundred and ten yards out, Francis and Eddie examined his lie, sitting down in a nest of greasy grass. He needed to make solid contact to clear the hazards ahead and reach the green.

"I can get a club on it," said Francis, and asked for his utility iron.

"Take your time," said Eddie.

Francis rehearsed the swing, then stepped out into the fairway and stared down toward the green until he saw the shot he wanted to play. He then played a precise left-to-right fade out of the rough that hugged the tree line before landing softly on the right side of the green, twenty-five feet from the hole. His best shot of the round.

Harry followed from the fairway with a clean wedge to within fifteen feet. Ted gripped his Snieler iron and dropped his ball twelve feet from the pin, leaving himself an uphill birdie putt to the cup. Putting cautiously, for the third time in the day Francis left his approach short, four feet from the hole down a dangerous sidehill slope. Harry and Ted both missed their birdie chances and tapped in for easy fours. Francis and Eddie lined up the putt and saw a nasty six-inch break to the right. Francis hit the putt firmly and confidently; any other stroke and he knew the ball wouldn't hold the line, but if he missed the hole, it would run ten feet past. Dead on line, it rattled off the back of the cup and stayed in for his four.

Francis and Harry all square, Ted one stroke back.

The fairway of the 420-yard fifth hole, Newton, runs toward the street that gives it its name. An elevated blind tee shot over a series of mounds, with a slight dogleg right downhill to a sharply sloping green, protected by bunkers to the left and a pot bunker and thick rough on the right. Dense woods and then out of bounds marked by a low stone wall ran all the way along the right side. Still holding the tee, Francis sent another well-struck drive right down the heart. Harry followed with his fifth dead-straight drive a few yards behind him. Still searching for his rhythm, Ted hooked his second consecutive tee shot long and left into the tall grass.

Playing first, off a slick downhill lie 225 yards from the green, Harry used a brassie and hit his first off-line shot of the day; the ball tailed slightly right, missed the front of the green, and settled in the rough. Playing next, Ted encountered some resistance getting his club through the high grass; the ball flew on line to the pin but landed twenty yards short of the green. A rustle of excitement ran through the crowd.

"They've left him an opening," said John Anderson.

"He'd better make the best of it," said Jerry Travers. "Those two might not make a mess of the same hole again today."

Throughout the crowd hushed voices asked a thousand variations on: *Can he reach the green and take advantage of it?* Marshals barked for order; the gallery settled again.

The rain had died back down to a swirling mist. Francis stared through it at the green.

"Let's have the spoon," he said.

Eddie toweled off the grip of his three-wood and gave it to him. The spoon had a small head and thin shaft and required a smooth, finessing swing, best encouraged by a lighter grip, but as Francis reached the top of his backswing, his palms slipped slightly; the entire club turned in his hands as it came down and made contact. Struck with a severely open club face, the ball shot almost dead right and hot, caromed through the trees and over the stone wall.

Out of bounds. The crowd gasped a collective *"Oh no!"* Francis stared after the ball for a moment in disbelief. A marshal stationed near the woods quickly emerged to confirm that the ball was gone; there was no point in even looking for it.

"What happened?" asked Eddie.

"The grip slipped in my hand," said Francis calmly. "Can't be helped. It was a bad shot."

He gestured for another ball. Eddie handed it to him. Playing today Francis would have been penalized both stroke and distance, but the USGA rule governing an out-of-bounds shot differed drastically in 1913, to the player's advantage: No penalty stroke was applied. As a referee came over to instruct him, Francis simply dropped a second ball over his shoulder within a club length of where he'd played his last; lying two, playing three. Francis immediately stepped behind the ball and lined up the shot to the green again.

"Sure you want to use that same club?" asked Eddie.

"It wasn't the club's fault, Eddie. It was mine."

Before the gallery had a chance to fully digest what had happened, or what he was doing in response, Francis walked up, took his stance, and made the swing he'd intended to the first time around. The ball soared high and straight toward the green, kicked right, and landed just inside and short of Harry's ball on the fringe.

The crowd roared. Francis smiled and handed the club back to Eddie as they started forward.

"That was the shot I meant to hit the first time," said Francis.

"Better late than never," said Eddie.

"Tremendous recovery," said Jerry Travers.

"But the door's open for Vardon and Ray now," said John Anderson. "A stroke in hand."

Francis and Eddie halted as Ted prepared to play his third shot, a short delicate pitch from twenty yards out. He swayed slightly forward as he came through with the Snieler niblick, which shut down the blade; the ball squirted out low and fast and ran all the way to the back of the green, twenty feet past the flagstick. A critical missed opportunity. Ted slammed the club into the ground in anger.

Now it remained to be seen if Vardon could capitalize. Concerned with getting his club face through the gnarled right side rough, Harry leaned on the swing a little too heavily and ran the ball eight feet past the stick, an equally crucial mistake. Francis now played his fourth, and best, shot of the hole, coaxing a chip to within a foot of the cup. He tapped in for bogey five and the crowd gave another sustained cheer. Unless one Englishman or the other canned his first putt, and neither was close to a gimme, Francis would escape any punishment for his errant shot.

For the first time that morning, Ted appeared visibly irritated by the emerging partisan sentiments. He made a point of waiting to even examine his line until the crowd went silent again. When they finally did, a photographer stepped out of the crowd to get a snapshot of Ted while he putted and a marshal shouted at the man to get off the course. Ted angrily swung around at the marshal.

"Are you going to talk, or am I going to putt?"

The marshal slunk away into the crowd. Ted turned back to his ball. After a long look at it, he sent his putt straight for the hole down the slanting sidehill green, but it avoided the cup by an inch. Harry's putt, an easier uphill eight-footer, gave his right hand its first stern test of the day; the muscle didn't jump, but his putt ran off line to the right. Both men tapped in, disappointed. Northcliffe looked mad enough to take his cane to both of them. All three scorers wrote down fives on the cards.

As Darwin added the fifth stroke, it occurred to him this salvaged five might do Francis more good than a birdie would have; sidestepping what had looked like certain disaster, Francis had halved the fifth hole.

Darwin was right. After Francis watched the other men putt out, he walked ahead to the next tee, empowered by a new insight: *They're not infallible*.

"I can play with these guys, Eddie," he said quietly.

"Yeah? Who said you couldn't?"

Harry betrayed no emotion as he walked to the next tee, but he seethed inside at his failure to cash in on Francis's mistake. If either he or Ted had converted, it might have opened a crack in the young man's unearthly composure. Harry had seldom seen the most hardened professional follow a butchered swing like that with such a dazzling recovery. He could only remember a handful of similar shots he'd made himself. But an amateur pulling off a shot like that under the pressure of an Open play-off? It was unimaginable.

Who does he remind you of, Harry?

Harry exchanged a glance with Ted—not worried, but concerned—and knew he was thinking exactly the same thing; the boy had demonstrated enough fortitude to show them he wasn't going to fold or fall apart. If they could no longer depend on Ouimet collapsing on his own—and to a measurable extent, even unconsciously, both men had—they would have to beat him straight up. Neither man had anyone to blame but themselves for their predicament, nor did they; they were paying the price for throwing away too many shots the day before. It should have been just the two of them out here today, playing for personal pride, and that was the assumption with which they'd started out. Trying to beat each other was challenge enough, but now it had turned back into a three-man race; in addition to all the inherent pressures of an Open play-off, they now felt the yoke of their nation's honor and sporting reputation pressing on their necks. Neither man could afford to squander another opportunity like the one Ouimet had just handed them at five. The next chance that came along, they had to bury him.

Opening feints and thrusts had all been made. Ted's three-putt at the third was all that separated them. The stakes had been raised; they could all feel it. The battle was joined.

Strike the blow now, thought Harry. *Before he feels the momentum lift him up. Strike a decisive blow.*

The sixth hole, Baker, was built on a lot purchased from Harriet Baker in 1898; uphill, 275 yards, par four. Francis led off at the sixth with another beautiful drive, in perfect position to attack the hole's vulnerable pin. Harry just outdrove him, along the same line, then met Ted's eye as the big man replaced him on the tee: *Now. Do it now.* Ted killed his first straight drive of the day, a real cloud buster that rainbowed down, flew by both other balls, and kicked forward up the hill, no more than forty yards from the green.

Francis approached first, a straight but slightly strong blind pitch that flew over the flag and settled eighteen feet past the hole. Harry waited for his caddie to walk ahead and line him up on the flagstick, then lofted a picture-perfect wedge dead toward the pin. The ball spun and stopped eight feet below the hole. Ted could see the flag from where his ball lay and he flew twelve feet long, on the same line with Francis's ball. Two good chances for birdie, and Ted would get a look at Francis's putt first; advantage Britain.

"You want to try for it?" asked Eddie, as they looked over Francis's ball at the back of the green. The putt ran straight down a sidehill slope to a hole cut halfway down a ridge. Not a likely birdie chance.

"A sure four's better than five," said Francis.

Eddie looked at him askance; was he advocating caution? Playing safe too early had handcuffed him yesterday, and he'd paid a stiff price for it. "Not gonna be a lot of chances out here today," said Eddie, giving him another opportunity to change his mind.

"We'll find them," said Francis. "Let's get this close."

Francis lagged his approach right on line to the hole. The ball stopped one roll short of falling in. He collected his par.

Smart, thought Harry. *He's playing the percentages.*

Ted rolled his first putt along the line he'd learned from watching Francis. Looking for a moment as if it would drop, the ball wandered just left at the end and he settled for four. Harry studied his eight-footer carefully, flexing his right hand repeatedly as he took his stance. He cajoled, threatened, and willed his damaged nerve not to jump. *Right, come on now, cooperate, damn you; we really need this one.* A sure, smooth stroke. Harry watched the ball roll straight into the hole for a birdie three.

"That's it," said Northcliffe.

A third of the way through the round, the first telling blow of the day had been landed: Harry led Francis by one stroke and Ted by two.

John Anderson felt some of the fragile confidence in the crowd around him go soft. Harry had missed one close putt after another all week; if he suddenly remembered how to putt now, it might be time to lower the lifeboats. The Brookline boys in the gallery urged Francis on as they walked to the seventh tee: *You can do it, Francis! Don't let 'em get you down! Straight and sure, Francis!*

"Don't worry," said Eddie. "We'll get that back."

But Francis wasn't worried. He couldn't prevent his opponents from making putts, or holing shots from 100 yards out for that matter. Following John McDermott's instruction to the letter, he paid no attention to what Harry and Ted were doing at all. All that mattered, all Francis could control at that moment was the next shot he had to play.

The first par three on the course, the 175-yard Plateau, named for its elevated green, was protected by large front bunkers left and right. For the first time all morning Francis relinquished honors on the tee; Harry sent a mid-iron over the left bunker into high rough, pin high, fifteen yards from the hole cut near the back. Francis landed his shot on line, six feet short of the green. Ted's drive held the same line, landed almost on top of the younger man's ball, and settled just shy in the fringe.

Francis's ball sat on the close-cropped chipping area, thirty paces from the cup, a couple of severe ridges and hollows to be negotiated over what appeared to be an exceedingly wet and slow green.

"This is a real surprise party," said Francis. "Let's putt it."

He immediately realized he had misjudged the effect of the moisture. The ball scooted through the chipping area without slowing at all and ran a good twelve feet past the hole. The worst putt he had struck all morning. This time profiting from Francis's mistake, Ted snuggled his shot right up to the flagstick and putted out for par. Harry had to slash an iron down into the rough to dig his ball out, and it ran thirty feet past the pin. Neither Harry nor Francis could sink his par putts coming back; both made four.

Ted had pulled even with Francis; they both trailed Harry by one stroke.

The 380-yard par four eighth, Corner, occupies what had originally been an outside corner of the club's property. Uphill fairway, left to right, to an elevated green. Now for the first time Ted led off, and the stroke he'd regained at seven had his blood pumping again. He slaughtered his tee shot straight down the middle. Francis and then Harry followed on line, short of Ted's but all in the fairway.

In order to watch the results of their blind approaches, a huge section of the gallery rushed ahead up the hill to surround the eighth green. All three men had landed on a short shelf below the steepest part of the incline, no more than ten yards apart. One hundred and sixty yards out, Francis looked up toward the crest of the hill and could just make out the top of the pin.

"I want to run it in there," said Francis. "Keep any mud off the ball."

Eddie handed him the mashie. "That's a good play. Keep it on line. I'll watch the ball."

Francis used a punched half-swing and liked it the minute he hit it. The ball bounced twice before passing out of sight over the brow of the hill and onto the green. A moment of silence, another, and then a tremendous explosion erupted from the gallery around the green.

"Your ball is stone dead," said Eddie with a grin.

Francis handed back the club. "I think I should have a chance for three."

Eddie shook his head. "Stone dead. Maybe in the hole."

Francis wouldn't allow himself the luxury of believing that, but before he could find out, they had to wait for Vardon and Ray. Both hit lofted irons onto the green; neither shot received the same reception. The moment the last ball was in the air, the gallery that had remained below rushed up the hill like a cavalry charge. Vardon and Ray were passed and nearly swallowed, Francis and Eddie had to run to stay in front of the advancing line. Tremendous applause greeted Francis from the crowd on top the moment he appeared over the rise.

Francis saw three balls on the green; the first two at least thirty and forty feet from the hole. The third sat within twelve inches of the cup. It was his.

"What did I tell you?" said Eddie. "Stone dead."

With his opponents' permission, Francis tapped in for his birdie three and then had to help the marshals ask the gallery for quiet. Ted fumed, again waiting for their celebration to end before he would even deign to look at his putt. What he saw didn't please him; forty feet away down a tenuous sidehill line. After thorough analysis Ted hardly tapped the ball, stood back, and watched it slide down the hill, take three distinct turns, and roll right into the cup. The crowd gasped. Ted had matched Francis's birdie.

"Good putt," said Francis. He couldn't help himself.

Ted acknowledged the compliment, tipped his hat, and smiled at him slyly; he knew he'd gotten away with one. Harry lagged his putt within inches and took four.

Another surprise party. All three men tied again through eight.

The ninth, a 520-yard par five, was called Himalaya for the craggy out-croppings of rock that rise sharply on each side of the fairway. An elevated tee overlooks a long narrow meadow, bisected by a brook that comes into play on the second shot, before another steep rise to the well-bunkered green. By the time they reached the tee box, lines of black-clad spectators crowned each ridge looking down along the fairway.

Ted held the honor again. His snorting, bull-like energy made it clear the last two holes had brought him back to life, eager to defy the crowd and continue his charge. His length gave him the best chance for birdie here, and he pounded a sensational drive deep down the right side, the optimum position to reach the green in two. Francis followed down the middle, taking the danger on the right out of play but trailing Ted by twenty yards. For the first time that day, Harry tried to match their drives, fell out of rhythm, and hooked his tee shot short and left into a nasty lie near the edge of the tree line.

"Nice drive, Harry," said Ted.

"Thank you, Ted," said Harry.

These were the first words they'd spoken to each other since the match began. Neither had said a word to Francis.

When he found his ball in high grass only inches from a gnarled root, Harry gave up any hope of getting home in two, or even crossing the creek; he laid up short of it, 200 yards from the green. Both Ted and Francis cleared the brook with their second shots, but the watery ground allowed no roll up the hill; Ted came up fifty yards short. A splendid third shot from Harry ran just over the back of the green. Francis pitched his third to within twenty feet, Ted followed and went him two feet better. Harry chipped down with a surgeon's touch to three feet below the hole. Both Francis and Ted took two putts to get down for par fives. They stood back and waited for Harry to finish.

A three-footer for par. The first he'd had all day. Uphill, straight in. Harry gripped his putter and moved it to the ball.

"They're going to be all even," said John Anderson.

"Not so fast," said Jerry Travers. "He missed more chokers than I did this week."

Unhurried, Harry stroked smoothly through the ball and sank the putt. In the crowd, Tom Vardon exhaled the breath he'd been holding in relief. *God knows how he does it*; the same question Tom had been asking himself for twenty years. As always, when it counted most, Harry somehow held his nerves in line.

The three men had gone through nine holes dead square, at even par 38, playing inspired golf under breathless pressure in dreadful conditions. Nine holes left to decide the championship. Tension began to mount with every step, slowly, exquisitely. The crowd, which had grown progressively larger throughout the morning, made a headlong flight to the tenth hole as it asked itself ten thousand questions: *Who will crack first? What if no one comes out on top? What if we have to go through another eighteen holes?*

The three players and their caddies paused briefly for water in the thatched hut on the way to the next tee. None of them said a word, but their eyes were on one another, meeting in darting glances. Ted appeared restless, lit up with excess energy. He and Eddie looked at each other; Eddie grinned and nearly made Ted laugh, which got a laugh from Eddie as well. Francis smiled broadly when he encountered and for a moment held Harry's eye.

He seems to be enjoying this, thought Harry. *Well, good for him. I used to as well, half a lifetime ago.*

Harry returned the look with his remote, Vardonic smile. But Francis didn't wilt at the sight of Harry's lofty self-possession as so many others had over the years. He knew enough about the man to know that smile was a weapon; that Vardon had tried to use it on him only made him appreciate the moment more.

You can't beat me that way, Harry; I know all your tricks. For the first time that day a thrilling thought entered his mind: *I might just beat you. I might just beat both of these guys.*

The steady drizzle that had been falling all morning at last began to fade. One by one umbrellas closed, put away. As the temperature rose and moisture condensed off the saturated course, the air grew positively steamy. Bernard Darwin made a point of looking at his watch; it was 11:45 when the players reached the tenth tee to begin the back nine.

The par three tenth, Redan, 140 yards, an elevated tee to an elevated green, protected by steep banks and bunkers, the only hole on the course that remained from The Country Club's original nine.

Ted stepped to the tee and confidently launched a high-iron tee shot onto the green about thirty-five feet to the left of the pin. Francis followed him, briefly stopping to consider his club selection.

"You want to try to run it up again?" asked Eddie, recalling the shot that had led to Friday afternoon's nearly disastrous double bogey.

Francis smiled. "That almost sunk us here yesterday, didn't it?"

Eddie nodded, afraid to say anything.

"They'll let us lift the ball out of a buried lie today," said Francis. "Let's fly it in."

Francis hit a beautiful short-iron that dropped onto the green twenty-five feet from the flag.

Harry followed with an equally effective tee shot, to the left of the flag near Ted, inside him by five feet. When they reached the green, they discovered all three balls were sitting up cleanly, but the pitch marks created by Vardon's and Ray's shots when they bit into the soggy grass lay directly along their line to the hole. The USGA had ruled that embedded balls could be lifted and cleaned, but added nothing about repairing divots. Francis's ball had spun slightly to the left when it landed; he alone had a clear path to the cup, although a small patch of mud had stuck to his ball.

The words Harry had spoken to him when they first met came back to Francis: *Some people have a talent for luck. It's a skill, you see, like any other. Maybe the most useful of them all.*

Ted putted first, aiming sharply left around the divot, a game effort, but without the proper line, he could get the ball no closer than six feet. Harry struck his first putt with a pronounced slicing action, actually trying to shape the shot around the crater in front of him, and the ball responded; he ended up less than four feet out. Mindful of how the mud on his ball might affect his line, Francis cautiously lagged his birdie putt inside of two feet and then immediately finished up for his three.

Ted settled over his ball to save par. The putt rolled on line but came up an inch short. Bogey four. Ted yanked it angrily out of the cup. Harry faced his third testing putt of the round, but this time the ball wouldn't drop. Bogey four. Both Harry and Ted had squandered earlier opportunities; now momentum began to swing toward the young American. For the first time that day, Francis took the lead. Rising excitement cranked the crowd up another notch; hoots and yells filled the air as they moved to the next tee. Ted looked annoyed again. For the first time that day, Bernard Darwin thought he saw a hint of fear beneath Harry's implacable mask.

The 390-yard par four eleventh was named Stockton for the original owner of this plot of land, one of The Country Club's earliest dedicated golfers. Long and uphill, with a pond protecting the right side on the drive. Francis took honors off the tee again. All three men hit sound drives in the center of the fairway, but again Francis outdistanced Harry and nearly matched Ted; he was swinging freely, his confidence growing with every shot. All three followed with superb irons onto the green; Ted landed closest, leaving him a makeable fifteen-footer. Francis and Harry sat twenty-five feet out. Three legitimate birdie opportunities.

Harry putted first but left his chance for three at least four feet short.

"His nerves are starting to show," said John Anderson.

"That putter's going to cost him sometime," said Jerry Travers.

"Par's a good score," said Eddie, now embracing prudence.

Francis played another safe lag and tapped in for four. Ted hit a solid stroke and creased the right edge with his birdie try, a fraction of an inch off line; he collected his four and stepped away, visibly disappointed. Harry hesitated longer than usual over his four-footer for par. Watching him linger, Tom Vardon feared the worst and could barely bring himself to watch. His brother stabbed at the ball unsteadily, a classically awful Vardon effort that barely trickled to the hole, trembled on the lip, and then dropped in. Harry had tried to shoot himself and dodged his own bullet.

All fours. Francis up by one on Vardon and Ray.

The 415-yard par five twelfth, Paddock, was built on the site of the old stables for the Clyde Park racetrack. Straight forward, up a long steep hill, it was a test of brute strength, pure and simple, with a slight downward slope at the end leading to a fiendishly subtle green. Francis led off with his best drive of the round, long and clean dead down the middle. Ted followed with another potent blast, but to his and everyone's amazement, when his ball stopped on the hill, they realized Francis had bested him by ten yards. Once again bringing up the rear, Harry reached down for something from his deep reserve and kept his ball in play just behind Ted.

Eddie knew Francis had gone into that place where no distractions reached him. He'd seen it come over him during those incredible first seven holes he'd played Friday morning. He had no idea how long this would last—six more holes would be too much to hope for—but Eddie kept his comments to a minimum now, the guardian of this perfect concentration, ready to throw himself between Francis and anything or anyone who might disrupt what he had going.

Harry played first, a hot brassie that scampered up the hill and took a hard bounce to the left, under an oak that sheltered the green. Ted's second landed just short; wet ground killed it. He'd taken one club less than he needed. Small mistakes from both men, but they might add up if Francis kept himself together.

"I'll try the mashie," said Francis.

"Keep your head down," said Eddie.

Francis followed his best drive of the day with his most purely struck iron. It flew straight as a rail to the green and settled eight feet from the pin. The crowd roared again; this time Francis didn't have to run up the hill to know he'd hit a perfect shot.

"That felt pretty good," said Francis.

"Pretty good?" said Eddie. "That was great."

The pressure shifted onto Harry's and Ted's short games. Ted pitched onto the green but landed on an upslope, killing its roll; the ball settled twenty feet short. Harry crafted an artful short wedge out of loose debris under the oak tree to roll the ball within six feet. Both in danger of making bogey, while Francis had an eight-foot putt for birdie.

Don't risk a three-putt here, instinct told Francis. *Four may be good enough. Make sure you get it.*

Francis tapped the putt cautiously and it came up a foot short—the crowd "oohed" their disappointment, but he was in first with his par.

He's managing the course, thought Harry as he watched him finish. *Managing himself. Something young players aren't supposed to be able to do.*

Ted hit a decent lag, but lost more ground to Francis. After coming up short on his last tester, Harry ran this one past the hole. He tapped in for five as well. The kid had played it safe, wisely, and made them both pay. Francis led them both by two strokes, with six holes left to play. He immediately walked ahead to the next tee, the crowd urging him on with what had by now become a crucial home field advantage. Every shot he hit went skyward accompanied by 10,000 prayers.

Harry and Ted fell into step together, speaking quietly without looking at each other.

"He's not cracking," said Ted.

"I couldn't help but notice," said Harry.

"I thought I'd only have you to worry about today, old man. Wasn't supposed to go this way."

"Seems that was our first mistake."

They reached the tee, watched Francis walking forward with his driver.

"If we're going to do anything about it, Harry, now would be the time."

"Right," said Harry. "At least let's make him fight for it."

The par four thirteenth, Maiden, 339 yards uphill and right, was named for its resemblance to the "Maiden" hole at Royal St. George's, Tom Vardon's old home course. Bernard Darwin described it best: "There stood the Maiden, steep and terrible, a bad, blind hole." But the Maiden didn't daunt Francis; he had picked up the first of the back nine birdies he'd so desperately needed here the day before. Brimming with confidence now, he led off with another perfectly placed drive down the left side of the fairway. Ted followed with a towering rip that passed Francis on the fly. Harry hit a textbook tee shot, following Francis's line down the left.

Harry laid a beautiful blind approach ten feet to the left of the flag. Francis followed with a gorgeous wedge shot of his own, bracketing the flag ten feet away on the right. Ted's joined them moments later on the green, fifteen feet short of the hole. Another birdie chance for all three. Ted putted first and missed by a hair. In for four; another chance squandered. Francis lined up his putt with Eddie and made a smooth stroke.

Collecting speed as it ran downhill for the hole—and what would be an almost insurmountable three-stroke lead—the ball caught the rim, spun 360 degrees around the lip, and shot back out a foot and a half the way it had come. The gallery staggered. Francis reacted evenly, showing no frustration. He tapped in for his par.

Now Harry stepped over his ball, eyes tracking the line like a sniper. Francis turned away: *Pay no attention.* Had he kept watching, he would have seen an exertion of the will he recognized. Harry applied an exact, untroubled stroke, without a tremor. The ball dropped for a birdie three. As Harry lifted it from the hole, he met Ted's eye and nodded: *Let's see if he cracks now.*

Harry had made his move. He was back within one stroke of Francis, leading Ted by one. Five holes to play.

"You okay, Francis?" asked Eddie, glancing at him sideways.

Francis smiled. "Never better. How are you?"

"Me?" He sounded surprised Francis had asked. "I'm okay. We just need pars now. They gotta do better than that to beat you."

"One shot at a time, Eddie."

"You said it." Then added, under his breath as Francis walked ahead of him: "But pars are all we need."

The par five fourteenth, Quarry, lay 470 yards from a severely elevated tee over a tumbling ridge of broken rocks that resembled a quarry in mid-excavation. Woods and out of bounds all the way along the left. Heavy rough, uneven lies to the right. The fairway runs uphill and then turns to the left to a small, well-protected green. The last true birdie opportunity on the course.

Harry had regained the tee for the first time in seven holes. Darwin noticed that the birdie at thirteen had snapped the steel back into his spine. Tom Vardon and Ted recognized the signs as well. The moment when this championship would be decided had arrived; "the Greyhound" had maneuvered into his favorite position for a finishing kick, closing from behind along the rail off the final turn. Would Francis hear his footsteps? As so many others had for the last twenty years, with Harry on his heels, would the young man falter coming down to the wire?

None of the three men looked at one another on the tee. Harry stared down at the fairway as he waited for his caddie to set up his ball. He would play it by the book: *Shape this one slightly left, down into that hollow at the bend of the fairway. The ball may run if it lands on the down slope and then you can get home from there.* But when he stepped up and took his swing, Harry overcooked this tee shot. Instead of drawing gently left, the ball hooked sharply, stopping in high rough just short of the trees. With the angle down the left side cut off, reaching the green in two from there was no longer an option.

Francis played another steady drive into the center of the fairway. Ted stepped up. He needed birdie more than Harry; if he didn't get at least one of those two strokes back here, short of an outright collapse by Ouimet, Ted figured his chances were growing cold on a slab. Ted came through; he airmailed a monstrous drive thirty yards past Francis's well-hit ball and for the moment kept his hopes alive.

Harry could barely see his ball down in the grass, near the same spot where on Wednesday John McDermott had found his resting on top of someone else's lost ball. The lie left him no choice but to bang a short recovery back toward the fairway and this he did; 120 yards out with a good angle to the green.

Francis studied his lie carefully. Two hundred and thirty yards to the green. The ball sitting on a gentle downhill slope. A slight embankment rose from the fairway about thirty yards directly in front of him. He could either try for the green with a wood, or play a cautious layup with a shorter iron. Francis ran both scenarios: He knew Vardon had only an outside chance now at birdie and Ted would have to gamble. As long as he kept this next shot on line to the green and stayed out of the bushes, Francis had nothing to lose and everything to gain. He had faith in his brassie, more than any other club in his bag.

"Brassie," he said to Eddie.

He was going for it; Eddie liked the decision. The caution of the last few holes had been hard for him to take, even if tactically sound.

"That's a downhill lie," said Eddie. "Keep your head down and make a good swing. I'll watch the ball."

With his feet above the ball Francis swayed slightly on his backswing; his weight drifted out over the outside of his right foot and he struggled to

keep his balance. His swing got too steep and when he made an adjustment with his hands to bring it back on plane, he hit only the top half of
the ball; the shot darted out low, smacked into the face of the embankment in front of him, tumbled forward another twenty yards, and stopped.
A forty-yard flub. One hundred and seventy yards left to the green.

Francis stared at it for a moment, his expression neutral. The first bad
shot he'd hit since going out of bounds on the fifth hole. The more inexperienced members of the crowd felt sure this spelled disaster, and they
indulged their fears: *This is the beginning of the end, the strain's too much,
he's finally cracking.*

"Easy, Francis," said John Anderson. "You're still in the fairway."

Showing no visible reaction, Francis handed the brassie back to Eddie.
"We can get home from there," he said, with such nonchalance that Eddie
thought he must be kidding.

"You topped it," said Eddie.

"At least it's not in the trees," said Francis, walking on.

Ted picked up his pace as he walked ahead to his ball; Francis had just
gift-wrapped the opportunity he'd hoped for. He lay only 200 yards from
the green, a clean level lie, both opponents in trouble; birdie and maybe
even eagle a possibility. No holding back now. With a wood in hand, Ted
took his stance, brought the club back, lurched forward, and lost his footing on the way down; the ball started on line but quickly cut right, landing amidst a cluster of scrub pines past the bunkers on the right, well
short of the hole. Ted cursed, slammed the club into the ground, tossed it
aside, and angrily stormed off after his ball. His chance had gone horribly
wrong.

And I won't have to worry about him again, thought Francis in a flash as
he watched Ted stomp away. *He's lost his focus.*

Francis looked over his third shot, decided on a mashie, and lofted a
long, beautiful straight shot that landed and settled on the green, twenty
feet to the right and dead level with the pin. On in three; the botched shot
hadn't hurt him. Harry pitched up from 120 yards out, but for the second
time in three swings, the shot hooked left, landing on the far back corner
of the green. Forty feet from the pin down a twisting sidehill slope. Not
much chance for birdie from there.

That's interesting, thought Francis. *Harry never pulls his irons, he plays from left to right with that club. I think he's more nervous than I am.*

When Ted reached his ball between the trees he discovered he still had a narrow opening between the pines and over a bunker to the front of the green. With exceptional touch he punched it cleanly through the gap. The ball landed short and trickled onto the front of the green. Despite Harry's foozled drive, and Ted and Francis's mis-hit second shot, all three men were on the green in three. No advantage. All three men took two putts to get down. All three made their par fives. Francis still up by one over Harry and two in front of Ted. Four holes to go.

The 370-yard par four fifteenth, Liverpool, was named for the Liverpool Jump on Clyde Park's old steeplechase course, which used to run near the main road that now cut across the fairway to the clubhouse. An elevated tee sets up a not overly difficult second shot to a slightly elevated green, provided the first one finds the fairway. The strings of suspense in the gallery were drawn so taut the tension had become physically unpleasant; bitter, gnawing, unrelieved. The crowd shuffled along silently as they lined the fifteenth fairway, deadened with anxiety. Bernard Darwin knew that however bad it might be for these spectators—himself included—by now the pressure on the players had reached intolerable levels; someone had to come to grief, and soon.

Harry and then Francis hit two more flawless tee shots into the teeth of a rising wind.

It'll be Ray, thought John Anderson, watching them set up on the tee. *He's ready to go.*

But Ted had one last lucky coin to cash in. His drive faded right off the tee, clearly headed for the rough, when it struck a man in the gallery on his bowler hat and bounced dead left back onto the fairway. The man was unhurt, but so distraught that he might have unwittingly helped the English cause that he immediately left the grounds. The crowd fell into morbid silence again, wondering if Ray could capitalize on this uncanny good fortune. Playing first, appearing increasingly distracted and taking far less time than he should over the ball, Ted also sliced his high arching approach. Throughout its flight the ball appeared to have a chance to catch the edge of the green, but a last-second dive to the right sent it straight down into the deep front bunker. Ted had under-clubbed himself again. Through fifteen holes, it was the first bunker any of the three men had landed in all day. Francis hit his approach safely onto the front right edge of the green. Harry knocked his second slightly long, on line with the pin but just over the back. They both walked up and waited for Ted to play out of the bunker.

The ball had buried right where it hit in the sand, within a foot of the bunker's steep face. Ted waded in, practiced the swing only once, hastily dug in his feet, and tried to blast out; the ball hit the front lip and fell back into the middle of the trap. Furious, Ted immediately swung down at it again, hard, caught the ball thin and knocked it through the green into the fringe on the far side. By the time he'd walked over to his ball, both Francis and Harry had chipped up to within two feet and secured their pars. Using his putter, Ted casually swiped at his ball in the fringe, running it down to within a foot of the hole and then tapped in for double bogey six. He was four strokes down, three holes to play. Ted stared at the ball in the cup for a long moment before lifting it out. He managed a rueful smile, slipped the ball into his pocket, then walked over to where Harry waited for him at the edge of the green.

"That's done for me," said Ted. "I'm well out of it, old boy. Godspeed."

Ted had cracked first. Now it was down to two.

Francis walked ahead to the sixteenth tee, the crowd swelling around him, urging him on. Three holes to play to win the U.S. Open, with a one-stroke lead over Harry Vardon. As Harry watched Francis walking ahead, the memory he'd been searching for earlier came to him: *He's playing just the way I did, against Taylor in the play-off at Muirfield in '96. The day I won my first Open.*

"Got a cigarette, mate?" Harry asked his caddie.

They stopped while the caddie pulled one out and lit it for him before they walked on to the next hole.

The 125-yard par three sixteenth, Clyde.

Still retaining the honor, Harry stood on the tee and stared out at the sixteenth green until he finished his cigarette. Drawing the smoke deep into his lungs, he didn't remove his eyes from that green, and the mesmerized crowd watched him without moving, hardly daring to breathe, for almost a minute. His mind settled, Harry flung the butt aside, pulled his club from the bag, took one practice swing. Calmly and efficiently he flew his tee shot straight over the flag and set it down fifteen feet past the hole.

Francis stepped up to the tee and looked things over: Pin toward the front. Traps left, front, and right. Disaster long. The hole had been nothing but uncommon trouble for him all week. He asked Eddie for his niblick. Eddie toweled off the grip and walked it over to him.

"One shot at a time," said Eddie. "Let's be putting after this."

Francis lofted a beautiful high iron that landed softly and settled on the green twenty feet to the right of the pin. The crowd hollered and let off some steam. When they had settled down again, Ted, in a bad mood and going through the motions, just cleared the bunkers in front to reach the fringe. Playing for three all the way, Francis lagged up to within inches and took his par. Harry's ball had a good look at birdie but he misread the line and it fell off just to the right. A collective sigh of relief from the crowd: Another chance for Vardon gone. Harry tapped in for par. His heart no longer in it, Ted blew his second putt well past the hole, three-putted for bogey, and fell five strokes behind Francis.

As Bernard Darwin finished marking Francis's score at sixteen, he glanced over to the crowd and noticed Northcliffe had gone as pale as a sheet after Harry's near miss. For once Darwin decided to stop worrying about his boss's emotional equilibrium. Being responsible for the young American's scorecard had impaired Darwin's ability to stand back and objectively observe with his reporter's voice and eye, and it created a delightfully liberating effect in him. Divided to this point in the play-off by his conflicted personal and professional sentiments, as the impossible edged another step closer to the inevitable, Darwin felt himself swept up by something larger and grander than petty nationalistic differences. He was not only one of the most devoted students of the game who ever lived, he was one of its greatest fans as well. Darwin discovered that as the last act of this back nine unfolded, great sport, riveting drama, and the steel-eyed courage Francis Ouimet apparently had to spare on this day transcended all his partisan loyalties.

Northcliffe's mission to take back the U.S. cup be damned, thought Darwin. *It would be a positive sin now if Francis didn't win.* With a sharp internal shock, this most English of Englishmen finally admitted to himself what he'd been feeling for some time: Along with every other man, woman, and child in that enormous crowd—save one—Bernard Darwin was rooting for Francis. *Yes, by God, let him do it.*

The 370-yard par four seventeenth was called Elbow, aptly describing its sharp dogleg left. A large bunker fiercely protecting that bend. One-stroke difference, two holes to play. Harry looked out at the fairway from the tee box set back among the trees. Getting the three he needed at the more difficult eighteenth would be improbable at best. If he was going to make up that shot, he'd have to do it right here, where Francis had caught them yesterday. Harry stared at that bunker in the joint of the dogleg. Cutting the corner straight with a drive over that trap would take fifty yards off the hole. His last best chance to make three.

He's not going to crack. I'll have to catch him. If I lay this drive dead over that bunker close to the green, he may feel he has to follow me around that corner. And that could reshuffle the deck . . .

Harry stepped up to the ball. Ted could see from his alignment where Harry intended to take it; Ted himself hadn't tried that flight path over the bunker all week, too high-risk, and he was the longest hitter in the world. But he understood; the time had come for desperate measures. Harry let the drive go, a perfect, soaring shot that drew slightly down the line toward that bunker. It appeared as if the ball would clear easily but it passed out of sight around the edge of the trees before it got there; no one could see where it landed from the tee box. For the moment the shot's fate remained unknown.

Francis walked up to the tee. He looked over at his house across the street through the woods. He looked at his mother and brother and sister in the crowd. He looked down at Eddie Lowery. He glanced over at Harry Vardon, then his eye picked out Johnny McDermott in the gallery; their gaze met briefly, Johnny nodded. Francis took a deep, shuddering breath.

Johnny's warning had been right on the money; Harry's trying to lead me down that left-hand side, into danger.

"Where you going with this, Francis?" asked Eddie.

Francis took the driver from him and hesitated another moment. Then he pointed.

"Out here, to the right," said Francis. "Away from that trap."

Francis drove his ball straight down the fairway, ending almost exactly where he'd landed yesterday afternoon; 170 yards out from the green, and perfectly safe.

Following Harry's lead, caution long since scattered to the wind, Ted hurled himself at the ball with seismic force and boomed his tee shot over the trees, over the bunker, over everything, into light rough less than sixty yards from the green. The line was viable, Ted's shot had proved it, but it remained to be seen if Harry's ball had cleared. The gallery charged ahead, the three players striding just in front of them. They turned around the bend in the trees and got their answer.

Harry's ball lay dead in the bunker. Buried against its steep front bank. No chance to advance it forward toward the green. Harry stared at it in disbelief, uncomprehending; he'd hit it hard enough, he'd hit it far enough. This shouldn't, this couldn't have happened. Someone who'd been standing at the elbow the entire time told Harry's caddie the ball had landed safely in the grass to the right, then kicked dead left into the trap.

Bad luck.

Eddie and Francis looked at each other without a word. They looked at his ball sitting neatly in the fairway. They looked at the green, at the hole cut halfway to the back on the left. For the first time they could admit it to themselves. The thought crept into their eyes, their bodies, their faces; the play-off, and the U.S. Open, was now his to lose.

"Any reason to do anything different than what we did yesterday?" asked Eddie.

"One doesn't come to mind," said Francis.

Eddie handed him the jigger he'd used to run his shot up Friday afternoon. Francis made the same crisp economic swing with his iron, landed the ball just short of the green, and ran it onto the upper tier about eighteen feet past the pin. On in two. The crowd let loose a tremendous roar.

A grim Harry took his niblick into the trap that has ever since been known as "Vardon's Bunker" and knocked his ball out sideways onto the fairway. He was ninety yards from the flag. He could still get up and down from here for a four, still hope against hope for one last miracle at eighteen. But he had at last run out of any room for error; Harry faced match point.

Using the same club, Harry sent the ball high and straight on line toward the pin, but when it landed on the green instead of pitching forward, the ball checked up and stopped short, twenty feet below the hole. Up ahead to the left, Ted prepared to play his second shot from the rough, but the cheers for Francis began again as he approached the green in the middle of Ted's swing. Ted stepped back and waited for complete order to be restored, openly annoyed, then played his second shot onto the green, a yard in front of Harry. Just as events had unfolded here yesterday afternoon, within moments the gallery enveloped the entire seventeenth green. Marshals and rope men struggled to hold them outside the lines. They could feel it coming now, something immense, unstoppable, close at hand. *He's going to do it. He's going to do it!* This was what they'd waited for, prayed for; primed, tortured, aching for relief and resolution.

The marshals wedged open a path for the three men to work their way through the crowd to the green. Harry would try his twenty-foot putt to save par first. Up shot the red flags, the marshals yelled for silence; they got it instantly. Eddie crossed his fingers behind his back for the second time that week, this time hoping someone would miss.

How much did Harry have left? Had he already acknowledged to himself that he was beaten? He didn't look any different, but then, he never did. He started the putt on line, but it was clear from the moment he let it go, the ball wasn't going to get there. Two feet short. Harry sighed, his shoulders slumped ever so slightly, then he walked over and tapped it in for five.

"Take all the time you need," said Eddie, handing Francis his putter. "It's only one o'clock. You've got till six o'clock tonight if you need it. Get this one dead, sure. Four is all you need."

Francis stood over his ball. His mind didn't race ahead to glorious dreams of victory or any of the thousand incomprehensible ways his life might be transformed. He didn't see himself with the trophy hoisted in his hands, or picture his photograph on the front page of nearly every newspaper in a dozen countries around the world. He stayed in that moment. Focused on the shot in front of him. Standing on the seventeenth green, less than 100 yards from his own front door, where he'd been sneaking out to practice before sunrise since he was six years old. When Francis moved inside this absolute concentration, as he did now, the pure center where his mind no longer felt the need to distinguish between action and intention, he knew exactly why he loved this game. Why he'd been so mysteriously drawn to it from his earliest living memory until now. He realized in that moment what he'd learned through the long journey of his improbable, extraordinary summer—that this was why he played; to stand in the still, perfect sweetness of this place outside of time, a club in his hand, looking down at a small white ball, knowing exactly what he was about to do.

Downhill and right. Eighteen feet. He barely touched it. The ball rolled and rolled and rolled down the slippery slope, and as it neared the hole no one around that green could any longer find a reason to hold back any of what they'd bottled up all day. Because here's the thing: Francis made the putt for three.

For a while it seemed all the world had lost its mind, and justifiably. The roars wouldn't stop. The crowd nearly rushed the green right then and there, but Francis stepped forward, Harry, too, holding up their arms to remind them that Ted still had to finish. Finally they relented and stepped back. With any and all reasons to try now gone, Ted needed three strokes to put it in the hole.

Francis led Vardon by three strokes, Ray by seven. The eighteenth would be a mere formality, the gallery spreading out all the way along its length to make it a celebration. Francis and Eddie walked through the crowd to the eighteenth tee. Hundreds reached out to touch him, shake his hand, pound them both on the back. They could hardly hear themselves above the nonstop cheering. Eddie looked at Francis as they reached the last tee box, his eyes lit up from within by some fantastic realization.

"Francis," he said, nearly shouting. "Francis, you need a four here to make seventy-two."

Francis felt a chill run right through him. He smiled. "That's what I'll do, then."

The par four eighteenth, 410 yards. Home.

Rope men took long excruciating moments to clear out the fairway. Marshals screamed and begged for silence but not until Francis stepped forward with the driver in his hand would they grant it. Then it came, sudden and absolute. Francis lashed one last perfect drive in the center of the fairway. Harry followed but couldn't match him; a drained, exhausted swing left him in the rough. Still showing his anger about the mob scene at seventeen, Ted swung fast and sliced down the right-hand side. The crowd chased them down the fairway. Harry made a last desperate attempt to reach the green but came up short in the front bunker. Ted quickly hit a towering brassie onto the green to within eight feet of the cup.

Now they all crowded in around every side of Francis. Although nothing short of a lightning strike could stop him at this point, anxiety raised its head one last time; a three-stroke lead could still vanish, stranger things had happened. To assure victory, he had to get this one on the green.

One hundred and eighty yards away. Francis took a practice swing, looked ahead. The rain had at last turned the racetrack in front of the green into a bog. *Just get it over that mud.*

He hit the ball straight and high at the pin and the moment everyone saw that his shot would clear that bunker, the last uncertainty disappeared. The ball danced as it landed and ran twenty-five feet past the flag, safely on the green. The celebration began in earnest; they cheered him the rest of the way in, Eddie walking alongside him step for step, a grin splitting his face from ear to ear. By the time they got there, the Home hole green had become an emerald amphitheater set amid a field of solid black. Harry blasted out of the bunker to the back of the green and needed three more quick, superfluous strokes to get down in six. Ted ran his first putt into the hole for a birdie that meant exactly nothing. Both men stepped back and cleared the stage for Francis. Darwin held the pencil poised above the card in his hand, prepared to add another stroke.

Francis stepped up to his ball. For the first time, all that day, the enormity of what he had done, of what he was about to finish, hit home.

I am about to become the national champion.

He stroked his first putt to within nine inches of the hole. As he followed it down, the shouts and cries and whoops increased tenfold again. They finally broke through his impregnable concentration, the veil that had covered and protected Francis from the first green onward shattered and fell away from him. As he stood over that nine-inch putt, his entire body began to tremble like a leaf. Shivering so hard, he could barely hold the putter still in his hands.

I am about to become the national champion.

Francis stepped back for a moment, looked up at the sky, looked over at Eddie, looked at the mob scene around him, and could not remotely comprehend where he found himself.

"One more stroke, Francis," said Eddie, at his side. "Just one more."

He stepped back to the ball and with the most conscious effort he'd had to expend all through the play-off, his last putt rolled into the final hole. The silence held for a moment. One momentous beat to let it sink in.

It was done. Francis had done it.

For the second time in as many days the multitude rushed forward as one and massed around him. For the second time they lifted him up onto their shoulders as cheer after cheer rang out. Women tore flowers from their bodices and hurled them at him. Hundreds pushed forward through the crowd just to touch him. Francis saw Eddie nearly swallowed up by that first rush and cried out to them: *Be careful, don't hurt him!* The warning spread quickly, and moments later Eddie was lifted up by friendly arms out of harm's way and joined him in the air. Eddie reached out to Francis and they shook each other's hands, both laughing and smiling. In every direction people staggered, exhausted, wrung out, more than a few self-medicated from a personal flask, all astonished by what they'd seen and been through, stunned by how they felt, more thrilled by such an experience than they'd ever known was possible.

Someone pressed a lucky horseshoe from the old racetrack into Francis's hand. Dozens others held up money they wanted him to take, large bills, trying to offer reward for the excitement he'd just given them. Francis shook his head and tried to wave them off. They didn't understand and he tried to explain: He was an amateur, he couldn't accept any money for what he'd just done. Those were the rules. They couldn't hear a word he said.

Bernard Darwin wrote down that final stroke on Francis's scorecard, added up his score, and then remembered nothing for the next few minutes, caught up in the joyous maelstrom. He remained fairly certain he had handed the scorecard to some appropriate official but retained no memory of doing it. He was later amazed to discover his handwriting was perfectly legible.

As Francis continued to refuse the money, he spotted John Anderson and Jerry Travers just below him and called down to them that they ought to pass the hat for Eddie Lowery. Jerry stepped forward to take charge and Anderson volunteered his bowler. A great cheer went up for Eddie. And then Francis saw a figure he thought he recognized push forward through the throng from about twenty feet away and stick the first dollar into John Anderson's hat. Within moments the bowler was filled to the brim with money. When the crowd blocking the line of sight between them shifted, Francis saw the face of the man who'd put in that first dollar; it was his father, Arthur.

Arthur looked up at Francis riding on the shoulders of the crowd; there were tears in his eyes. He raised a hand straight into the air, held it there, palm open to Francis, a wave or a salute. Francis waved back to him and smiled. Instead of heading for the locker room, this time the crowd conveyed Francis toward the clubhouse where the U.S. Open trophy waited. As they carried him away, Francis lost sight of his father, but he could still see Arthur's hand thrust into the air above the faceless crowd.

Harry and Ted walked quickly through the crowd and away from the green as the throng converged on Francis. They shook hands, said not a word, a wry smile for each other: *Nothing to be done.* Moments later a pleasant young USGA official stepped forward to meet them near the clubhouse steps.

"The secretary wanted me to ask," said the young man, "if you gentlemen would like to be part of the presentation of the trophy."

Absolutely, they said, and looked at each other. *Part of the job.*

"And do either of you happen to know, will Lord Northcliffe be joining us for the ceremony?"

Neither man could look at the other for a moment, for fear of laughing. Both worked to keep a smile off their faces.

"I don't believe he will," said Harry.

"Sends his apologies," said Ted. "Urgent business."

A few minutes later the USGA's secretary, John Reid Jr., stepped forward and called the crowd to order from the front of the clubhouse. The trophy and the medals rested on a table beside him on the porch.

"I can find no words to express my feelings," said Reid, capturing exactly the mood of so many in the crowd. "The event is too much for me. I should like to begin by congratulating our two visitors for their outstanding play today and throughout this tournament. We shall never forget them. We also hope they understand that although they have both won many championships around the world, we here in America have never seen anything quite like this before, so I should like to apologize—in a slight way—for any outbursts of cheering which may have come during the course of play at inopportune times."

Both Ted and Harry graciously signaled their appreciation for Reid's gesture; the crowd liked them all the more for it.

"In third place," said Reid, "it gives me pleasure to introduce Mr. Edward Ray. If he is not quite as well known as Harry Vardon, he is a bit younger—"

"Quite a bit," said Ted, getting a laugh.

"—and I think it safe to say that if we all live for a number of years longer, we may be able to behold in him another five-time Open champion."

Ted stepped forward to shake Reid's hand and receive his check. Three great cheers went up and he acknowledged them gallantly by doffing his hat and bobbing his head in each direction.

"It gives me the greatest pleasure," said Ted, "to congratulate Mr. Ouimet on his splendid victory. I have no hesitation in saying that he played better golf the whole four days than any of us. His was the best golf I have ever seen in my time in America. It has been an honor to play with him and no dishonor to lose to him."

More cheers as Ted stepped aside, hat in hand. John Reid introduced Harry by way of saying he required no introduction. A long ovation for Vardon as he stepped forward and took off his cap; Harry smiled broadly, visibly moved by their display of appreciation, then finally had to ask for silence.

"Ladies and gentlemen—ladies and gentlemen . . ." The crowd finally settled. "We have no excuses to make today, for we were both defeated by the highest class of golf. We were trailing all the time, for our opponent left us not a single opening. We made mistakes and Mr. Ouimet, like a wise man and good golfer, took advantage of every one of them. His play was so excellent and so steady, all hope was kept out. We do not begrudge him this victory. America should be nothing but proud of her new champion. He has proved himself to be a superior golfer and a courageous fighter."

Harry turned to Francis behind him on the porch and met his eye with genuine warmth and admiration. Francis nodded his thanks and waved back shyly. The crowd bathed them both in cheers and applause. When they subsided again, Harry continued.

"There exists a special bond between our two countries, and it is my firm belief that this great sport played in the spirit of friendly competition over time can only make it stronger. This is my second time in America, which I count as one of the great privileges of my life. I hope it is not my last, and for the great kindnesses and hospitality accorded me, I wish to thank all of you. I assure you that, for my part, they are returned with nothing but the deepest and most lasting affections."

After receiving his check from Reid, Harry moved aside. Reid now lifted the first-place gold medal from the table and beckoned to Francis, who stepped hesitantly forward to meet him. Without a word Reid slipped the ribbon of the medal around his neck to thundering acclaim and then picked up the U.S. Open trophy.

"Francis, the only thing I can think of to say is that because of what you, alone, have done here today, this cup which I hold in my hands will not be making a journey overseas—" That prompted another rousing outburst from the crowd. "Generally, when this trophy is awarded, the USGA requires the winner's home club to provide some security for the safety of our prize, but the only security we are going to ask from the Woodland Club today is that they insist you keep practicing your game."

A great laugh erupted and with that Reid handed him the trophy. Francis had never seen the cup this closely before. He regarded it in wonder as he held it in his hands, then lifted it up carefully for the crowd to see and they went wild. Cries of "Speech, speech!" rent the air. Francis tried to modestly wave off the request, but they would not be denied. Finally, he acknowledged his willingness to speak, the crowd gave a cheer, and then went silent again.

"I can assure you that no one here is more surprised than myself," he said, his eyes shining. "Naturally it was my hope, but this is so far beyond anything I ever dreamed to do that I never once expected I would win. My only thought was to play as well as I could for eighteen holes and let the score stand, for good or bad. I did the very best I could, and tried hard to keep the cup from going to our friends across the water." He turned to nod at Harry and Ted, who snapped a salute at him. "I am happy indeed that it gets to stay. I am very glad to have helped in every way I could."

Francis waved modestly and stepped back. The cheers poured down harder than yesterday's rain. They expanded to once again include all three players on the porch as USGA and club officials moved forward to shake their hands. With that the formal ceremony and the gathering casually dissolved. The three men were asked to pose together for a phalanx of photographers in front of a flowering hedge outside the clubhouse, Francis standing between Harry and Ted, holding one of their hands in each of his, the Englishmen with their lit pipes going in the other, all of them smiling. Each man then took his turn in the press tent, patiently answering any and all questions about the events of the day.

Playing for the U.S. Open Championship, on a drenched, unyielding, backbreaking course, in front of the largest crowd to ever witness a round of golf in the United States, Francis had not missed a single fairway. He did not send one single approach shot into a bunker. He did not three-putt a single green. The final scores, the prize money, and their modern equivalent:

First place:	Francis Ouimet	72	Amateur
Second place:	Harry Vardon	77	$300 ($5,390)
Third place:	Ted Ray	78	$150 ($2,695)

NEARLY AN HOUR after his last putt had been struck, Francis collected his trophy from the porch and began slowly working his way back through the crowd to the locker room, hundreds still milling around him, friends and strangers alike shaking his hand, patting him on the back, reaching out to touch the silver cup. Eager to steal a private word with the new champion, Bernard Darwin moved toward him, then caught sight of a small, beaming, gray-haired lady stepping into his path. Francis leaned down and they embraced. Darwin couldn't quite hear what the woman said to him, but he did hear Francis's soft reply: "Thank you, Mother. I'll be home soon." When Francis moved on, Bernard decided not to follow him.

More than enough time to talk about it later, thought Darwin. *Let the young man have his moment.*

Marshals standing guard outside saw to it no one from the crowd followed him into the sanctuary of the locker room. Francis set the trophy on the bench and sat down beside it. He studied every inch of it, ran his fingers across the list of names engraved along the base: *Horace Rawlins, James Foulis, Joe Lloyd, Fred Herd, Willie Smith, Harry Vardon, Willie Anderson, Lawrence Auchterlonie, Alex Smith, Alex Ross, Fred McLeod, George Sargent, John McDermott.* His name would join them, right there, right after Johnny's.

He heard Dan McNamara's voice behind him. "Francis? Someone here to see you." Francis looked up; Dan had escorted Eddie into the locker room. Eddie's eyes went straight to the trophy.

"Is that it?" he asked.

"That's it," said Francis.

Eddie walked over to examine it more closely. "Can I touch it?"

"Of course."

Eddie ran his fingers over the gleaming silver surface, tracing the engravings. "Real silver."

"That's right."

"You gonna take it home with you?"

"Soon. I'll have to give it back first so they can put my name on it," said Francis. "Down here, see?"

Eddie looked at the engraved names around the base, his lips moving as he read a few of them off, then he looked back at Francis with absolute wonder. "Isn't that something."

"Isn't that something."

"Francis, you can't believe it, look," said Eddie, reaching into his coat pocket. "They gave me all this money, I didn't even ask 'em for it, they just gave it to me." Eddie showed him the thick, hastily folded roll.

"That's great. How much do you have there?"

"I only counted it once, but I think it's almost a hundred dollars. That's more money than I've ever seen in my whole life."

"That's wonderful." Francis reached into his pocket. "I want you to have this, too, Eddie."

Francis held out one of the two golf balls he'd finished playing the round with.

"Really?" Eddie stared at the ball.

"I told those reporters the same thing I want to tell you," said Francis. "I hope you can hear me say this: I could not have done this without you. I think I was able to do what I did here . . . because you believed I could."

Eddie accepted the ball, gripped it as if trying to feel the full weight of what Francis had given him. Then he looked up at Francis again.

"We shot seventy-two," he said.

"Yes, we did."

Eddie nodded, shoved his money back into one pocket, put the golf ball in another. Francis stuck out his hand; they shook one last time.

"I'll see you soon, Francis."

"See you soon, Eddie. Out at Woodland. Maybe we'll play a round together."

That put the biggest smile on Eddie's face so far. "It's a deal."

Eddie walked out with Dan. "Mr. McNamara, I heard somebody say that truant officer's out there looking for me. You know, I hope he is; I got a couple of things to tell him."

Francis showered and shaved, dressed in some fresh clothes, and was getting ready to leave when he heard two more voices issuing from around a corner in the locker room.

"What time's the train, then?"

"Five o'clock. Into New York by ten, they say."

"Hope we've got time for a drink first," said Ted. "I'm bloody knackered."

"Never despair, old boy, there's always time for a drink," said Harry. "Where are the clubs?"

"I've had them sent directly to the station."

Francis turned the corner and found the two English pros emptying their lockers and closing up their kit bags.

"Well done," said Harry. "I've called ahead, they'll send our bags on from the hotel. Tickets are waiting. All we have to do is present ourselves."

Prepared now to leave, they turned and saw Francis.

"Well, Master Ouimet," said Ted, friendly and brisk. "Shaven and shorn, ready to face the evening."

"What's on for you this fine Saturday, then, Francis?" asked Harry.

"Oh, I'm not sure. Some friends want to take me into Boston for dinner," said Francis.

"Good. See to it you go out and paint the town," said Ted, laying a big sociable hand on his shoulder. "Grab hold tight to every last minute of this day, my young friend, that's my advice to you. And from this moment forward. You'll find it's going to be quite a ride."

"I will. I will," said Francis. "What's on for you, then?"

"Train to catch," said Ted. "Places to go. Never enough time."

"We've a match scheduled tomorrow morning," said Harry. "Alex and Mac Smith. A club somewhere outside New York City."

"Good Lord, you have to play again tomorrow?"

"The professional's life, Francis," said Ted. "Three more weeks on the road before we even sail for home. Hope you're not planning to turn pro anytime soon."

"No, I hadn't planned on it."

"Count yourself among the lucky, then. Dreadful way to make a decent living," said Ted, shouldering their bags. He shook Francis's hand vigorously. "Well, I'm sure we'll meet again. Come look us up in London, we'll show you the sights."

"I've never really thought about traveling overseas."

"Trust me," said Ted. "You will now."

"I'd like to take you up on that," said Francis, warming to the idea. "I'd like that very much."

"Depend on it, then. We'll await your arrival on our shores. And Francis, it's your turn now: Enjoy yourself." Ted winked at him and went out the door.

Harry lingered for a moment, set down his bag, struck a match, and lit his pipe.

"I was lucky out there today," said Francis, to fill the silence.

"No," said Harry. "That wasn't luck. I didn't underestimate you, Francis. You showed us too much yesterday for that. But I didn't think you'd be able to sustain that into a play-off. That was my mistake."

Francis nodded shyly, and looked down. Harry shook out his match and tossed it aside.

"Someone mentioned to me you live quite nearby," said Harry.

"Just across the street, near seventeen," said Francis.

Harry's ears perked up. "So you grew up right there, did you? Across from the course."

"That's right."

Just as I did. Now it begins to make sense. "And I imagine you've played the game your whole life."

"As long as I can remember. I caddied here. My brother got me started."

Yes. I was even more right than I knew: A second young Harry.

Harry paused, never taking his eyes off Francis, then nodded slightly. Francis couldn't read his look exactly, but it seemed as if some satisfying private instinct had been confirmed. "Your family must have been here today to watch you, then."

"Some of them were," said Francis.

Harry picked up a hesitation in his tone. "What does your father do?"

"He's a gardener." Francis thought Harry seemed unusually interested, perhaps even emotionally moved for some reason, by that answer.

"Really? Does he approve?"

Francis hesitated again. "I don't know. In the past, I can't say . . . but no. No, not really."

Harry gave him a long, understanding look. "That's all right, Francis." He held out his hand. Francis shook it. "We approve."

"Thank you, Mr. Vardon," said Francis.

Harry smiled. A horn honked impatiently outside, then Ted yelled for him. Harry picked up his bag, held up a hand in farewell, and left without another word.

Francis sat down on a bench and looked around the empty locker room. After a time he took out an old and weathered golf ball from his pocket and studied it for the longest while. An old treasure. There appeared to have been some writing on it once—a name, perhaps one starting with a *V*—but whatever it was had long since faded with age. A smile crossed his face.

When he heard voices calling his name outside, Francis slipped out the locker room's side door where no one waited for him, into the cool and welcome silence of late Saturday afternoon. The rain had stopped, he could hear birdsong for the first time in two days, and it looked now as if the sun might even show itself before the day was done. With all the time in the world, Francis walked down alone across the wide, empty fairways, his steps measured and his direction sure, past the seventeenth green, through the stand of beech trees, across the street, and up the stairs of 246 Clyde Street to home.

PART THREE

AFTERWARD

FRANCIS, TOP; EDDIE, FRONT AND CENTER.

DURING THE TWO days preceding Francis's victory, and in the days immediately afterward, the name Ouimet was used more than any other word on the nation's telegraph and cable wires. It crossed their desks so often that telegraph operators on either side of the Atlantic had only to tap out the three long Morse code dashes for O and the rest was understood. Bernard Darwin had been the first to cable Francis's name beneath the sea to England three weeks before at Garden City. His predictions for the young American's eventual success now seemed more like prophecy.

In its Sunday September 21 edition, *The New York Times* featured a story about the sport of golf, and its conquering young hero, on the front page for the first time in its history. Nearly every other major newspaper in America, Great Britain, and Western Europe followed suit. Borrowing a phrase from the American Revolution, the fateful strokes on which their play-off battle turned quickly became known as "the shots heard around the world." In one day, with no intention of doing anything other than playing the shot in front of him, Francis had elevated his sport to a national prominence it had never experienced before and from which it has never retreated.

Francis did go into Boston for dinner with his friends on that Saturday night, if for no other reason than to escape the constant stream of well-wishers who swarmed the Ouimets' front door. After dining at a Boylston Street café, the young men attended a performance of a touring Broadway comedy called "The Merry Martyr" at the downtown Colonial Theater. When Francis was recognized during the intermission by a number of people in the audience, it led to his presence being announced by an actor from the stage before the second act. The audience gave him a standing ovation; Francis sheepishly stood up and acknowledged their acclaim. As it would always throughout the rest of his life, public recognition made him profoundly uncomfortable.

The weather in Boston improved dramatically the next day, the start of an Indian summer, and The Country Club's members threw a day-long celebration in honor of Francis's victory that Sunday. Francis, who had risen at his usual early hour and eaten a huge breakfast cooked up by his mother and sister, walked over from home to hit a few practice shots and joined the party around 11:00; the festive gathering lasted most of the rest of the day. Bernard Darwin got his chance to sit down privately in the clubhouse with the new champion and found him remarkably unchanged from the modest young man he'd met only three weeks before at Coney Island. On that gilded Sunday afternoon Francis appeared as lighthearted and carefree as he had been grave and purposeful yesterday. He reiterated his intention to Darwin to always remain an amateur. The life of a professional golfer was not for him; he not only had his sights set on making a go of it in the business world, winning the National Amateur Championship still remained his greatest ambition in golf. Although many of the adults on the grounds that day appeared to be enjoying stronger beverages, Francis, who was still eight months under the legal drinking age, downed one "Horse's Neck" after another, a refreshing blend of ginger ale and lemonade.

As Ted Ray had predicted, Francis's entire way of life would undergo a complete transformation, and the first indications came his way quickly on that same Sunday. Officers of The Country Club announced to the crowd that they had decided to accord Francis playing privileges on their course for the coming year. Within minutes representatives of six other private clubs around the Boston area, not to be outdone, presented him with identical honorary memberships. Before the day was through, Francis took a trip out to attend a brief reception at his home course, Woodland, where banners had been put up throughout the clubhouse in his honor ("Ouimet the enemy and he is ours!"). His old friends there showered him with gifts and extended him a hero's welcome.

When he returned home on Sunday evening, Francis discovered that reporters from all over the northeast had descended on the Ouimet home. In their Monday edition the *Boston Globe* ran a huge special front-page feature on the champion and his family's home life, featuring photographs of the Clyde Street house and his mother, brother, and sister. Their excitement and pride in Francis is palpable; his father Arthur is conspicuous by his absence. His sister, Louise, exercising the skills she was learning in stenographic school, stationed herself at the family telephone, efficiently writing down the dozens of messages and requests that poured in. Throughout the day a parade of telegraph delivery boys beat a steady path to their front door, delivering congratulatory greetings from distinguished players and dignitaries around the country. Francis politely responded to every one of them with a personal letter. Among the two he most prized: one from Boston's Mayor John F. Fitzgerald, the maternal grandfather of John F. Kennedy, another from the man whose keen eye for talent had picked him out of the crowd during Tuesday's qualifying round, former U.S. President William Howard Taft.

More perks came his way: George Wright called the house to tell Francis not to come to work on Monday; George had decided to give him another paid week of vacation, starting immediately. Later that day Francis learned he had been named as a last-minute addition to Massachusetts's five-man team for The Lesley Cup, an annual competition for top amateur players from Massachusetts, New York, and Pennsylvania, scheduled to take place at The Country Club the following weekend. Tremendous excitement surrounded the announcement because it meant that at some point during the tournament Francis would meet the New York team's captain, Jerry Travers; that would be the first amateur match ever played in the United States between the country's standing National Amateur and National Open champions.

The *Globe's* reporter also visited the home of Eddie Lowery earlier that Sunday, calling him "the most envied and happiest boy in Newton." Eddie, his brother Jack, and their mother invited the reporter in and gave him a delightful exclusive about life in the rowdy Lowery household, but only after Eddie made certain he wasn't a truant officer; according to a front-page feature in the Sunday *Boston Globe* that same relentless Inspector Javert was still hot on Eddie's trail. (When the man did finally put the hook on Eddie the following day, the boy's new popularity made it impossible to punish him.) Sounding now like a sage and savvy veteran of his sport, Eddie was quoted by the reporter as saying: "I knew Francis would win the title, because I've followed his game pretty well the last three years. And another thing, he's going to win that Lesley Cup next week because there is not anybody who can beat him."

Among the many millions across the country who were thrilled to read accounts of Francis's victory that Sunday morning was an eleven-year-old caddie at Apawamis Country Club in Rye, New York. Small for his age, the son of Sicilian immigrants, Eugenio Saraceni became so excited at the idea of a fellow caddie beating the English champions that he made up his mind right then and there that come what may, he was going to become a professional golfer. He immediately adopted Francis's interlocking grip from a photo in the newspaper and tried to mimic his graceful swing, bragging to the other caddies that "This is the way Ouimet does it." His best friend and fellow caddie, an Irish kid named Ed Sullivan—who later in life wouldn't do too badly himself, working the entertainment side of show business—believed even then that little Eugenio had the potential to go far in the sport. At the age of eighteen, Saraceni saw his name in the papers for the first time after scoring a hole in one and decided it sounded more like a violinist than a golfer. Two years later the up-and-coming pro "Gene Sarazen" had the honor of playing a pro-am event in Houston with Francis, which Francis won. Afterward the older man took young Sarazen aside to tell him: "Son, I think that with your swing, you should go a long way." Francis took Sarazen under his wing—among their many common interests, they shared an enthusiasm for fast greens—and not long afterward predicted to the great sportswriter Grantland Rice that his young friend would someday win the Open, and soon. Gene Sarazen won his first U.S. Open Championship at Skokie, Illinois, in 1922, the very next year. One of the most dominant and popular players of all time, Sarazen would go on to win six more majors, and when the Masters was added to the rotation in 1934, two years later he became the first player to complete the modern Grand Slam. He and Francis remained close friends for the rest of their lives.

News of Francis's victory did not go down quite so smoothly in England. Although the only British eyewitnesses to the event gave Ouimet all the credit in the world, and Bernard Darwin continued to lead the choir singing his praises in print, the pros and press back in Britain who'd not been there to see it happen found it harder to accept that such a stripling had beaten their two champions at their own game and struck such a punishing blow to their national pride. J. H. Taylor labeled the loss "humiliating." One after another English veteran player chimed in, damning Francis's achievement with faint praise or rationalizing it away by saying Ouimet was too young to even know what he'd been up against, and played so well only because he'd started with nothing to lose. Just wait until the boy got older, they said, and years of tournament pressure began to exact a toll on his nerves. You could practically picture the teacups rattling in their hands, like some hospitalized platoon of shell-shocked infantry. The game's Scottish professionals, on the other hand, evinced a much more generous public reaction to Francis's win; in their responses you can glean a hint of secret delight that the English, who not so long ago had wrested dominance from Scotland of her beloved ancient and national sport, already faced a similar displacing at the hands of the upstart Americans.

In all their published and private statements for years to come Harry and Ted continued to offer nothing but the deepest regard for what Francis had accomplished at The Country Club. Only they knew just how hard each had tried to beat him and what the stakes had been both physically and emotionally, although the evidence was there for all to see when they experienced an immediate and public post-tournament letdown of their own. After catching the late train out of Boston to New York that Saturday night, at 9:00 Sunday morning Harry and Ted began play in a thirty-six-hole best-ball challenge match against brothers Alex and Macdonald Smith at Mac's home club, Wykagyl Country Club in Westchester. The Smith brothers had not remained in Boston to watch the play-off, traveling south a day early to get in a practice round. Worn out by his battle with Francis, Harry didn't record a par in the match until the eleventh hole.

With Mac leading the way, the Smith brothers handed Harry and Ted the first and only team defeat of their entire American tour, 3 and 2.

After a welcome day off in New York City, Harry and Ted's tour headed south again, with stops in Philadelphia, Delaware, Virginia, and North Carolina. One of the last exhibitions they played took place in early October in Georgia at Atlanta's East Lake Country Club. In the gallery watching them that day was a local eleven-year-old phenom, son of a prominent Atlanta lawyer, who had been playing the game since he was five on a two-hole course he and a friend had built in the family's backyard. Daily accounts of Francis Ouimet's tremendous victory in the papers had excited the young boy no end, but the sight of the two great champions he'd defeated—Vardon's easy grace, Ted's awesome power—inspired him to work harder at his game than anything he'd ever seen before on a golf course. Three years later he qualified in his first entry into the National Amateur Championship and went on to reach the quarterfinals, at the ripe old age of fourteen. The game's next immortal had announced his arrival. His name was Robert Tyre Jones Junior. Family and friends called him Bobby.

At the end of his paid week's vacation, Francis concluded the greatest seven days of his early life by fulfilling another of Eddie Lowery's predictions: He defeated Jerry Travers in the match play Lesley Cup finals at Brookline. Although it took him twenty holes to finish Travers off—creating a national sportsmanship controversy when the partisan Boston crowd cheered the wayward shot that precipitated Jerry's defeat—Francis led his Massachusetts team to victory in the process. The excitement Ted Ray had foreseen for the young champion did not stop there. His local supporters honored Francis with a grand ceremonial dinner for 200 people at the Exchange Club in downtown Boston before the month was out. Francis's once prescribed world and future expanded out in every direction on the compass. He soon received a raise from Wright & Ditson and with it came increased responsibilities as a representative of the company. Over the course of that winter a number of prominent wealthy patrons offered to organize a collection so that Francis could voyage to England and the Continent the following summer to compete in their amateur and professional championships. Francis readily agreed.

When Francis boarded the ship along with friends Jerry Travers and

Chick Evans in May of 1914 to make his first-class passage to England, over a dozen reporters and a horde of photographers awaited him at the Boston docks. His departure made headlines on every sports page in the country. From out of nowhere Francis had become an overnight national folk hero. Since his win at last September's championship, golf had become America's new sensation, hundreds of thousands were now taking up the game. Francis inspired an entire generation of young players like Gene Sarazen who would not so long from now make America's dominance of the game absolute. If he had been older or richer, or even a professional, his victory might have provided no impact on the game at all. He was none of those things; he was a boy-next-door amateur, young and modest and free from affectation. From his exemplary behavior during the intervening months, it was already abundantly clear he would never allow the many consequences of worldly achievements to go to his head. However reluctant he might have been to live the life of a public figure, which truly ran counter to his self-effacing temperament, Francis understood that with great success came great responsibilities. He took what was asked of him seriously, and because of his abiding respect for the game he loved, he never hesitated to fulfill a champion's obligations. Those fortunate enough to ever cross his path came away with the rare and delightful realization that the hero they'd admired from afar was up close an even better human being, warm, generous and full of kindness, invariably more interested in learning about the many people he met than in talking about himself. In the decades ahead of him his early success would continue to shape Francis as a man in a profoundly affirmative way because, as it turned out, he had been a great man to begin with.

Francis stood on the bridge, the captain's guest of honor, as the ocean liner pushed away from port. A few minutes later he excused himself from his friends and walked around to the stern to watch the city of Boston recede as the ship moved out to sea. He'd never seen his hometown from this angle before. A thought came to him as he stood at the rail, made him smile, and then almost laugh at its absurdity. When it occurred to him again, for the first time he felt it find a home inside him and it filled him with a deep and quiet satisfaction.

America's national champion, setting sail to the land of the game's birth.

EDDIE AND FRANCIS AT THE U.S. OPEN,
THE COUNTRY CLUB, 1963.
(COURTESY OF THE OUIMET FOUNDATION)

AFTERMATHS

THE IMMIGRANT SMITH brothers from Carnoustie, Scotland, Alex and Macdonald, continued their high level of professional play for many years. As late as 1922, at the age of forty-nine, Alex finished fifth in the Open at Skokie, tied with a young Bobby Jones, as Gene Sarazen won his first championship. Having tutored Jerry Travers early in his career, Alex developed a reputation as one of the first great teachers in American golf. He died in 1930, living just long enough to see his friend Bobby Jones win his unprecedented Grand Slam.

Despite nearly forty career PGA victories and a string of heartbreaking second-place finishes in important tournaments, Macdonald Smith would never win a U.S. or British Open, or any other major title, in over thirty years of trying. Twelve times he finished within three strokes of the lead. In 1925 he took a five-stroke lead into the final round of the British Open at Prestwick, only to shoot an 82 and lose by six. In 1930 he finished second to Bobby Jones when he won the first leg of his legendary Grand Slam in the British Open at Hoylake. "The best player ever to have never won a Major," that dubious title now passed down from one generation's greatest hard luck player to the next, was originally coined for Macdonald Smith. Five years after his death in 1949, he was voted into the Professional Golfers Association's Hall of Fame.

Their middle brother, Willie, won 1899's U.S. Open by eleven strokes, a record margin that stood for 100 years until Tiger Woods broke it recently at Pebble Beach. Willie and Alex are still the only brothers to have both won the national championship. All three Smith brothers also won the important Western Open—Willie won the first in 1899—the tournament considered America's second major until the PGA and Masters came along. After failing to make the cut in the 1913 Open at The Country Club, Willie returned to his new job as professional at the first private country club ever built in Mexico City. Eighteen months later, when the Mexican Revolution that had begun in the country's northern and southern border states finally reached the nation's capital in its center, Willie got caught in the crossfire. His country club was attacked and shelled by Zapata's rebel forces as a symbol of the corrupt ruling class establishment. Refusing to abandon his post, although he'd been given adequate warning to flee well ahead of the attack, Willie took shelter in the building's cellar. When the rebels moved on after leveling the building, Willie was found crushed under a fallen beam, severely wounded by shrapnel. In poor condition, he died shortly thereafter. When the tragic news reached them weeks later in the States, at his brothers' request Willie's body was sent all the way home to Scotland for burial in their family plot.

TRANSPLANTED ENGLISHMAN LONG Jim Barnes, all six four of him, went on to a long and successful professional career on both sides of the Atlantic. Like so many other early professionals, he began his career in England as a caddie and club-maker before immigrating to the west of the United States not long after the turn of the century. He remained such a quiet, modest man, not much is known about him as a player until he turned up and placed second at the Canadian Open in 1912. After his fourth-place finish in the Open in 1913, he duplicated the feat two years later and improved to third the following year. He won America's inaugural match play PGA Championship in 1916. After a three-year lapse due to World War I, Long Jim won the second PGA Championship as well in 1919. Barnes lost to Walter Hagen in the finals of the PGA in both 1921 and 1924. After a sixth-place finish in the 1920 U.S. Open at Inverness, he finally broke through to win his first Open in 1921 held at Columbia Country Club in Maryland. President Warren G. Harding, an avid golfer, was on hand to present Barnes with the U.S. Open trophy. After a number of high finishes in the sport's oldest championship, including second in 1922, he bested Macdonald Smith in the final round at Prestwick in 1925 to win the British Open. In the years before the Masters joined the list of majors in 1934, Jim Barnes is one of only eight men to ever win the other three major championships. Add to his five major titles seventeen additional tournament wins in the United States before the regular PGA tour invented itself and you're looking at one of the great neglected careers in the history of the sport. A dedicated student of the game, Barnes published two instruction guides to golf in his lifetime, including the first to use a series of still photographs on flip pages, creating the illusion of motion to illustrate the full swing. Jim Barnes died in 1966 at the age of seventy-nine and was inducted to the PGA's Hall of Fame in 1989.

NEITHER OF THE first two great Massachusetts golf professionals, Tom McNamara and Mike Brady, ever realized their dream of winning a U.S. Open, although near misses continued to distinguish and define both their playing careers; they were the perennial bridesmaids of American golf. Tom finished second in the championship for a third time in 1915, this time by only a single stroke, and took third in the 1919 Open at Brae Burn, at which point his star began to dim. Although he'd been the first homebred to ever get close to the national title, in 1909, the trophy remained forever just out of his reach. Mike Brady had four close calls at the Open, losing in play-offs twice, the last time in 1919 to Walter Hagen after entering the final round with a five-stroke lead. Prior to Hagen's ascendance, who during those years had become one of his closest friends, Brady was recognized as America's best-known touring professional golfer, holding course records all over the country. Although he never won the Open, a dozen victories in lesser but still significant tournaments later earned the sport's first "King" a place in the PGA Hall of Fame. He died in 1972 at the age of eighty-five.

FRENCHMAN LOUIS TELLIER emigrated to the United States with his wife, Wilfred Reid's sister, before the outbreak of World War I. He accepted his first job as a professional in America at Canoe Brook Country Club in New Jersey in 1914, and while there set the course record of 63. Two years later, trading on experiences and social connections he made during the 1913 Open, Louis accepted an invitation to become resident professional at The Country Club in Brookline. Louis remained at the post for the next three years, when he moved on to nearby Brae Burn. He was succeeded at The Country Club by former caddie master and Francis's old friend and supporter Dan McNamara. Content to live his life as an itinerant American club pro, Louis Tellier played less and less competitive golf and was never again a factor in another major championship.

WILFRED REID AND his wife followed through with their plans to avoid the English Inland Revenue and joined his sister and Louis Tellier in the United States in 1914 shortly after the outbreak of the war. His friendship with members of the DuPont family led to Wilfred's first job stateside as an American golf professional at the Summit Country Club in Wilmington, Delaware. Although he joined the American PGA in 1917 and remained a competitive golfer for another ten years, Reid had already left his best years as a player behind. Always a deadly iron player, he scored a phenomenal twenty-six holes in one during his playing career. Wilfred's second career as a resident professional eventually took him to some of the finest country clubs in America; Detroit C.C., the Broadmoor in Colorado, and Seminole Golf Club in Florida, where he eventually settled. After obtaining United States citizenship in 1921, Reid entered into a distinguished third career as a golf course architect and designer; fifty-eight courses and forty-three remodels around America, England, and France to his credit before he retired in the early 1950s. Wilfred and Ted Ray patched up their differences a few months after their altercation at the Copley Square Hotel; Reid even contributed a chapter about the short game to Ted Ray's entertaining first book, *Inland Golf*, published in 1915. Eventually becoming an established member of West Palm Beach society, Wilfred Reid died there in 1973 at the age of eighty-nine.

ALTHOUGH BUSINESS OBLIGATIONS had prevented him from being at Brookline to see his win in person, Old Man Walter Travis wrote glowingly about Francis's victory for months in *The American Golfer*. He continued to publish and edit his magazine for another decade, riding the boom years inspired by Ouimet, forever a tireless supporter of the game and its players in the United States. At the age of forty-eight, after over 200 tournament victories in an almost-twenty-year career, Travis finally retired from competitive amateur golf in 1915. He went out in style. After the National Amateur, the Metropolitan Championship of New York was considered the second most important American amateur tournament. The match play quarterfinals of the Metropolitan found Travis pitted one last time against his perennial archrival Jerry Travers, who was now almost exactly half his age. Travis had lost his last five matches to Jerry; each had cost him a fifth National Amateur Championship. On this day Travis turned back the clock and played what he considered to be the one perfect round of his life. Jerry matched him shot for shot in the greatest duel of their magnificent rivalry, until the Old Man sank a twenty-footer on the thirty-sixth and final green to win the match. Travis went on to defeat John Anderson in the finals to win the 1915 Metropolitan and immediately thereafter announced his retirement. Fittingly, the last stroke Walter Travis ever played in competition was a forty-five-foot putt that dove straight into the hole. Travis now turned his attentions to *The American Golfer* and his burgeoning golf course design business. In addition to being the first great American golf writer and philosopher, he is also considered to be one of the most original and influential architects the game has ever known. The Grand Old Man of American Amateur golf died in 1927, from emphysema brought on by his ever-present cigars, at the age of sixty-five.

. . .

JERRY TRAVERS, THE rich man's kid from Oyster Bay, won his fourth and last National Amateur title in 1913, a record only equaled since by Bobby Jones. Jerry would reach the finals of the event one more time, the following year in 1914. In 1915 the match play genius surprised himself and the rest of the world by becoming only the second amateur, after Francis, to win the U.S. Open, at Baltusrol, edging out Tom McNamara. Two weeks later, wearying of the competitive grind, Jerry lost that epic match in the finals of the Metropolitan Open to Walter Travis. Not long afterward, when the Old Man hung up his clubs, the much younger Travers announced his own surprise retirement as well and did not even return to defend his Open title the following year at Minikahda, when Chick Evans became the third American amateur to win the national championship in four years. The first great player to really focus and rely on the importance of the short game, Jerry never did establish reliable command of his driver. He played a number of wartime charity exhibitions but never returned to the highest levels of competitive golf. When the Great Depression hit, Jerry lost the family fortune that had sustained him throughout his carefree life. Unable to support himself in any other way, the forty-three-year-old Travers turned professional and attempted a comeback, but by then the game had passed him by. Barely eking out a living as a humble club pro and driving range instructor, Jerry abandoned golf altogether with the outbreak of World War II. He spent the last ten years of his life working as an aircraft engine inspector for Pratt and Whitney. He died in 1951, at the age of sixty-four.

AFTER THE 1913 Open, Alfred Harmsworth, Lord Northcliffe, accompanied Bernard Darwin to Chicago on newspaper business before returning to England. Although he remained a fanatical supporter of British golf, events in the world were about to shut down all of life's pleasantries and wrench Great Britain and the rest of Europe into hellish, self-destructive world war. Wielding enormous social and political influence from his editorial pulpit in *The Times* and the *Daily Mail*, Northcliffe's hawkish, predatory personality helped stir up anti-German sentiments and push England into the conflagration. Some of his contemporaries later claimed that his irresponsible warmongering had done more than any other single living man to bring about World War I. The aggressive grammar of battle suited Northcliffe all too well; his penchant for crushing his enemies, at home and abroad, found endless new sources of justification. Soon he was meddling in affairs of state, attacking national hero and Secretary of State for War Lord Kitchener and eventually demanding and bringing about the resignation of Prime Minister Herbert Asquith, whom he accused of "appeasing the Hun." His replacement, new Prime Minister David Lloyd George, privately considered Northcliffe to be "the most unscrupulous man in the country" and a menace to public life. George was also smart enough to realize that the one way to muzzle Northcliffe was to bring him into government and ship him out of the country; in 1917, Northcliffe accepted an appointment from Lloyd George to head the British War Mission in the United States.

Northcliffe's personal life was equally tumultuous; flagrantly promiscuous, with his wife of many years unable to conceive, he fathered three illegitimate children by one of his many mistresses, a widowed woman named Mrs. Wrohan. Although she and her children were frequent guests at the Northcliffe country estate, often for weeks at a time, Lady Northcliffe later claimed never to have known their true identities, demonstrating a gift for self-deception that rivaled her husband's for deceit. When Northcliffe returned from Washington and accepted a post as Lloyd George's Director of Propaganda in Enemy Countries, his behavior grew increasingly erratic. He was chronically hypochondriacal, sustained himself with a pharmacopoeia of illegal substances, and flew into frequent uncontrollable rages. On one occasion he ordered workers at one of his newspapers to line up according to height, then appointed the tallest man in charge of the department. He often demanded that employees bow down before him; others he just as arbitrarily showered with wildly capricious rewards. When the war finally ended, Lloyd George dismissed Northcliffe immediately and soon afterward retaliated in a rival's newspaper for all the years of abuse he'd suffered at Alfred Harmsworth's hand, accusing him of "black crimes against humanity" prompted by his "diseased vanity."

Lloyd George wasn't far from the mark; whatever internal spiritual darkness had driven Northcliffe throughout his chaotic, careening life, it at last took root in his physical body. A series of progressively more serious illnesses deprived him of his demonic energy. His personal appearance deteriorated drastically. His behavior grew increasingly irrational and paranoid, imagining dire plots against him everywhere he looked. On a trip to Germany after the armistice, he accused the German chancellor of trying to serve him poisoned ice cream. During a visit to the Fontainebleu in France, he was seen trying on Napoleon's tricornered hat—a sure sign of incipient madness if ever there was one—and claimed that it fit him perfectly. He increasingly relied on morphine to calm his nerves and insisted that all his secretaries carry concealed firearms to guard against the threat of unknown assassins. Although a precise diagnosis was never officially made public for fear of scandal, by the early 1920s Northcliffe was exhibiting all the classic symptoms of late stage neurosyphillis. His descent into full-scale dementia proceeded rapidly; his family finally fulfilled Northcliffe's deepest fears of conspiratorial action by taking custody and confining him behind closed doors at his palatial family estate. Using a soft pencil, he wrote a will in July of 1922 that began: "I, Alfred Charles William Harmsworth, Viscount Northcliffe, being in good mental state, though suffering from one dangerous disease, Indian Jungle Fever, and another unknown to any doctors in Great Britain, poisoning by ice cream supplied on the Belgian frontier, where I was unfortunately recognized by my enemies." He died one month later on August 14, 1922, at the age of sixty-one.

JOHN MCDERMOTT RETURNED to his home in Atlantic City, New Jersey, after the 1913 Open. His disappointment at Brookline weighed on him heavily for months; without the title of national champion propping Johnny up, he had little else to sustain his precarious emotional balance. In a desperate attempt to recoup the fortune he'd recently lost in the stock market, he ventured into a series of increasingly risky investments, all of which failed. Feeling that playing and winning at golf offered the only way out of his dilemma, he spent most of the winter in Florida and recovered enough confidence in himself to sail over and attempt to qualify for the 1914 British Open. The morning of his first scheduled round, he missed by minutes the ferry he needed to take in order to get to Prestwick in time for his tee off. By the time he finally reached the course, the qualifying round had already begun. Compassionate British officials offered to let him begin play out of turn but the sportsman in McDermott wouldn't take them up on it; not fair to the other players, he said. Returning immediately to London, depressed, alone, and unrecognized, he bought a ticket back to New York on the *Kaiser Wilhelm II*, the fastest luxury liner in the Atlantic fleet. As the ship left Southampton and crept out into a heavy fog blanketing the English Channel, a commercial cargo carrier appeared out of the mist without warning. Despite both captains' desperate attempts to avoid a collision, the carrier's bow sliced into the *Kaiser Wilhelm*'s hull amidships and opened a gaping hole. Sitting in the *Wilhelm*'s barbershop getting his morning shave when the two vessels collided, McDermott nearly had his neck slashed open by the barber's razor. Johnny and the rest of the passengers were quickly loaded into the lifeboats; the *Kaiser Wilhelm* went down within an hour. After helping the survivors on deck and spending six hours huddled in the small boat, McDermott and the other passengers were safely plucked from the frigid mist. Although he was physically unharmed, this near brush with death further undermined John's fragile state of mind.

After returning home, he entered the 1914 Open at Midlothian Country Club near Chicago and made the cut but was never close to being a factor in the tournament. Many who watched him play there felt the competitive fires that had always driven America's first native-born champion had gone cold. Later that summer, heading to work one day at his country club in Atlantic City, he experienced a blinding panic attack as he entered his pro shop; Johnny blacked out and had to be hospitalized. When after a week his condition didn't improve, the twenty-three-year-old McDermott was taken back to his parents' house in Philadelphia. Shortly thereafter doctors made a chilling diagnosis; Johnny had suffered a shattering nervous breakdown. He vanished from public life. Most of his old friends in the game never saw him again and he never played another competitive round of golf in his life. His mind and spirit broken, Johnny spent the rest of his days living with his parents, and in and out of a succession of rest homes. Within a few years, as the American players he'd once led to victory made great leaps and bounds in the game throughout the world, John McDermott had become a completely forgotten man.

When the 1971 U.S. Open was played at Merion Golf Club, near John's old home outside Philadelphia, a local reporter wrote a story commemorating the sixtieth anniversary of John's first U.S. Open victory. After a little sleuthing by the same reporter, it was discovered, to everyone's amazement, that America's lost champion was not only still alive, he practically lived within walking distance of Merion in nearby Yeadon, Pennsylvania. After their gentle inquiries were met with expressions of guarded interest, with admirable care and concern for his well-being, the USGA quietly arranged for John McDermott to make his first public appearance in fifty-six years. As Johnny watched the first and last days of the 1971 Open as a special guest of honor in the Merion clubhouse, an entire new generation of players passed through to pay homage to the man who'd started it all. Although he granted no interviews, by all accounts Johnny enjoyed the experience enormously. He died peacefully in his sleep not long afterward, only one month shy of his eightieth birthday.

JOHN G. ANDERSON'S vivid reporting of Francis's victory at The Country Club in *The Boston Transcript* was immediately picked up by wire services and published around the country; for millions of readers in America, John's faithful, stirring account of the play-off at Brookline served as their first introduction to the game's new hero. The newspaper world took note and before long John accepted a job with the *New York Sun* as their principal golf correspondent and his column was soon being syndicated from coast to coast. Soon afterward Wanamaker's department store in New York offered him a job to represent its new line of golf equipment. John's new position took him all over the country and he made the crossing to Europe no less than twenty-two times. A dedicated track man in college, after moving to New York he also became involved with America's premier track and field event, the annual Milrose Games at Madison Square Garden. He served as chairman for the Milrose Association for thirteen years; the 1,600-meter John G. Anderson Relay is still run in his honor.

John Anderson remained active as a top-rank amateur golfer throughout his professional career, finishing as runner-up in the National Amateur for the second time in 1915, and he played a significant role in the formation of the American Professional Golfer's Association. Although he never turned pro, the PGA named him an honorary member in 1920. The crowning achievements of Anderson's playing career came when he twice won the French Amateur, in 1924 and 1926. He won at least one tournament every year he played between the ages of eleven and forty-three. John and Francis remained close friends throughout their lifetimes; they traveled and played together frequently all over the world. One of the most admired human beings ever involved with the sport of golf, John died tragically in 1933 after a brief undiagnosed illness at the age of forty-nine. His obituary in the *New York Post* summed up his career this way: "Johnny Anderson was the friend of all golfing souls. He breathed the spirit of the game, and year after year added to its glory with his mere presence. Golf has lost a friend it could ill spare. We shall not see your like again." Two months later John's home club of Winged Foot Country Club conducted the first Anderson Memorial. Nearly seventy years later, the Anderson is considered the amateur game's most coveted four-ball competition.

BERNARD DARWIN RETURNED to London and resumed a similar dual career to John Anderson's as his country's preeminent golf journalist and one of its finest amateur players. He reached the semifinals of the British Amateur for the second time in 1921, and frequently represented England in the prestigious Home International matches with Scotland, Ireland, and Wales. In 1922 the reluctant traveler returned to America for his second and last visit to cover for *The Times* the inaugural Walker Cup competition, named in honor of its founder, George Herbert Walker, former president of the USGA and President George W. Bush's paternal great-grandfather. When British team captain Robert Harris became too ill to play, at the age of forty-six Darwin ably stepped in as his substitute and defeated U.S. captain Bill Fownes in their singles match.

In shocking contrast to his mild, retiring personality as a writer,

Bernard's success as a player appears to have been limited by his perfectionist's explosive temper, frequently throwing clubs and cursing wildly at his own mistakes, which took him out of many matches. After Lord Northcliffe, the man who'd hired him in 1907 as the world's first full-time golf correspondent and whom Bernard found consistently terrifying, went mad and died in 1922, Darwin remained at *The Times* for another thirty years. During that time he published over thirty books on golf and a wide variety of other subjects. He also became known as one of his country's leading scholars on Charles Dickens, who had been a close friend of Darwin's father.

Beloved by his readers and subjects alike, Bernard Darwin went out of his way to befriend three generations of American golfers who traveled overseas to play in Great Britain's championships. Instead of bemoaning the inevitable loss of his country's supremacy in golf, he championed Ouimet, Hagen, Jones, Sarazen, and Hogan, each in his turn, always taking the larger view that the game transcended national borders. In 1932 Darwin wrote the introduction to his good friend Francis Ouimet's autobiography, in which he said: "My only misgiving about his book is that he may be too modest." Three years later Bernard was chosen to serve in their game's ultimate position of honor, as captain of the Royal & Ancient Golfing Society of St. Andrews.

A series of illnesses, including degenerative arthritis and Dickensian gout, forced his retirement from the game as a player in 1940 and his lyric, bittersweet tribute to the sport that had been the cornerstone of his life is heartbreaking reading. ("To have done the only kind of work that one could have liked, in green and pleasant places and amid pleasant, friendly people—that is something to be grateful for, and the wind is still blowing on the heath.") Bernard Darwin is one of the most important figures in the history of golf; his still vibrant eyewitness histories and profiles span the ages from Old Tom Morris to Ben Hogan. Shortly after his professional retirement from *The Times* in 1953 Darwin became the first member of golf's Hall of Fame to be admitted as a writer. He died in 1961 at the age of eighty-five.

WALTER HAGEN RETURNED to Rochester after the 1913 Open at The Country Club profoundly discouraged by his fourth-place finish. To his mind he should have won the damn thing and the way he saw it, he had no one to blame but himself. He promised a local writer that "There is plenty of time ahead, and with another year's experience I'll show 'em all how to play this game." When the Rochester Country Club and every other course in upstate New York shut down that winter, Walter took his clubs south to Florida for the first time and while there flirted with his other passion, baseball. Hagen later claimed he had an invitation to join the Philadelphia Nationals training camp as a pitcher that spring; impossible to verify now but practically a one-way ticket to Cooperstown to hear Walter's version of it. When he returned to Rochester and announced he would be throwing his energies toward baseball from that day forward, a friend convinced him not to abandon golf until he played in one more U.S. Open. Remembering that he'd also promised the press, the USGA, and Francis he would return, Hagen decided to give golf one last try and spent the next three weeks sharpening up his game. He had his fancy tournament outfit dry-cleaned but made one significant substitution, exchanging his infamous rubber-soled shoes for a pair of hobnail boots that gripped the ground.

In June of 1914 Hagen traveled west for the first time in his life to the Midlothian Country Club outside Chicago. Feeling flush and eager to live the high life, the night before the tournament began Walter treated himself to a huge lobster dinner with oysters on the half shell for a starter. Deathly ill all night with food poisoning, he staggered through his first round the next day and somehow, in classic Hagen fashion, set a new course and U.S. Open scoring record of 68. Although Francis remained right on his tail with an opening 69, Hagen stayed hot all week and led the tournament wire to wire, defeating Chick Evans by a stroke and tying George Sargent's record low score in an Open of 290. Walter Hagen never had to worry about a newspaper misspelling his name again, although his victory didn't get as much ink as he would have liked; war had erupted in Europe. He took the train back to Rochester clutching the Open trophy, his name already engraved on the base right after Francis Ouimet. Golf's gain was baseball's loss; Hagen's future in the sport was secure. Now he took to playing and studying the game in earnest, and the Hagen of legend began to emerge. World War I suspended championship golf for a few years, but that didn't prevent Walter from earning a respectable upper-middle-class wage in challenge and exhibition matches. He was on his way to making his first million, although for the rest of his life Walter's income was chronically and perpetually exceeded by his outgo. He soon bought the first of dozens of flashy sports cars and affected the flamboyant wardrobe of a silent movie lothario both on and off the course. A brief marriage predictably failed but a son he adored, Walter Jr., resulted; poor Mrs. Hagen never stood a chance with Walter's roving eye spending so much time on the road.

When the war ended and the U.S. Open resumed play in 1919 at Brae Burn Country Club not far from Brookline, Walter quickly jumped into the thick of the race for his second national championship. Spending more time chasing showgirls with his headliner friend Al Jolson instead of playing practice rounds didn't seem to hurt him; tied after the end of regulation play, Hagen spent the entire night out partying with Jolson, then won his play-off with Mike Brady the next day by a single stroke. Hagen dominated American golf throughout that year, also winning the Metropolitan, Western, North, South, and Florida Opens; by the end of 1919 he had become the sport's undisputed heavyweight champion. Sufficiently emboldened by this extraordinary run, Walter took the unprecedented step of severing his relationship with his home club—he saw to it that Mike Brady was hired to replace him—and became the first full-time touring golf professional in the sport's history. Free now to travel where he liked, defying universal predictions that this risky move would land him flat on his empty wallet, Walter Hagen went on to blaze more trails than Daniel Boone.

The Haig made his first voyage to England in 1920, and although he played poorly in his first exposure to British links courses, he made an even more important contribution to the pro game, one that would soon help break down the age-old English prohibition against professional golfers setting foot in private clubhouses. Ignorant of these stringent regulations upon his arrival, Walter was asked to leave the clubhouse at Deal when he went in to change his shoes. One look at the shabby shack reserved for visiting pros infuriated him and he refused to use it. When Deal held firm on barring him from the clubhouse, Hagen responded with pure audacity: He arranged for his chauffeur to meet him in a rented Daimler limousine each day after his round less than fifty feet from the eighteenth green, where delighted crowds watched Hagen climb in and ostentatiously change his shoes. When he was also denied the use of the clubhouse grill room for lunch between rounds, Walter had his chauffeur drive out a catered meal and he shared an elaborate picnic on the front lawn with some of the other players, right outside the restaurant's window. On another occasion he hired a private plane and between rounds had the pilot fly Walter and a couple of other pros to a nearby four-star restaurant. His outrageous behavior raised a considerable furor in print and old establishment circles, but fellow pros and his public loved him for it. Despite finishing fifty-third in a field of fifty-four at Deal and earning the scorn of the British sporting press, Walter left with a smile and an enigmatic warning that Arnold Schwarzenegger later co-opted without attribution: "I'll be back." No less an august presence than his old acquaintance from Brookline Harry Vardon stood up for Walter in the London *Times* by predicting that "Hagen will win our Open Championship not once, but several times." Harry underestimated slightly; Hagen would win four British Opens during the 1920s, on four different courses, starting in 1922 at Royal St. George's when he became the first American player to ever capture Great Britain's national championship.

As dominant a presence as he'd become in stroke play competition, Walter may have been even more commanding in match play. His bullet-proof confidence laid such an emotional burden on his opponents, he started almost every match with a three-shot advantage. In the process he became one of the great masters of psychological gamesmanship, honing in on a player's weaknesses, subtly pushing his buttons at precisely the right moment. Hagen won his first match play PGA Championship in 1921, beating Jim Barnes 3 and 2. In 1923 he lost in a play-off to one of the few men who ever proved himself immune to his bag of tricks, Gene Sarazen. In 1924 Hagen began one of the most amazing streaks in the history of any sport, running off the first of four straight PGA Championships. When he finally lost the title in 1928 and officials asked him where the PGA's trophy was before the awards presentation, Walter replied, "I don't know. Must have left it in a cab." (It eventually turned up.)

By this time Walter had firmly established himself as the sport's first superstar and household name. He gave exhibition matches with the other greats in the game around the country, charged a dollar a head at the gate, and kept all of it. Befitting his celebrity, he spent a couple of years in Hollywood and cashed in on his fame by appearing in a couple of dreadful movies. If you'd known Walter Hagen during his prime in the roaring twenties, who was on a first-name basis with everyone from kings to chambermaids, you were only one degree of separation from nearly every famous person on the planet.

After his eleventh and final major win, at the British Open in 1929 at the age of thirty-six, Hagen settled into the cosseted life of a celebrity who'd earned a free pass to the world, relying on endorsements and exhibitions to pay the bills. Walter spent the balance of his long, happy existence traveling to every corner of the globe, sampling the banquet that life had to offer, and loving every minute of it. Wherever Hagen went, a floating house party followed him; his appetite for wine, women, and song never faltered. Generous to a fault, a soft touch to fellow pros in need, he became a friend for life to anyone who ever met him. No one ever reported finding a mean bone in his body. Nearer the end, when the money ran low and the spotlight finally passed him by, a touch of sadness tinges Walter's last chapter; fewer friends to hear the old familiar stories, the grand piano around which they used to all carouse sitting silent in the corner, an extra highball or two to assuage an old man's loneliness. But the Haig never asked anyone to feel sorry for him—he certainly never did himself—he just wanted the party to go on forever. But the party ended for good in October 1969; Walter Hagen died of throat and lung cancer at the age of seventy-six. Of all the contemporary greats who owed their success on tour, even the existence of the PGA tour itself, to him, only the Haig's friend Arnold Palmer attended his funeral.

HARRY VARDON AND Ted Ray returned to London together in October of 1913 to find their country anxious and on edge, already hearing the distant drumbeats that within months would lead to war. The following spring Harry's father, Phillip, died at the age of eighty-six; Harry returned to the Isle of Jersey for the first time in many years for the funeral. Harry was amazed to discover that the humble little cottage where he and Tom grew up had become a local landmark. Although much of the British press hung on to their sullen disappointment about Harry and Ted's loss to Francis, Harry won them back over in the summer of 1914.

Harry established a two-stroke lead over J. H. Taylor on the first day of play at the 1914 British Open at Prestwick, where he had won the championship twice before. The random draw paired the old friends and rivals together for the second and final day's play. By the end of the third round on Friday morning, their positions were reversed, with Harry two shots down to Taylor, and Taylor's lead increased to three by the third hole of the final round. Then Harry began the last and perhaps greatest of his backstretch runs after the brittle Taylor lost his temper when a fan snapped his photograph in the middle of his backswing. By the day's end Harry had captured his sixth British Open victory over Taylor by three strokes—the sixteenth and last ever won by one of the Great Triumvirate—climbing one win ahead of both Taylor and Braid for the final time. At the age of forty-four Harry Vardon became the oldest man to ever put his name on the Claret Jug. This was the last championship to be played in England or Europe for the next five years. Two weeks later an Austrian prince was shot and killed in Sarajevo, and darkness descended on the world.

The next British Open (made notorious by Walter Hagen's duel with the Deal clubhouse officials) would not be played until 1920. George Duncan won that tournament, Ted Ray took third, while Harry finished far back and well out of the running. Now fifty years old, deprived of half a decade's income by the war and facing at best an uncertain competitive future in his sport, Harry convinced Ted Ray that the time was right for a return trip to America. They engaged a tour manager to arrange a two-month exhibition schedule, with the climax to come, as it had on their last tour, at the U.S. Open, being held that year at Inverness Country Club in Toledo, Ohio. The two men sailed over in July and again received warm, enthusiastic welcomes wherever they traveled, spending some cherished extra time in Chicago with Tom. The touring Jerseymen discovered that not only had golf courses vastly improved, so had the level of their competition. It soon became apparent that the passage of time and the rapid improvement of American players inspired by Francis's victory had deprived

Harry and Ted of their former invincibility; they still won many more than most, but lost over a dozen matches before even reaching Inverness.

In the qualifying rounds as well as on the first day of play in the 1920 U.S. Open, Harry found himself paired with eighteen-year-old Bobby Jones, making his debut in the national championship. Defending champ and pre-tournament favorite Walter Hagen never became a factor at Inverness, and Jones was just getting his feet wet at the championship level; they finished in eleventh and eighth place, respectively. During the final day of play one after another of the other American contenders fell to the wayside, leaving only Harry Vardon and Ted Ray.

Harry pulled into the lead at the end of the third round, two strokes in front of Ted, and after a brilliant front nine, he stepped to the twelfth hole in his final round having increased that lead to four shots. Then it was as if the gods conspired against him; on what had been a mild Midwestern summer afternoon, a violent gale blew in off Lake Erie out of nowhere, directly into the face of Harry Vardon as he stood on the twelfth tee. The fierce wind knocked down his drive and he needed four shots to reach the green, dropping a stroke. His stamina broken by the appearance of the strange and savage weather, Harry's right hand began jumping and he three-putted the next three holes. Harry ended up playing the final seven holes in seven over par for a final round 78 and as a result he lost the 1920 U.S. Open by one stroke. To Ted Ray. Harry was nearly inconsolable; he said later that to have won another major title at the age of fifty would have been the greatest achievement of his life. Instead, crushing disappointment. The fact that his great friend Ted Ray captured the cup in his place, and became the first Englishman to win the U.S. title since Harry himself had done it twenty years before, went a long way toward mending the wound. It would be nearly fifty years before a third Englishman, Tony Jacklin, added his name to the U.S. Open trophy. One great advance that benefited every person in the sport: For the first time, Inverness made the use of their entire clubhouse facilities available to every player in the field, professional and amateur alike. From that moment forward the pros were no longer considered second-class citizens.

To celebrate his victory, and perhaps in response to Inverness's decision, Ted's home club in Oxhey, Hertfordshire, soon afterward named him as an honorary member, the first time any British club admitted a professional golfer to its ranks. Between Hagen's protest at Deal and Ted's appointment to Oxhey, the walls that had separated the amateur from the professional in Britain at last began to crumble. Within months the home clubs of the Great Triumvirate—J. H. Taylor, James Braid, and Harry Vardon—all followed suit. For the first time in their lives the three men who had single-handedly carried British golf into the twentieth century were allowed to enter the locker rooms, restaurants, and clubhouses of the establishments that had hired them so many years before.

Not only Harry was nearing the end of his years at the top. Ted Ray was forty-three when he won the U.S. Open at Inverness, and he's still the oldest man to ever hold the title. Ted would later finish second to Jim Barnes in the 1925 British Open, and he continued to play in the event until 1932. He also played a major role in initiating the first Ryder Cup competition and played on Great Britain's inaugural team in 1927. Actively competitive until the mid-1930s, Ted remained at his post as resident professional at Oxhey until 1941. He died two years later on August 23, after a heart attack at the age of sixty-five.

WHEN HARRY RETURNED to England after his 1920 tour, he found an unexpected compensation for the loss of his professional success. As detailed recently for the first time in Audrey Howell's loving and intimate biography of him, while playing an exhibition at Hoylake, Harry met a twenty-eight-year-old music hall dancer named Matilda Howell who was staying at the same hotel. Her own career as part of a song and dance act with her sister was coming to an end after her sister's recent decision to retire, and Matilda was still grieving the death of her fiancé in the Great War. An immediate spark flew between the young dancer and the distinguished older man, although it appeared that nothing more would come of it when Harry left to resume his busy touring schedule. But the lithe young beauty lingered in Harry's mind. He made no attempt to contact her, but when they met again at the same hotel a year later, where Matilda was now working, their attraction evolved into a serious romance; in the autumn of his life, for the first time Harry had found a real consuming love. Obstacles to their complete happiness remained; Harry could not bring himself to leave Jesse after so many years, even when Matilda became pregnant in 1925. Unwilling to risk the social destruction of his spotless reputation with public acknowledgment of an affair with a younger woman and an illegitimate child, Harry agreed to financially help her raise the boy she gave birth to, but reluctantly told Matilda he could not in any other way act as his father. Daunted by England's stern, unforgiving cultural bias against unwed mothers, Matilda gave their son, Peter, to her sister and her husband to raise as their own. She remained in London to be closer to Harry, until loneliness for Peter prompted her to move back to Liverpool. Harry became a frequent visitor in their home, always bringing expensive presents for the boy, who never knew Harry was his father. When Peter grew old enough to become curious about exactly who "Uncle Harry" was, Matilda realized the visits would have to stop. Difficult as it was for him to accept, Harry realized it was best for the boy. Soon afterward, perhaps inevitably, Harry and Matilda grew apart. Although his financial support never ceased, Matilda eventually found work as a live-in housekeeper. Harry returned to Liverpool less and less frequently, and then stopped altogether. If Jesse ever knew about the entire affair, she never breathed a word of it to anyone.

Harry now returned to his position at South Herts and for the first time in over thirty years settled into the quiet life of a club professional. He threw himself enthusiastically into teaching, and made occasional forays into golf course architecture; fourteen original designs and eight revisions. One of the courses Harry redesigned was the nine-hole track near Mundesley sanatorium, where as a patient he scored his only hole in one. In the early 1930s Harry wrote his autobiography, *My Golfing Life*, which quickly became a best-seller in Great Britain. By 1935 the earlier ravages of tuberculosis exacerbated by his lifelong smoking began to wear down his once limitless strength; within a year he could no longer even climb a flight of stairs. Just as he had when his disease first laid him low, Harry insisted on fulfilling his obligations at South Herts. In early 1937 a series of tests revealed that Harry was now battling lung cancer. Weeks later he insisted on giving a scheduled lesson in the chill spring wind; the severe cold he caught soon turned into pneumonia. Harry died one week later on

March 20, 1937, at home in his own bed, within sight of his favorite garden, where the spring flowers were in early bloom. He was sixty-six years
old. Both Harry and Ted bequeathed all of their championship medals to
the Jersey Museum in Grouville, the town of their birth.

The club at South Herts closed for the day of Harry's funeral service,
held in his local parish church and filled with admirers from around the
world. J. H. Taylor, James Braid, Sandy Herd, Tom Vardon, and Ted Ray carried him to his rest. In the back of the church, unnoticed and unknown, a
woman in early middle age dressed in black stood alone, quietly weeping:
Matilda Howell. Years later she finally told her son, Peter Howell, the truth
about his real father. Now retired from a life in business, Peter never took
up the game of golf very seriously, although it's clear some part of the Vardon
talent came through him; Peter was at one time England's national croquet
champion. Peter's wife, Audrey, eventually wrote her aforementioned book
about Harry, which first made their family's story public.

Millions of golfers around the world still use the Vardon grip, although
most may not immediately connect the name with the man. "The Harry
Vardon Trophy" is awarded each year by both the American and European
PGA to the players on their tours who post the lowest scoring average, a
fitting tribute to his unsurpassed dedication to excellence; at least the
game's professionals still remember Harry. For many years whenever the
Ryder Cup was played in England, the visiting American team went out of
its way to make a pilgrimage to Harry's grave in Totteridge. In light of the
unfortunate animosity the competition has kicked up over the last decade,
a revival of this custom would be a welcome remembrance. Harry's record
of six British Open victories has never been matched; Peter Thompson and
Tom Watson have come the closest, with five each. That record may still
one day be broken—most are—but if Harry Vardon had not lost his putting
stroke and seven years of his prime to tuberculosis, and five more years to
World War I, it's safe to say that for as long as the game is played, no one
would ever have come within a Ted Ray drive of it.

THE U.S. OPEN trophy that had passed through the hands and bore
the names of so many of the men mentioned in this chronicle finally made

its second crossing across the pond to England with Harry Vardon and Ted
Ray in 1920; Ted shipped it back to the USGA when his reign ended a year
later. In 1946, the original trophy was destroyed in a fire while in the possession of then champion Lloyd Mangrum's home club, Tam O'Shanter,
outside Chicago. The USGA briefly considered replacing it with a newly
designed trophy, but decided instead to re-create the original with a full-
scale replica. That substitute trophy followed the same tradition as its pre-
decessor, passing from the hand of one champion to another, until 1986,
when it was permanently retired to the USGA Museum in Far Hills, New
Jersey. From 1986 forward, the U.S. Open champion has received custody
of a second full-scale replica. At the end of their year with the sterling silver cup, each host site and champion are permitted by the USGA to produce a ninety percent replica for their public and personal collections.

THE MAGIC FRANCIS created at the seventeenth green of The
Country Club in Brookline lingered and never went away. "Vardon's
Bunker" is still there; members still refer to it by name and it came into
play again when the U.S. Open returned to The Country Club in 1963 to
commemorate the fiftieth anniversary of Francis's victory. At the conclusion of the final round, two former Open champions, Arnold Palmer and
local favorite Julius Boros, walked off the course trailing a young tour
player from Texas named Jackie Cupit by two strokes. Both men thought
their tournament was over—Boros had already started cleaning out his
locker—when Jackie Cupit stepped to the seventeenth tee. Cupit landed
his drive in Vardon's Bunker, had to punch out sideways, and ended up taking a double bogey six. After he parred eighteen, the three men finished in
a dead heat; the next day the second three-man play-off for the U.S. Open
title at The Country Club got under way. Boros built an early lead but
Palmer was right in it until experiencing an eerie echo of the freak lie that
befell Walter Hagen in 1913; Palmer hooked his drive into the woods on
the eleventh hole and found his ball sitting on top of a rotten tree stump.
More than any other modern player who'd come along, Palmer's fearless,
slashing style of play most resembled Hagen's, which helped account for
both men's enormous popularity, and they'd become good friends after

Arnold burst onto the scene in the mid-1950s. (Another strange coincidence: Arnold had come down with a case of food poisoning from a bad lobster on the eve of the tournament, just as Hagen did at the 1914 Open.) Palmer decided against declaring his stump ball an unplayable lie and taking a penalty stroke, but then needed three strokes to get his ball back on the fairway; he was done. Boros went on to win the play-off and his second U.S. Open title when Jackie Cupit once again put his drive on seventeen into Vardon's Bunker.

In 1988, now honoring the seventy-fifth anniversary of Francis's win, the U.S. Open returned to Brookline for a third visit. American Curtis Strange led defending British Open champion Nick Faldo by one stroke heading into the fourth round and they found themselves paired in the final twosome. After nine holes they were all square, but Faldo had pulled ahead by a single stroke on the back when they reached the seventeenth. Strange birdied the hole—sinking a long putt very similar to Francis's—to pull even with Faldo, and then made a spectacular sand save on the eighteenth hole to maintain the tie. Once again, for the third time a U.S. Open at The Country Club would be decided by an eighteen-hole play-off. The next day Strange holed a clinching putt on the seventeenth green and won the first of his two consecutive U.S. Opens. Years later the blunt Strange, a student of history, put the similarities to Francis this way: "We both faced the reigning British Open champion in a play-off at an Open at Brookline, and we both kicked their butt."

The Ryder Cup visited The Country Club for the first time in the early fall of 1999. After the first two days, the biannual competition between American and European players appeared to be going Europe's way for what would have been an unprecedented third consecutive victory. The European team held a commanding lead heading into the last day of twelve singles matches, until the Americans mounted one of the greatest comebacks in the history of organized sports.

With the sudden melodramatic shifting of focus peculiar to the Ryder Cup, the pivotal match in the entire competition came down to Justin Leonard versus Spain's José Maria Olazabal. In front of a swarming gallery of family, peers, and over-amped partisan fans, not to mention a worldwide television audience, playing for nothing less than national pride and global bragging rights, Leonard had clawed his way back from four holes down through twelve, to all-square, when they reached the seventeenth green. Olazabal was lying two, inside Leonard by twenty feet on the same line. Leonard was also lying two but faced a forty-five-footer, running up onto a subtle ridge with a harrowing right-to-left bias. He needed to secure at least a tie in his match to ensure a United States victory. Leonard made the putt, and the crowd erupted in a green-trampling frenzy, stirring up a much more bitter international controversy about American vulgarity than Francis's had caused in 1913, primarily because Olazabal could still win the match and his putt mattered. Although he later claimed not to have been upset by all the premature celebration, when he missed the putt, Olazabal did say he had been bothered by the traffic and honking horns on nearby Clyde Street. Leonard won the match, America took back the Ryder Cup, and in the process revived for the first time in many years memories of Francis's great victory. At least one veteran reporter claimed Francis Ouimet must have been there in spirit at seventeen to guide Leonard's improbable putt into the hole. American team captain Ben Crenshaw was later presented with a commemorative statue of Francis and Eddie by the U.S. team's caddies.

EDDIE LOWERY CADDIED frequently for Francis at Woodland Golf Club in the weeks and months after their partnership at the Open. When Francis sailed to Europe in the summer of 1914, Eddie was there at the docks to see him off. Like many of the early American players facing their first exposure to the windy British links courses, Francis did not fare well at either the British Open or Amateur Championships. He did, however, take Ted Ray up on his invitation to see the sights, and spent many delightful evenings away from the course in the company of both Ted and Harry. Francis recovered enough of his game in time to win the 1914 French Amateur Championship, on an inland course, before sailing for home.

Francis immediately traveled to Midlothian Country Club outside Chicago to defend his championship in the 1914 U.S. Open. He finished a respectable fourth but took considerable delight in watching his friend

Walter Hagen win his first major title. Francis then returned to Brookline and successfully defended his Massachusetts State Amateur title. Throughout his young life Francis's sustaining dream had always been to win the U.S. National Amateur Championship. In the summer of 1914 at Ekwanok Country Club in Manchester, Vermont, Francis again finished one stroke behind the leaders in the qualifying rounds, defeated Bill Fownes in the semifinals, and ended up facing his pal Jerry Travers for the championship. Re-creating the excitement and tension of their match the previous year at Garden City, the two men stayed within one hole of each other all through their morning round, but in the afternoon Francis corrected a flaw in his putting stroke and quickly built a commanding lead. Up six holes with six to play, they halved the thirteenth and the match was over; so lost in his habitual fog of concentration he wasn't even aware of the score, Travers pulled out his driver and headed to the next tee. When USGA president Robert Watson, who was refereeing the contest, pointed out that the match was actually over, Travers apologized profusely and congratulated Francis with all his heart. His lifelong ambition realized, Francis had become the first American player to ever win both the USGA's professional and amateur titles.

All this success finally won Francis's father over. When in 1915 Francis decided to break away from Wright & Ditson and establish his own Boston sporting goods business, Arthur Ouimet became one of his principal investors. Concurrently the USGA announced a new series of punitive restrictions on the eligibility of amateur golfers, to now preclude anyone who worked as a golf architect or sold golf equipment for a living. Francis's store stocked equipment for every recreational sport, not just golf, but to his own shock and the dismay of his fans around the country, the USGA came down hard on the one man who had done more to advance and promote the game than any American in history; Francis Ouimet had been effectively banned from competitive amateur golf. Unwilling to give up his successful new business for an arbitrary ruling he believed was unjust, for the only time in his life Francis briefly considered becoming a professional. To protest the USGA's ruling, the Western Golf Association, at that point a separate organization, invited Francis out to Chicago and welcomed him into their amateur championship with open arms. He promptly won the tournament. With neither side willing to give an inch, Francis and the USGA locked horns in a stalemate, broken only when the United States officially entered World War I in 1917. Francis enlisted, and quickly rose to the rank of lieutenant. He organized and performed in countless fund-raising golf outings for the Red Cross all across the East Coast and New England. During a leave from the army, Francis married his longtime sweetheart, Stella Sullivan, sister of his business partner and old school chum John Sullivan, in 1918. When the war ended the next year, the Red Cross awarded Francis its special prize medal, in recognition of his "Aid to Humanity in World War I."

Following in Francis's footsteps, Eddie Lowery began his own playing career during the war years and in 1919 won the first of his two Massachusetts Junior Amateur Championships. The following year he was named the caddie master at Woodland Country Club. Eddie held on to his celebrity status long after the 1913 Open; he loved being recognized, and he embraced the spotlight as fervently as Francis avoided it. Eddie became a stagestruck fan of show business. Walter Hagen's pal Al Jolson took a liking to young Eddie and whenever he came to Boston always invited him to shows with backstage passes and the glamorous parties that followed after the curtain came down. Shortly thereafter Eddie left Woodland to become a sportswriter for the Boston Traveler, covering a variety of local teams and events. Wherever he went for the rest of his life, Eddie loved being near the action; he was usually right in the middle of it.

The USGA finally came to its senses during the war years about where they'd drawn the line between amateur and professional, in effect admitting they had been overzealous with regard to Francis's case. In early 1919 Francis was quietly reinstated as an amateur player in good standing. Despite the pain and suffering their decision had cost him, he never uttered a single negative word about the USGA. Francis jumped back into competition immediately; he won his fourth Massachusetts Amateur title in the summer of 1919 and the following year finished runner-up to Chick Evans in the National Amateur, beating the nearly-arrived Bobby Jones in the process. Francis also had the pleasure of reuniting with Harry and Ted when they returned to the States in 1920. Francis covered the Open at Inverness that year as a correspondent for a Boston newspaper, an inside-the-ropes eyewitness to Harry's stunning collapse and Ted's U.S. Open victory. When the two Jerseymen came through Boston at the end of their tour, the old friends staged a private, friendly reunion of their 1913 play-off at The Country Club, playing Francis and a local pro in a four-ball exhibition match. The Englishmen exacted some small measure of revenge by winning the match one-up, although the stakes this time were slightly lower; after the round, Francis bought the drinks.

The 1920s did not offer Francis the same level of success on the golf course he'd met with during the previous decade. Stella gave birth to two daughters, Janice and Barbara, and the demands of family life and making a living took Francis happily away from full-time sport. His fellow amateur and great friend Bobby Jones had by now ascended to full immortal status, presenting an immovable obstacle to the National Amateur title; Francis reached the semifinals five times in the twenties but couldn't get past the now invincible Jones. Always preferring the excitement and risk-taking of match play to the habitual caution of stroke competition, Francis entered only one U.S. Open during the decade, and it was to be his last. In 1925 at nearby Worcester Country Club, at the age of thirty-two Francis demonstrated he could still play with the best in the game. He led the field after an opening round 70 and went on to finish tied for third, only two strokes away from the lead. Francis also became a perennial figure on the United States Walker Cup Team, the biannual amateur competition between America and Great Britain, playing on the first six squads, serving as player-captain for the next two, then as non-playing captain on every team until the outbreak of World War II, and twice more after competition resumed when the war ended. During his long tenure with the Walker Cup team, for which he held the record number of both appearances and victories until the 1980s, the United States lost the cup only once.

The happiest achievement in the later stages of Francis's playing career occurred in 1931, when seventeen years to the day, and almost to the minute after his victory in the Amateur at Ekwanok, he won his second National Amateur Championship at Beverly Country Club in Chicago. Francis reached the semifinals again when he defended his title the following year and in 1932 won his sixth Massachusetts Amateur Championship; the first title he had won in 1913 would, nineteen years later, also be his last. Now describing himself as a "businessman golfer," Francis dedicated more and more time to family and career; his years of playing at the top of the game were over and he never regretted it.

"Golf and business don't mix very well," he said. "You can have a choice, but you can't have both. One day I woke up to the fact that I had a wife and two little girls to look after, and that I'd better get busy doing it. I'm glad I did."

Neither his wife nor his daughters ever took up the game. He published his autobiography, *A Game of Golf*, in 1932. With characteristic modesty, Francis devoted only ten pages of the 274-page book to his win in the 1913 Open, beginning the chapter by saying, "There is little to be said about the championship itself."

In 1932 The Country Club organized a black-tie invitation dinner to commemorate its fiftieth anniversary. Francis served as the guest of honor and featured speaker, and after the dinner gave a lovely, lyrical speech recalling the events of the 1913 Open. He summed up his feelings for The Country Club this way: "To me the property around here is hallowed. The grass grows greener, the trees bloom better, there is even warmth in the rocks you see around here. And I don't know, gentlemen, but somehow or other the sun seems to shine brighter on The Country Club than on any other place I have seen."

Francis had by now fulfilled his other life's ambition by becoming a respected member of Boston society, a pillar of the community. An aristocrat in the best sense of the word, he was known and appreciated wherever he went for his courtly manners, unstinting generosity, gifted public speaking, and great good humor. He never forgot a face or a name, and went out of his way to compliment others, even when he was supposed to be the focus of an event. Francis also loved to sing and was for many years the tenor in a popular barbershop quartet. With his inherited musical talent, he frequently entertained at civic and private dinners, accompanying himself on the piano as he composed on-the-spot, extemporaneous, good-natured ditties about people in the room. He moved fluidly throughout his business career between the financial world and as an executive in professional sports, serving for many years as president of the Boston Bruins hockey team, vice president of the Boston Braves baseball team, and then as chairman of the

Boston Arena Authority. He spent the early part of his investment career at the brokerage firm of Harrison & Bromfield in Boston, and the majority of his later years as a senior broker at the Boston blue-blood investment firm of Brown Brothers, Harriman. They later named their boardroom in his honor.

Eddie Lowery reached the pinnacle of his playing career with a victory in the 1927 Massachusetts Amateur Championship at the age of twenty-four. Francis was there to see him do it. Eddie always idolized Francis, and freely acknowledged he owed everything in his life to their association, although not when Francis was around; he preferred to give Eddie all the credit. They remained devoted, lifelong friends despite, or perhaps because of their sharply contrasting personalities. Francis matured toward gentility and classic Old Boston virtues, a fixture at Red Sox games in his seersucker suit and bow tie. Eddie hustled his way ahead in the world with the gift of gab and aggressive entrepreneurial instincts. He moved from covering golf and hockey at the *Boston Traveler* into advertising when he figured out that's where the dough was, married for the first time, then moved up to a job as the advertising sales manager for the *Boston Herald*. His first wife died of pneumonia during the early 1930s; two years later Eddie married a local socialite he'd known for years. During the Great Depression Eddie carved out a successful niche for himself as national advertising director for National Beef Wholesalers. That job took him often to California, where the freewheeling Gold Rush mentality that still prevailed captivated him; he felt right at home. In 1937 Eddie and his second wife moved to San Francisco, where Eddie took a job as a senior car salesman with a large Lincoln/Mercury dealership. Within a few years Eddie was running the company's wholesale division, and when the owner decided to retire shortly thereafter, Eddie bought him out. During the 1940s and 1950s Eddie built the most successful Lincoln/Mercury dealership on the West Coast, eventually opening a second showroom in Palm Springs where he spent the winters. His personal life had its share of tragedy; his first child, Eddie Junior, entered the Air Force with the outbreak of World War II and died during a training mission. His second wife died of cancer shortly after the war ended. In 1950 Eddie married for the third time; his secretary Margaret, a woman fifteen years his junior. It would prove to be a long and happy marriage.

Eddie remained active as an avid amateur golfer and generous financial supporter of the game. He was instrumental in helping his old friend and fellow former caddie Bing Crosby organize and develop his annual clambake/pro-am golf tournament at Pebble Beach. Eddie was a fixture in the tournament for many years and he won the event in 1953 with his professional playing partner Byron Nelson. He also had a keen eye for talent, and became the first sponsor and mentor to a young Northern California player named Ken Venturi, who would eventually go on to win the 1964 U.S. Open. Eddie introduced Ken to his old buddy Francis Ouimet, who became Ken's friend and stockbroker.

After retiring as a player Francis also remained devoted to the game of amateur golf. He served for eight years on the USGA's Executive Committee, the last two of those as vice president. In 1944, along with his friends Bobby Jones and Gene Sarazen, Francis was elected as one of the four original members of the Golf Hall of Fame. In 1951, at the behest of his old friend Bernard Darwin and the many others he'd met during his numerous visits to Great Britain, Francis became the first American to ever be named Captain of the Royal & Ancient Golf Club of St. Andrews, his sport's oldest and highest office. This was one public honor Francis didn't have to be persuaded to accept. The Captain's only requisite duty is to appear at 8:00 A.M. on the morning of the opening of the R&A's spring meeting and hit a ceremonial first drive on the St. Andrews opening hole. The church bells rang, the drums beat, the signal cannon was fired, and the club's caddies lined the fairway. Francis chose to hit a Spalding Dot One, emblazoned with both a red British lion and a blue American eagle. The lucky caddie who retrieved the ball for him received from Francis a five-dollar United States coin from 1913. Francis proudly posed for a majestic oil portrait in his red captain's hunting jacket; when his wife, Stella, saw it for the first time she asked him: "Where's your horse?"

In 1949 Francis realized another lifelong dream when with the help and encouragement of his friends in the Boston business community he organized a college scholarship fund for underprivileged caddies from throughout Massachusetts. His friends insisted it be called the Francis Ouimet Caddie Scholarship Fund, although Francis needed some convincing; only when they persuaded him his name would allow them to raise more money did he acquiesce. In the fund's first year, thirteen young caddies received a total of $4,600 in tuition assistance. With the support of some of the game's greatest names, during the intervening years the Ouimet Fund has helped over ten thousand caddie/students, grown to a multimillion-dollar endowment, and in the year 2002 for the first time passed the million-dollar mark in awarded annual scholarships. The fund also maintains a museum outside Boston that honors Francis's life and playing career. Many of the fund's recipients have gone on to distinguished careers in many walks of life in Boston, New England, and throughout the world. A compelling tribute of charity and generosity inspired by his own humble beginnings among the impoverished Boys from Brookline who always loved and supported him, the fund was privately considered by Francis to be the most important achievement of his entire life.

Francis remained a member of Woodland Country Club his entire life, although he played and was welcomed at clubs throughout Boston, the state of Massachusetts, and the world. The Country Club named him an honorary member for life in 1953. In 1963 when the U.S. Open returned to Brookline for the fiftieth anniversary of his win, Francis served as honorary chairman, appeared at a number of functions throughout tournament week, and presented the Open trophy at the awards ceremony to winner Julius Boros. Always reluctant to have people treat him as someone special, Francis agreed to be honored at a gala dinner that week, but only if the proceeds went to benefit his caddie fund. Eddie Lowery returned to Boston as an honored guest of the tournament as well and the two friends spent every precious minute they could together. The two men, now sixty and seventy years old, gave a touching interview to a local television crew as they walked some of The Country Club grounds, reliving the grand excitement from fifty years before. Eddie lived another twenty-one years; he eventually retired as an extremely wealthy man to Palm Springs and died there of respiratory failure in 1984, at the age of eighty-one. In his will Eddie left a substantial sum to the Ouimet Scholarship Fund, which has since created a special scholarship endowment in his name for each year's most outstanding caddie.

Francis lost his beloved wife, Stella, in 1965. He continued to live alone in the house in Wellesley they'd shared together since 1936. Two years later, after enjoying a quiet dinner at his daughter's house on a hot August night, Francis returned home and soon afterward took ill. Although reluctant as always to trouble anyone, he felt in such acute distress, he called his daughter, who immediately telephoned for an ambulance. The previous week young Boston Red Sox star outfielder Tony Conigliaro had been hit in the head by a pitch during a game; he suffered serious head and eye injuries that would soon prematurely end his career, and the news was still very much in people's mind. When the ambulance crew took him to Newton-Wellesley hospital and doctors there realized who he was, Francis received immediate red-carpet treatment. Modest and unassuming as always, Francis told them: "Such a fuss. You'd think I was Tony Conigliaro." Francis had suffered a serious heart attack. With his daughters at his side, Francis died nine days later on Saturday, September 2, 1967. He was seventy-four years old. The world of golf had lost its greatest friend. Three days later he was laid to rest beside Stella after a requiem mass at St. Paul's Church in Wellesley Hills. Friends from around the world gathered to attend the service. Gene Sarazen was one of his pallbearers. So was Eddie Lowery. When the memorial service at the cemetery ended, Gene Sarazen was the last to linger. He knelt beside the grave, sprinkled a handful of dirt onto the casket, and whispered: "Fast greens, Francis. Fast greens."

In 1980 the USGA announced it had named the handsome silver cup awarded to the winner of their Senior Open Championship "The Francis Ouimet Trophy." In 1988 the U.S. Postal Service issued a Ouimet commemorative stamp; in his sport only Bobby Jones and Babe Zaharias had been so honored. In 1993, to commemorate its 100th anniversary, the USGA chose as their centennial celebration logo the silhouettes of two figures walking side-by-side down a fairway, a tall, slender player and his intrepid little caddie, inspired by the famous photograph of Eddie Lowery and Francis Ouimet.

GAMES ARE CENTRAL to the human experience. Outlets for aggression, universal forms of entertainment, metaphors for the struggle to survive. The cathartic experience of participating in a hard-fought contest takes us one step closer to an understanding of our mysterious, questing nature. The old saw leaned on by coaches in professional sports that their game builds character doesn't always hold true, when winning is the only thing and rules are only there to be bent or broken in service of that goal. Golf alone demands a self-administered adherence to its rules, and along with its other more palpable benefits, that discipline does contribute something of measurable value to the human heart: self-reliance, restraint, courtesy, purpose, humility, and pride in authentic achievement. This legacy of excellence is golf's greatest gift to us, and the men in this book saw to it that it has been passed down through the generations.

They're all gone now. All those champions and challengers. All the men who breathed life into an obscure Scottish pastime that has grown to proportions none of them could have imagined in their wildest dreams. Every tournament you see today that thrills you with its twists and turns, reversals of fortune, triumphs and tragedies, owes an enduring debt of gratitude to this pioneering generation. Every man or woman who's ever collected a paycheck from the game of golf can give thanks to the sacrifices made by J. H. Taylor, John McDermott, Walter Hagen, Ted Ray, and Harry Vardon, and countless others, for their livelihood. Every one of us who casually or passionately plays the game for fun, companionship, competition, or recreation should be forever grateful that Francis Ouimet looked out at that private, privileged world across the street from the house where he grew up, and found somewhere within himself the courage to cross that street.

Golf is master of us all.
—HARRY VARDON

ACKNOWLEDGMENTS

Seven years ago I had the pleasure of introducing my good friend and literary agent Ed Victor to the game of golf, the sport that has consumed the better part of my spare time for the past twenty years. Ed has since repaid this apparent act of kindness—which on occasional despairing afternoons can seem more akin to an act of cruelty—in ways too numerous to count, but never more so than on a transcontinental flight we shared during the summer of 2001. In the course of discussing an upcoming golf outing, I recounted to Ed the story, to the limited extent I then knew it, of Francis Ouimet and his landmark victory in the 1913 U.S. Open. With the sudden, fierce conviction that those who know him will recognize as characteristic, Ed locked eyes with me and said: "Mark, this is a book." Thanks to Ed, whose interest and support knows no limits, now it is.

Re-creating the life and times of Francis, Harry, Eddie, Ted Ray, Walter Hagen, and the sport of golf in 1913 began with a phone call to Randon Jerris, chief historian in charge of the library at the USGA's headquarters in Far Hills, New Jersey. Rand's formidable knowledge of the game's history and his encyclopedic command of its most extensive American archive proved to be the skeleton key for unlocking the mysteries of a nearly forgotten era. He is also one swell guy, whose unassuming modesty—not unlike Francis in that regard—I hope will not be offended by my saying so. With Rand and his incredibly capable assistant Patty Moran as my guides, the USGA's resources provided me with a portal to the past, and I spent many happy days lost in their voluminous stacks. Tanya Steffan and Shannon Doody, also of the USGA, provided timely and valuable assistance as well. As I absorbed the journals and books and newspaper accounts of the early twentieth century, slowly the facts and figures of these events began to acquire the necessary human form. Many of the story's more vivid characters came to life without much prompting: Walter Hagen, Ted Ray, Johnny McDermott, Walter Travis, and Harry Vardon didn't require detective work to find a voice; theirs quickly turned out to be inimitable. But in spite of the fact that a fair amount had been written about him—although never the full biographical treatment he so richly deserved—Francis Ouimet proved elusive; his reticence and humility, the qualities that made him such a remarkable human being, turned out to be serious obstacles to fuller understanding.

From there the trail led to Boston and two men without whose assistance this story would have lacked a center. Robert Donovan, executive director of the estimable Francis Ouimet Scholarship Fund (Golf House, 300 Arnold Palmer Boulevard, Norton, MA 02766 (774) 430-9090; www.ouimet.org) and its museum, can best be described as caretaker of the Ouimet legacy. That he felt secure enough to entrust me with his thoughtful insights into the psychology and conflicts of Francis and his family brought a pulse to the heart of the book. Robert then introduced me to J. Louis Newell, archivist and historian for The Country Club at Brookline. Louis not only toured their storied course and clubhouse with me and shared the treasures of their archives, he provided a living link to Francis; as a young fellow he knew and on occasion played golf with "Mr. Ouimet"—who called him "Master Newell"—and in Louis's generous and gentlemanly manner I found a warming echo of the man who lived across the street. Also many thanks to Michael Daly for his introduction to the venerated Garden City Golf Club, and a memorable round of golf.

As the manuscript took shape I am, as ever, grateful to my assistant Susie Putnam for her tireless research and sharp eye for detail. Many thanks to my publisher at Hyperion, Will Schwalbe, with whom I've been down this road before, and to my editor Gretchen Young, with whom I haven't but now hope I will again. I wish to also thank my friends David Steinberg, Sonny Van Dusen, Paul Thayer, Peter Gethers, Bill Shinker, Ian Chapman, Bruce Vinokour, Adam Krentzman, and Stephen Kulczycki for their thoughtful early reads and responses. Similar thanks for that, and so much more, to my wife Lynn and my parents Warren and Virginia Frost; I've learned, as Francis did along the way, that belief in one's self will only take you halfway home unless those closest and dearest to you share your dreams.

A NOTE ON THE WRITING

In employing dialogue to bring these scenes to life, I used source material for direct attribution whenever possible. In its occasional absence I attempted to infer intent from prose or reportage, remaining as true as possible to what I understood to be the spirit of the moment. In rare exceptions, with a dramatist's license, and in the utter want of an eyewitness, I took the liberty of elaborating on those perceptions beyond what I could absolutely verify. It is my hope and belief that in no instance did I violate the underlying truths, laboring only to illuminate them.

THE PLAY-OFF. FRANCIS, KNEELING LEFT, LINES UP HIS FINAL
PUTT, WATCHED BY HARRY, CENTER, AND TED, RIGHT.

INDEX